CALL to FAITH

GRADE 1
Teacher Edition

Harcourt Religion Publishers
www.harcourtreligion.com

Nihil Obstat
Rev. Richard Schaeffer

Imprimatur
✠ Most Rev. Jerome Hanus, OSB
Archbishop of Dubuque
June 2, 2004

The Imprimatur is an official declaration that a book or pamphlet is free of doctrinal or moral error. No implication is contained therein that anyone who granted the Imprimatur agrees with the contents, opinions, or statements expressed.

The Ad Hoc Committee to Oversee the Use of the Catechism, United States Conference of Catholic Bishops, has found this catechetical text, © 2005, to be in conformity with the *Catechism of the Catholic Church*.

Harcourt Religion Publishers

CALL to FAITH

SCHOOL 1

Grade 1 Contents

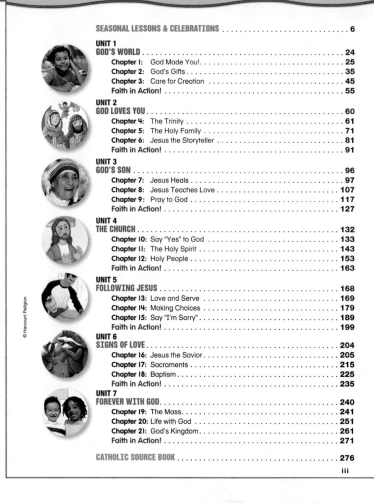

iii

© Harcourt Religion

UNIT 1
GOD'S WORLD 24

1 God Made You! 25
- God created everything. All that God made is good.
- God knows and loves everyone.
- Wonderful Things

SCRIPTURE
The First Humans
Genesis 2:7–22

2 God's Gifts 35
- God's world is a gift to you.
- You can learn about God and his love from the world he made.
- We Use God's Gifts

SCRIPTURE
What God Made
Genesis 1:5–25

3 Care for Creation 45
- All creation is a gift from God.
- Everyone must help care for God's world.
- Taking Care

SCRIPTURE
All Creation
Genesis 1:26–30

Faith in Action! 55
Catholic Social Teaching:
Care for God's Creation

Unit 1 Review 58

UNIT 2
GOD LOVES YOU 60

4 The Trinity 61
- The Holy Trinity is God the Father, God the Son, and God the Holy Spirit.
- Jesus is the Son of God.
- Three in One

SCRIPTURE
God the Father
John 14:7–9

5 The Holy Family 71
- Jesus is both God and man.
- Jesus, Mary, and Joseph are the Holy Family.
- Jesus' Family, Your Family

SCRIPTURE
The Boy Jesus
Luke 2:51–52

6 Jesus the Storyteller 81
- Jesus told stories, or parables, to teach about God's love.
- The Bible is God's word written in human words.
- The Bible

SCRIPTURE
The Lost Sheep
Luke 15:3–6

Faith in Action! 91
Catholic Social Teaching:
Life and Dignity of the Human Person

Unit 2 Review 94

UNIT 3
GOD'S SON 96

7 Jesus Heals 97
- Jesus' healing actions show God's power and love.
- Faith is the gift of believing in God.
- Sharing God's Love

SCRIPTURE
Have Faith
Luke 8:40–56

8 Jesus Teaches Love 107
- The Great Commandment is one of God's laws.
- You are to love God above all else and love others as you love yourself.
- Showing Love

SCRIPTURE
Loving Others
Luke 10:25–28

9 Pray to God 117
- Prayer is talking and listening to God.
- Jesus taught his friends how to pray the Lord's Prayer.
- The Lord's Prayer

SCRIPTURE
How to Pray
Ephesians 5:18–20

Faith in Action! 127
Catholic Social Teaching:
Rights and Responsibilities of the Human Person

Unit 3 Review 130

© Harcourt Religion

iv

v

© Harcourt Religion

Welcome to
Call to Faith!

The following pages provide an opening lesson that will help you and the children get better acquainted with one another and with this textbook. The introductory pages will introduce the children you teach to the text that they will be exploring during the coming year. Together you will form a faith-sharing community with an open, trusting environment and a sense of fun and enthusiasm. Here's a brief look at the components of the opening lesson and how they will help children become more familiar with the catechetical process.

About You

This page, along with the Activity Master that appears on page 5A, will serve as an "ice-breaker" to get your group talking, sharing, interacting, and having fun together.

About Your Faith

The activities and suggestions on this page will help you assess where children are on their faith journeys. Children are called to share what they already know about the Catholic faith, the Bible, and Church Tradition—topics they will build on as they grow in faith with your help and the guidance of the entire Church community.

About Your Book

Both you and the children will get a "sneak preview" of the textbook and become familiar with the features and symbols that will guide you through the lessons, stories, activities, and celebrations included in every chapter.

A Call to Faith

During this prayer celebration, you and the children will bond as a community of faith through ritual, Scripture, discussion, prayer, and song.

May **you** and the **children** find **holiness, joy,** and **many blessings** during your year of **discovery** and **faith!**

SCHOOL BUS

Student Editions (Grades K–6) help children deepen their faith through compelling stories and Scripture, appealing visuals, activities, prayers, and seasonal celebrations. Family Faith pages help families participate in their children's faith formation. (Available for school, parish, and bilingual programs)

Lectionary Links: Breaking Open the Word (Grades K–6) visually displays the Sunday lectionary readings along with compelling faith-sharing questions for different ages in an interactive format. Lectionary Links are available for Years A, B, and C.

Teacher and Catechist Editions (Grades K–6) provide all the tools for success—easy-to-use planners, Catechism and GDC connections, a simple three-step catechetical process, a wealth of resources and optional activities, plus activity and assessment reproducibles. (Available for school, parish, and bilingual programs)

People of Faith Collection (Grades K–6) includes 133 vibrantly illustrated cards—each with a brief biography and prayer. These cards are excellent tools for encouraging children to learn from examples set by people of faith.

Music CDs (Grades K–6) offer a repertoire of liturgical music to accompany every chapter and seasonal celebration. Each grade set includes 30 songs on two CDs.

The Catholic Family in a Changing World, by Reverend Robert Hater, Ph.D., offers pastoral insight and spiritual wisdom to the real-world faith lives of today's Catholic families. Personal stories and biblical stories of the Holy Family offer guidance and inspiration—a valuable resource for families and those that minister to them.

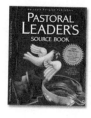

Pastoral Leader's Source Book (Grades K–6) provides practical resources including professional development articles, implementation models, sources for parish adults, parent and catechist orientation sessions, plus a separate section for implementing whole community catechesis.

Praying All Ways: A Multiple Intelligences Approach to Prayer, by Caroljean Willie, SC, Ph.D., provides a fresh perspective on the many ways we can pray. Through a myriad of prayer models, this personal source book helps adults deepen their life of prayer.

Faith at Home: Nurturing Households of Faith (Grades K–6) features practical suggestions, tips for sharing and celebrating faith at home, a section on using *Call to Faith* at home, and more—all in an engaging magazine.

Planning the *Year*

Consider the Basics

- How many times a week will I teach religion?
- What is the time frame for each lesson?
- How many sessions are scheduled for the year?
- What impact will other parish and school activities (retreats, liturgies, assemblies) have on my lesson schedule?

Celebrating the Seasonal Lessons

- Eight lessons are tied to the seasons and feasts of the liturgical year.
- The teaching year may be planned to determine where each lesson will fit best.
- Lessons are flexible and can be adapted for either 20- or 60-minute sessions.
- Lessons may be taught individually or may accompany a chapter that discusses the relevant season.
- The Family Faith page is a reproducible master and includes a background on the season, a family prayer, and a family activity.

Using the Catholic Source Book

- The Source Book is an age-appropriate resource for young learners.
- It has five sections: Scripture, Creed, Liturgy, Morality, and Prayer.
- Optional activities appear in designated boxes in the Teacher edition of the Catholic Source Book.

Covering the Chapters

- *Call to Faith* contains seven units and twenty-one chapters.
- Each chapter is divided into five sessions of approximately 30–40 minutes each.
- Each chapter wrap-up provides a review of material and suggestions for families.
- Activity Masters are fully integrated into the chapter theme and can be used before, during, or after a session.
- Review features provide a quick assessment of what students have learned and offer an immediate application of each lesson.
- Unit reviews and tests measure students' progress in the acquisition of religious knowledge, beliefs, and practices; they also promote students' development of a faith vocabulary.

Benefiting from Faith in Action

- *Call to Faith* contains seven Faith in Action sessions, one at the end of each unit. Each of these sessions corresponds to one of the Catholic Social Teaching themes.
- These sessions may be used in a flexible time frame—in 20-minute sessions over three days, or as one 60-minute session.

The Vocation to Teach

Sustaining the vocation to teach as Jesus did takes time and rarely happens without some struggle. At the beginning of each chapter in this Teacher Edition, you will find short essays designed to help you sustain your spirit. These essays will assist you in the ongoing process of assessing the spiritual dimensions of your catechetical commitment, reviewing the expectations that put your vocational commitment at risk, and examining proactive ways of adapting to those challenges.

Perhaps the essence of the grandparent's message was this: The task of sustaining your call is about representing the faith, deeply and authentically, to those you teach.

 GO ONLINE
Visit www.harcourtreligion.com for more Sustaining the Spirit resources.

Sustaining Your Spirit

Some years ago, a new catechist was struggling to meet the requirements and expectations of effective religious education. Challenged by striving for creative activities and perfectly facilitated classroom discussions, the new catechist felt her commitment beginning to fade.

One day a grandparent arrived early to pick up a student. Instead of waiting in the parking lot, this woman lingered just outside the open door of the classroom, listening to the closing prayer.

Shortly after dismissal, she appeared in front of the catechist and, without a word of introduction, nodded toward the classroom window. The catechist could see students waiting for their rides—the younger children running, playing, and laughing, and the older ones standing in tight circles sharing accounts of the day's events.

It was the landscape of the young—fully alive. The grandparent looked directly at the catechist and said with feeling and certainty: "You may be the only Bible that they ever *really* read."

Your students may not remember all of the material and experiences that you offer them, but they will remember the way that your life and your presence reveal your faith. Your dedication to the commitments and challenges of this ministry will help shape others' lives.

Reaching ALL LEARNERS

A student's intelligence is not the only factor in how he or she will learn. Learning is also affected by family situations, learning disorders, and mental or physical impairments. The lessons and teaching methods in *Call to Faith* have been carefully crafted in order to meet the needs of all learners.

A special feature in your Catechist Edition, called "Reaching All Learners," will provide you with tips, suggestions, and proven ways to include students with different learning styles and abilities in your lesson. Some of the suggestions, will help you make provisions for physical and mental challenges your children may face, while other suggestions will help you respond to the diverse ways children learn and experience the world. By varying your teaching strategies, you can help students enhance the range of their learning capabilities.

Be alert for signs that students are experiencing difficulty learning or relating to others. If you notice a student is struggling, contact the director of your program and the appropriate family member. The following are examples of impairments or situations that may cause serious difficulty for students.

Physical Impairment Difficulty with motor skills, hearing loss, speech or visual problems

Cognitive and Emotional Impairment ADHD, dyslexia, behavioral issues, impulse control

Home Situations death, divorce, single parent, foster home, abuse

"People learn and grow in many different ways"

Multiple Intelligences

Educational research proves that there are different ways in which people learn. The names of these different ways of learning, or intelligences, follow.

Verbal/Linguistic learning occurs best through reading, writing, telling stories, and discussing ideas.

Musical learning occurs best through singing, listening to music, and remembering melodies.

Mathematical/Logical learning occurs best through solving problems, analyzing, and applying logic.

Visual/Spatial learning occurs best through visualizing, looking at pictures, drawing, and creating.

Bodily/Kinesthetic learning occurs best through physically moving, processing knowledge through bodily sensations, dancing, and acting.

Interpersonal learning occurs best through interviewing people, sharing about one's feelings, and cooperating with others on tasks.

Intrapersonal learning occurs best through working alone and reflecting.

Naturalist learning occurs best through exploring nature and living things.

Dr. Howard Gardner, of Harvard University, revolutionized education with his theory of multiple intelligence. He theorized that there was not only one kind of intelligence. Rather, there were different ways in which people learned. Applying this theory to faith formation shows that there are also many different ways in which people come to know God.

The most common and recognizable form of intelligence is **verbal/linguistic.** People who learn in this way prefer parables, story telling, and creative writing when learning new faith concepts. Those with **musical** intelligence learn best through listening to different kinds of music, making up songs, or singing throughout the lesson.

Those with **logical/mathematical** intelligence enjoy studying the origins of different religions, using clues to identify Biblical characters, or examining the true cost of poverty.

Learners with **visual/spatial** intelligence put faith concepts into concrete terms through painting, photography, or unique inventions. The learners eager to act out a story or to dance a prayer are those with **bodily/kinesthetic** intelligence, they who feel comfortable using their bodies to take in information.

Those with **interpersonal** intelligence thrive on community and cooperation, and those with **intrapersonal** intelligence know themselves well and enjoy journaling and reflection.

Those with **naturalist** intelligence use God's creation to learn.

Using Gardner's theory in the faith formation classroom is an opportunity to reach all students, regardless of their learning styles.

Catholic Social Teachings

Seven Principles of CATHOLIC SOCIAL TEACHING

> Care for God's Creation

> Life and Dignity of the Human Person

> Rights and Responsibilities of the Human Person

> The Dignity of Work and the Rights of Workers

> Solidarity of the Human Family

> Call to Family, Community, and Participation

> Option for the Poor and Vulnerable

For the past 115 years or so, Catholic social teaching has grown to occupy an increasingly important place in catechesis and in Catholic life. Recently, Church leaders have urged all those in the ministry of catechesis to include the social teachings of the Church in all aspects and at all grade levels of religious instruction and faith formation.

Call to Faith is the first elementary religion series to provide a curriculum for Catholic social teachings. Following the recommendations of a task force convened by the U.S. Bishops in 1995, *Call to Faith* provides a comprehensive, age-appropriate lesson at the end of each unit that correlates to the text.

Following this *Call to Faith* curriculum, students of every age will be deeply motivated by the Catholic social teaching and ready to live it. For parish programs, the complete program is available on-line at **www.harcourtreligion.com**.

Faith in Action lessons follow a three-step process:

- **Discover** This step describes the Catholic social teaching being presented in the unit and engages the learner in understanding it.

- **Connect** This step gives interesting examples and the witness of people and groups who are living out the teaching.

- **Serve** This step allows students to makes choices about how he or she can practice the principle.

  Parish Directors and Coordinators of Religious Education can integrate these lessons into the regular calendar or use them for family or intergenerational sessions.

GO ONLINE The complete Social Justice program is available on-line at www.harcourtreligion.com

1st GRADE
Six- and Seven-year-olds

Suggestions

- To help children who do not make friends easily, be sure to involve all children in classroom activities. Rotate partners and group memberships frequently.

- At six or seven years of age, children are capable of making moral choices. Provide them with good examples and clear moral guidelines. This will help them choose between right and wrong.

- First graders can plan and carry out simple tasks and responsibilities. Ask them to assist you with classroom tasks and needs.

- A child of this age is beginning to understand that actions have consequences. They may be motivated by a strong desire to please family members and others in authority, as well as a need to conform with their peers. Help them see the consequences of their behavior, both good and bad.

- Children at six and seven love to celebrate. Use drama, music, and ritual to involve the senses of your children.

Know The CHILD

The first grader is making an important transition from the family circle into the wider world. Even children who have been in full-time day care, preschool, and kindergarten situations will find first grade a new and different experience. Allow children opportunities to try out their new status. Expect occasional regressions as children resist leaving early childhood behind.

Friends are especially important to first graders. It's common for six- and seven-year-olds to feel intense, though brief, attachments. First graders have new "best friends" every few days.

While children of this age go through many different moods, prolonged sadness or anger in a first grader may indicate emotional problems, reaction to a difficult home situation, or frustration resulting from learning disabilities. Follow school or parish policies for offering help to troubled children.

Whether you are an experienced catechist or a beginner, it is always important to keep in mind the emotional and developmental progress of your children. Doing so will give you perspective on your work with them.

The way of teaching that we learn from the Gospels is called, in the *General Directory for Catechesis*, the "pedagogy of Jesus." This method allows gradual learning about Christ and the Church through age-appropriate words and activities.

Households OF FAITH

The first catechists in any student's life are the family members with whom he or she lives. What happens at home—both positive and negative—provides lessons for life. In the family, faith is shared as part of the unfolding of daily life. The home or "domestic Church" provides a real place in which a child learns to *live* his *or* her *faith* as well as to understand it.

Call to Faith is committed to partnering with parents and guardians to develop households in which the faith is shared and lived with vigor. Toward that end, *Call to Faith* is written with the family and household in mind.

- Family connections are made throughout the program.
- Each chapter includes a Family Faith page with suggestions for taking the lesson home.
- *Faith at Home: Nurturing Households of Faith* is a yearly magazine for families who wish to provide in-home catechesis for their children. It empowers parents and guardians in their role as the primary religious educators of their children.
- Harcourt Religion Publishers is committed to providing an array of resources on our Web site, **www.harcourtreligion.com**, for all families and households.

GO ONLINE Visit www.harcourtreligion.com for weekly scripture readings and seasonal resources.

Suggestions

- Create an environment for prayer within your classroom. This space can serve as a center to help students understand the beauty, depth, and sublimity of prayer.

- Make the Celebrate step in *Call to Faith* an integral and important part of each lesson.

- Have students memorize certain prayers so that they can pray them spontaneously.

- Use a Bible or the Lectionary when proclaiming Scripture during prayer celebrations.

- **Lectionary Link**—this feature, found on the Celebrate page of each chapter, helps you connect the Sunday readings to life through a process called "Break Open the Word." The readings for each week are found on the Web site.

- **Liturgy Link**—this feature, found on the Celebrate page of each chapter, gives practical tips for engaging students in the closing prayer celebration.

The songs in *Call to Faith* come from the *Singing Our Faith* hymnal.

Visit **www.harcourtreligion.com** for a correlation between *Call to Faith* music track numbers and *Singing Our Faith* song numbers.

Prayer and Worship

Catechesis always leads into prayer. Through prayer, Christians develop a close relationship with Jesus Christ, with God the Father, and with the Holy Spirit. In prayer, believers allow the Lord to touch their hearts, to lead them with his teachings, and to unite them with fellow Christians.

Thus, prayer is essential for anyone growing in faith. It is an important mission of catechesis to help students grow in their appreciation of prayer and to model a life of prayer for them.

Break Open the Word

1. Prepare minds and hearts to listen to God's word.
   a. Light a candle.
   b. Move the group to a special environment for prayer.
   c. Invite students to quiet their thoughts.
   d. Ask students to listen to what God is saying in this reading.
2. Proclaim the Gospel.
3. Allow for a moment of silent reflection.
4. Read the sharing question.
5. Share responses to the question.

Grade 6

- God reveals himself and his plan of salvation through Scripture.
- The most important truth of both Sacred Scripture and Tradition is that God is faithful and wants you to live with him forever.
- The stories of creation in Genesis reveal that God alone created the universe.
- God created humans in his own image to live in harmony with him forever.
- God fully revealed his faithfulness to humans by sending his only Son, Jesus.
- Humans have the ability to live in friendship with God.

Ruth 1:1–17, Genesis 1:1–30, 2:4–25   CCC: 51–55, 214, 108; 279–289, 355–361, 373; 396–411, 1730, 1468, 396

- God calls you on a journey of faith toward salvation.
- The path toward salvation is paved with prayer.
- God rescued the Hebrews from slavery and sent his Son to save all people.
- The Passover and the Eucharist celebrate God's saving actions.
- The Ten Commandments are the laws of God's covenant with the Israelites.
- The Ten Commandments help you stay close to God and in right relationship with others.

The Book of Genesis,   CCC: 176–184, 2570–2572, 183; 62–64, 1150–1151,
The Book of Exodus   430–431; 1961–1966, 1949–1953

- In Old Testament times, God chose leaders like Saul and David, who were anointed kings.
- God the Father anointed his Son Jesus to be prophet, priest, and king.
- The Bible teaches that true wisdom comes from trusting God and obeying his law.
- Jesus is the wisdom of God, sought in every age by those who are wise.
- Prophets of the Old Testament spoke for God, telling people to repent and obey God.
- Jesus is the Messiah described by the Old Testament prophets.

1 Samuel and 2 Samuel, 1 Kings, Job,   CCC: 59–64, 695, 218–221; 156–158, 215–217,
Isaiah and Zechariah   1950; 2581–2584, 711–714, 702

- The Gospels are the good news of Jesus; they proclaim his life and teachings.
- The Gospels are interpreted by the Church through Tradition.
- Jesus founded the Church through his life and teachings. He sent the Holy Spirit to help the Church fulfill its mission.
- The Holy Spirit continues to animate the Church today.
- The Church is one, holy, catholic, and apostolic.
- The Church is a community, united in faith, working together to share the Gospel.

Luke, Acts of the Apostles, 1 Cor 3:16, 12:12,   CCC: 124, 109–119, 772; 763–768, 849–854,
Eph 1:22–23, 2:19–20   737–747; 811–813, 830–831, 823

- The Great Commandment allows you to achieve happiness and holiness.
- The Beatitudes and precepts of the Church help the faithful live holy lives.
- Working toward justice means respecting the dignity of persons and peoples.
- Justice is giving what is due to God and others.
- Your conscience helps you know when you have sinned.
- Through the sacrament of Reconciliation, God forgives sins and restores us to his friendship.

Matthew 17:1–8, 18:23–35, 22:37–40,   CCC: 1716–1729, 2041–2043; 1939–1942, 2304–2306,
Micah 6:8   1807; 1777–1782, 1440–1445

- The mission of the Church is to proclaim the Gospel in word and deed.
- Through the Sacraments of Initiation, Christians are given new life.
- All of the baptized are called to follow Christ by serving others.
- Ordained ministers serve God through preaching the word and through celebrating the sacraments.
- The Church celebrates marriage through the Sacrament of Matrimony.
- This sacrament helps a man and woman grow in love and holiness.

Acts 8:26–39, John 13:1–15   CCC: 849–856, 1212, 1285; 897–900, 1548–1553, 900; 1612–1617, 1646–1651, 2204

- Members of the communion of saints can intercede, or pray to God for others.
- The communion of saints includes all holy persons, both living and dead, who are united in the Eucharist.
- Christ desires the unity of all his disciples.
- Ecumenism is the work of Christians toward unity.
- God will triumph over evil when Christ comes again in glory.
- In the new creation, God will reward good and punish evil.

Acts of the Apostles,   CCC: 2634–2638, 946–948; 820–822, 813–819,
The Gospel according to John   992–996, 1038–1041, 1042–1047, 991

People of Faith

Grade K
Saint Catherine of Siena
Saint Pier Giorgio Frassati
Simeon
Saint Philip the Apostle
Moses
Saint John the Baptist
Saint Therese of Lisieux

Grade 1
Blessed Mother Theresa of the Child Jesus
Blessed Pedro Calungsod
Frederick William Faber
Mary, Mother of God
Michelangelo
Pope John XXIII
Saint Albert the Great
Saint Angela Merici
Saint Dominic
Saint Emily de Vialar
Saint Frances Cabrini
Saint Giuseppina Bakhita
Saint Louise de Marillac
Saint Moses the Black
Saint Nicholas
Saint Patrick
Saint Pedro de San Jose Betancur
Saint Teresa of Jesus of the Andes
Saint Thomas of Villanova
Venerable Father Solanus Casey
Zechariah, Elizabeth, and John

Grade 2
All Saints
Bishop James Healy
Blessed Julian of Norwich
Blessed Mariano de Jesus
Blessed Marguerite Bays
Blessed Teresa of Calcutta
David
Mary, Mother of God
Pope John Paul II
Pope Saint Victor
Saint Anthony Claret
Saint Brigid of Kildare
Saint John Berchmans
Saint Juan Diego
Saint Luke
Saint Paul
Saint Peter
Saint Pius X
Saint Tarsicius
Saint Teresa Margaret Redi
Venerable Pierre Toussaint

Grade 3
Blessed Bartholomew Osypiuk
Blessed Joseph Vaz
Blessed Luigi & Blessed Maria
Jean Donovan
Pierre Teilhard de Chardin
Saint Clement of Rome
Saint Dismas
Saint Elizabeth of Hungary
Saint Francis of Assisi
Saint Genevieve
Saint Gregory the Great
Saint Isaac Jogues
Saint John of Matha
Saint Margaret of Scotland
Saint Mary Ann of Quito
Saint Mary Magdalene

Saint Peter Canisius
Saint Pio (Padre Pio)
Saints Perpetua and Felicity
Thea Bowman
Thomas Merton

Grade 4
Aaron and Miriam
Blessed Frederic Ozanam
Blessed Kateri Tekakwitha
Catherine de Hueck Doherty
Cesar Chavez
Korean Saints and Martyrs
Mary, Mother of God
Naomi and Ruth
Saint Bede
Saint Charles Lwanga
Saint Teresa Benedicta
Saint Jane Frances de Chantal
Saint Joan of Arc
Saint John of God
Saint Katharine Drexel
Saint Margaret Mary Alacoque
Saint Martin de Porres
Saint Mary Magdalen Postel
Saint Maximilian Kolbe
Saints Anne and Joachim
Venerable Matt Talbot

Grade 5
Blessed M. V. Rosal Vasquez
Dorothy Day
Michael the Archangel
Queenship of Mary
Saint Athanasius
Saint Augustine
Saint Benedict
Saint Catherine of Siena
Saint Cecilia
Saint Clare of Assisi
Saint Cyril of Jerusalem
Saint Francis Xavier
Saint Hildegarde of Bingen
Saint Jerome
Saint John Vianney
Saint Marguerite Bourgeoys
Saint Paul Miki
Saint Robert Bellarmine
Saint Stephen Martyred
Saint Thomas Aquinas
Saint Thomas More

Grade 6
Blessed Dorothy C. Orozco
Blessed Fra Angelico
Blessed Peter to Rot
John Carroll
Saint Birgitta of Sweden
Saint Charles Borromeo
Saint Teresa Benedicta
Saint Elizabeth Ann Seton
Saint Faustina Kowalska
Saint Hilda of Whitby
Saint Ignatius of Loyola
Saint J.B. de la Salle
Saint John the Baptist
Saint John Neumann
Saint John the Evangelist
Saint Matthias
Saint Monica
Saint Rose Duchesne
Saint Teresa of Avila
Venerable Catherine McAuley
Women Martyrs of El Salvador

Call to Faith Scope and Sequence

	Grade 4	Grade 5
Revelation	• God loves and cares for all creation and has a plan for the world. • All God wants you to know about him is in Scripture and Tradition. • God's covenant with Abraham reveals that God is always faithful to his people. • Sin is present in the world because of human choice. • The Ten Commandments help you be faithful to him and his covenant. • The commandments tell you ways to love God and others. **Jonah, Genesis 3, 12, 15, 17, 21, 37, 42, 44, 45, Exodus 2, 5, 14, 17–20** CCC: 302–308, 80–83, 50; 59–61, 385–389; 2055, 2060–2061, 577–580	• True happiness can come only through communion with God. • Religion expresses relationship with God through beliefs, prayer, and practices. • Humans share in the Creator's loving plan by caring for creation. • God's providence is his care and plan for all creation. • God communicates through signs. • Through the signs and symbolic actions of the sacraments, God's life becomes truly present in your life. **John 4:7–29, Psalm 98:4–9, Exodus 3:1–15** CCC: 27, 28, 142–143, 153–155, 160, 162; 307, 302, 2404; 1147, 774, 1152
Trinity	• Every person is worthy of respect because he or she is created in God's image. • Each person has a soul that will live forever. • God created people for one another, and all must work for the common good. Such love of neighbor reflects the love of the Holy Trinity. • No one can believe alone, just as no one can live alone. • God has given you free will so that you can make good choices. • Your conscience is in the "inner voice" that helps you choose what is good. **Genesis 1:27, Acts 2:42–45, Luke 10:30–37** CCC: 355–357, 362–366, 1928–1933; 1905–1906, 1878, 1757; 1706–1786, 1804-1806	• The Trinity is the central mystery of Christian faith and life. • Virtue is the habit of doing good. The theological virtues are faith, hope, and love. • Prayer and worship are ways to show love for God. • When we pray and worship, God fills us with joy, strength, and hope. • The Great Commandment states that you will love the Lord, your God, with all your heart, soul, and mind and your neighbor as yourself. • The cardinal virtues play a central role in helping people lead morally good lives. **John 1:32–34, 2 Samuel 6:1–15, Mark 12:28–34** CCC: 234, 1813, 253–255; 1083, 2638, 1082, 1071, 2565; 1804–1809, 1811
Jesus Christ	• The Beatitudes describe the reign of God that Jesus announced. • The Beatitudes show you how to live and act as a follower of Jesus. • The Great Commandment is to love God with all your heart, strength, and mind and to love your neighbor as yourself. • The Great Commandment sums up all the teachings of the Ten Commandments. • The first three commandments are to honor, respect, and worship God. • These commandments tell you believe in, trust, and love God. **Matthew 5:1–10, Matthew 19:16–22, Exodus 32:1–20** CCC: 1716, 1720, 1723, 1078–1079; 2055, 2083, 2196, 2447; 2062, 2077, 2113	• The Incarnation is the belief that the Son of God became a human being. • Jesus is both human and divine, truly God and truly human. • God's kingdom is present and grows until God's reign comes in fullness. • Jesus proclaimed the kingdom of God through his actions and parables. • Through the sacraments, Christ unites his followers to his passion, death, Resurrection, and Ascension. • Jesus Christ is the Redeemer of the human race. **Luke 8:5–8, 24:5–9** CCC: 461, 464, 1701–1702; 763–769, 546–547, 567; 1076, 618, 654
The Church	• Every person is called by God to a vocation. • Through your vocation, you can help God increase his reign. • The Church's holiness shines in the saints. All who live their love of God are saints. • Mary is the perfect model of holiness, and she is called the Mother of the Church. • Jesus gave the leaders of the Church the authority to interpret Scripture and Tradition for the faithful. • The Holy Spirit directs the Church in teaching and guiding the People of God. **Jeremiah 1:5–8, Luke 1:46–50, Mark 8:27–30** CCC: 941, 2046, 2030; 828, 829; 85, 87, 940–943	• As members of the Church, we are all united in living out the mission of Christ. • Church is expressed in the images of the Body of Christ and the People of God. • The Apostles proclaimed God's good news and cooperated with God's reign. • Under the guidance of the Holy Spirit, the pope and the bishops continue the Apostles' mission to teach. • Mary and the saints provide the Church with models of holiness. • Canonization declares that a model Christian is enjoying eternity with God. **I Peter 2:4–5, Matthew 16:15–19, 28:19–20, Luke 1:30–31, 38** CCC: 811, 776, 775; 551, 85–86, 863; 1173, 828, 2013
Morality	• God created humans to live in strong, loving families. • The fourth, sixth, and ninth commandments provide basic laws of family love and respect. • All human life is sacred because it comes from God. • The fifth commandment forbids anything that takes a human life. • Because God is truth, his people are called to live in the truth. • The eighth commandment forbids lying. **Luke 2:41–52, Matthew 5:43–45, John 8:31–32; 14:6** CCC: 2203, 2197, 2204, 2380, 2233; 2258, 2268, 2303–2304; 2465, 1741, 2467	• Evil is the result of humans' turning away from God's goodness. • God sent his Son to redeem people from the power of sin and evil. • The process of becoming Catholic is called the Rite of Christian Initiation of Adults. • The Sacraments of Initiation are Baptism, Confirmation, and Eucharist. • The Church receives God's forgiveness through the Sacraments of Healing. • The Sacrament of Reconciliation includes contrition, confession, penance, and absolution. **Romans 5:19, 6:10–11, Luke 15:11–32** CCC: 311, 614, 1854–1863; 1232, 1233, 1212, 1231; 1421, 1491, 1527
Sacraments	• The Church year celebrates the Paschal mystery. • The seasons of the liturgical year include Advent, Christmas, Lent, Easter, and Ordinary Time. • The seven sacraments are signs, instituted by Christ, that give grace. • The Sacrament of the Eucharist is at the heart of Christian life. • God's forgiveness is offered to all who seek it. • Reconciliation and the Anointing of the Sick celebrate God's healing love. **Ecclesiastes 3:1–8, Luke 22:17–20, 19:1–10, John 9:1–38** CCC: 1067, 1171, 1140; 1210, 1407, 1370; 1489, 1421	• The wheat bread and grape wine become the Body and Blood of Jesus in the Sacrament of the Eucharist. • In the liturgical assembly, the Holy Spirit strengthens the community. • The word of God is conveyed through Scripture and Tradition. • Jesus is truly present in the word as it is proclaimed and preached in the liturgy. • The Eucharist is the source and the summit of the Catholic Church. • The Eucharist closely unites Christ's followers to him and to one another. **Colossians 3:16, Matthew 26:26–28** CCC: 1374, 1141, 1378; 80–82, 1088, 108; 1324, 1372, 1398
The Kingdom of God	• The commandments call you to be generous and to have the right attitude toward possessions. • The goods of the earth are meant for the benefit of the whole human family. • The Church's mission is to proclaim the Gospel and to work for the good of all. • The Church is made up of people from many cultures united by belief in Christ. • The Church teaches that at the end of time, all will be raised from the dead. • All will come into the presence of Christ to be judged. **Mark 12:41–44, Matthew 25:34–40, 28:18–20** CCC: 299, 2402, 2407; 849, 1807, 942; 681, 682, 671	• The vocations of ordained and married people build the reign of God and serve others. • The Sacraments of Service are Holy Orders and Matrimony. • Faith in the Resurrection is the source of hope in eternal life and happiness. • Last rites of the Church include the Sacraments of Healing and the Eucharist. • The Church's mission is to bring the good news to all people everywhere. • Every baptized person has the responsibility of sharing the good news. **Matthew 9:35–38, 25:31–40, Luke 4:16–21** CCC: 1534, 1535, 1635; 989, 1525, 1024; 849, 863, 2820

Grade 2

- God is the creator of all that is good.
- Jesus is God's greatest gift. Jesus is the Son of God.
- God sent his Son, Jesus, to bring all people back to his friendship.
- Jesus is the Savior and the Good Shepherd.
- God tells us about himself through the Bible.
- The Bible is God's word written by humans.

Psalm 8:2, 7–9, Genesis 2–3, 6–9, John 10:11–14, Matthew 4:23–25
CCC: 290, 355, 422–464, 2415–2418; 430, 220, 389–390, 1441, 1846; 51–55, 80–82

- You can call God "Father" because he created you and cares for you like a good parent.
- You can trust in God because he loves you.
- Jesus is the beloved Son of God.
- Jesus is the Savior of the world.
- The Holy Trinity is the three Persons in one God.
- The Holy Spirit guides the Church and helps you to be a disciple.

Matthew 6:26–32, Luke 1–2, 2:41-52, 3:13–17, John 14:15–26, Acts 1–2
CCC: 355–356, 238–242; 461, 495, 437, 464–469; 685, 253, 1831, 1845, 731, 249–253

- The Ten Commandments are God's laws to his people.
- Jesus teaches you to love God above all things and to love others as you love yourself.
- Conscience is God's gift that helps you know right from wrong.
- Sin is a free choice to do what is wrong.
- God is merciful and forgiving.
- God will always forgive you if you are truly sorry.

John 15:12, 18:17–18, 25–27, Luke 10:25–37, 15:11–32
CCC: 2060–2068, 2055, 1730–1731, 1847, 1996–2005, 1786–1789; 1428, 2839, 1846, 1870

- Grace is sharing in God's life.
- Sacraments are holy signs that come from Jesus and give grace.
- In the Sacrament of Reconciliation, you receive God's forgiveness.
- This sacrament also celebrates your friendship with God and the Church.
- The Church year celebrates the life, death, and Resurrection of Jesus.
- The Resurrection is the mystery of Jesus being raised from death.

Genesis 6:14–22, 7:1–23, Acts 8:4–12, Luke 14:16–23, 7:36–50, John 14:25
CCC: 1131, 1996–1997, 1212, 1113–1130; 1849, 1440–1448; 1168, 1169, 1194

- The kingdom of God is love, peace, and justice for all.
- Everyone is welcome in God's kingdom and the Catholic Church.
- Jesus' disciples share in his life and in his work.
- Followers of Jesus are to proclaim his good news to the world.
- Prayer is being with God in your heart and mind.
- Jesus taught his followers the Lord's Prayer.

Luke 19:1–8, Matthew 6:5–9, 19:13–15, 28:20, John 15:4–5
CCC: 541, 543–544, 1826–1827, 2816; 1716–1717, 747, 902; 2762-2763, 2620, 2564

- Mass is another name for the celebration of the Eucharist.
- The assembly uses songs, prayer, and actions to worship.
- In the Liturgy of the Word, God's word is read from the Bible.
- We say what we believe about God and pray for the needs of the Church and the world.
- The Eucharist is a memorial of the sacrifice of Jesus.
- The Liturgy of the Eucharist is the second main part of the Mass.

Acts 2:42–47, Matthew 13:31–32, 19:21–22
CCC: 1071, 1167, 1083, 1140–1144; 546, 1349, 1354, 101–104; 1357, 1374, 1356–1381

- Through the Eucharist, Jesus' followers are united with him and one another.
- The gift of Holy Communion is received with reverence.
- The Church's mission is to share Jesus' message of love and to spread the news of the kingdom of God.
- All members of the Church share in its mission.
- Heaven is life and happiness forever with God.
- The Eucharist is a sign of joy and of what heaven will be like.

Luke 9:10–17, 14:15–23, Acts 10:42–48, Matthew 22:2–10
CCC: 1358, 1390; 846, 791, 850, 849–856; 542–543, 545, 546

Grade 3

- God created everything. All creation shows God's goodness.
- God created humans in his image and likeness.
- The Bible is the word of God written in human words.
- The Church is the People of God gathered in the name of Jesus.
- Children first learn about God's love through their families.
- The family home is called the "domestic Church."

Genesis 1:1–2:3, Acts 2:42–47, Luke 1:39–56
CCC: 315, 355, 293–301; 831, 836, 771; 1657, 1666, 2204–2207

- The Holy Trinity is three Persons in one God.
- Jesus, God the Son, taught about God the Father and God the Spirit.
- The Mass is the Church's most important form of worship.
- In the Mass the Church remembers what Jesus did at the Last Supper.
- Prayer is the raising of one's mind and heart to God.
- Prayer is an important part of a Christian's daily life.

John 14:6–7, 16–17, Luke 18:9–14, 22:14-20, Matthew 6:5–8
CCC: 253, 240, 243, 234; 61, 69, 1083; 2559, 2659, 2688

- Jesus shared the good news about God's kingdom of justice, love, and peace.
- Jesus is the Messiah, the chosen one, and Savior.
- Jesus died and rose to new life to save all people from the power of sin.
- The Church celebrates the Paschal mystery in all the sacraments.
- The Church is the Body of Christ to which all members belong.
- Church members continue Jesus' work when they help others.

Luke 4:16–22, John 20:11–18, Matthew 25:34–40
CCC: 546, 1154, 2688; 613, 2099–2100; 521, 1267, 2427–2428

- The bishops are the successors of the Apostles.
- The pope, bishops, and pastors lead and guide the Church.
- The Holy Spirit unites the Church and makes its members holy.
- Many cultures together make up the unity of the Church.
- The Church's mission is to share Jesus' good news with the people of all nations.
- The Church is catholic because it is everywhere and welcomes everyone.

Matthew 16:15–19, 26:69-75, John 21:15–17, Luke 1:46–50, 1 Corinthians 3:5–9
CCC: 880, 884, 890; 813, 791, 957; 831, 830, 864

- Jesus' law of love is to love one another as Jesus loves each of us.
- Jesus teaches that we should love and forgive our enemies.
- God's gifts of faith, hope, and love help you live a good and moral life.
- Christians are called by Jesus to be the light of the world.
- The Holy Spirit and the teachings of the Church help you make good choices.
- Your conscience and grace also help you follow God.

Matthew 5:14–16, 43–48, Acts 9:1–30
CCC: 1822, 1825, 1970; 1813, 2105, 1697; 2041, 1496, 1444

- Sacraments are signs that come from Jesus and give grace.
- The Sacraments of Initiation are Baptism, Confirmation, and Eucharist.
- The Sacraments of Healing are Reconciliation and Anointing of the Sick.
- In these sacraments the Church prays for spiritual and physical healing.
- The Sacraments of Service are Holy Orders and Matrimony.
- These sacraments celebrate people's commitment to God and the community.

Acts 2:38–41, Luke 8:40–42, 49–56, 1 Corinthians 4:1–2
CCC: 1229, 1271, 1272; 1421, 1514, 1531; 1534, 1535

- God kept his promise to be forever faithful when he sent his Son, Jesus.
- The Church continues to be a sign of God's covenant.
- All members of the Church share in its mission to work for peace and justice.
- The Church is a sign of the kingdom of God.
- People who die in God's friendship live forever in God's presence.
- At the end of the world, Christ will judge all people on the way they lived their lives.

Matthew 10:5–14, Revelation 21:1–4, 22:13
CCC: 781, 1612, 813–822; 2046, 2443, 2448; 673, 681, 1041

Call to Faith Scope and Sequence

	Grade K		Grade 1	
Revelation	• God made the world. • God made people to be like him. • God made people to love him and others.		• God created everything. All that God made is good. • God knows and loves everyone. • God's world is a gift to you. • You can learn about God and his love from the world he made. • All creation is a gift from God. • Everyone must help care for God's world.	
	Psalm 148:7–10, Genesis 1:27–28, 6–8, 1 Corinthians 13:4–7	CCC: 337; 356; 288	Genesis 2:7–22, 1:5–25, 1:26–30	CCC: 282, 286–287, 290, 299, 355–361, 364; 32, 297, 301, 293–295; 2402
Trinity	• God shows his love through others. • When we pray, we are talking to God. • All people care for God's world.		• The Holy Trinity is God the Father, God the Son, and God the Holy Spirit. • Jesus is the Son of God • Jesus is both God and man. • Jesus, Mary, and Joseph are the Holy Family. • Jesus told stories, or parables, to teach about God's love. • The Bible is God's word written in human words.	
	1 John 3:1, 1 Thessalonians 5:16–18, Genesis 1:28–30, 6–8	CCC: 238; 278; 373	John 14:7-9, Luke 2:51–52, 15:3–6	CCC: 232–234, 240, 423, 458–459, 516; 464, 531–533; 105–110, 136
Jesus Christ	• Jesus is the Son of God and the Son of Mary. • Jesus taught us to live through his life. • All Christians are called to follow Christ.		• Jesus' healing actions show God's power and love. • Faith is the gift of believing in God. • The Great Commandment is about love of God and others. • You are to love God above all else and love others as you love yourself. • Prayer is listening and talking to God. • Jesus taught his friends how to pray the Lord's Prayer.	
	Luke 2:1–7, 6:27–36, 10:25–37, Mark 1:16–19	CCC: 422, 723; 561; 940–942	Luke 8:40–56, 10:25–28, Ephesians 5:18–20	CCC: 547–550, 153, 1814; 2052–2056, 2196; 2560, 2564, 2601, 2607, 2759, 2761
The Church	• The Church is a large family that belongs to God. • The Holy Spirit helps the Church family to love. • Each person has special talents to serve others.		• God invites everyone into his kingdom. • The Church is people who follow Jesus and say "yes" to God's call. • God the Holy Spirit is the third Person of the Holy Trinity. • The Holy Spirit fills people's hearts with love and guides the Church. • Saints are friends of God who can show you how to live. • People in the Church are called to live holy lives, as the saints did.	
	Colossians 3:12–17, Acts 2:1–4, Matthew 25:42–46, Luke 2:1–20	CCC: 751, 752; 253, 791; 910, 2447	Genesis 6:14–22, 7:1–23, Luke 14:16–23, John 14:25–26	CCC: 541–545, 551, 781–782, 768; 243, 685; 684, 688, 731–733, 828, 829, 1023, 825, 956
Morality	• Love one another as Jesus loves you. • God's rules help people make good choices. • Tell others when you are sorry.		• Jesus' words and actions teach us how to love and serve God. • When you serve others, you are serving God. • The Ten Commandments are God's laws to help people love God and others. • God gives people the freedom to choose. • God always forgives those who are truly sorry and want to do better. • God asks that we forgive others and ourselves.	
	John 15:9, 11, Matthew 18: 21–35, 19:18–19	CCC: 1825; 2472; 270; 1421, 2227, 1435	John 13:4–17, Deuteronomy 10:12–13 Luke 18:9–13	CCC: 565, 459, 2825; 2053, 2058, 2067, 1730–1734; 982, 1431, 2840, 1446–1450
Sacraments	• The words and actions of the sacraments show the wonders of God. • Water is a source of life and also brings new life. • The bread becomes Jesus at Mass.		• God loves you so much that he sent his Son to save you. • Jesus died and rose to new life. • The Church has seven sacraments. They are signs of God's love. • Jesus gave the sacraments to remind people that he is with them always. • Your sharing in God's love and life is called grace. • Baptism is your welcome into the Church family.	
	Mark 8:22–26, 14:22–31, Acts 8:35–40	CCC: 459, 1749, 1131; 1, 1218, 1228, 1333, 1337, 1341	Luke 23–24, John 14:18–19 Acts 1:5, 8	CCC: 416–418, 422, 601, 654–655, 683; 1113, 1130, 1123; 1279, 1263–1270
The Kingdom of God	• God is great and we must serve him first. • The saints pray for us to God the Father every day. • To praise God for the wonderful thing he does is adoration.		• At Mass the Church family celebrates God's love. • Jesus gives himself to us in the Eucharist. • Heaven is being happy with God forever. • God invites all people to heaven. All who show love will go to heaven. • The signs of God's kingdom are justice, peace, and love. • Christians work here and now to help God bring his kingdom to its fullness.	
	1 Corinthians 2:9, Matthew 25:35–39, Luke 24:1–12	CCC: 30, 1844, 223; 833, 958, 955; 54, 2639, 2097	I Corinthians 11:23–25, John 14:1–3, 16:22, Romans 14:17–19	CCC: 1359–1361, 1374, 1325; 1024, 1023; 2819, 2818, 543–554

Call to Faith

Catechetical Process

Call to Faith uses a proven three-step catechetical process: Invite, Explore, Celebrate.

Invite   This step invites the learner into the catechetical process through simple and engaging reflections that draw out the life experience of the learner.

Explore   This step explores, in an age-appropriate way, the living Tradition of our Catholic faith as it is expressed in Scripture and doctrine. Through the use of a variety of stories, literary forms, and questions students enter more deeply into the chapter content and are helped to connect faith with their lives.

In order to show reverence for the word of God, Scripture is clearly labeled and set apart in each lesson. The "Words of Faith" feature included in this step helps build a common language of faith.

Celebrate   In this step, students celebrate what they believe through prayer celebrations that model the diverse ways in which Catholics pray. Prayers of praise, meditations, litanies, and celebrations of the word are included.

Music and song are included in each celebration. The Call to Faith music CD tracks are listed by chapter for ease of use.

Call to Faith Activity Process

Each chapter includes an integrated activity strand designed to lead the student from personal faith reflection to communal participation.

Let's Begin helps children reflect on their own varied experiences.

Share Your Faith helps children dialog with others and act on their faith.

Connect Your Faith helps children connect with the faith life of the Church.

Live Your Faith helps children put their faith into action.

The Family Faith page also includes a "Live Your Faith" activity, emphasizing that it is in the family setting—the "domestic Church"— that students primarily live out their faith.

Generations of Faith & CALL to FAITH

Lifelong Catechesis and *Call to Faith*

"Continuing formation in the faith is directed not only to the individual Christian, to accompany them in their journey towards holiness, but also to the Christian community as such so that it may mature also in its interior life of love of God and of brethren as well as in its openness to the world as a missionary community." *(GDC 70)*

Call to Faith incorporates lifelong catechesis in its curriculum. Through regular moments of faith sharing, connections to the Sunday lectionary, and options for family-centered catechesis and adult formation, *Call to Faith* engages not only the specific learner but the larger community of faith.

Today, parish and school leaders are seeking ways to meet the catechetical needs of several generations. They want an approach to catechesis that provides a systematic and comprehensive presentation of the faith while using a pedagogy that itself is drawn from the teaching style of Christ. They want to serve the entire community, giving parents, grandparents, guardians, and other adults the tools they need to develop households of faith. And they want to encourage everyone to participate fully in parish life, especially in the Sunday Liturgy.

To help leaders meet these goals, Harcourt Religion Publishers has partnered with the Generations of Faith Project of the Center for Ministry Development. The Generations of Faith approach enables the parish community to create a program of lifelong faith formation that is centered in the events of church life. It embraces all ages and generations, promotes faith growth at home, and, most importantly, promotes participation in Church life.

Generations of Faith and *Call to Faith*, working together, will provide you with an innovative approach to lifelong faith formation that engages all generations. All members of the community are invited to learn and grow in faith together.

Liturgical catechesis

Call to Faith includes a generous amount of liturgical catechesis to help students and families become, as the Second Vatican Council's document on the liturgy expressed, "full, conscious, and active" participants of the assembly at Mass. *Call to Faith* students who learn by celebrating the rites and feasts, rather than by merely reading about them, are formed for life in the rich liturgical tradition of the Catholic Church.

Lectionary-connected catechesis

For Catholics, the Scriptures are proclaimed week after week in the Liturgy of the Word at Sunday Mass. The "Break Open the Word" feature in *Call to Faith* provides an ongoing opportunity to reflect on these Scriptures. Care is also taken to provide opportunities to reflect on the readings for the seasons and feasts of the Church year. Harcourt Religion Publishers' Web site, **www.harcourtreligion.com**, serves the entire catechetical community in this effort.

 Visit www.harcourtreligion.com for weekly scripture readings and seasonal resources.

Catechetical approaches in CALL to FAITH

Because of the many ways children learn, and because of the communal nature of the Church itself, *Call to Faith* uses a variety of catechetical approaches, which are designed to help you succeed and be faithful to the task of catechesis.

Content-centered catechesis

The presentation of the core elements of the faith is essential in religious formation and instruction. *Call to Faith* provides you with accurate and comprehensive content based on Scripture and the *Catechism of the Catholic Church*, as well as a teaching method that will help you effectively communicate the content to your students.

Catechesis in the whole community

Call to Faith is the first textbook series designed for use in a catechetical program that encompasses the whole parish community. Although these textbooks are designed for children of various ages, they are also specifically designed to be the basis for catechesis in the rest of the community. The *Pastoral Leader's Source Book*, which accompanies *Call to Faith*, provides resources that will extend catechesis to the entire faith community.

Doctrine Each lesson of *Call to Faith* draws on and instructs in Church doctrine in ways that help students, catechists, and families understand and appreciate the Church's teachings as they apply to life today.

Lives of Saints and People of Faith *Call to Faith* takes seriously the importance of models and witnesses of faith as a factor in the faith development of both children and adults. The story of one person of faith whose life witnesses to the lesson theme is presented at the end of each lesson, and stories of other saints and people of faith are interwoven into the lessons when appropriate.

Cultural Customs and Celebrations Many communities have customs and devotions that address or celebrate the faith. These customs and devotions involve the lived experience and wisdom of the Christian community, and they respect the context and the culture of the local community. The inclusion of many of these rituals and customs is a unique component of *Call to Faith* and assists parishes in making the curriculum their own.

CALL to FAITH

Philosophy

Call to Faith is shaped around the following catechetical principles:

• **Conversion is central to catechesis.** The aim of *Call to Faith* is to form participants into disciples who act with the mind and heart of Christ.

• **Catechesis is a lifelong process.** Catechesis is gradual, systematic, and lifelong. We are touched and transformed by the living God and by the lived Tradition of the community throughout our lives.

• **Catechesis is the responsibility of all baptized members of the Church.** The whole parish community (including parents, family members, catechists, and pastors) is called to hand on the faith through faith sharing and the witness of daily life.

Sources of Catholic Wisdom

Call to Faith is deeply rooted in Church Tradition. In its dependence on and faithfulness to both the *Catechism of the Catholic Church* and the *General Directory for Catechesis*, it remains true to the *magisterium*, or teaching office of the Church, and draws from the following sources of Catholic wisdom:

Scripture In *Call to Faith*, the treasure of God's word is highlighted and integrated into the program's instruction, reflection, sharing, and prayer. Throughout the program students, catechists, and families are provided with both the content and the tools necessary to explore the Scriptures and to enrich their faith.

Let Us Pray

Oh God, Teacher and Giver of Life,
    we begin today a new journey,
    a journey of faith.
We are ready to learn from each other in this ministry,
    to support one another in love,
    and to work together as Church.
Grant us your wisdom
    to deepen our understanding of you.
Grant us your love
    to grow in our love for each other.

Walk with us on this journey
    as we answer the call to faith
    and help others do so as well.
Lead us to make loving choices in everything we do.
Guide us with the witness of the saints,
    the words of Sacred Scripture,
    and the teachings of the Church.

We pray for these gifts,
    confident in your goodness,
    through Jesus Christ, our Lord. Amen.

Opening Prayer

Sign of the Cross

In the name of the Father,
    and of the Son,
    and of the Holy Spirit.
                Amen.

We Are Called

Come! Live in the light!
Shine with the joy and the love of the Lord!
We are called to be light for the kingdom,
    to live in the freedom of the city of God!

Refrain:
We are called to act with justice,
we are called to love tenderly,
we are called to serve one another;
    to walk humbly with God!

Come! Open your heart!
Show your mercy to all those in fear!
We are called to be hope for the hopeless
    so all hatred and blindness will be no more!

¡Canten un cántico nuevo!
¡Anuncien el día de la salvación!
Reinará el Señor y su pueblo estará caminando
    en fraterna unión!
Dios nos llama a amar tiernamente y a
    servirnos unos a otros, caminando
    junto con Él.

Sing! Sing a new song!
Sing of that great day when all will be one!
God will reign, and we'll walk with each other
    as sisters and brothers united in love!

David Haas, © 1988, 2004, GIA Publications, Inc.

CONTENTS

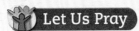

About You

About You

Objective: To look forward to the year ahead

Let Us Pray

Leader: Please bless us, God.

"May God be gracious to us and bless us."   *Psalm 67:2*

All: Please bless us, God. Amen.

Let Us Pray

Have children move to your classroom prayer space. In the space, have a crucifix and a Bible opened to the psalm verse. Begin with the Sign of the Cross. Pray aloud the opening prayer and have children respond.

Activity — Let's Begin

Welcome First grade is a great grade. You will learn many new things. You will learn about God's love for you. You will also grow as Jesus' friend.

You will spend time with your teacher and classmates. Why don't you share something about yourself?

Draw something special you can do!

Activity

- Tell children that this new year together is a new beginning for you, too, and that you are looking forward to getting to know them better. Read aloud "Let's Begin."

- Begin this activity by telling children something interesting about you. Invite volunteers to share something about themselves.

- Encourage each child to think about something special he or she can do well, and then have children draw pictures of themselves engaged in that activity in the space provided.

1

OPTIONAL ACTIVITY

Predictions Children will enjoy guessing what the year ahead will bring.

- Ask volunteers to suggest things they think the class may do during the year, such as singing or performing a play.

- Children's suggestions may provide activities they will enjoy.

Multiple Intelligence: Mathematical/Logical

★ REACHING ALL LEARNERS

Physical Activity First graders need periods of physical activity within their lessons.

- First graders can sit and pay attention for only a short time, but movement will help alleviate boredom.

- Physical activity can convey content as well as use up excess energy. Plays, pantomimes, dance, gestures, and active games can help children internalize religious concepts.

Objective: To explore knowledge of the Catholic faith and how this book will be used

About Your Faith

Invite volunteers to tell how they learn new things. Responses will vary.

• Point out that we learn new things every day, and that there are many people in our lives who help us learn. Ask volunteers to name some of those people. Responses will vary.

• Read aloud the text.

• Ask children why it is important to learn more about God and the Church community. Possible responses: Learning more about God helps you know how much God loves you; learning more about the Church helps you grow in your friendship with God.

Activity

• Invite volunteers to share some things they know about God.

• Ask children how they came to know these things.

• Ask children for questions they have about God. Tell children that together you will try to find answers to these questions.

During the year you will lear many things.

You will hear stories about God's love. You will get to kno God's Son, Jesus.

Your family and parish will help you.

Activity

Share Your Fai

Think: What is something you know about God?

Share: Talk to a small group about how you learned this.

 **Act:** As a class work with your teacher to make a list of questions you have about God.

QUICK TIP

Assess Prior Learning The activity above gives you an opportunity to learn how far children have already come on the journey of faith.

• Listen for any misunderstandings that you may need to correct as they discuss what they know about God and how they learned it.

About Your Book

Your book has many things in it.

It has stories about God and his Son, Jesus.

It also has stories about Jesus' followers.

Your book has prayers, songs, and activities, too.

Activity Connect Your Faith

Seek and Find To get to know your book better, look at the pictures below. Then find an example of the pictures in your book.

3

About Your Book

Summarize the text.

• Tell children that the textbook is like a map or guidebook that will help them on the journey of faith.

Activity

• Explain the concept of a Seek and Find because some children may not have participated in one.

• Explain the activity directions. Ask children to raise their hands when they discover one or more of the pictures in their texts.

• Give children sufficient time to find the pictures throughout their texts.

• Explain that each picture is a symbol for an activity or information that can be found near that picture.

• Ask volunteers to suggest what the other pictures might stand for.

OPTIONAL ACTIVITY

Scavenger Hunt Expand on the activity in the book by having a scavenger hunt within your room.

• Before class, place objects around the room such as a crucifix, a candle, and a rosary.

• Explain to children they are to look for items that tell them something about their Catholic faith.

Multiple Intelligence: Bodily/Kinesthetic

CATECHIST BACKGROUND

Textbook Features

• Biographies help children relate the content to their lives.

• Words of Faith define important vocabulary.

• Faith Facts are quick ways to arouse interest.

• People of Faith stories are about saints.

• Focus questions give a context for information.

A Call to Faith

Objective: To respond to the call to be followers of Jesus

 Let Us Pray

Tell children that in this celebration they will learn how Jesus calls people to be his followers.

Prepare

Choose one child to lead the group in the opening Sign of the Cross.

 Use the *Call to Faith* 1 CD, track 9, to rehearse the suggested song.

Gather

Have children move to the prayer space and sit comfortably on the floor, facing you and the prayer table.

Leader's Prayer: **Jesus, help us learn to follow you always.**

Listen to God's Word

Follow the order of prayer on pages 4–5.

- Read aloud the first Reflect question. Allow time for children to think before calling on them.
- Tell children that each of them received a call to be a follower of Jesus at Baptism.

A Call to Faith

Gather

Pray the Sign of the Cross together.

Leader: The Lord be with you.

All: And also with you.

Leader: Let us pray.

Bow your heads as the leader prays.

All: Amen.

Listen to God's Word

Leader: A reading from the holy Gospel according to Mark.

Read Mark 1:16–20.

The Gospel of the Lord.

All: Praise to you, Lord Jesus Christ.

Reflect

What did Jesus ask Simon and Andrew? What does Jesus ask of you?

4

 SCRIPTURE BACKGROUND

The First Followers of Jesus Jesus called as his first followers ordinary men and women.

- Simon, Andrew, James, and John were going about their daily business of fishing when they were called.

- Jesus continues to call us to follow him while we are about our daily business of school, work, or play.

 LECTIONARY LINK

Break Open the Word Read last week's Sunday Gospel. Invite children to think about what the reading means to them as they try to follow Jesus. For questions related to the weekly Gospel reading, visit our website at **www.harcourtreligion.com**.

 Visit www.harcourtreligion.com for weekly scripture readings and seasonal resources.

Sign of the Cross

Leader: In the name of the Father,

All: In the name of the Father,

Leader: and of the Son,

All: and of the Son,

Leader: and of the Holy Spirit.

All: and of the Holy Spirit.

Leader: Amen.

All: Amen.

Go Forth!

Leader: Let us begin this new year with all the joy and love that comes from Christ.

All: Thanks be to God.

 Sing together.

We are called to act with justice,
we are called to love tenderly,
we are called to serve one another;
to walk humbly with God!

"We Are Called" © 1988, 2004 GIA Publications, Inc.

• Read aloud the second question. Encourage responses that include actions outside of church, such as sharing and helping.

Sign of the Cross

• Have children stand facing you. Then turn around so that children can follow your gestures correctly.

• Remind children which hand they will use to make the Sign of the Cross by raising your right hand.

• Begin the Sign of the Cross, slowly and prayerfully. Ask children to repeat both words and gestures after you.

Go Forth!

• End the celebration with enthusiasm and joy.

• Have children sing the song once while they are still in the prayer space.

• Invite children to line up behind you with their texts and process around the classroom while singing the song again.

 LITURGY LINK

Making the Sign of the Cross At every liturgy, the priest and assembly gathered begin the celebration with the Sign of the Cross.

• Making the Sign of the Cross reminds us that we are called by Jesus to follow him. It is our sign of discipleship. It is our sign of belonging. We belong to and follow Jesus, whose life was given up for us on a cross.

Family Faith

You belong to Jesus. You belong to the Church community. You belong to your family and friends. You are special!

Use the drawing spaces to draw pictures of some of the people and groups to whom you belong.

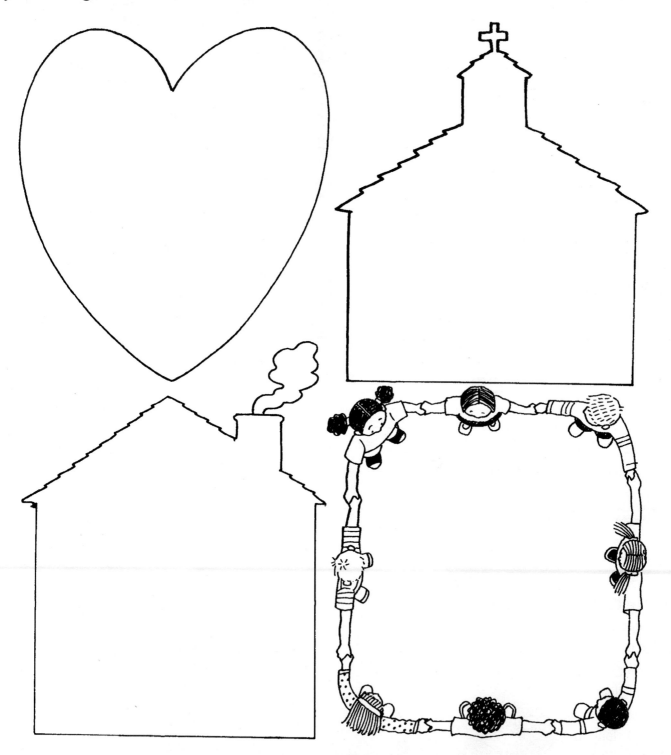

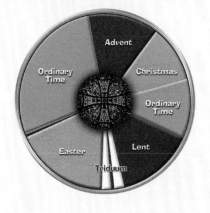

Seasonal Lessons

By means of the yearly cycle the Church celebrates the whole mystery of Christ, from his incarnation until the day of Pentecost and the expectation of his coming again.

General Norms for the Liturgical Year and the Calendar, 17

Liturgical Environment

Since these celebrations are meant to have a different tone and flavor than the other lessons, the environment you set for them is important. Factors to include in setting the environment are:

- Color
- Silence
- Music
- Symbols

The heart of these sessions is the celebration. Take time to determine whether your prayer space is appropriate for the ritual or if there is something else, such as moving furniture, adding plants or flowers, or moving to another place that would create a more reflective prayer-filled environment. Use the appropriate liturgical colors for seasons and feasts:

- Green for Ordinary Time
- White or gold for Christmas and Easter
- Purple for Advent and Lent
- White for Feasts of Mary
- Red for Pentecost

The use of primary symbols, water, oil, the cross, the Scriptures, and candles is very important. Display them prominently and reverently in your prayer space.

The Role of Music

Besides the music from the *Call to Faith* and *Singing Our Faith* CDs suggested in your Teacher Edition, use of meditative music at the beginning of a service or during a meditation time will also enhance a prayerful atmosphere for the children. Do not be afraid of silence. It is good for students to have time to reflect.

The Church Year

Within the flow of what most people experience as a calendar year, from January first to December thirty-first, there is another year—the liturgical or Church year. This year, which is not dependent on the civil calendar, begins on the first Sunday of Advent or the fourth Sunday before Christmas and ends on the feast of Christ the King, the last Sunday of Ordinary Time. For Christians, as it unfolds each year, the liturgical year is a time of grace and favor because it celebrates and remembers the person of Jesus Christ and the Paschal mystery of his life, death, and Resurrection. Easter, the feast of Jesus' Resurrection, is the most important and principal feast of the Church year. Another significant feast is Christmas—the celebration of the birth of Jesus. These feasts determine the flow of the Church year. Each of them is preceded by a season of preparation: Advent for Christmas and Lent for Easter. Each feast is followed by a number of weeks of celebration called the Christmas season and the Easter season. There are also thirty-three to thirty-four Sundays of the Church year called Ordinary Time. Ordinary Time celebrates the events and teachings of Jesus' public life. During the year, as the Church celebrates the mysteries of Christ, the Church also honors Mary, who is closely linked to the saving actions of her Son, and the saints, who are faithful examples of how to live the Christian life.

In these eight sessions you will find a celebration for each of the liturgical seasons of the Church year including the Triduum and a celebration for Mary and one of the saints. Use your class calendar to plan ahead for each of these lessons to coincide with the season or feast during Ordinary Time.

Liturgical Catechesis

These celebrations follow a process of liturgical catechesis which includes forming children in the language, rituals, structure, and order of the liturgy. The process of liturgical catechesis contained in each session includes:

- A reflection about the context of the feast being celebrated.
- A ritual celebration built around a text taken from the Book of Rites or Lectionary. Within the celebration there is always participation in some ritual action.
- An opportunity for reflection and action that flow from the celebration.

The Scriptures

The scripture readings in these sessions are meant to be proclaimed and probed with children. Give them ample time to respond to the dialogue questions. The purpose of the dialogue is to find out what children heard in the proclamation of the word and to explore their thoughts. Always ask open-ended questions and refrain from trying to control the dialogue.

The Students

Elementary grade children bring an innate sense of wonder, awe, and imitation to ritual prayer. They are quieted through the creation of a prayerful environment. They are caught up by the use of signs and symbols and need little explanation of them as long as they are prominently displayed and reverently used. Make your gestures large and inclusive. For example, when you sign children with the Sign of the Cross, sign with large gestures. Use slow and reverent gestures, such as bowing before the Scriptures, and lighting the candle slowly in silence. Children will imitate you and will learn far more by your movements during ritual than by your words.

Special Times

Families share special times together. Birthdays and holidays are often spent with family and friends.

The Church shares special times together, too. The Church celebrates events in the lives of Jesus, Mary, and the saints.

The Church uses words and actions to celebrate.

Words and Actions

Hands are folded in prayer.

Heads are bowed in silence.

The Sign of the Cross is marked on foreheads, hearts, and lips.

During the year, your class will use these words and actions to celebrate, too.

6

The Church Year

Advent

Christmas

Ordinary Time

Ordinary Time

Lent

Easter

Triduum

Ordinary Time

Mother Mary

As it celebrates the mystery of Christ in the yearly cycle, the Church also venerates with a particular love, Mary, the Mother of God and sets before the devotion of the faithful the memory of the martyrs and other saints.

General Norms for the Liturgical Year and Calendar, 8

Catechist Formation

At the birth of their child most Christian parents share their delight with family and friends. Parents also proudly give their child a name. It was really no different in first century Israel. Mary, a variation of Miriam, was born to Jewish parents, Joachim and Ann. Although we have no record of her childhood, we assume she grew up participating in all the Jewish customs and laws of her time.

Through the scripture stories, we know that God found favor with Mary and asked her to be the mother of his son, Jesus (*Luke 1:26–38*). It is her willingness to say "yes" to God that Catholics continue to celebrate today.

Throughout the liturgical year, there are many feasts honoring Mary. In all of them the Church celebrates Mary's favor with God and her willingness to become the Mother of God, and an instrument in our salvation. Mary's birth is celebrated on September 8, nine months following the Church's celebration of her Immaculate Conception on December 8. The celebration of Mary's birthday in the Church calendar is unusual. In most cases the Church celebrates a saint's feast on the date of their death which is seen as their birth into eternal life. Mary and Saint John the Baptist are the only two people whose human births are celebrated in the liturgical year. In celebrating Mary's birthday the Church gives expression to her birth as a special moment in salvation history. She would give birth to Jesus, the Savior.

Reflect ***Which qualities of Mary do you most admire?***

Environment

Materials:

Prayer table
White cloth
Bible
Statue of Mary
Battery operated or electric candle
Paper and crayons
Call to Faith Grade 1 CD

- Place the prayer table in the center of the prayer space, and cover it with the white cloth.
- Place the statue of Mary on the table, and light the candle.
- Arrange the prayer space so that children can kneel.

8A   Mary Background

Ordinary Time

Parents are very special people. We are born to them, and they continue to nurture, support, and care about us for the rest of their lives. It is interesting to reflect on the fact that the role of mother or father never ends. No matter how old, wise, or accomplished their child becomes, they are still the parents. The celebration of Mary's birthday in the Church calendar on September 8 is unusual. In most cases the Church celebrates a saint's feast on the date of his or her death which is seen as his or her birth into eternal life. Mary and Saint John the Baptist are the only two people whose human births are celebrated in the liturgical year. In celebrating Mary's birthday the Church gives expression to her birth as a special moment in salvation history. She would give birth to Jesus, the Savior. She is the Mother of God.

By celebrating Mary's birthday, we rejoice that she was open to God's invitation to become the Mother of Jesus. We rejoice that through her Jesus came into the world, and she continues today to be our mother.

Family Celebration

Read together the story of the Wedding Feast of Cana *(John 2:1–11)*. Talk with one another about how Mary recognized a need and went to Jesus. Discuss how Jesus responded. Together think about needs you have as a family that you would like to bring to Mary in prayer. Pray the Memorare together.

> **Memorare**
> Remember, most loving Virgin Mary, never was it heard
> that anyone who turned to you for help was left unaided.
> Inspired by this confidence, though burdened by my sins,
> I run to your protection for you are my mother.
> Mother of the Word of God, do not despise my words of
> pleading but be merciful and hear my prayer.
> Amen.

Family Activity

One of the ways to celebrate the birth of Mary is to honor mothers you know.

- Talk about the many "mothers" who have helped you in your life. Include your own mother and grandmother as well as aunts, mothers of friends, and others.

- Brainstorm what special thing each of you can do to honor one of the mothers you have talked about. Possibilities might be to bring them flowers, write a note, draw a picture for the person, or pray for the person.

Mother Mary

- Ask children what they know about Mary. Possible response: She is Jesus' mother.
- Invite children to study the picture on page 8.
- Ask what is happening in the picture. The angel is asking Mary to be Jesus' mother.
- Elicit what feelings Mary might have had when the angel asked her to be Jesus' mother. Possible responses: happy, afraid
- Read aloud the first five lines of text.
- Invite children to draw a face that shows how they feel about what you just read.
- Invite volunteers to share their faces with the group.
- Summarize the rest of the text. Emphasize the importance of Mary's "yes."

Ordinary Time

Mother Mary

You are God's child.

Because God is your Father, Jesus is your brother.

The mother of Jesus is Mary.

Mary is your mother, too.

Mary's birthday is on September 8.

Mary said "yes" to God's plan, and the Son of God became man.

8

 SEASONAL RESOURCES

Books Many resources are available to supplement your lesson about Mary.

- *Mary's Journey.* Rev. Louis Cameli (Christian Classics). This book is a meditation on Mary based on Scripture, Church teaching, and worship.
- *How to Talk with Your Children about Mary.* Cindy Cavnar (Our Sunday Visitor). This book will help you explain Mary's role in the Church.

 CULTURAL CONNECTION

Marian Devotions Many of today's popular devotions to Mary have grown over the years and enhanced people's faith.

- Devotion to the Rosary was spread by Saint Dominic in the thirteenth century.
- Devotion to the Miraculous Medal was initiated by Zoe Labore, a Daughter of Charity of St. Vincent in the nineteenth century.

Celebrate Mary

Gather

Sing together the refrain.
Ave, Ave, Ave, Maria.
Ave, Ave, Maria.

"Immaculate Mary" Traditional

Pray the Sign of the Cross together.

Leader: Blessed be God.

All: Blessed be God forever.

Leader: Let us pray.

Bow your heads as the leader prays.

All: Amen.

Listen to God's Word

Leader: A reading from the holy Gospel according to Matthew.

Read Matthew 1:18–23.
The Gospel of the Lord.

All: Praise to you, Lord Jesus Christ.

Go Forth!

Leader: Let us go to share God's peace and love.

All: Thanks be to God.

9

Celebrate Mary

Gather

- Gather children for worship with a moment of silence.
 Lead children in singing the opening song using the *Call to Faith* 1 CD, track 1.
- Lead them in the Sign of the Cross.
- Leader's prayer: **O God, we thank you and we praise you for giving us Mary, our mother.**

Listen to God's Word

- Have children remain standing for the Gospel.
- Proclaim the Gospel.
- Use a hand gesture to invite children's response to the Gospel.
- Pause for a moment of silence.
- Have children kneel and say the Hail Mary together.
 Have children stand and then lead them in singing the refrain.

Go Forth!

- Dismiss children with the final blessing.

 RITUAL

Kneeling This is one of the postures of prayer. It expresses submission, adoration, reverence, and humility.

- It is a deep posture of penitential character.
- It is also an expression of devotional piety and the posture of the individual engaged in private prayer.
- During the celebration, it is an expression of reverence and honor of Mary.

 LECTIONARY LINK

Matthew 1:18–23 The gospel reading for the celebration of Mary's birthday tells the story of how she became the Mother of Jesus.

- This reading is the first infancy narrative in the Gospel according to Matthew.
- It proclaims that the conception of Jesus was the work of the Holy Spirit.

Advent

Waiting for Jesus

Advent is thus a period for devout and joyful expectation.

General Norms for the Liturgical Year and Calendar, 39

Catechist Formation

Expecting a child takes much preparation and energy. Time is spent preparing a space for a new baby. Parents and siblings dream about what this new child will bring and how their lives will be changed by his or her coming. For centuries the people of God waited for the coming of a savior. They, too, wondered about what this savior would bring and how they might be changed by his coming. In the years leading up to the birth of Christ, God prepared his people through the ministry of the prophets who heralded his coming and awakened expectation in their hearts.

Each year, the Church prepares to celebrate Christ's coming in Advent—the four weeks before Christmas. The Advent season also marks the beginning of the liturgical year. Through Scripture, music, and ritual actions, the worshiping assembly renews the ancient expectations and promises of the Messiah. The color purple, which symbolizes that the hearts of the gathered community are in preparation, adorns the sanctuary and is the color of the vestments worn by the priest. By sharing in Advent celebrations the faithful renew their sense of desire to see and know Christ when he comes again.

The celebration of Advent takes place both communally and in people's hearts. It is a time for reflection and preparation, not only remembering Christ's first coming, but preparing for Christ's second coming at the end of time.

Reflect   ***How will you prepare your heart for Christ's coming this Advent?***

Environment

Materials:

Prayer table
Purple cloth
Advent Wreath
Bible
Call to Faith Grade 1 CD

- Cover the prayer table with the purple cloth.

- Place the Advent Wreath in the center of the prayer table.

- Obtain necessary permission to light the candles on the wreath.

Advent

Each year during Advent, the Church prepares for Christ's coming. The Advent season also marks the beginning of the liturgical year. Through Scripture, music, and ritual actions, the worshiping assembly renews the ancient expectations and promises of the Messiah. The color purple, which symbolizes that the hearts of the gathered community are in preparation, adorns the sanctuary and is the color of the vestments worn by the priest. By sharing in Advent celebrations, the faithful renew their sense of desire to see and know Christ when he comes again.

The Advent season is a good time for reflection. During this period of preparation, families are called not only to remember Christ's first coming, but are called to mindfully prepare for his second coming at the end of time.

Family Celebration

Use the following prayer to bless your Advent wreath.

> **Blessing of the Advent Wreath**
>
> **Leader:** Celebrating the endless circle of God's love, we join together around this Advent wreath in his name.
>
> **All:** Amen.
>
> (Extend hands over the wreath in a gesture of blessing.)
>
> **Leader:** As our family's Advent wreath stays evergreen and alive, and the candles mark the weeks of anticipation ahead, nurture in us joyful hope. We ask this in your name.
>
> **All:** Amen.

Family Activity

Create an Advent wreath.

1. Begin by gathering evergreen branches from your yard or from a Christmas tree lot.

2. Using white or purple ribbons attach the branches to a Styrofoam™ ring.

3. Place the candles evenly in the Styrofoam™ ring between the branches.

4. After the wreath is completed, bless the wreath using the Family Prayer.

5. Light the first purple candle, and sing "O Come, O Come Emmanuel." Do this for each week during Advent, lighting the pink candle during the third week as a symbol of joy and hope.

©Harcourt Religion

Waiting for Jesus

- Ask children to share some experiences of waiting. Possible responses: the birth of a sibling, a parent to come home
- Ask children what they do and how they feel when they are waiting. Responses will vary.
- Emphasize responses which indicate longing or preparation.
- Explore the feelings God's people must have had waiting for the Messiah—tired of waiting, worried, excited. Have children share their responses.
- Read aloud the text

Advent

Waiting for Jesus

The days before Christmas are called Advent.

Advent means coming.

We celebrate Jesus' coming to us.

People waited many years for God to send a savior to earth.

Finally, Jesus the Savior was born in Bethlehem.

10

SEASONAL RESOURCES

Books Many resources are available to supplement your lesson.

- *An Advent Source Book.* Thomas O' Gorman (Liturgy Training Publications). Contains Scripture, poetry, hymns, homilies, letters, fiction, folklore and liturgy.
- *Advent Arts and Christmas Crafts: With Prayers and Rituals for Family, School and Church.* Jeanne Hieberg (Paulist Press).

CULTURAL CONNECTION

Advent in Germany Germans follow a custom of giving and using Advent calendars.

- Traditionally, on the first Sunday of Advent children receive an Advent calendar.
- It has colorful pictures on each small paper window.
- Children open a "window" each morning, counting the days toward Christmas.

Celebrate Jesus

Gather

Sing together the refrain.

Rejoice! Rejoice! Emmanuel
Shall come to you, O Israel.

"O Come, O Come, Emmanuel," Traditional

Pray the Sign of the Cross together.

Leader: The Lord be with you.

All: And also with you.

Leader: Let us pray.

Bow your heads as the leader prays.

All: Amen.

Listen to God's Word

Leader: A reading from the prophet Isaiah.
Read Isaiah 40:9–10.
The word of the Lord.

All: Thanks be to God.

Go Forth!

Leader: Let us go forth to wait for Jesus.

All: Thanks be to God.

11

Celebrate Jesus

Gather

- In the prayer space gather children around the Advent wreath. Explain that it helps us remember we are waiting for Jesus.
- Light the appropriate number of candles on the wreath.

 Lead children in singing the song using the *Call to Faith* 1 CD, track 2.

- Leader's prayer: **God our Father, we wait for Jesus. Help us prepare a place for him in our hearts.**

Listen to God's Word

- Have children remain standing for the Gospel.
- Proclaim the Gospel.
- Use a hand gesture to invite children's response to the Gospel.

Go Forth

- Invite children to extend their hands over the wreath as you pray the final prayer.
- Encourage children to respond with enthusiasm.

RITUAL

Advent Wreath   The ritual of Advent wreaths began in pre-Christian Germany. In winter people made wreaths with evergreens and candles as a sign of hope.

- Christians kept this popular tradition alive to symbolize Advent hope in Christ our Light.
- You may wish to repeat this ritual in your class several times during Advent.

LECTIONARY LINK

Isaiah 40:9–10   This reading is part of the first reading on the Second Sunday of Advent during Year B of the Lectionary cycle.

- These verses proclaim a powerful and strong God.
- Chapters 40–55 in the Book of Isaiah were written at a time when Israel was discouraged. These chapters paint a picture of hope for then and now.

Christmas

The Light of Christ

Next to the yearly celebration of the Paschal Mystery, the Church holds most sacred the memorial of Christ's birth and manifestations. This is the purpose of the Christmas season.

General Norms for the Liturgical Year and Calendar, 32

Catechist Formation

The Christmas Season begins with the celebration of Christ's birth on December 25th and ends with the celebration of the Baptism of the Lord in January. The Christmas liturgy sings the glory of the night when the angels appeared to the shepherds in the region of Bethlehem and proclaimed the good news that the Messiah is born.

The gathered assembly meets Christ in the Word of God and, filled with joy, they celebrate the arrival of the Messiah. The people of God go forth from the Christmas liturgy to spread the good news that God became man. During the Christmas season several feast days frame the brilliance of the Incarnation, namely the feasts of the Holy Family, Epiphany, and the Baptism of Jesus.

Christ's Incarnation is important to our salvation, for without God's gift of his Son, we would not know redemption. While on earth, Jesus taught that his Incarnation is embodied in the commandment of love—loving those who are oppressed. Christ is incarnate in the lives of those around us. The Christmas season celebrates the light of Christ found in one another.

Reflect **How is God made flesh in your actions and words?**

Environment

Materials:

Prayer table
White cloth
Manger scene
Cutouts of a star, an evergreen branch, and a baby
Evergreens
Bible and lights
Call to Faith **Grade 1 CD**

- Place the manger scene on the prayer table so children can gather around it. Decorate the table with evergreens and lights.

- Arrange the space so children can process.

Christmas

All too often Christmas is celebrated in the weeks before Christmas as we prepare, rather than in the true Christmas season that follows the birth of Christ. The Church celebrates the Christmas season beginning with the celebration of Christ's birth on December 25th and ending with the celebration of the Baptism of the Lord in January. No one knows the exact date of Jesus' birth. The early Christians chose the December date—a time in mid-winter, the darkest time of the year—to emphasize that Christ brings light into the darkness of the world.

In the liturgies of the Church, the people of God celebrate the Incarnation of the Word, listening to the Christian story of joyous shepherds, the arrival of the magi, and prophecies about Jesus' life. We celebrate the gift of light evident throughout the church. White linens, a symbol of new life, adorn the crèche as the image of the Christ child is placed in the manger. The Church celebrates Christ incarnate in one another. As a family, it is important to continue the celebration in your home.

Family Celebration

Say this prayer before your evening meal during the Christmas season.

> **Leader:** Lord Jesus,
> in the peace of this season
> our spirits rejoice:
> With the beasts and angels,
> the shepherds and stars,
> with Mary and Joseph,
> we sing God's praise.
>
> By your coming
> may the hungry be filled with good things,
> and may our table and home be blessed.
> Glory to God in the highest.
>
> **All:** And peace to his people on earth.

Family Activity

Here are some suggestions for family activities during the Christmas season.

- Gather around your family crèche. Ask your family to extend their hands over the crèche in a gesture of blessing. Say: "May our Christmas manger be a reminder that our hearts are a home for Jesus."

- Have each family member welcome Jesus to the world with a word or gesture. Possible examples: A simple word of welcome, or placing infant clothing by the manger to donate to a needy family after the Christmas season.

The Light of Christ

- Show children pictures or cutouts of a star, an evergreen, and a baby.
- Ask children what the symbols have in common. Elicit *Christmas* as a response.
- Invite children to look at the illustration in the text.
- Ask them to share what they know about the visit of the wise men to the Christ child.
- Emphasize that the wise men followed the star which lit their way to Jesus.
- Read the text aloud.
- Invite children to share ways they can light the way to Jesus for others. Possible response: Be kind to a classmate on the playground.
- Make a list of children's suggestions, and place it in a prominent place.

Christmas

The Light of Christ

The star of Bethlehem pointed the way to the baby Jesus.

When you look at the star on your tree, think of the three wise men.

You will be wise, too, if you look for Jesus.

Are you a star?

You can be a star by lighting the way to Jesus.

SEASONAL RESOURCES

Books   Many resources are available to supplement your lesson about Christmas.

- *Keeping Advent and Christmastime* (Liturgy Training Publications). This prayer book contains prayers for Advent and Christmastime.
- *Behold This Child: The Gospel Stories of Jesus' Birth.* Anthony Scanell (Saint Anthony Messenger Press).

CULTURAL CONNECTION

Epiphany Cake   A common custom in many European cultures thought to have pagan roots is the Epiphany cake.

- Originally the cake contained one to three trinkets or beans and the person who found it became the king or queen of the feast.
- The tradition is adapted for Christians today so that persons finding the hidden trinket do something special for the others.

Celebrate Christmas

Gather

Sing together the refrain.

O come, let us adore him,
O come, let us adore him,
O come, let us adore him,
Christ, the Lord.

"O Come, All Ye Faithful," Traditional

Pray the Sign of the Cross together.

Leader: The Lord be with you.

All: And also with you.

Leader: Let us pray.

Bow your heads as the leader prays.

All: Amen.

Listen to God's Word

Leader: A reading from the holy Gospel according to Matthew.

Read Matthew 2:9–11.
The Gospel of the Lord.

All: Praise to you, Lord Jesus Christ.

Go Forth!

Leader: Let us rejoice in the birth of Jesus.

All: Thanks be to God.

13

Celebrate Christmas

Gather

 Practice the hymn before gathering children for worship. Use the *Call to Faith* 1 CD, track 3.

- Gather children in a single file, and process around the room, to the prayer table while singing the refrain.
- Lead children in the sign of the cross and opening prayers.
- Leader's prayer: **God, our Father, we give you thanks for the gift of your Son, Jesus. Help us to follow his light.**

Listen to God's Word

- Proclaim the Gospel.
- Use a hand gesture to invite children's response to the Gospel.

Go Forth

- Give the final blessing and then gesture for children to respond.
- While singing the refrain together, lead children in procession around the room back to their places.

 RITUAL

Procession Processions have long been a part of religious ceremonies.

- Processions may recall holy events, as the procession with palms on the Sunday before Easter, or be functional, as the entrance procession for Mass.
- Children will easily relate to a procession as a "holy parade."

 LECTIONARY LINK

Matthew 2:9–11 This reading is a part of the Gospel proclaimed on the feast of the Epiphany.

- The Magi represent the world outside of Judaism. The event of their visit proclaims that Jesus came for all people.
- Gold represents the kingship of Christ; frankincense, his divinity; and myrrh, his suffering.

Ordinary Time

"The saints of universal significance have celebrations obligatory throughout the entire Church. Other saints either are listed in the General Calendar for optional celebration or are left to the veneration of some particular Church, region, or religious family."

General Norms for the Liturgical Year and the Calendar, 9

Catechist Formation

Ordinary Time is the longest portion of the Church year. It is divided into two parts. The first begins immediately after the Christmas season and continues until Ash Wednesday, when Lent begins. The second begins immediately after Pentecost and continues until the first Sunday of Advent. Right now you are probably in the first part of Ordinary Time. The word *ordinary* in Ordinary Time does not mean "as usual" or "common." Rather it comes from the word "ordinal," which simply means counted time (12th Sunday of . . .). While Ordinary Time does not celebrate a specific aspect of the mystery of Christ as Christmas and Easter do, it is devoted to the mystery of Christ in all its aspects.

The Church year is also structured in two major cycles: the temporal cycle and the sanctoral cycle. The temporal cycle refers to "time" and is the recurring series of the main *times* or *seasons* of the Church year. The sanctoral cycle refers to "saints" and is the recurring series of *the feasts of the saints.*

As Bishop of Geneva, Switzerland, in the seventeenth century, Francis de Sales started catechetical instructions for the faithful, both young and old. He was known for his goodness, patience, and mildness. Francis loved the poor. He identified with them and lived a simple life in order to be able to provide more abundantly for the wants of the needy. Together with St. Jane Frances de Chantal, he founded the Institute of the Visitation of the Blessed Virgin.

Reflect **Which saints are your favorites?**

Environment

Materials:

Prayer table
Green cloth
Bible
Battery operated or electric candle
Bowl of holy water
Call to Faith 1 CD

• Place the prayer table in the center of the prayer space, and cover it with the green cloth.

• Place the Bible and bowl of holy water on the table, and light the candle.

Ordinary Time

Ordinary Time is the longest portion of the church year. It is divided into two different parts. The first begins immediately after the Christmas season and continues until Ash Wednesday, when Lent begins. The second begins immediately after Pentecost and continues until the first Sunday of Advent. Right now you are probably in the first part of Ordinary Time.

The word *ordinary* in Ordinary Time does not mean "as usual" or "common." Rather it comes from the word "ordinal," which simply means counted time (12th Sunday of . . .). While Ordinary Time does not celebrate a specific aspect of the mystery of Christ as Christmas and Easter do, it is devoted to the mystery of Christ in all its aspects. The Gospel Readings of Ordinary time proclaim the life and teachings of Jesus.

Family Celebration

During Ordinary Time the gospels proclaim the events in the life of Jesus. Have each member of the family choose his or her favorite Gospel Story. Gather several times over dinner or at some other appropriate time, and have family members share their Gospel Story. At the end of the sharing, pray the Act of Love together.

> O my God, I love you above all things, with my whole heart and soul, because you are all good and worthy of all my love. I love my neighbor as myself for the love of you. I forgive all who have injured me, and I ask pardon of all whom I have injured. Amen.

Family Activity

Make a tablecloth of Ordinary Time memories.

• Obtain a plain white tablecloth, an undercloth, and a variety of colorful permanent markers.

• On the Sundays of Ordinary Time, gather at mealtime to discuss the scripture readings.

• Mark off a segment on the tablecloth for each Sunday.

• After discussion invite family members to draw pictures or write words that are important to them in the designated space.

Family Faith Copy Master 14B

Saint Francis

- Ask children what they know about saints. Possible responses: They are holy; they are God's friends.
- Invite children to study the picture of Saint Francis de Sales.
- Summarize the text.
- Remind children that everyone is called to be a saint.

Saint Francis de Sales

Francis lived in France. He was a wise and wealthy man. Francis heard God calling him, and he became a priest.

Francis helped people learn about the Catholic Church. He became a bishop and wrote many books.

The feast of Saint Francis is January 24.

14

SEASONAL RESOURCES

Books and Videos   Many resources are available to supplement your lesson.

- *Radical Grace: Daily Meditations*. Richard Rohr (St. Anthony Messenger Press). A collection of meditations following the Church's liturgical cycle.
- *The Angel's Church Year Lesson* (12 min). Twenty-Third Publications. This videotape is part of a series which tells what happened to Jesus in each of the seasons of the Church year.

CULTURAL CONNECTION

Patron Saint   Patron saints are chosen as special protectors or guardians over many areas of life. Saint Francis de Sales is patron of:

- authors, educators, journalists, teachers, writers, Catholic press.
- confessors, deaf people, deafness.

Celebrate Service

Gather

 Sing together the refrain.

Sing to the Lord a new song,
for he has done marvelous deeds.

"Psalm 98: Sing to the Lord a New Song" *Lectionary for Mass* © 1969, 1981

Pray the Sign of the Cross together.

Leader: Blessed be God.

All: Blessed be God forever.

Leader: Let us pray.

Bow your heads as the leader prays.

All: Amen.

Listen to God's Word

Leader: A reading from the holy Gospel according to Luke.

Read Luke 22:24–30.
The Gospel of the Lord.

All: Praise to you, Lord Jesus Christ.

Go Forth!

Leader: Let us go out to serve the Lord.

All: Thanks be to God.

Celebrate Service

Gather

 Use the *Call to Faith* 1 CD, track 4 to sing the opening song.

- Lead children in the Sign of the Cross and opening prayers.
- Leader's prayer: **God, our Father, we praise and thank you for the lives of all the saints who show us how to live humbly as your children.**

Listen to God's Word

- Have children remain standing.
- Proclaim the Gospel.
- Use a hand gesture to invite children's response to the Gospel.
- Invite children to think quietly about how they serve others.

Go Forth

- Have children gather around the prayer table.
- Using the holy water, sign each child on their hands with the Sign of the Cross and say: **(Child's name), in Baptism, you are called to serve others.**
- Pray the final blessing.

 RITUAL

Signing Signing children with the Sign of the Cross is a multi-layered ritual.

- It is a reminder of their Baptism.
- It recalls the cross of Christ and the call to discipleship and service.

LECTIONARY LINK

Luke 22:24–30 This Gospel reading is sometimes proclaimed on the feast of saints who were pastors.

- It is part of the farewell that Jesus gives to his disciples before his passion.
- It is a reminder that the mark of true discipleship is service.

Lent

Lent is a preparation for the celebration of Easter.

General Norms for Liturgical Year and Calendar, 27

Catechist Formation

Lent is a forty-day journey toward conversion and change of heart. The journey includes fasting, prayer, and penance. These practices open you to the presence of God in your life as well as the areas in your life which are in need of conversion. They prepare you to more fully enter into the celebration of Easter when we celebrate that Christ wins our salvation through his Resurrection.

The Church celebrates the forty days of Lent beginning with Ash Wednesday. The signing of a person with ashes with the words "Turn away from sin and be faithful to the gospel" is done in the spirit of repentance. The spirit of repentance is reflected in the use of the color purple for church vestments and the stark, desert-like environment created for the liturgy. The Alleluia is neither said nor sung during the Lenten season. This practice reminds the community of both their constant need for God and their hunger for the joy of the risen Christ.

Lent is also a time of intense preparation for those who will receive the sacraments of initiation at the Easter Vigil and for the baptized to reflect on their baptismal promises which they will renew at Easter time.

Reflect *How will you practice repentance during Lent?*

Environment

Materials:

Purple cloth
Prayer table
Bible
Crucifix
Call to Faith Grade 1 CD

• Place the prayer table in the center of the prayer space, and cover it with the purple cloth.

• Place the crucifix on the prayer table.

• Arrange the prayer space to provide space for children to kneel.

Lent

Have you ever had an experience that has caused you to have a change of heart? Lent, meaning springtime, is a forty-day journey toward conversion, or change of heart, that includes fasting, prayer, and penance.

The Church celebrates the forty days of Lent beginning with Ash Wednesday. The signing of a person with ashes with the words "Turn away from sin and be faithful to the gospel" is done in the spirit of repentance. This spirit of repentance can also be seen in the use of the color purple for church vestments and the stark environment created for the liturgy. The Alleluia is neither said nor sung during the Lenten season. This practice highlights the longing of the community for the joy of the risen Christ.

Family Celebration

Say this prayer together as a mealtime prayer during Lent.

> **Prayer for Mercy**
> Merciful God, you called us forth from the dust of the earth; you claimed us for Christ in the waters of Baptism. Look upon us as we live in these Forty Days. Bless our journey through the desert of Lent to the font of rebirth. May our fasting be hunger for justice; our alms, a making of peace; our prayer, the chant of humble and grateful hearts. All that we do and pray is in the name of Jesus.

Family Activity

Lent is a time for prayer and repentance.

- Create a prayer space in your home where the family can either gather together at special times or spend individual quiet time.

- You will need a purple tablecloth, the family Bible, a cross, a candle, and a small table.

- Cover the table with the purple cloth, and place the Bible in the center with the cross and candle around it.

Lent

- Invite children to imagine they are going on a trip.
- Ask what they will need to take with them. Possible responses: clothing, water, food, and so on
- Brainstorm with children other things one does to prepare for a trip.
- Compare the journey of Lent to the discussion of the imaginary trip. You may make a chart comparing the two on the board or on chart paper.
- Read aloud the text.
- Discuss the significance of ashes. They mark the beginning of our Lenten journey. They remind us that we are on a journey to Easter.

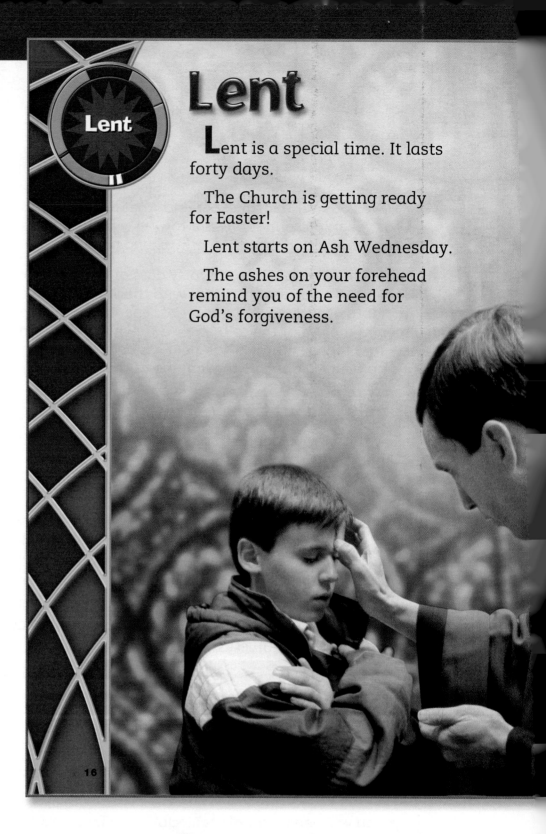

Lent

Lent is a special time. It lasts forty days.

The Church is getting ready for Easter!

Lent starts on Ash Wednesday.

The ashes on your forehead remind you of the need for God's forgiveness.

16

SEASONAL RESOURCES

Books and Videos Many resources are available to supplement your Lenten lesson.

- *The Big Book of Catholic Customs and Traditions* (Our Sunday Visitor). This book has many ideas for teaching the Church Year.
- *Lent: Celebrating the Season* (12 min). St. Anthony Messenger Press. This video explains Lenten practices to children.

CULTURAL CONNECTION

History of Ashes The Old Testament has references to people covering themselves with ashes as a sign of repentance. *(Jonah 3:6; Daniel 9:3)*

- In the early Church sinners seeking reconciliation were signed with ashes at the beginning of Lent.
- In the 11th century, ashes were used for everyone at the beginning of Lent.

Celebrate Lent

Gather

 Sing together.

Jesus, remember me
when you come into your
Kingdom.

"Jesus, Remember Me" ©1981, Les Presses de Taizé,
GIA Publications, Inc., agent

Pray the Sign of the Cross together.

Leader: Blessed be God.

All: Blessed be God forever.

Leader: Let us pray.

Bow your heads as the leader prays.

All: Amen.

Listen to God's Word

Leader: A reading from the holy Gospel
according to Mark.
Read Mark 1:12–13.
The Gospel of the Lord.

All: Praise to you, Lord Jesus Christ.

Go Forth!

Leader: Let us go out to do good deeds for
the Lord.

All: Thanks be to God.

17

Celebrate Lent

Gather

- Call children to worship with a moment of silence.

 Lead children in singing the opening song using the *Call to Faith* 1 CD, track 5.

- Lead children in the Sign of the Cross and opening prayers. Then ask children to kneel and repeat the following prayer after you.

- Leader's prayer: **God, our Father, sometimes we do not act as your children. (pause) We ask your forgiveness and mercy. (pause) Lord have mercy, (pause) Christ have mercy, (pause) Lord have mercy.**

Listen to God's Word

- Invite children to stand.
- Proclaim the Gospel.
- Use a hand gesture to invite children's response to the Gospel.

Go Forth!

- Give the final blessing.
- Gesture children to respond, "Thanks be to God."

 RITUAL

Lord Have Mercy This prayer is often prayed at the beginning of the Mass during the Penitential rite.

- The *Lord Have Mercy* unites the worshiping in asking for God's mercy.
- The *Lord Have Mercy* may be done as a call and response. Pray "Lord have mercy." Have children respond, "Christ have mercy."

LECTIONARY LINK

Mark 1:12–13 This section of the Gospel according to Mark is read on the first Sunday of Lent during Year B of the Lectionary cycle.

- The use of the images of wild beasts and angels shows that both forces of good and evil were present to Jesus.
- This Gospel is meant to remind us that Lent is a time for us to grapple with good and evil in our world.

new Life

[T]he Easter Triduum of the Passion and Resurrection of Christ is the culmination of the entire liturgical year.

General Norms for the Liturgical Year and Calendar, 18

Catechist Formation

Most Americans are familiar with instant replay—it is very much a part of watching a sporting event on television. With the help of video, one can easily see the best play of a game again and again. The celebration of the Easter Triduum, the three days leading up to Easter, is much more than a replay of historical events leading toward Christ's Resurrection. The liturgical celebration of the Triduum makes real God's accomplishments, allowing the assembly to enter into the lived mystery.

Lent ends and the Triduum begins at sundown on Holy Thursday. It ends with evening prayer on Easter Sunday. During these three days the whole Church fasts and prays with anticipation and hope. The assembly gathers for the washing of the feet and the Lord's Supper. They participate in the Adoration of the Cross, and await Christ's Resurrection, which is celebrated in a most solemn way during the Easter Vigil.

Through the symbols of water and the cross, and the liturgical actions of blessing and kissing the foot of the cross, the historical events of Jesus' life, death, and Resurrection are made real in the here and now. In these liturgical actions the Triduum is more than a reminder of what God did long ago. Instead, it is a continuous celebration of the Church's salvation today.

Reflect ***What are ways you can participate in the Triduum this year?***

Environment

Materials:

Prayer table
White Cloth
Bible
Glass bowl with holy water
Green branches
Call to Faith Grade 1 CD

- Place the prayer table in the center of the worship space.
- Cover the table with the white cloth.
- Place the glass bowl with holy water in the center of the table. It will be the focal point of the celebration.

Triduum

The Triduum begins at sundown on Holy Thursday and ends at sundown on Easter Sunday. During these three days the whole Church fasts and prays with anticipation and hope. The assembly gathers for the washing of the feet and the Lord's Supper. They participate in the Adoration of the Cross, and await Christ's Resurrection, which is celebrated in a most solemn way during the Easter Vigil. In these liturgical actions the Triduum is more than a reminder of what God did long ago. Instead, it is a continuous celebration of the Church's salvation today.

Family Celebration

On Good Friday, the Church venerates the cross. Make the cross the focal point of your prayer and say the following together.

> Lord, send your abundant blessing upon your people who devoutly recall the death of your Son in the sure hope of Resurrection. Grant us pardon; bring us comfort. May our faith grow stronger and our eternal salvation be assured. We worship you, Lord, we venerate your cross, we praise your Resurrection. Through the cross you brought joy to world.
>
> This is the wood of the cross, on which hung the Savior of the world.
>
> Come, let us worship.
>
> (Reverently touch or kiss the foot of the cross.)

Family Activity

The Seder meal is a celebration of the Hebrew Passover. Jesus celebrated the Passover on Holy Thursday. Celebrate this Holy Thursday by having a family celebration.

- Set your table in a festive manner.

- Buy bread that has no yeast—Matzoh or pita both work.

- Include bitter herbs as part of your recipe for this evening's meal—parsley dipped in saltwater—and pour glasses of wine or grape juice.

- Read *Luke 22:7–20* aloud. Begin the meal by breaking bread and sharing the cup.

New Life

- Ask children to share experiences of losing something very important to them and then finding it. Possible responses: a toy, a pet
- Discuss the feelings they had during those experiences. Possible responses: fear, sadness, joy, happiness
- Explain that these feelings are similar to the ones the Apostles felt during the time of Jesus' death and Resurrection.
- Tell children that we remember these events every year in three special days before Easter Sunday.
- Read aloud the text.
- Clarify what events each day of the Triduum remembers.

Triduum

New Life

Jesus gave us a special gift. He gave his life for our sins. He died, but he was raised to new life.

The Church celebrates Jesus' dying and rising in a special way during the three holiest days of the year.

- Holy Thursday
- Good Friday
- Holy Saturday

18

Books and Videos   You may wish to use these additional resources.

- *What Am I Doing for Triduum this Year?* Paul Turner (Liturgy Training Publications). A book to help you make your own personal retreat during the Triduum.
- *Jesus Promises: Part II of the Life of Jesus* (15 min). St. Anthony Messenger Press. This video recounts Holy Week events for young children.

Good Friday   This day has had several names.

- The earliest was "*Pascha*," which refers to the Jewish Passover celebrated at this time.
- Other names: "Day of the Lord's Passion," and "Day of the Cross."
- "Good Friday" is an English name. It reflects the joy of redemption and protests against superstitious notions that all Fridays are "unlucky."

Celebrate New Life

Gather

Pray the Sign of the Cross together.

Leader: The Lord is risen, alleluia.

All: Alleluia, alleluia.

Leader: Let us pray.

Bow your heads as the leader prays.

All: Amen.

Listen to God's Word

Leader: A reading from the holy Gospel according to Mark.

Read Mark 16:1–6.
The Gospel of the Lord.

All: Praise to you, Lord Jesus Christ.

Go Forth!

Leader: Let us go out to praise the Lord.

All: Thanks be to God.

 Alleluia, alleluia, alleluia!

"Alleluia" Lectionary for Mass © 1969, 1981, 1997

19

Celebrate New Life

Gather

- Gather children in silence and lead them in the prayer.
- Leader's prayer: **Lord God, we praise and thank you for these holy days. We remember your dying on the cross and your rising.**

Listen to God's Word

- Proclaim the Gospel.
- Invite children to answer "yes" to the questions you will ask them. Say that you will bless them with holy water as a sign of Baptism.
- Ask: **"Do you believe in God the Father?"; "Do you believe in Jesus, God's Son, who died and rose?"; "Do you believe in God the Holy Spirit?"**
- Using the green branches, sprinkle children with holy water.

Go Forth!

- Give the final blessing.

 Use the *Call to Faith* 1 CD, track 6, to sing the song.

 RITUAL

Baptismal Promises One of the highlights of the Easter Vigil is the Baptism of the elect and the renewal of baptismal promises by the faithful.

- The sprinkling with holy water is called the *asperges*.
- Remind children that everytime they enter the church and bless themselves with holy water, they remember their Baptism.

LECTIONARY LINK

Mark 16:1–6 The reading from the Gospel according to Mark is proclaimed at the Easter Vigil when the readings are taken from Lectionary Year B.

- This Gospel emphasizes the empty tomb.
- Other Gospels stress the importance of the appearances of the risen Jesus to his disciples.

Easter Joy

The fifty days from Easter Sunday to Pentecost are celebrated in joyful exultation . . .These above all others are the days for the singing of the Alleluia.

General Norms for the Liturgical Year and the Calendar, 22

Catechist Formation

Though part of the human condition, the experience of loss is a difficult one to overcome. Imagine the elation and even confusion the followers of Christ must have felt after learning that Jesus was alive! On Easter morning, the Church rejoices as disciples of Christ. We celebrate as people of God who have received the extravagant gift of salvation.

The celebration of the Easter season includes the fifty days following the Triduum. The Easter liturgies of these eight weeks reflect the joy of salvation in song and in action. The Alleluia not only returns to the repertoire, but also expresses whole-heartedly the joy of the Body of Christ. The Church renews their baptismal commitments in the sprinkling rite. The Gospels unpack the meaning of the Easter event and help the assembly to celebrate and remember that what God the Father did in his son Jesus, he is doing in the lives of his people. In this period of mystagogy following Christ's Resurrection, the assembly is sent out from the Easter celebration to spread the good news.

Easter is about the bareness of winter and Lent giving way to Christ's light and life. Jesus' Resurrection is a sign of new life; it is about Christ's triumph over death. Jesus turned the darkness of sin into the light of love. You are called to rejoice and spread the good news. Allow your Easter joy to translate to action.

Reflect **How do you celebrate the joy and good news of Easter on a daily basis?**

Environment

Materials:

Prayer table
White cloth
Easter lily(s)
Bible or lectionary
Alleluia banner (optional)
Cross

- Cover the prayer table with the white cloth.

- Place the Easter lily in front of the cross and place the Bible in the center of the table on a stand.

- Arrange the space so children can process.

Easter

Think about the elation and even confusion the followers of Christ must have felt after learning that Jesus was alive! On Easter morning, the Church rejoices. We celebrate as People of God who have received the gift of salvation.

The celebration of the Easter season includes the fifty days following the Triduum. The Easter liturgies of these eight weeks reflect the joy of salvation in song and in action. The Alleluia not only returns to the repertoire, but also expresses whole-heartedly the joy of the Body of Christ. The Church renews their baptismal commitments in the sprinkling rite. The Gospels unpack the meaning of the Easter event and help the assembly to celebrate God's saving power.

The Church is an Easter people. You are called to rejoice and be glad in it! You and your family can let this joy translate to action.

Family Celebration

Continue celebrating the joy of the season during the eight weeks of Easter. Say this prayer before your Sunday meal during the Easter season.

> **Leader:** We joyfully sing your praises, Lord Jesus Christ, who on the day of your Resurrection was recognized by your disciples in the breaking of the bread. Remain here with us as we gratefully partake of these gifts, and at the banquet table in heaven welcome us, who have welcomed you in your brothers and sisters, for you live and reign forever and ever.
>
> **All:** Amen.

Family Activity

Be an Easter family. Spread the joy of the Resurrection by celebrating new life. Here are two ideas to help celebrate life.

• Contact your local Respect Life chapter or shelter for battered women. They are always in need of new and used baby items. As a family purchase diapers, baby clothes, or formula that you can donate.

• Contact a local environmental group or your park district. There is always a need for new plant life. Purchase plants or flowers together, and plant them where needed. Follow up to make sure the plants are getting the care they need. Nurture them together.

Easter Joy

- Have children look at the prayer table. Ask them what has changed. Possible responses: color, flowers
- Write their responses on the board or on chart paper.
- Be sure that children see that the starkness of the Lenten decorations has turned to joyous abundance.
- Read aloud the text with enthusiasm.
- Talk with children about why Easter is a joyful season. It helps us remember that Jesus is alive; he had power over death; he lives in us.
- Talk about the reasons the Church celebrates Easter and why it is the most important holiday.
- Organize the group in four smaller groups, and assign each group one of the last four sentences in the text.
- Do a dramatic choral reading with children.

Easter

Easter Joy

Jesus was dead, but three days later he rose from the dead to new life.

Jesus was alive.

What great power God showed!

Jesus is risen!

Now he lives in us!

20

SEASONAL RESOURCES

Books   Many resources are available to supplement your Easter lesson.

- *Song of the Morning.* Compiled by Pat Alexander (Lion Publishing). A collection of inspiring Easter stories and poems.
- *Three Easter Journeys.* Robert Willoughby (Abingdon Press). A children's book tells of Jesus' journey to Jerusalem, the women's journey to the tomb, and Peter's journey with Jesus.

CULTURAL CONNECTION

Easter Clothes   It has become a tradition that people get new clothes at Easter time.

- When catechumens are baptized at the Easter Vigil, they are given a white garment to represent that they have put on Christ and have become a new creation in him.
- For the faithful, new clothes can also call to mind the new life of this baptismal season.

Celebrate Easter

Gather

Sing together the refrain.

Alleluia, alleluia,
give thanks to the risen Lord.
Alleluia, alleluia,
give praise to his Name.

"Alleluia, Alleluia, Give Thanks," Traditional

Pray the Sign of the Cross together.

Leader: The Lord be with you, alleluia.

All: And also with you, alleluia.

Leader: Let us pray.

Bow your heads as the leader prays.

All: Amen.

Listen to God's Word

Leader: A reading from the holy Gospel according to John.

Read John 20:19–22.
The Gospel of the Lord.

All: Praise to you, Lord Jesus Christ.

Go Forth!

Leader: Go out to celebrate new life, alleluia.

All: Thanks be to God, alleluia.

21

Celebrate Easter

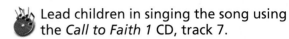

Gather

 Lead children in singing the song using the *Call to Faith 1* CD, track 7.

- Lead the opening prayers.
- Leader's prayer: **Lord, through your cross and Resurrection, you have set us free and made us your followers. Thank you.**
- Gather children for a procession.
- Lift up the lectionary or Bible.
- Process to the prayer table singing the refrain. Place the lectionary or Bible on the prayer table.

Listen to God's Word

- Bow deeply toward the prayer table to reverence the Scripture.
- Proclaim the Gospel.
- Use a hand gesture to invite children's response to the Gospel.
- Lead children in singing the refrain.

Go Forth

- Lead the final blessing and dismissal.

 RITUAL

Alleluia and Procession The word *alleluia* comes from the Hebrew verb *hallel*, "to praise," and from *Yah*, a shortened form of the name "Yahweh." Together it means, "Praise Yahweh!"

- The ritual of processing the Gospel book and singing the *Alleluia* is a way to honor and praise the Gospel as God's word.

LECTIONARY LINK

John 20:19–22 This reading from the Gospel of John is proclaimed on Easter Sunday during Year B of the Lectionary cycle.

- This Gospel is proclaimed at some time in all three cycles.
- Jesus' action of breathing on the disciples as he gives them the gift of the Holy Spirit reminds us that through him comes new spiritual life.

Pentecost

The Spirit of Jesus

The weekdays after the Ascension until the Saturday before Pentecost inclusive are a preparation for the coming of the Holy Spirit.

General Norms for the Liturgical Year and the Calendar, 26

Catechist Formation

Jesus' Apostles and disciples were expecting the Holy Spirit. The Risen Lord had told them to remain in Jerusalem to wait for "the promise of the Father about which you have heard me speak; for John baptized with water, but in a few days you will be baptized with the Holy Spirit." (Acts 1:1–5) The disciples gathered in an upper room during the Jewish Feast of Pentecost. There were many people in Jerusalem at that time because for the Jews, this was one of three great feasts that required a pilgrimage to the Temple. Originally, it was an agricultural festival celebrating the "first fruits" of early spring also known as the *Feast of Weeks*. Later it developed into a celebration recalling the making of the covenant, fifty days after Passover. It appears that the Apostles were in the upper room awaiting the end of the festival when the Holy Spirit came to them.

Today the Church celebrates the arrival of the Holy Spirit on Pentecost. This Christian feast celebrates the new covenant of God with his people. Pentecost Sunday is an enthusiastic and uplifting celebration of God's ongoing work in the world. The assembly celebrates an active renewal of the Church's purpose and mission through the renewal of Baptismal vows and the Dismissal, when they go forth to continue serving as Christ did.

Reflect ***How does the Holy Spirit act in your life?***

Environment

Materials:

Prayer table
Red tablecloth
Bible
Symbol of the Holy Spirit
Cross
Battery operated or
    electric candle
Bowl of holy water
Call to Faith Grade 1 CD

• Cover the table with the red cloth.

• Place the cross, candle, bowl of holy water, opened Bible, and a symbol of the Holy Spirit on the table.

Pentecost

The Church celebrates the arrival of the Holy Spirit on Pentecost. Falling on the seventh Sunday of Easter, it was originally an agricultural festival celebrating the "first fruits" of early spring called the Feast of Weeks.

On Pentecost, the sanctuary colors and priest's vestments are red symbolizing the fire of Pentecost and the empowerment of the Holy Spirit. In the scripture readings, the liturgical music, and the gestures of the assembly, the Church celebrates God's enabling activity through the gifts of the Holy Spirit. An active renewal of the Church's purpose and mission takes place through the renewal of Baptismal vows and the Dismissal, when the celebrant sends the assembly forth to continue serving as Christ did. The gifts of the Holy Spirit give the Church the wisdom and the strength to carry on the mission of Jesus. Sent forth from the celebration of Pentecost, your family can begin the work of the Holy Spirit.

Family Celebration

Lead this blessing for your family around your prayer table or at your evening meal.

> **Leader:** This day the Father of light has enlightened the minds of the disciples by the outpouring of the Holy Spirit. May he bless you and give you the gifts of the Spirit for ever.
>
> **All:** Amen.
>
> **Leader:** May almighty God bless you, the Father, and the Son, and the Holy Spirit.
>
> **All:** Amen.

Family Activity

Central to the Feast of Weeks was the offering of two loaves of bread *(Lev. 23:17)*. The historic festival concluded with a communal meal to which the poor and strangers were invited. You can carry out this Jewish Pentecost tradition, too.

- Bake two loaves of bread. Take one loaf to a needy family in your parish, and save the other for an evening meal.

- Invite a new neighbor to dinner or someone you know who is lonely or in need of good company. Perhaps there is someone in your family whom you could invite.

- Break bread together as a symbol of being one in Christ.

The Spirit of Jesus

- Ask children about a time they have been lost, perhaps at a store, or at the park or zoo.
- Discuss the feelings that came from that experience. Possible responses: frightened, lonely
- Use this discussion to talk about how the Apostles must have felt after Jesus returned to his Father.
- Read aloud the text.
- Go over some of the gifts of the Holy Spirit—wisdom, courage, strength.
- Talk about how the Holy Spirit is always with us.

Pentecost

The Spirit of Jesus

A cheer shows spirit.

You cannot see spirit, but you know when people have it.

After Jesus was raised from the dead, he sent the Holy Spirit.

The Holy Spirit helped the Apostles remember what Jesus told them.

You cannot see the Holy Spirit. The Holy Spirit is always with you.

 SEASONAL RESOURCES

Books You may wish to use additional resources for your lesson.

- *Christ is Risen: Celebrating Lent, Easter and Pentecost.* Theresa Cotter (St. Anthony Messenger Press). This book contains projects.
- *Spirit With Us.* Judith Dunlap and Mary Cummins Wlodarski (St. Anthony Messenger Press). This children's book has stories that show the Holy Spirit's work in the Church.

 CULTURAL CONNECTION

Jewish Feasts The three major religious feasts of the Jewish people developed out of their agricultural roots. They travel to the Temple for each of these feasts.

- Passover was the beginning of the harvest.
- Pentecost was the end of the harvest of the corn.
- The Feast of Tabernacles was the end of the harvest of fruit, oil, and wine.

Celebrate the Spirit

Gather

Sing together the refrain.

Spirit of God's people,
Spirit Friend.

"Spirit Friend" © 1969, 1987, Hope Publishing Co.

Pray the Sign of the Cross together.

Leader: The Lord be with you.

All: And also with you.

Leader: Let us pray.

Bow your heads as the leader prays.

All: Amen.

Listen to God's Word

Leader: A reading from the Acts of the Apostles.

Read Acts 2:1-4.
The word of the Lord.

All: Thanks be to God.

Go Forth!

Leader: Let us go forth to live in God's Spirit and share joy, peace, and love.

All: Thanks be to God.

23

Celebrate the Spirit

Gather

 Lead children in singing the song using the *Call to Faith 1* CD, track 8.

- Lead children in the opening prayers.
- Leader's prayer: **Come Holy Spirit, fill us with your gifts of life and love.**

Listen to God's Word

- Proclaim the Gospel.
- Use a hand gesture to invite children's response to the Gospel.

Go Forth

- After a moment of silence, call children forward one by one.
- Using the holy water, mark each child on the forehead with the Sign of the Cross saying: (Child's name) **I bless you, in the name of God the Father, God the Son, and God the Holy Spirit.**
- Give the final dismissal, and send children forth.

 RITUAL

Blessing For Jews and Christians *blessing* is a ritual of praising God and giving thanks.

- Blessing one another can be a part of how Christians interact with the world and the community.
- Blessings are a part of our Christian heritage and have a variety of meanings, such as a gift, a word of praise, or a making holy.

 LITURGY LINK

Acts 2:1–4 This reading of the events of Pentecost is proclaimed on Pentecost Sunday during all three Lectionary cycles.

- The symbols of wind and fire are associated with the power of the Holy Spirit.
- They also point to a new covenant between God and his people.

Teacher's Notes

UNIT 1
God's World

Chapter 1 God Made You!
Who loves you?

Chapter 2 God's Gifts
What has God made?

Chapter 3 Care for Creation
How can you thank God for his gifts?

Faith in Action!   **Catholic Social Teaching Principle:**
Care for God's Creation

24

© Harcourt Religion

UNIT 1 OPENER

Preview Unit Content

Tell children that Unit 1 is about God's world.

- Invite a volunteer to read aloud the chapter title and question for Chapter 1. Ask children what they think they will learn in this chapter.

- Repeat this for Chapters 2 and 3.

- Tell children that at the end of the unit they will learn how one organization cared for the gifts of God's creation.

God Made You!
CHAPTER BACKGROUND

Faith Focus

- **God created the universe and all that is in it. Everything he created shares in his goodness.** *(CCC 282, 286–287, 290, 299)*
- **God created humans in his image, to know him and to love him.** *(CCC 299, 356–358)*

Catechism Connection

The *Catechism* emphasizes that humans are the only earthly creatures who are capable of sharing in God's own life. *(CCC 355–361, 364)*

GDC Link

The *Directory* states that no teaching "method," however sound, can deprive the catechist of a central role in passing on the faith to children. *(GDC 156)*

 God created man in his image;
in the divine image he created him;
male and female he created them.

Genesis 1:27

In God's Image

You have had a fight with a friend or spouse; your kids are yelling at one another. When it has been one of those days, it is easy to forget God's infinite love for you. Your path through life can become cluttered with distractions and overshadowed by feelings of resentment, guilt, and loneliness. It can be a difficult task to stay on the path at all.

Focus on the thought that, as a person, you are created in the image of God. You possess the dignity of a being who mirrors something of his splendor and his goodness. Remember, too, that no matter what your faults, no matter how difficult your life may be, God's love for you, his image, can never fail.

The Love of the Creator

Gazing upon a newborn baby for the first time, a parent falls in love—each tiny feature is an image of himself or herself. With this love comes a parent's great desire to shower this child with tokens of love. A parent wants to give this tiny infant everything needed for survival. So it is with God, the Father of us all. When we were lost, he held out his hand to us, sending us the savior to show us the way home.

Reflect How do you see God's love working in your life right now?

An Ongoing Process

Six-year-olds are mostly interested in what they can see and touch. God is spirit, and therefore invisible. So how do you teach about God our Creator? Start by imitating the teaching methods used in the student text.

- Each chapter of the text starts with familiar material—something to which children can relate. Whenever you introduce a concept, begin with what they already know. Then make the connection to the unfamiliar.

- Each chapter is story-based. Stories captivate six-year-olds. Add a personal touch, such as gathering children around you to listen to the story. Tell children to listen for something in the story, and you've got active learning going on.

- Knowing God means having a relationship with God. A relationship isn't formed in one lesson or in two. Knowing God is an ongoing process.

Being Acknowledged

- I like being acknowledged. Learn my name as quickly as you can.

- I am interested in rules. Make them clear to me.

- I have a vivid imagination. Help me use it to learn.

Listening to the Call of Vocation

The word *vocation* comes from the root word *vocare*, which means "to call." Where do you think the call of vocation comes from?

- The call of vocation comes from God. You may try to discern your vocation by praying or submitting your will to the will of God.

- You may also look inward, analyzing your talents and interests to find out what comes naturally for you.

Research indicates that the way you view a vocation directly affects your ability to discern and sustain it.

Reflect **In which direction do you usually turn to hear the call?**

Teacher's Prayer

God our Creator, I praise you! Thank you for calling me to share my faith with these children. May they know you in the kindness and care I show them. Amen.

Weekly Planner

		Objective	Materials	Prayer & Scripture
DAY 1 Invite	**God Made You!** Page 25	**Objective:** To identify God as the one who made everything	☐ Art supplies ☐ Pencils	**Let Us Pray** Psalm 139:14
DAY 2 Explore	**God Loves You** Pages 26–27	**Objective:** To explain that humans learn from the Bible that God is the Creator	☐ Board or chart paper ☐ Crayons or markers ☐ Bible ☐ Index cards ☐ Copies of Activity Master 1, p. 34A	**Let Us Pray** Psalm 139:14 ✝ **Scripture:** Genesis 2:7–22 ✝ **Scripture Background:** God Created Humans, p. 26
DAY 3 Explore	**God Knows You** Pages 28–29	**Objective:** To conclude that God created people to know him and to love him	☐ Board or chart paper ☐ Art supplies ☐ *On the Day You Were Born* by Debra Frasier (Harcourt, 1991) ☐ Nature CD	**Let Us Pray** Psalm 139:14
DAY 4 Explore	**Wonderful Things** Pages 30–31	**Objective:** To identify some gifts of God's creation	☐ Board or chart paper ☐ Art supplies ☐ Small squares of gift wrap ☐ Construction paper "bows"	**Let Us Pray** Psalm 139:14
DAY 5 Celebrate	**Prayer of Praise** Page 32	**Objective:** To praise God for being wonderfully made	☐ Hymnals ☐ Music CD	**Let Us Pray** **Prayer of Praise** 🎵 **Hymn:** "All Things Bright and Beautiful"

Chapter 1 Wrap-Up: Review and Apply p. 33 • Chapter 1 Assessment p. 25E

Activities	Enrichment
Let's Begin: Who Made Everyone?, p. 25 Multiple Intelligence: Verbal/Linguistic OPTIONAL Beginning the Year, p. 25 Multiple Intelligence: Interpersonal	
Share Your Faith: Think, Share, Act, p. 27 Multiple Intelligence: Verbal/Linguistic OPTIONAL Activity Master 1: Wonderful Me!, p. 27 Multiple Intelligence: Visual/Spatial	• **Teacher Background:** The Bible, p. 26 • **Justice and Peace:** In God's Image, p. 27
Connect Your Faith: What God Made, p. 29 Multiple Intelligence: Visual/Spatial OPTIONAL Cross-Curricular: Reading, p. 28 Multiple Intelligence: Verbal/Linguistic OPTIONAL Sounds of Creation, p. 29 Multiple Intelligence: Musical	• **Quick Tip:** Celebrating Friendship, p. 28 • **Reaching All Learners:** Physically Challenged, p. 29
Live Your Faith: Draw Your Family and Friends, p. 31 Multiple Intelligence: Visual/Spatial OPTIONAL Cross-Curricular: Science, p. 30 Multiple Intelligence: Naturalist OPTIONAL Make a Bulletin Board, p. 31 Multiple Intelligence: Visual/Spatial	• **Quick Tip:** Provide Prompts, p. 30 • **Christian Living Skills:** Reverencing the Ordinary, p. 31
	• **Liturgy Link:** Get Ready to Pray, p. 32 • **Lectionary Link:** Break Open the Word, p. 32

Multimedia Resources

BOOK
Conan, Sally Anne. *Look and See What God Gave Me.* Paulist Press. 1997. Rhyming text celebrates the uniqueness of each child created in God's image.

VIDEO
The Beginner's Bible: The Story of Creation (30 min). SONY Wonder. 1999. An animated version of the creation stories from Genesis.

 Teacher Resources
www.harcourtreligion.com
• For interactive lesson planner, chapter resources, and activities
• For free materials and information

 Home Connection
Chapter 1 Family Faith, p. 34
Take-home activities, chapter content review, saint features and prayer

For more family activities
www.harcourtreligion.com

God Made You! 25D

Name _____ Date _____

Ⓐ Work with Words   Write the word from the Word Bank that best completes each question.

WORD BANK
God
Creator

1. Who made you?   _____
_ _ _ _ _ _ _ _ _ _ _ _ _ _ _ _
_____

2. What is one name for God who made everything?

_____

_ _ _ _ _ _ _ _ _ _ _ _ _ _ _ _

_____

Ⓑ Check Understanding   Draw a line to the best ending for each sentence.

3. God's word written down by humans is the

a. Bible.

4. God created the

b. good.

5. Everything God made is

c. world.

©Harcourt Religion

ASSESSMENT

Answers can be found in the back of the Teacher Manual.

Chapter 1 God Made You!

Invite

Let Us Pray

Leader: God, help us to learn about all you have made.

"I praise you, so wonderfully you made me; wonderful are your works!"

Psalm 139:14

All: God, help us to learn about all you have made. Amen.

Activity Let's Begin

● **Who Made Everyone?**

Antonio and Pamela,
Roberto and Erin.
God made us all!
Maria, Tyrone, and Omar,
God loves us all!

• Who loves you?

_____

_____

_____

Make a Thank You Card Make a card for the person you named. Thank him or her for loving you and taking care of you. 25

OPTIONAL ACTIVITY

Beginning the Year Here are two ideas for children's first gathering of the year:

• Give them some time to explore their new books. Invite children to point out things that look interesting or fun.

• Make simple name tags for children. Greet each child with a handshake and present his or her name tag.

Multiple Intelligence: Interpersonal

Objective: To identify God as the one who made everything

Open

Prayer Space Have children move to your classroom prayer space. In the space, have a crucifix and a Bible opened to the psalm verse.

Let Us Pray Invite children to gather in the prayer space and make the Sign of the Cross. Have them raise their arms and pray the psalm.

Build

Activity

• Read the poem "Who Made Everyone?"

• Ask everyone to stand. One by one, invite each child to say his or her name. After every fourth child pronounces his or her name, lead everyone in saying "God made us all!" When everyone has been introduced, read the question and invite children to write their response in the lines provided.

Extension Activity

• Tell children that they will be making a thank-you card for the person that they named in the last activity.

• Distribute art supplies to children.

• Allow children time to complete their cards.

• Ask volunteers to share their cards with the class.

Close

Have children tell what they learned about God's love.

Objective: To explain that humans learn from the Bible that God is the Creator

Open

 Let Us Pray Invite children to pray the psalm verse on page 25 with you.

Focus **Who is the Creator?** List children's answers on the board or on chart paper.

Build

God Loves You

Read aloud the first paragraph.

- Show a Bible and tell children that it is a holy book. It is God's book.
- Hold up an index card with the word *Bible* on it. Have everyone read it.
- Read the second paragraph.

The First Humans

- Proclaim the scripture story.

- **What else did God create?** List children's responses on the board or on chart paper.

Explore

God Loves You

Focus **Who is the Creator?**

You are God's child. God knows you and loves you. The **Bible** has many stories about God's love for all of us.

Listen to this Bible story. This story is about God and how he made the first humans.

✝ **SCRIPTURE** Genesis 2:7–2

 Read to Me The First Humans

A very long time ago, God created a man. God breathed into the man, and the man began to live. God loved the man and wanted him to be happy. God created a woman to be the man's partner. The man's name was Adam. His wife's name was Eve.

Based on Genesis 2:7–22

❓ What else did God create?
Responses will vary.

26

✝ **SCRIPTURE BACKGROUND**

God Created Humans (Genesis 1–2) The scripture stories about the creation of man and woman tell of the magnitude of God's love.

- Humans were created in God's own image and likeness.
- They were created to live together in joy and peace with God and with each other.

 **TEACHER BACKGROUND**

The Bible The Bible is God's holy book. It contains stories about his love.

- God inspired the humans who wrote down his words in the Bible.
- The Bible is made up of two parts, the Old Testament and the New Testament.

od Made You!

God made everything. Everything
d made is good. God is the **Creator**.
d gave you life. He brought you into
s world.

God Made You!

Hold up an index card with the word *Creator* and explain that this is a name for God.

- Share the information in the paragraph. Allow children time to look at the photograph.
- Point to several children, one at a time, and ask "Who made you?"

Activity

- Assign each child a partner. Have children take a few moments to explain to each other one reason why they like being who they are.
- Invite each child to print his or her name on the line provided.

Close

Remind children that Christians learn about God from the Bible. One thing the Bible tells them is that God is the Creator of everything.

Activity

Share Your Faith

Think: What do you really like about being you?

Share: Tell your partner.

Act: You are special. So is your name. Print your name here.

_____

- - - - - - - - - - - - - - - - -

27

Activity Master 1: Wonderful Me! Distribute copies of the activity found on page 34A.

- Tell children they will be drawing and coloring.
- As an alternative, you may wish to send this activity home with children.

▲ Activity Master 1
page 34A

In God's Image God created humans "in our image, after our likeness" (*Genesis 1:26*). You show respect for people by addressing them by their name.

- A name is an important gift that has been given to a person by his or her family. Invite children to learn each other's names as quickly as they can.

Catholic Social Teaching: Life and Dignity

Objective: To conclude that God created people to know him and to love him

Open

Let Us Pray Invite children to pray the psalm verse on page 25 with you.

Focus **What is one way you can be God's friend?** List children's answers on the board or on chart paper.

Build

God Knows You

Read aloud God Knows You.

- Explain that humans cannot see God, but they know what he is like from the things that he has made and from the Bible. Say that God is greater and more wonderful than anything people can imagine about him.

❓ **What is one thing you know about God?** Help children generate ideas from the teachings.

Explore

God Knows You

Focus **What is one way you ca** **be God's friend?**

Those who love you know you best God knows you better than anyone knows you. He wants you to know him, too.

God loves you very much. He is your friend. God wants you to be friends with others, too.

❓ **What is one thing you know about Go** Responses will vary.

28

OPTIONAL ACTIVITY

You may want to read aloud the book *On the Day You Were Born* by Debra Frasier (Harcourt, 1991).

- After reading, have children draw self-portraits on drawing paper.
- Display children's artwork. Remind children that every person is an image of God.

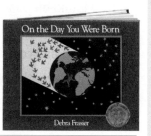

Multiple Intelligence: Verbal/Linguistic

od's World

d created a wonderful world.
is filled with lots of good things.

here are mountains and rivers,
d fish in the stream,

rds soaring high
d good things to dream.

here are flowers and forests
d puppy dogs, too,

ut the best thing of all is that
od made you!

Connect Your Faith

 What God Made Draw your favorite thing that God made.

29

God's World

Ask children to stand to celebrate God's wonderful world.

• Read God's World. Then have children work together to invent gestures to go with each line of the poem. Read aloud the poem a second time while children use the gestures.

Activity

• If you need to save time, call the drawing activity a "fast draw." Set a time limit. Make the drawing a game so that children will not become frustrated.

• Walk around the room as they are drawing. Ask children to describe their drawings. Give positive feedback.

Close

Remind children that no one can see God, but we know a lot about him through his creation.

★ REACHING ALL LEARNERS

Physically Challenged   Be sensitive to the feelings of physically-challenged children.

• A child in a wheelchair will not be able to stand as the activity asks. Invite this child to show enthusiasm by doing something physical that he or she can do well.

OPTIONAL ACTIVITY

Sounds of Creation   Bring in a nature CD that has the sounds of nature—birds singing, wind blowing, thunder booming, etc.

• Have children guess what the sounds are. Tell them God made all of these things.

• Or demonstrate the sounds yourself by using wind chimes, drums, or cymbals.

Multiple Intelligence: Musical

Objective: To identify some gifts of God's creation

Open

Let Us Pray Invite children to repeat after you the psalm verse from page 25.

Focus **Where can you see God's gifts?** List children's responses on the board or on chart paper.

Build

Wonderful Things

Read aloud the first paragraph to summarize responses to the Focus question.

- Direct attention to the text on the page, which is designed as a picture puzzle, or rebus.

- Have children follow along as you read aloud each statement. When you come to a picture, pause and have children say aloud the object represented.

❷ **Why did God give you all these gifts?** Invite children to respond.

Explore

KEY

birds

children

families

flowers

fruit

moon

sun

trees

Wonderful Things

Focus **Where can you see God's gifts?**

God made so many wonderful things God's gifts are all around you.

God gave people the and the .

God gave people and .

God gave people that grow

God gave people other to play wi

Best of all, God made all the

who love you and take care of you.

❷ **Why did God give you all these gifts?**
Possible responses: because he loves me, because he wants me to be happy, because I need them.

30

Cross-Curricular: Science Have children work in groups to list gifts of God in nature.

- Take children outdoors or have them look out the windows.
- Have each group write or draw five things they see in nature that are gifts from God.

Multiple Intelligence: Naturalist

QUICK TIP

Provide Prompts Young children often require prompting to carry out brainstorming activities or discussions.

- Resist the temptation to put words in children's mouths or supply answers too quickly. Use questions as prompts.
- When children supply off-topic responses, don't cut them off. Thank them and lead the discussion back to the topic with specific questions.

Live Your Faith

 Draw Your Family and Friends Draw a picture of people who love you and care for you.

God made special people to love and care for me!

31

- Read aloud the directions for the activity.
- Provide art materials, and allow time for children to work independently on their drawings.
- Invite a volunteer to read aloud the text from the drawing frame.
- Encourage children to share their drawings with family members and friends.

Close

Lead children in spontaneous prayers of thanks for God's gifts, including the people who take care of them.

CHRISTIAN LIVING SKILLS

Reverencing the Ordinary Young children sometimes define a "gift" as something exotic or costly, given on a rare occasion. Help children see that their everyday lives are full of simple gifts—the wonders of nature, the joys of time shared with friends, the love shown by family members.

- Invite children to thank God for these "ordinary blessings" in their night prayers.

OPTIONAL ACTIVITY

Make a Bulletin Board Title a bulletin board or poster with *We Are God's Gifts.*

- Give each child a small square of gift wrap and a "bow" cut from construction paper.
- Help them tape drawings of themselves to the gift-wrap squares and attach the paper bows. Then attach the "gifts" to the bulletin board or poster.

Multiple Intelligence: Visual/Spatial

Objective: To praise God for being wonderfully made

Prepare

Choose three children to be leaders. Show them which words to say.

 Use the *Call to Faith 1* CD, track 1, to rehearse the song.

Gather

Invite children to assemble in the prayer space. Tell them to be very quiet and to be ready to talk to God. Read the name of the prayer as they follow along in their books.

Pray

A Prayer of Praise

 **Let Us Pray**   Follow the order of prayer on page 32.

- Optional music from *Singing Our Faith:* "Praise and Thanksgiving," #148, "Sing, Sing, Praise and Sing," #159, "For Your Gracious Blessing," #285.

Celebrate

A Prayer of Praise

Let Us Pray

Gather and begin with the Sign of the Cross.

Leader: God, we praise you!
We are wonderfully made!

All: God, we praise you!
We are wonderfully made!

Leader: We praise you, God, for our minds!

All: We can think.
We can imagine.

Leader: We praise you, God, for our bodies.

All: We can play.
We can grow.

Sing together the refrain.

All things bright and beautiful,
All creatures great and small,
All things wise and wonderful,
The Lord God made them all.

"All Things Bright and Beautiful," Traditional

32

 LITURGY LINK

Get Ready to Pray   Explain to children what they should do whenever they pray together.

- Show children where the prayer space is.
- Tell them to move quietly to that area when you ring the bell indicating that it is time to gather for prayer.
- Show them how to fold their hands when they pray.

 LECTIONARY LINK

Break Open the Word   Read last week's Sunday Gospel. Invite children to think about what the reading means to them as they try to follow Christ's example. For questions related to the weekly Gospel reading, visit our Web site at **www.harcourtreligion.com**.

 Visit www.harcourtreligion.com for weekly scripture readings and seasonal resources.

CHAPTER 1
Review

A Check Understanding

1. Draw your face in the circle. On the line, write who made you.

_ _ _ _ _ _ _ _ _ _ _ _
God (p. 27)

2. Circle the best answers for these sentences.

God made the world. (p. 29)

(**Yes**)   **No**

God loves everyone. (p. 25)

(**Yes**)   **No**

3. Circle the word that finishes the sentence.

God is our _____. (p. 27)

(**Creator**)   **pet**

B Make Connections Trace the letters to tell about God's gifts.

God made __Adam and Eve__. (p. 26)

God made __everything__. (p. 25)

God made __me__! (p. 27)

33

Review

A Check Understanding
Have children draw their face in the circle and then write who made them on the lines provided for them. Then have children circle the best answers for these sentences.

B Make Connections
Have children trace the letters to tell about God's gifts.

Assessment

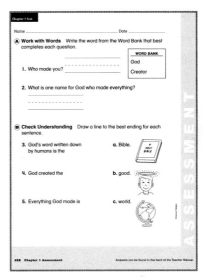

▲ **Chapter 1 Test page 25E**

Answers to the Chapter Test can be found in the back of the Teacher Manual.

OPTIONAL ACTIVITY

Sign Language Children have learned that God loves them. Teach them the American sign language for "I love you."

- Extend thumb, index finger, and little finger toward the person addressed.

Multiple Intelligence: Bodily/Kinesthetic

OPTIONAL ACTIVITY

Celebrating Uniqueness Give children an opportunity to reflect upon and celebrate the qualities that make each of them unique.

- Distribute crayons and a blank piece of paper cut into the shape of a simple human figure to each child.
- Ask children to color their figures to depict a special interest, skill, or talent.

Multiple Intelligence: Visual/Spatial

Family Faith

Remind children to discuss the Family Faith page at home. Encourage them to read the scripture passage from the Book of Genesis with their families.

Activity

- Explain the activity. You may want to hand out pre-cut stars.

People of Faith

Tell children about Michelangelo.

- When Michelangelo was a boy, he liked drawing better than his schoolwork. Michelangelo sometimes painted himself into scenes from the Bible.

- You may wish to have children start a People of Faith album. Have them cut out and paste the People of Faith feature into booklets. Have children add Michelangelo to their People of Faith albums.

- Encourage them to pray the prayer at home with their families.

  Visit **www.harcourtreligion.com** for weekly scripture readings and seasonal resources.

Unit 1: CHAPTER 1

Family Faith

◉ Catholics Believe

- God created everything. All that God made is good.

- God knows and loves everyone.

✝ SCRIPTURE

Read Genesis 1:9–13 to find out about some of God's creations.

GO ONLINE **www.harcourtreligion.com**
For weekly Scripture readings and seasonal resources

Activity
Live Your Faith

Praise One Another Give each perso in your family a paper star. Print your names on the stars. Take turns telling one good thing you know about each person in your family. Then say each time, "You are God's child." As you do this, glue a gold star on that person's paper star. Keep your stars. Try to remember to say one nice thing to eac other every day.

▲ Michelangelo, 1475–1564

People of Faith

Michelangelo was born in Italy more than five hundred years ago. He spent his life painting, making statues, and writing poetry. Michelangelo was hired by the pope to paint the ceiling of the Sistine Chapel in the Vatican. He painted for four years, sometimes lying on his back. Some of the pictures are about creation. Every year people of all religions come to see these pictures. They make people think about God the Creator.

🙌 Family Pra

Dear God, thank you for creating us. Help us use our talents to tel others about you wonderful gifts. Amen.

In Unit 1 your child is learning about REVELATION.
34 **CCC** *See Catechism of the Catholic Church 295, 299 for further reading on chapter content.*

❓ HOW DID I DO?

This week my religion classes were

☐ *some of the best ever!* ☐ *pretty good.* ☐ *in need of improvement.*

In what discussions and activities were children most interested?

_____

What activity did I most enjoy teaching?

_____

In what area do I need to improve?

_____

Name _____ Date _____

Wonderful Me!

Make the drawing look like you.
Color the things that tell what you can do.

God's Gifts

CHAPTER BACKGROUND

Faith Focus

- God's world is a gift to humans. *(CCC 356, 358)*
- You can learn about God and his love from the world he made. *(CCC 32, 286–287, 297, 301)*

Catechism Connection

The *Catechism* points out that God created the world freely, for no other reason but to display his love and generosity. His purpose was to call into existence creatures who could "share in his being, wisdom, and goodness." *(CCC 293–295)*

GDC Link

The *Directory* notes that "God . . . offers to men a constant evidence of himself in created things." *(GDC 36)*

How varied are your works, LORD!
In wisdom you have wrought them all;
the earth is full of your creatures.

Psalm 104:24

God's Great Gift

Genesis begins with two creation stories which were probably told and retold separately for centuries before they were joined together. The first creation story (*Genesis 1:1–2:4*) represents the creation of humanity as the climax of all God's works. According to the second creation story, the first human was created before all the plants and animals, which God subsequently produced for his sustenance, comfort, and delight (*Genesis 2:4–25*). Common to both stories is the idea that all the other wonders of creation are gifts from God to humanity, gifts that humans have a responsibility to cherish.

Honoring Creation

Belief in the goodness of creation was one of the most important convictions that the people of ancient Israel bequeathed to the Catholic Church. The Church has defended this doctrine against false teachers who claimed that matter was intrinsically evil. Gratitude for creation is a central theme of all Christian prayer. The sacraments that Christ instituted in his Church employ the good things of earth—water, wine, oil, and grain—to bring about human salvation.

When you are working or taking care of children, you may easily overlook the glories of creation. Yet God bestows new gifts on us every day.

Reflect **Where have you seen the Creator's glory today?**

Knowing God

In this chapter children focus on knowing God through his gift of creation. Using their senses, they perceive his gift of the world.

- Children this age relish gifts. They love shaking the box, tearing the wrapping paper, and peeling off the layers until the gift is revealed.

- Lead children to discover that they are surrounded by gifts from God—in the sky, in the water, on the earth. Throughout the chapter children will be "shaking, ripping, and peeling"— uncovering and celebrating God's gifts to them.

- You also will help broaden children's concept of gift. God's gifts do not usually come wrapped, and they do not arrive only on Christmas and birthdays.

Exploration

- I like to explore God's world. Help me to appreciate what I find.

- Praise helps me learn what's expected of me. Be generous in your praise.

- I like using my eyes, ears, nose, mouth, and hands to learn.

The Vocation to Teach

The vocation to teach develops differently for each person. Teaching as a vocation has a unique flavor to it. You cannot change its flavor or its taste. Just as root beer and orange soda each taste a certain way, so does the vocation to teach. Some people claim they always knew they would teach. Others never imagined they would be involved in education.

- This vocation comes with the conviction that you can succeed despite economic, domestic, or institutional deficits.

- It also comes with moments of doubt about your effectiveness.

Reflect **Which of these two flavors do you taste more frequently in your catechetical vocation?**

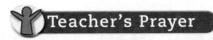 Teacher's Prayer

God our Creator, the world abounds with your wonders. I thank you for the colors, aromas, textures, and tastes that enrich my life. Amen.

Weekly Planner

		Objective	Materials	Prayer & Scripture
DAY 1 Invite	**God's Gifts** Page 35	**Objective:** To express delight in creation	☐ Pencils	**Let Us Pray** *Psalm 111:2*
DAY 2 Explore	**God's Big Gift** Pages 36–37	**Objective:** To describe the world as God's gift to people	☐ Board or chart paper ☐ Index card	**Let Us Pray** *Psalm 111:2* ✝ **Scripture:** *Genesis 1:5–25* ✝ **Scripture Background:** The First Creation Story, p. 37
DAY 3 Explore	**Use God's Gifts** Pages 38–39	**Objective:** To conclude that every good thing is a gift from God	☐ Board or chart paper ☐ Copies of Activities Master 2, p. 44A ☐ Pencils ☐ Crayons	**Let Us Pray** *Psalm 111:2*
DAY 4 Explore	**The Gift of Food** Pages 40–41	**Objective:** To describe ways that people use God's gifts	☐ Board or chart paper ☐ Pencils ☐ Food Pyramid ☐ English muffins, pizza sauce, cheese, toppings	**Let Us Pray** *Psalm 111:2*
DAY 5 Celebrate	**Prayer of Praise** Page 42	**Objective:** To praise the Lord for the great things he has done	☐ Hymnals ☐ Music CD ☐ Index cards	**Let Us Pray** **Prayer of Praise** 🔔 **Hymn:** "Psalm 98: Sing to the Lord a New Song"

Chapter 2 Wrap-Up: Review and Apply p. 43 • Chapter 2 Assessment p. 35E

Words of Faith

Praise

Activities	Enrichment
Let's Begin: A Moment in Summer, p. 35 Multiple Intelligence: Bodily/Kinesthetic	• **Reaching All Learners:** Movement, p. 35
Share Your Faith: Think, Share, Act, p. 37 Multiple Intelligence: Interpersonal OPTIONAL A Moment in Summer, p. 36 Multiple Intelligence: Visual/Spatial OPTIONAL Caring for Creation, p. 37 Multiple Intelligence: Verbal/Linguistic	• **Quick Tip:** Graphic Organizer, p. 36
Connect Your Faith: Special Gifts, p. 39 Multiple Intelligence: Visual/Spatial OPTIONAL Activity Master 2: Gifts from God, p. 39 Multiple Intelligence: Visual/Spatial	• **Teacher Background:** Icky Things, p. 38 • **Justice and Peace:** Looking After God's Beautiful World, p. 38 • **Quick Tip:** God's Gifts, p. 39
Live Your Faith: Match the Gifts, p. 41 Multiple Intelligence: Visual/Spatial OPTIONAL Make Pizzas, p. 40 Multiple Intelligence: Bodily/Kinesthetic OPTIONAL Cross-Curricular: Health, p. 41 Multiple Intelligence: Naturalist	• **Quick Tip:** Food in the Classroom, p. 40 • **Christian Living Skills:** Giving Thanks, p. 41
	• **Liturgy Link:** Music and Prayer, p. 42 • **Lectionary Link:** Break Open the Word, p. 42

Multimedia Resources

 BOOK
Conan, Sally Anne. *Thank You, God!*
Paulist Press. 1997. Children give thanks for God's gifts.

 VIDEO
Great Bible Adventures: Look What God Made! (30 min). Questar, Inc. Children learn about the wonders of God's creation.

 Teacher Resources
www.harcourtreligion.com
• For interactive lesson planner, chapter resources, and activities
• For free materials and information

Home Connection

Chapter 2 Family Faith, p. 44
Take-home activities, chapter content review, saint features and prayer

 For more family activities
www.harcourtreligion.com

Name ______________________ Date ______________

(A) Work with Words Circle the word that best completes each sentence.

1. God's gift to you is the ________.

sea  **world** 

2. The ________ tells that God made the world.

Bible 

arithmetic book 

3. God made the ________ to give light at night.

sun  **moon** 

(B) Check Understanding Draw a line to the best ending for each sentence.

4. God created the world to show his

5. Praise God because he is

a. good. 

b. love. 

©Harcourt Religion

ASSESSMENT

Answers can be found in the back of the Teacher Manual.

Chapter 2 God's Gifts

Invite

 Let Us Pray

Leader: God, we thank you for your many gifts.
"Great are the works of the LORD,
to be treasured for all their delights."
Psalm 111:2

All: God, we thank you for your many gifts. Amen.

Activity Let's Begin

A Moment in Summer

A moment in summer
belongs to me
and one particular
honey bee.

A moment in summer
shimmering clear
making the sky
seem very near,
a moment in summer
belongs to me.

Charlotte Zolotow

• What is one thing you like about summer?

_____

_ _ _ _ _ _ _ _ _ _ _ _ _ _ _ _ _ _ _ _

_____

Act It Out With a small group, act out something that is fun to do in the summer.

35

⭐ REACHING ALL LEARNERS

Movement Some children are more energetic than others. They may be kinesthetic and active learners. They tend to express their ideas and feelings through movement.

• Give these children opportunities to move around the room every once in a while. For example, when you read "A Moment in Summer," ask them to buzz about the room like bees.

Objective: To express delight in creation

Open

Let Us Pray Have children move to the classroom prayer space. Tell them that *Lord* is another name for God. Teach them the response to the psalm verse. Pray the psalm verse, and then invite children to pray the response with you.

Build

Activity

• Read aloud the poem "A Moment in Summer." Ask children to picture in their minds what they hear.

• Organize children in three groups. Have one group say "A moment in summer" on your cue; have the second group make soft buzzing sounds on your cue; have the third group point to themselves when you read the words, "belongs to me." Then read the poem a second time, and have the three groups perform their roles.

• Ask children to respond to the question.

Extension Activity

• Arrange the class into small groups.

• Have groups prepare a skit on something that is fun to do in summertime.

• Invite groups to present their skits.

Close

Have children tell what they learned about God's gift of summer.

Objective: To describe the world as God's gift to people

Open

Let Us Pray Invite children to pray the psalm verse on page 35 with you.

Focus **What has God made?** List children's answers on the board or on chart paper.

Build

God's Big Gift

Lead children through God's Big Gift.

- Draw the graphic organizer on the board or on chart paper.
- Tell children that God gives us the gift of the world and all that is good in it.
- Using an index card, introduce the word *praise*.

❷ **What are some of the gifts in God's world?** Write children's responses on the board or on chart paper and draw a line connecting them to the graphic organizer.

Explore

God's Big Gift

Focus **What has God made?**

Faith Fact

The Bible has two stories about God's creation of the world.

God gives you a very, very big gift.

Stretch your arms wide. God's gift is bigger than that!

God's gift is too big to wrap. It is so big that no ribbon can be tied around it.

Can you guess what it is? God gives you the world. God filled the world with many gifts!

Praise God for these gifts.

❷ **What are some of the gifts in God's world?**
Possible responses: animals, water, people, flowers

36

A Moment in Summer Have children draw a picture of their favorite moment of the summer that has just passed. Invite those who know how, to write "Thank You!" at the bottom of the picture to show they are grateful for that moment.

Multiple Intelligence: Visual/Spatial

QUICK TIP

Graphic Organizer

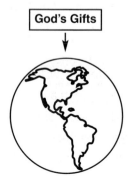

God's Gifts

Bible Story

God made many good things. God made the world to show his love. Before God made Adam and Eve, he made the world.

Praise is giving God honor and thanks because he is good.

SCRIPTURE
Genesis 1:5–25

What God Made

Long ago, God made the sky, the land and the seas. The earth was empty. There were no trees to climb. No flowers swayed in the breeze.

So the Lord God created a beautiful world. God filled the garden with creatures. Birds flew in the sky. Many animals lived on the earth. God created fish and whales to swim in the seas. All that God made was good.

Based on Genesis 1:5–25

What things in God's world can you see, hear, and touch? Responses will vary.

Activity — Share Your Faith

Think: Think about God's gifts to the world.

Share: Talk about the gifts in a group.

Act: Bring some of God's gifts to school to share with the class.

37

A Bible Story

Gather children around you.

- Read aloud the paragraph to prepare them for the scripture story they are going to hear.

What God Made

Proclaim the scripture story. Then proclaim the scripture story a second time, asking children to raise their hands every time they hear the name of one of God's gifts.

- Tell children that you will point to either your eyes, ears, or hands. Have them think of something good that they experience in God's world through that sense. Responses will vary.

❷ **What things in God's world can you see, hear, and touch?** Write all responses on the board or on chart paper.

Activity

- Organize children into small groups. Tell them they can bring either a "gift," or a picture of it to the next session.

Close

Emphasize that the whole world and everything in it is God's gift to us.

✝ SCRIPTURE BACKGROUND

The First Creation Story *Genesis 1—2:4* affirms several vitally important truths:

- God created the earth and everything in it.
- The world that God created was both orderly and good.
- God created man and woman to be the stewards of his creation and to care for all living things.

OPTIONAL ACTIVITY

Caring for Creation Have children name familiar characters in movies, television shows, or advertisements who promote caring for the earth. Ask children to explain what kind of actions each of these characters promotes or discourages.

Multiple Intelligence: Verbal/Linguistic

Objective: To conclude that every good thing is a gift from God

Open

 Let Us Pray Invite children to pray the psalm verse on page 35 with you.

 Focus **What good things are made from God's gifts?** List children's answers on the board or on chart paper.

Build

Use God's Gifts

Explain that everything we eat, wear, or use is made from one or more of God's gifts.

Wiggle Worms

• Direct attention to the repeated action words in Wiggle Worms and tell children that they will be acting out those lines.

• Do the actions yourself while reading the story. Ask children to do the actions this time while you read the story again.

Explore

Use God's Gifts

Focus **What good things are made from God's gifts?**

Everything around you is a gift from God. Paper was once part of a tree. Foo is made from animals or plants.

A STORY

WIGGLE WORMS

Worms move in the earth.
Wiggle, wiggle, wiggle.

Wormy wiggles put air in the so
Puff, puff, puff.

Now the farmer digs some holes
Deep, deep, deep.

In the holes go the seeds.
Plop, plop, plop.

38

JUSTICE AND PEACE

Looking After God's Beautiful World God put humans in charge of taking care of the earth. But at times humans do things that damage the land, water, and air.

• Have children think of ways they could take better care of the earth. For example, Ask them how they could reduce the amount of water they use each day.

Catholic Social Teaching: Care for Creation

TEACHER BACKGROUND

Icky Things Some children don't like worms. Point out that without worms, farmers couldn't grow the grain that they eat.

• Tell them even scary things serve useful purposes in God's creation. For example, bats may be scary, but they make people's lives easier by eating mosquitoes and other insects.

Wheat grows straight and tall.
Up, up, up!

Stalks get cut and ground
into flour.
Smash, smash, smash.

Wheat flour is turned to dough.
Roll, roll, roll.

Bread is eaten warm and tasty.
Yum, yum, yum.

**What are three gifts from God
that help to make this bread?**
Possible responses: worms,
the farmer, wheat

Connect Your Faith

Special Gifts Draw a line from each gift to show how it helps God's world.

God's gift	How it helps
	gives light at night
	gives shade
	makes the day bright
	makes the ground soft

39

❷ **What are three gifts from God that help to make this bread?** Invite children to respond.

- Call attention to the matching activity. Lead children in reading the names of the two columns.
- Explain the directions. Because some children are just learning to read, they may feel more comfortable working in pairs. Or, you may work along with children, going through one entry at a time.

Close

Remind children that if God had not given humans his gifts, people could not make any of the foods, toys, or other good things that they enjoy.

QUICK TIP

God's Gifts Children enjoy activities that help illustrate a lesson while allowing them to participate.

- To help them understand the concept of God's intangible gifts, bring a large gift bow to class.
- Allow each child a turn to place the bow on top of his or her head while stating one reason why he or she is a gift from God.

OPTIONAL ACTIVITY

Activity Master 2: Gifts from God Distribute copies of the activity found on teacher page 44A.

- Tell children to circle in crayon the hidden food and animals.
- As an alternative, you may wish to send this activity home with children.

▲ **Activity Master 2 page 44A**

Explore

Objective: To describe ways that people use God's gifts

Open

Let Us Pray Invite children to repeat after you the psalm verse from page 35.

Focus **How do people use the things God made?** List children's responses on the board or on chart paper.

Build

The Gift of Food

Read aloud the introductory text.

- Have children follow along as you read aloud the captions to the pictures.

- Pause after reading each caption to make sure children understand the sequence of changing natural substances into prepared foods.

❷ **What other things can you make from God's gifts?** Invite children to respond.

Explore

The Gift of Food

Focus How do people use the things God made?

God gave people many gifts to use. People take the things he made. They use them to make things they need.

You use God's gifts to make the food you eat.

Dough is made from wheat flour.

Sauce is made from tomatoes.

Cheese is made from the milk of cows.

All together they make pizza!

❷ What other things can you make from God's gifts?
Responses will vary.

40

Make Pizzas Have children assemble and share mini-pizzas from prepared ingredients.

- Supply prepared English muffin halves, pizza sauce, shredded cheese, and other non-meat toppings such as chopped broccoli, olives, or pineapple.

- As children put together the pizzas, talk about the origins of each ingredient.

Multiple Intelligence: Bodily/Kinesthetic

QUICK TIP

Food in the Classroom Always follow these important rules when sharing food in the classroom:

- Obtain information about food allergies and sensitivities before allowing children to taste foods. Avoid all nuts and shellfish, as these can cause serious allergic reactions even in small amounts.

- Follow food safety practices such as keeping foods at proper temperatures and having children wash their hands before preparing or eating foods.

Live Your Faith

✎ **Match the Gifts** Draw lines to match the gifts of God with the things made from them.

Gift of God   **What You Make from It**

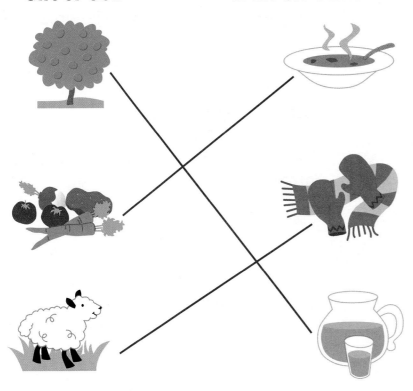

✎ **Trace the Words** What can you say to God for giving us all these gifts? Trace the words below.

Thank you, God!

- Read aloud the directions for Match the Gifts.
- Go through the pictures in both columns with children, making sure they can identify them.
- Have children work in pairs to do the matching activity.
- Review the matches with the class.
- Read aloud the directions for Trace the Words.
- Have children work independently to trace the words.
- Ask a volunteer to read aloud the traced sentence.

Close

Invite children to think about the gifts of God that they will share at lunch today.

CHRISTIAN LIVING SKILLS

Giving Thanks Remind children that they give thanks for God's gifts that are made into food when they pray grace, or the blessing before meals.

- Teach or review with the children a favorite meal blessing.
- Remind children that they can thank God by saying grace at family meals or even silently before any meal.

OPTIONAL ACTIVITY

Cross-Curricular: Health Review with children the healthful eating pyramid.

- Invite children to name examples of favorite foods in each food group.
- Have children tell where these foods are found in God's creation.

Multiple Intelligence: Naturalist

DAY 5

Objective: To praise the Lord for the great things he has done

Prepare

Invite children to look over the index cards to find the word that refers to God. *Creator*

 Use the *Call to Faith 1* CD, track 2, to rehearse the song.

Gather

Invite children to assemble in the prayer space.

Pray

A Prayer of Praise

 Let Us Pray Follow the order of prayer on page 42. Take the leader's part yourself.

• Optional music from *Singing Our Faith:* "Psalm 146: Praise the Lord, My Soul," #53, "Praise and Thanksgiving," #148, "Praise to God," #155.

Celebrate

A Prayer of Praise

 **Let Us Pray**

Gather and begin with the Sign of the Cross.

Leader: Sing praise to the Lord with harps and trumpets!

All: Let the sea crash and the sea creatures sing!

Leader: Let the rivers clap and the mountains shout "Hooray!"

All: Praise the Lord! He has done great things!

Based on Psalm 98

 Sing together.

Sing to the Lord a new song, for he has done wondrous deeds.

"Psalm 98: Sing to the Lord a New Song" © 1969, 1981, and 1997, ICEL.

42

 LITURGY LINK

Music and Prayer Whenever possible, have children sing the song or refrain suggested on the Celebrate page in each chapter.

• Children of this age love to sing.
• You will help them discover the Church's treasury of sung prayer.
• You will help build habits of active liturgical participation.

 LECTIONARY LINK

Break Open the Word Read last week's Sunday Gospel. Invite children to think about what the reading means to them as they try to follow Christ's example. For questions related to the weekly Gospel reading, visit our Web site at **www.harcourtreligion.com**.

 Visit www.harcourtreligion.com for weekly scripture readings and seasonal resources.

CHAPTER 2
Review

Ⓐ Check Understanding

1. Draw one thing that God created.

2. Why did God create the world? Circle the best answer. (p. 37)

   to do some work   (to show his love)

3. What gift from God do you like best?

   _____

   -
   Responses will vary.
   _____

Ⓑ Make Connections Name one way you use God's gifts. Draw a picture of the gift.

_____

- -
Responses will vary.
_____

43

Review

Ⓐ **Check Understanding**   Have children draw one thing that God created in the space provided. Have children circle the best answer. Then have children write the response to the question in the lines provided.

Ⓑ **Make Connections**   Instruct children to name one way they can use God's gifts and have them draw a picture of the gift in the space provided.

Assessment

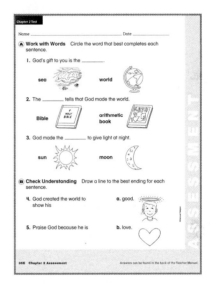

▲ **Chapter 2 Test page 35E**

Answers to the Chapter Test can be found in the back of the Teacher Manual.

OPTIONAL ACTIVITY

Our Families—God's Gift   Invite children to bring to class duplicate copies of photos of their parents or guardians and of their brothers and sisters. (Request parents to write on the back of the photos the full names of the people shown.) Make a poster with the photos. Title it: "Our Families—God's Gift to Us."

Multiple Intelligence: Interpersonal

OPTIONAL ACTIVITY

Cross-Curricular: Reading   You may wish to read aloud *Each Living Thing* by Joanne Ryder (Gulliver Books/Harcourt, 2000).

- This book reminds children to be aware of and to care for all God's creatures.

Multiple Intelligence: Verbal/Linguistic

Family Faith

Remind children to discuss the Family Faith page at home. Encourage children to read the scripture passage from the Book of Genesis with their families.

Activity

• Explain the family project. Suggest that children initiate the project at home.

People of Faith

Tell children about Saint Nicholas.

• Nicholas' parents died when he was a young man. He was left with money, which he shared with the poor. He is especially known for his love of children. Thousands of churches have been named after the generous Saint Nicholas.

• Remind children to add Saint Nicholas to their People of Faith albums.

• Encourage them to pray the prayer at home with their families.

Visit **www.harcourtreligion.com** for weekly scripture readings and seasonal resources.

Unit 1: CHAPTER 2

Family Faith

 Catholics Believe

■ God's world is a gift to you.

■ You can learn about God and his love by looking at the world he made.

† SCRIPTURE

Read Genesis 1:27–31 to find out more about God's creation.

GO ONLINE www.harcourtreligion.com
For weekly Scripture readings and seasonal resources

Activity
Live Your Faith

A Nature Walk Take a walk outside to collect things that are gifts from God.

• Bring these things inside to put them in a special prayer space.

• Gather in the space. Thank God for all his marvelous deeds!

▲ Saint Nicholas, 270–310

People of Faith

Nicholas tiptoed to the open window. The family inside was asleep. Nicholas tossed in a bag of gold coins. It landed on the floor with a soft thump. Then he hurried away. Nicholas liked helping people who were poor. He was a bishop in Asia Minor. Nicholas was so kind that people still remember him today. They try to be generous like he was. Saint Nicholas is the patron saint of children. The Catholic Church celebrates his feast day on December 6.

 Family Prayer

Dear God, help us be like Saint Nicholas so that we may give gifts of kindness and care to family and friends. Amen.

In Unit 1 your child is learning about REVELATION.
44 **CCC** *See Catechism of the Catholic Church 315, 319 for further reading on chapter content.*

? HOW DID I DO?

This week my religion classes were

☐ *some of the best ever!* ☐ *pretty good.* ☐ *in need of improvement.*

In what discussions and activities were children most interested?

_____

What activity did I most enjoy teaching?

_____

In what area do I need to improve?

_____

Name _____ Date _____

Gifts from God

God gives a world full of gifts. Circle the hidden food and animals that are gifts of God.

cat	feather	duck	loaf of bread	snake
rabbit	crab	bird	apple	frog
octopus	cow	carrot	turtle	flower

Care for Creation

CHAPTER BACKGROUND

 God looked at everything he had made, and he found it very good.

Genesis 1:31

Responsibility

In the first creation story in the Book of Genesis, God created every living thing and then entrusted all to the care of humans. Only after he had given care of the earth over to the man and the woman was he able to rest "from all the work he had done in creation" (*Genesis 2:3*). God gives humans the responsibility and stewardship of his creation.

Called to share in God's power, humans have the ability and responsibility to care for other creatures. Yet, many continue to turn their backs on this responsibility. The repercussions on the rest of creation have been tremendous. The earth is suffering in many ways today because of human callousness.

What Can Be Done

As a steward of creation it is important that you take the time to enjoy creation and pass on to future generations this respect for what God has given you. Lead by example. Teach respect by taking time to praise God for the food on the table. Be respectful of the neighbors' garden and lawn. Pick up the paper that litters sidewalks and streets. Take a long walk or hike on a Sunday afternoon. Praise God for flowers, trees, and plants. Show love for him by loving the earth. Take care of creation as Jesus himself would do.

Reflect As a steward of God's creation, what can you do to fulfill your responsibility right now?

Respect

Children focus on knowing God through his gift of creation. Using their senses, they perceive his gift of the world.

- Connecting the theological concepts of the chapter to children's experiences should not be difficult. Most young children naturally delight in the wonders of nature and have an innate attraction to living creatures.

- Most young children have been taught basic protocol in receiving presents and gifts. Through stories you will lead children to see that care given to a gift shows respect for the gift giver. When people care for the earth, they show love for God, the Creator.

- Today's young children are exposed to sophisticated knowledge. They are aware that the earth and its resources are fragile and many living creatures are endangered. Give children opportunities for age-appropriate and satisfying acts of care for creation.

Caring

- I am beginning to see myself as part of the world.
- I am capable of practicing caring deeds and interactions.
- I need you to affirm and confirm my caring behavior.

Blessed Assurance

Catechesis can be risky. You place yourself before students, parents, and administrators. Some of us become timid and fearful about embracing the possibilities that arise from teaching. Teachers who place themselves in front of students faithfully and with confidence have much to gain.

Many have discovered that this kind of quiet confidence comes from their past. Their confidence came from some person or group that assured them that they were trustworthy and capable.

Now and then, you may need to revisit that person or group to renew your confidence. This will help you recapture and reclaim that blessed assurance.

Reflect **Who comes to mind as one that gave you such a blessed assurance about yourself?**

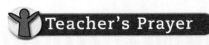

Teacher's Prayer

Help me care for the world, O Lord. May I work to repair the damage already done and work to protect that which could be saved. Help me teach the children to be caretakers of your creation. Amen.

Weekly Planner

	Objective	Materials	Prayer & Scripture
DAY 1 Invite	**Care for Creation** Page 45	**Objective:** To recognize that living things need care	☐ Art supplies ☐ Pencils	**Let Us Pray** *Psalm 150:6*
DAY 2 Explore	**Many Gifts** Pages 46–47	**Objective:** To describe how cooperation can make a difference in the world	☐ Board or chart paper ☐ Art supplies ☐ Index card ☐ Small cups of soil ☐ Seeds	**Let Us Pray** *Psalm 150:6*
DAY 3 Explore	**God's Command** Pages 48–49	**Objective:** To identify ways to show God love and thanks	☐ Board or chart paper ☐ House Plant ☐ Index card ☐ Pencils ☐ Crayons or markers ☐ Drinking straws ☐ Scissors	**Let Us Pray** *Psalm 150:6* ✝ **Scripture:** *Genesis 1:26–30* ✝ **Scripture Background:** Genesis 1:26–30, p. 48
DAY 4 Explore	**Care for Yourself** Pages 50–51	**Objective:** To identify ways to care for oneself	☐ Board or chart paper ☐ Art supplies ☐ Pencils ☐ The Best Part of Me by Wendy Ewald (Little Brown, 2002)	**Let Us Pray** *Psalm 150:6*
DAY 5 Celebrate	**Thank You, God!** Page 52	**Objective:** To give thanks to God in prayer for a wonderful world	☐ Music CD	**Let Us Pray** **Thank You, God** 🎵 **Hymn:** "Sing Out, Earth and Skies"

Chapter 3 Wrap-Up: Review and Apply p. 53 • Chapter 3 Assessment p. 45E

Words of Faith

creation

caretaker

Activities	Enrichment
Let's Begin: Sam's Fish, p. 45 Multiple Intelligence: Visual/Spatial	• Teacher Background: Blessing of Animals, p. 45
Share Your Faith: Think, Share, Act, p. 47 Multiple Intelligence: Visual/Spatial (OPTIONAL) Play "I Care," p. 47 Multiple Intelligence: Interpersonal	• Quick Tip: Rooted in Understanding, p. 46 • Justice and Peace: Don't Waste, p. 46 • Teacher Background: A Children's Garden, p. 47
Connect Your Faith: What I Will Do, p. 49 Multiple Intelligence: Visual/Spatial (OPTIONAL) Activity Master 3, p. 49 Multiple Intelligence: Visual/Spatial (OPTIONAL) Animal Care, p. 49 Multiple Intelligence: Verbal/Linguistic	• Reaching All Learners: We Care, p. 48
Live Your Faith: Talk about Pictures, p. 51 Multiple Intelligence: Visual/Spatial (OPTIONAL) Act It Out, p. 50 Multiple Intelligence: Bodily/Kinesthetic (OPTIONAL) Cross-Curricular: Health, p. 51 Multiple Intelligence: Visual/Spatial	• Christian Living Skills: Honoring the Body, p. 50 • Quick Tip: Share Poetry, p. 51
	• Liturgy Link: Making Prayer Expressive, p. 52 • Lectionary Link: Break Open the Word, p. 52

Multimedia Resources

BOOK

Sasso, Sandy Eisenberg. *A Prayer for the Earth: The Story of Naamah, Noah's Wife.* Jewish Lights Publishing. 1996. A folk tale about the ark teaches caring for creation.

VIDEO

The Magic School Bus in the Rainforest (30 min). A-Vision. A class learns about an important and endangered part of creation.

 Teacher Resources
www.harcourtreligion.com

• For interactive lesson planner, chapter resources, and activities
• For free materials and information

Home Connection

Chapter 3 Family Faith, p. 54
Take-home activities, chapter content review, saint features and prayer

 For more family activities
www.harcourtreligion.com

Name _____ Date _____

A **Work with Words**   Write the word from the Word Bank that best completes each sentence.

```
┌─────────────────────────────┐
│          WORD BANK          │
│  _____│
│  everything      creation   │
└─────────────────────────────┘
```

1. Creation is _____ God made.

2. You can care for all God's _____ .

B **Check Understanding**   Put an X next to the three things a good caretaker would do.

_____ 3. Be kind to pets.

_____ 4. Throw away a dull pencil.

_____ 5. Dump milk in the lunch garbage.

_____ 6. Save water.

_____ 7. Recycle cans.

_____ 8. Throw out cardboard boxes.

Answers can be found in the back of the Teacher Manual.

ASSESSMENT

Chapter 3 Care for Creation

Invite

 **Let Us Pray**

Leader: God, teach us to care for your world.
"Let everything that has breath
give praise to the LORD!
Hallelujah!"

Psalm 150:6

All: God, teach us to care for your world. Amen.

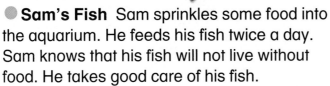

Activity **Let's Begin**

● **Sam's Fish** Sam sprinkles some food into the aquarium. He feeds his fish twice a day. Sam knows that his fish will not live without food. He takes good care of his fish.

• What living things do you take care of?

_____

_____

_____

_____

Draw a Picture Think of the living things that you take care of. Draw a picture of yourself caring for a pet or a plant.

45

TEACHER BACKGROUND

Blessing of Animals Often on October 4, the feast of Saint Francis of Assisi, parishes may ask parishioners to bring in their pets to be blessed. This is done on his feast day because Saint Francis called all creatures Sister and Brother. Francis is the patron saint of those who care for creation.

DAY 1

Objective: To recognize that living things need care

Open

 **Let Us Pray** Tell children to move to the classroom prayer space. Pray the psalm verse and ask children to wave their arms in the air as they praise God for creation.

Build

Activity

• Read aloud Sam's Fish. Have children search the page for the word *care* and circle it.

• Direct attention to the photo of Sam. Invite children to make up a story about Sam and how he shows he cares. Ask volunteers to share their stories.

• Ask children what living thing they take good care of. Possible responses: a pet, a plant, a family member

Extension Activity

• Tell children that they will be drawing a picture of themselves caring for a pet or a plant.

• Allow children time to draw.

• Ask each child to share his or her drawing.

Close

Have children tell what they learned about caring for living things.

Care for Creation 45

DAY 2

Objective: To describe how cooperation can make a difference in the world

Open

 Let Us Pray Invite children to pray the psalm verse on page 45 with you.

Focus **How can you share the gifts of God's creation?** List children's answers on the board or on chart paper.

Build

Many Gifts

Read the paragraph aloud.

• Hold up an index card with the word *creation* written on it. Explain the meaning of the word *creation*.

Miss Sandy's Garden

Read aloud Miss Sandy's Garden.

• Ask children what Miss Sandy's problem was. Her land was too weedy and too big for her to clear all by herself.

❓ **Why would you work with Miss Sandy?** Ask volunteers to share their responses.

Many Gifts

 Focus **How can you share the gifts of God's creation?**

All **creation** is a gift from God. Find out how Miss Sandy cared for God's creation.

A STORY

MISS SANDY'S GARDEN

Miss Sandy's large plot of land was full of weeds. She loved it anyway. She wanted to share it with others. She knew that clearing the land was a big job. Miss Sandy thought, "I need people who like work in the garden!"

Miss Sandy placed an ad in the paper. It said, "Come plant a garden to share." She brought the seeds. To Miss Sandy's surprise, different stores dropped off bags of rich soil, wood, and hay. Many children came ready to work.

Possible responses: It's fun; it's good to help.

❓ **Why would you work with Miss Sandy?**

QUICK TIP

Rooted in Understanding Give children a first-hand glimpse of gardening by giving each child a small disposable cup half-filled with potting soil. Provide easy-to-grow seeds for the children to plant in the soil, and encourage them to bring the planted seeds home and water them regularly. Remember to ask how the mini gardens are faring at future sessions.

JUSTICE AND PEACE

Don't Waste Expand children's understanding of care by talking about not wasting food or water. Supermarkets give young children the inaccurate impression that there is an endless supply of food. Guide children to make rules for not wasting food.

Catholic Social Teaching: Care for Creation

GARDENING FUN

Every day the children worked.

They dug holes and planted.
They watered and they weeded.
They shoveled and they hoed.
Before they knew what happened,
everything began to grow.
Beans popped up by the dozen,
black-eyed Susans by the bunch,
tomatoes by the bushel—
they ate them all for lunch!

The children shared flowers and food
from the garden with their neighbors.

**❓ What happened when everyone
worked together?**
The garden grew and everyone enjoyed it.

Words of Faith

Creation is everything that God made. All that God made is good.

Activity

Share Your Faith

Think: Think about what you might like to grow in a garden.

Share: Talk about different things you can put in a backyard garden.

 Act: On a piece of paper, draw your own garden. Fill it with your favorite flowers and vegetables that God has made.

47

Gardening Fun

Finish reading the story.

- Have children stand and act out the three sentences that describe the work the children did.
- Ask children to tell what they liked about the story.

❷ What happened when everyone worked together? Ask volunteers to share their responses.

Activity

- Set a time limit for the drawing. Have each child share his or her picture with someone who sits nearby.

Close

Remind children that creation is everything that God made. When people work together, they can accomplish great things.

OPTIONAL ACTIVITY

Play "I Care" Ask a volunteer to call out the name of any living thing.

- Encourage children to name things that are found in their everyday environment.
- Invite another child to describe one way of caring for the creature the other child named.

Multiple Intelligence: Interpersonal

TEACHER BACKGROUND

A Children's Garden The story about Miss Sandy is based on the development of a children's garden in Colorado.

- Community businesses donated materials, and many children spent the whole summer working there.
- The flowers and vegetables grown in the garden were shared with people in care centers.

DAY 3

Objective: To identify ways to show God love and thanks

Open

 Let Us Pray Invite children to pray the psalm verse on page 45 with you.

◎ Focus **What does God ask you to do?** List children's answers on the board or on chart paper.

Build

God's Command

Read aloud the introductory paragraph. Explain that children worked hard in the garden to thank Miss Sandy for sharing her land.

• Explain that in the following story, God tells humans how to show him love and thanks for creation.

All Creation

Proclaim the scripture story.

• Discuss with them ways that they can show care for the Earth.

❷ What did God ask Adam and Eve to do? Ask children for responses.

Explore

God's Command

◎ Focus What does God ask you to do?

The children worked hard to make a garden. They wanted to thank Miss Sandy for sharing her land. Listen to what God asked the first man and woman to do.

✝ SCRIPTURE   Genesis 1:26–3

 All Creation

God made Adam and Eve to be like him. He said to them, "Have children to fill the earth. Use the earth for what you need. Here are plants with seeds, and animals, and birds. Take care of all that I have given you."

Based on Genesis 1:26–30

❷ What did God ask Adam and Eve to do?
Possible responses: to have children; to take care of the animals and plants

48

★ REACHING ALL LEARNERS

We Care Children with disabilities may feel left out when they hear the story about Miss Sandy's garden.

• Show them that they too can play a role in caring for creation by obtaining an easy-care house plant for your room.

• Assign these children the task of caring for it by watering it and making sure it has enough light.

✝ SCRIPTURE BACKGROUND

Genesis 1:26–30 This passage comes at the end of the first creation story in the Book of Genesis.

• The scripture story affirms that humans are the only creatures whom God made in his own image.

• God tells humans to have children and settle the whole earth.

• Everything else was created for humanity's benefit, but God ordered humans to take good care of everything.

how Thanks

God told the first man and woman care for his creation. God asks you be a good **caretaker**, too.

When you care for living things, you how your love for God. Caring is way to thank God for all that e has given you.

How can you thank God for his gifts?
ossible responses:
ay with and feed
ets; share food;
ray

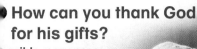

Activity

Connect Your Faith

What I Will Do Draw a line to match each action to a picture.

Save water.

Clean up trash outside school.

Be kind to pets.

49

Words of Faith

A **caretaker** is a person who treats everything with care and respect.

Show Thanks
Read aloud Show Thanks.

- Hold up an index card of the word *caretaker*. Invite children to name some habits a good caretaker should have.

Activity

- Direct children's attention to the activity and the good habits that are pictured in the photos. Ask volunteers to describe other good habits that they have seen people display.
- Give children the directions for completing the activity.

Close

Emphasize that God put humans in charge of taking care of his creation.

OPTIONAL ACTIVITY

Activity Master 3: Be a Caretaker Distribute copies of the activity on teacher page 54A.

- Tell children they will make a work of art reminding them to be caretakers.
- As an alternative, you may wish to send the activity home with children.

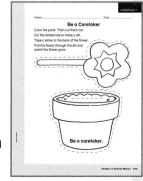

▲ Activity Master 3 page 54A

OPTIONAL ACTIVITY

Animal Care Ask children to think of a television show or movie that has an animal in it. Let children tell how the animal is cared for. If the observations are scarce, make up an animal for a television show or movie, and let children suggest good ways to treat it.

Multiple Intelligence: Verbal/Linguistic

Objective: To identify ways to care for oneself

Open

 Let Us Pray Invite children to repeat after you the psalm verse from page 45.

◎ Focus **How do you help take care of yourself?** List children's responses on the board or on chart paper.

Build

Care for Yourself

Read aloud the first paragraph.

- Point out the lists of ways to care for the body and for the mind.

- Have children follow along as you read aloud the lists.

- Direct attention to the pictures, and ask children to explain how the children depicted are taking care of themselves.

❷ **What other things can you do to take care of yourself?** List responses on the board or on chart paper.

Explore

Care for Yourself

 Focus How do you help take care of yourself?

You are one of God's greatest gifts! He made your body and your mind. God loves and cares for you very much. He wants you to help take care of yourself.

Ways to Take Care of Your Body

✔ Eat good foods.
✔ Keep your hair, teeth, and body clean.
✔ Play and get exercise.
✔ Get enough sleep at night.

Ways to Take Care of Your Mind

✔ Listen to stories.
✔ Do your best in school.
✔ Make something.
✔ Learn to do a new thing.

❷ What other things can you do to help take care of yourself?
Responses will vary.

50

OPTIONAL ACTIVITY

Act It Out Have children act out situations in which children are not taking care of their bodies and minds.

- Invite children to form small groups to plan and carry out their dramatizations.

- Have the class respond to each dramatization by suggesting better choices.

Multiple Intelligence: Bodily/Kinesthetic

🖐 ❤ CHRISTIAN LIVING SKILLS

Honoring the Body As Catholics, we are rooted in an incarnational theology that respects the body as the temple of the Holy Spirit.

- Encourage children to show respect for their own health and safety and that of others.

- Remind children that God calls us to respect bodies of all sizes, shapes, ages, colors, and levels of ability.

Live Your Faith

Talk About Pictures Look at the pictures. With a partner, talk about how the children in the pictures are helping to take care of themselves.

✎ **Write About Yourself** Name one way you can take care of yourself this week.

_____
- -
_____
_____
- -
_____

51

- Ask children to choose partners.
- Read aloud the directions for Talk About Pictures.
- Allow time for the pairs to discuss the pictures.
- Invite pairs to share their responses with the class.
- Read aloud the directions for Write About Yourself.
- Have children work independently.
- Invite volunteers to share their responses.

Close

Play lively music and invite children to thank God for their bodies by dancing.

QUICK TIP

Share Poetry You may wish to share with children selections from the book _The Best Part of Me: Children Talk About Their Bodies in Words and Pictures_ by Wendy Ewald (Little, Brown, 2002). It is a collection of childrens poems and photos.

OPTIONAL ACTIVITY

Cross-Curricular: Health Have children work together to make a mural illustrating the consequences of making bad choices about health.

- Divide the class into groups, and let each group select a bad health choice to illustrate.
- Ask children to draw both the choice and the consequences.

Multiple Intelligence: Visual/Spatial

Objective: To give thanks to God in prayer for a wonderful world

Prepare

Have children run their fingers down the page and notice all the times the words *"thank you"* are used.

- Divide the class into small groups, and assign each group a line to remember to say. All should say the thank-you lines together.

 Use the *Call to Faith 1* CD, track 3, to rehearse the song.

Gather

Take children outdoors for prayer if possible.

- Have the members of each small group stand together to say their lines.

Pray

Thank You, God

 Let Us Pray Follow the order of prayer on page 52.

- Conclude with the song.

Celebrate

Thank You, God!

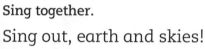 **Let Us Pray**

Gather and begin with the Sign of the Cross.

Leader: God made a wonderful world! Give thanks to God for his wonderful world.

All: Thank you, thank you, thank you, God.

Leader: For pets and trees and carrots and peas And birds that fly and sing.

All: Thank you, thank you, thank you, God.

Leader: We sing our thanks and praise to you Every day and night! We'll care for all that you have made, We'll try with all our might!

Sing together.

Sing out, earth and skies!
Sing of the God who
  loves you!
Raise your joyful cries!
Dance to the life
  around you!

"Sing Out, Earth and Skies," Marty Haugen
© 1985, GIA Publications, Inc.

52

LITURGY LINK

Making Prayer Expressive Children will naturally respond to some of the words in this prayer, such as *thanks*, *wonderful*, and *praise*. Encourage them to say those words with expression. Invite them to make vigorous arm movements when they pray "Thank you."

LECTIONARY LINK

Break Open the Word Read last week's Sunday Gospel. Invite children to think about what the reading means to them as they try to follow Christ's example. For questions related to the weekly Gospel reading, visit our Web site at **www.harcourtreligion.com.**

 GO ONLINE Visit www.harcourtreligion.com for weekly scripture readings and seasonal resources.

CHAPTER 3
Review

A Check Understanding Look at each picture. Draw a line from the word to the picture that shows how you can care for God's creation.

Water   Keep Clean   Feed

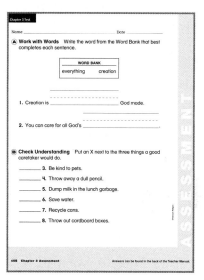

B Make Connections Name or draw a picture of one way you can take care of your body.

Responses will vary.

53

Review

A Check Understanding Have children do the matching activity by themselves.

B Make Connections Have children respond in the lines or blank space provided to them.

Assessment

▲ **Chapter 3 Test page 45E**

Answers to the Chapter Test can be found in the back of the Teacher Manual.

CULTURAL AWARENESS

Protecting God's Creatures The people of Japan were alarmed by the many building projects that encroached on the habitats of Golden Eagles. In fact, today only 134 pairs of Golden Eagles remain in Japan.

• After a three-year research project, there was a significant decrease in land development and wildlife protection areas were increased. The Forestry and Environment agencies prepared guidelines for protection of these birds.

TEACHER BACKGROUND

In the Beginning According to the *Catechism*, "Creation was fashioned with a view to the sabbath and therefore for the worship and adoration of God" (*CCC 347*). On the seventh day, God rested, and we celebrate all of his creation each Sunday at Mass.

Family Faith

Remind children to discuss the Family Faith page at home. Encourage them to read the scripture passage from the Gospel according to Luke.

Activity

• Suggest that children watch for the parts of creation that need a good caretaker the next time they go to the park with their family.

People of Faith

Tell children about Saint Albert the Great.

• Albert taught people about what he learned. He also wrote and illustrated many books about God's world. Albert is the patron saint of scientists.

• Remind children to add Saint Albert the Great to their People of Faith albums.

• Encourage them to pray the prayer at home with their families.

  Visit **www.harcourtreligion.com** for weekly scripture readings and seasonal resources.

Unit 1: CHAPTER 3
Family Faith

◎ Catholics Believe

■ All creation is a gift from God.

■ Everyone must help care for God's world.

✝ SCRIPTURE

Read Luke 13:6–9 about a fig tree that had no fruit. Do you think it had fruit after the gardener cared for it? Why or why not?

 www.harcourtreligion.com
For weekly Scripture readings and seasonal resources

Activity
Live Your Faith

Be a Caretaker Go to a local park with the family. Watch an ant do its work. Look at a sunset. Talk about what you see in the shapes of the clouds. Name the things you see that God has made. Look for parts of creation that need a good caretaker. Choose a way to help.

People of Faith

Albert was the oldest son of a wealthy military family. Albert liked to learn about God's world. He looked carefully at spiderwebs. He studied the stars and the way they move. Albert hiked for miles just to be around the animals and plants of nature. People called Albert "the bishop of the boots." The Catholic Church celebrates Saint Albert's feast day on November 15.

▲ **Saint Albert the Great, 1206–1280**

Family Pray

Saint Albert, pray for us that we may enjoy the outdoor Help us care for a living things. Ame

In Unit 1 your child is learning about REVELATION.

54 CCC *See Catechism of the Catholic Church 374–379 for further reading on chapter content.*

 HOW DID I DO?

This week my religion classes were

☐ *some of the best ever!* ☐ *pretty good.* ☐ *in need of improvement.*

In what discussions and activities were children most interested?

_____

What activity did I most enjoy teaching?

_____

In what area do I need to improve?

_____

Name _____ Date _____

Be a Caretaker

Color the parts. Then cut them out.

Cut the dotted line to make a slit.

Tape a straw to the back of the flower.

Pull the flower through the slit and
watch the flower grow.

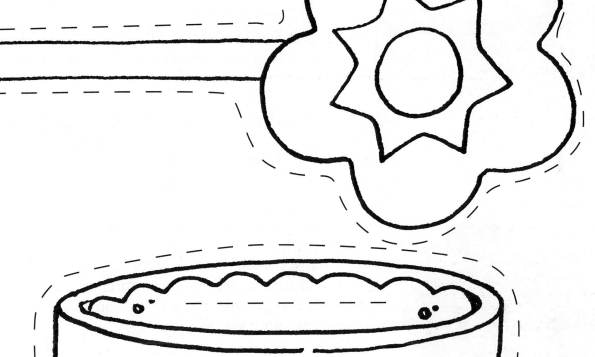

Be a caretaker.

Seven Principles of CATHOLIC SOCIAL TEACHING

> **Care for God's Creation**

> Life and Dignity of the Human Person

> Rights and Responsibilities of the Human Person

> Dignity of Work and the Rights of Workers

> Solidarity of the Human Family

> Call to Family, Community, and Participation

> Option for the Poor and Vulnerable

Faith in Action!
CATHOLIC SOCIAL TEACHING

Connect to Unit 1

This unit's Faith in Action feature teaches first graders the principle of caring for God's creation. It connects to topics covered in this unit.

Children learned that
- God made all things.
- People use the gifts of creation that God made.
- God calls people to help care for creation.

Discover Catholic Social Teaching

Principle: Care for God's Creation

Technological advancement, with all its positive aspects, can also serve to alienate us from the natural world. As more and more people live in larger and larger urban areas, we lose touch with the wonders of creation. We are more likely to neglect our responsibility to care for the natural world. That's why the Church continually reminds us that all that we have and all that we are comes to us from God as gift. We are entrusted with creation as stewards.

Catholic tradition calls us
- to renew our connections with the natural world.
- to be thankful for all the gifts of God's creation.
- to work for the preservation and care of the natural environment.

Reflect **How can you maintain a close and caring relationship with the natural world God created?**

Catholic Social Teaching Document

"The Bible, from the first page on, teaches us that the whole of creation is for humanity, that it is men and women's responsibility to develop it by intelligent effort and by means of their labor to perfect it, so to speak, for their use. If the world is made to furnish each individual with the means of livelihood and the instruments for growth and progress, all people have therefore the right to find in the world what is necessary for them."

From *Populorum Progressio (On the Development of Peoples)*, Pope Paul VI, 1967

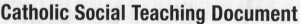

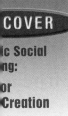

COVER

ic Social
ng:

or
Creation

Faith in Action!
CATHOLIC SOCIAL TEACHING

In this unit you learned that God made all people and things. People care for the gifts of God's creation.

Be My Helpers

You can be a good helper. You can help your family at home. You can help your teacher at school.

God asks you to be his helper, too. You can help take care of the gifts of God's creation. You can help by planting flowers and vegetables. You can feed wild birds. You can take care of your pets. You can also help keep parks and playgrounds clean.

❓ **Why should you take care of the gifts of creation?** Possible responses: to keep the air and water safe, to keep plants and animals alive

55

DISCOVER

Catholic Social Teaching

 Let Us Pray   God our Creator, show us how to care for the world you made.

Faith in Action
Read aloud the first paragraph.

• Ask children to name gifts of God's creation.

Be My Helpers
Read aloud the first paragraph.

• Ask children to listen carefully as you read about ways to be a good helper.

• Read aloud the second paragraph.

• Invite children to suggest other ways to help take care of creation.

❓ **Why should you take care of the gifts of creation?** Discuss the question as a class.

QUICK TIP

Cross-Curricular: Science   Share with children one of these books about God's creation.

• *Wonderful Nature, Wonderful You* by Karin Ireland (Dawn Publications, 1996)

• *A Place to Bloom* by Lorriane Siomades (Boyds Mills Press, 1997)

OPTIONAL ACTIVITY

Draw Pictures   Give children art materials, and have them draw pictures of themselves helping to care for God's creation.

• Display the completed art work on a bulletin board titled *We Are God's Helpers.*

Multiple Intelligence: Visual/Spatial

CONNECT

With the Call to Justice

From Concrete to Garden

Read aloud the introduction in the margin.

- Direct attention to the photographs, and ask children to guess what the story on this page is about.

- Read aloud the first two paragraphs.

- Ask children why they think the people at Cardinal Bernardin chose to make a garden.

- Finish reading aloud the story.

❷ **How are the children, teachers, and parents of this school acting as God's helpers?** Arrange the class in small groups to discuss the question.

CONNECT

**With the
Call to Justice**

God calls everyone to help care for creation. Let's look at how one Catholic school community answered that call.

From Concrete to Garde

The children of Cardinal Bernardin Early Childhood Center live in a big ci in Illinois. Cities like Chicago are full concrete and brick. There is not much room for nature.

The children, teachers, and parents this school wanted a garden. They dug up a blacktop schoolyard. They brough in lots of good soil. They planted flowe and vegetables. They even made a sma pond and filled it with turtles, frogs, and fish.

It was hard work, but now they see butterflies and hummingbirds. Children listen to stories or play in the garden. They harvest the fruits and vegetables. They share them with people who have little money for food

❷ **How are the children, teachers, and parents of this school acting as God's helpers?**
Possible responses: They are taking care of nature, they are feeding the poor.

56

✦ TEACHER BACKGROUND

CBECC Garden The Cardinal Bernardin Early Childhood Center garden has won numerous awards and has inspired similar projects at other schools. It is featured in the book, *Schoolyard Mosaics: Designing Gardens and Habitats,* available from the National Gardening Association.

OPTIONAL ACTIVITY

Gardens Tour Arrange for the children to meet with the parish groundskeeper.

- If possible, have the groundskeeper take the children on a tour of the parish grounds and explain the importance of caring for God's creation.

Multiple Intelligence: Naturalist

Reach Out!

SERVE
Your Community

Plan a Garden

Pretend you are going
to plant your own garden.
Finish the drawing below
to show what will grow in
your garden. Draw
yourself working to
care for the flowers
and plants.

Make a Difference

Make Bird Feeders With your teacher's help,
make bird feeders from recycled milk or soda
bottles. Fill the feeders with seed. Hang or place
them outside where you can watch the birds eat.

57

 SERVE

Your Community
Reach Out!

Plan a Garden

Activity

- Read aloud the directions for Plan a Garden.
- Provide children with drawing materials.
- Allow time for children to work independently on their drawings.
- Invite volunteers to share their work.

Make a Difference

Activity

- Read aloud the directions.
- Supply materials, and assist children in making bird feeders from recycled materials. (See Quick Tip below.)
- Help children fill and hang or place bird feeders where they can be viewed from the classroom, if possible.

Encourage children to share what they have learned with friends, family members, and other classes.

QUICK TIP

Bird Feeders Have children research at the library or on the Internet simple patterns, materials lists, and instructions for making bird feeders from recycled materials.

OPTIONAL ACTIVITY

Cross-Curricular: Science Have children grow and care for bean plants.

- Give each child a paper cup three-quarters filled with potting soil and help them plant, water, and sun their beans.
- Help children keep picture diaries of their plants.

Multiple Intelligence: Naturalist

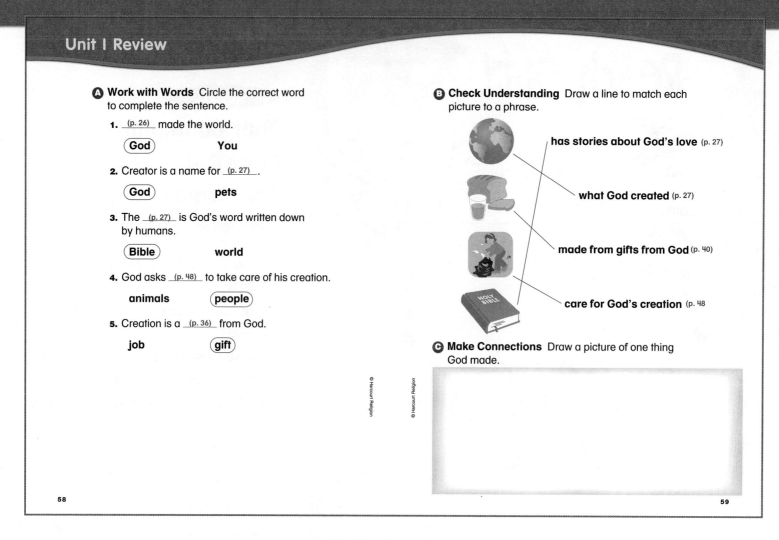

A **Work with Words** Circle the correct word to complete the sentence.

1. __(p. 26)__ made the world.

   (God)   You

2. Creator is a name for __(p. 27)__.

   (God)   pets

3. The __(p. 27)__ is God's word written down by humans.

   (Bible)   world

4. God asks __(p. 48)__ to take care of his creation.

   animals   (people)

5. Creation is a __(p. 36)__ from God.

   job   (gift)

© Harcourt Religion

B **Check Understanding** Draw a line to match each picture to a phrase.

has stories about God's love (p. 27)

what God created (p. 27)

made from gifts from God (p. 40)

care for God's creation (p. 48)

C **Make Connections** Draw a picture of one thing God made.

© Harcourt Religion

58

59

Unit Review

The Unit Review is designed to prepare children for the Unit Assessment. Have children complete the Review pages. Then discuss the answers as a class. You may wish to review any concepts with which children are having difficulty before the Unit Assessment.

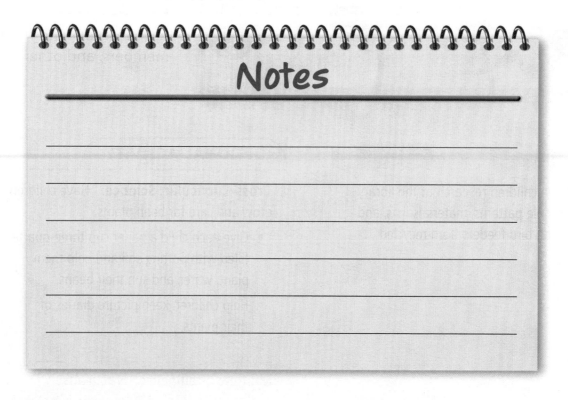

Notes

Name _____ Date _____

(A) Work with Words Write the word from the Word Bank that completes the sentence.

WORD BANK

loves

Creator

good

1. God is the _____ who made everything.

2. Everything God made is _____.

3. God knows and _____ everyone.

(B) Check Understanding Circle the best answer.

4. Everything around you is a _____ from God.

   person    **gift**

5. The story of creation is in the _____.

   Bible    **box**

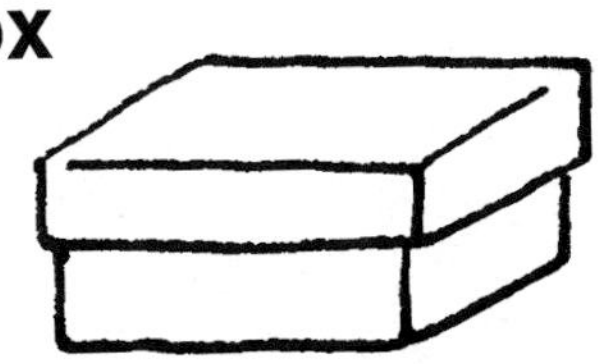

6. God is our loving _____.

   Angel    **Father**

©Harcourt Religion

Answers can be found in the back of the Teacher Manual.

Name _____ Date _____

ⓒ Make Connections   Draw a line to the best title for each picture.

7.

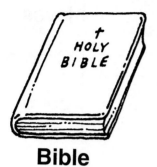

Bible

the first humans

8.

praise

God's word

9.

Adam and Eve

everything God made

10.

creation

give honor and thanks to God

ASSESSMENT

©Harcourt Religion

Answers can be found in the back of the Teacher Manual.

UNIT 2
God Loves You

Chapter 4 **The Trinity**
What do you call God?

Chapter 5 **The Holy Family**
Who is Jesus?

Chapter 6 **Jesus the Storyteller**
Where do you find Jesus' stories?

Faith in Action! Catholic Social Teaching Principle:
Life and Dignity of the Human Person

60

© Harcourt Relig...

UNIT 2 OPENER

Preview Unit Content

Tell children that Unit 2 is about how God loves you.

- Invite a volunteer to read aloud the chapter title and question for Chapter 4. Ask children what they think they will learn in this chapter.

- Repeat this for Chapters 5 and 6.

- Tell children that at the end of the unit they will learn how a group of people discovered that everyone has gifts to share.

The Trinity

CHAPTER BACKGROUND

Faith Focus

- The Holy Trinity is God the Father, God the Son, and God the Holy Spirit. *(CCC 232–234, 238, 240–244)*
- Jesus is the Son of God, who reveals the Father and his love to humans. *(CCC 423, 458–459, 516)*

Catechism Connection

The *Catechism* affirms that the mystery of the Trinity "is the central mystery of the Christian faith." *(CCC 261–262)*

GDC Link

The *Directory* teaches that catechesis attends to the innermost being of God, who is revealed to be a Trinity of Persons. The Holy Trinity in turn shows that human communion is a reflection of the nature of God. *(GDC 100)*

 Do you not believe that I am in the Father and the Father is in me? The words that I speak to you I do not speak on my own. The Father who dwells in me is doing his works.

John 14:10

God the Father

The fatherhood of God is a theme found throughout Scripture. From an early date, the Israelites conceived of their God as the Father of his chosen people, and of themselves as his first-born son. (See *Exodus 4:22*.) Jesus invited his disciples to address God as "Abba," the affectionate Aramaic word for "father." Saint Paul describes how Christians have received a "spirit of adoption" that inspires them to call God by this name. (See *Romans 8:15*.)

Father and Son

Through his mother, Jesus Christ belonged to the human family. However, he was God's Son in a unique and privileged sense. He was and is the true and perfect image of his heavenly Father. The works of charity, compassion, and self-sacrifice that he performed on earth were the works of the Father who dwelt in him. For this reason, the life and death of Jesus are the supreme revelation of the Father's love for humanity. Jesus Christ, God's incarnate Son, revealed the Father's true nature to humans in a way that no mere prophet or teacher, however wise and good, could have done. Jesus came bearing God the Father's love, and he challenges his Church to share this divine love with others.

Reflect *How can you be God's loving arms for others?*

The Experience of Love

Jesus shows us that God the Father loves unconditionally and forgives mercifully.

- Families are central to the life of first graders, so the image of God as a loving parent is one to which many children can easily connect. Today's children, however, have had diverse experiences of family. Some children have not had loving fathers. Others have had no contact with their fathers at all. Such children may need other models to help them understand their relationship to God.

- Talk to children about any adults whose actions have been for them a sign of God's love.

- In himself, God is infinitely greater than any earthly image. He loves each child more than anyone else, even a parent, can.

Listening and Doing

- I like listening to stories. Use them to teach me about God the Father.

- My eye-hand coordination is developing. Use it in activities that help me to learn.

- I like to take things home to share.

Engagement with Others

Blessed assurance in yourself is important. It is also important to experience significant and constructive engagement with others. Doing so enables you to

- see firsthand the goodness of others.

- recognize that sometimes a task is best addressed by a team.

- replenish your level of empathy.

- see that you can still benefit from different styles and approaches.

Engagement with others sustains your spirit by pulling you past your own limitations and by restoring your faith in yourself and others.

	Lone Ranger				Engaged with Others
Reflect **Rate yourself**	1	2	3	4	5

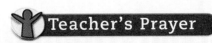 Teacher's Prayer

God the Father, your love for me is greater than that of any parent. Thank you for the gift of all those who helped me grow and taught me about your love. Amen.

Weekly Planner

Chapter 4

		Objective	Materials	Prayer & Scripture
DAY 1 Invite	**The Trinity** Page 61	**Objective:** To explore the idea of lighting other people's way	☐ Board or chart paper ☐ Pencils ☐ Strips of heavy paper cut for bookmarks ☐ Colored pencils	🎁 Let Us Pray *Psalm 96:3*
DAY 2 Explore	**Help Others** Pages 62–63	**Objective:** To consider the value of having friends	☐ Board or chart paper ☐ Art supplies	🎁 Let Us Pray *Psalm 96:3*
DAY 3 Explore	**God's Love** Pages 64–65	**Objective:** To discover what Jesus reveals about his Father	☐ Board or chart paper ☐ Index cards ☐ Pencils	🎁 Let Us Pray *Psalm 96:3* ✝ **Scripture:** *John 14:7–9* ✝ **Scripture Background:** "Show Us the Father," p. 64
DAY 4 Explore	**Three in One** Pages 66–67	**Objective:** To name the Persons of the Trinity	☐ Board or chart paper ☐ Pencils ☐ *God is Like* by Julie Walters (Waterbrook, 2002)	🎁 Let Us Pray *Psalm 96:3*
DAY 5 Celebrate	**Prayer of Praise** Page 68	**Objective:** To pray to the Holy Trinity	☐ Music CD	🎁 Let Us Pray **Prayer of Praise** 🎵 **Hymn:** "Psalm 113: Blessed Be the Name"

Chapter 4 Wrap-Up: Review and Apply p. 69 • Chapter 4 Assessment p. 61E

Words of Faith

Jesus

Holy Trinity

Multimedia Resources

Activities	Enrichment
Let's Begin: A Light, p. 61 Multiple Intelligence: Interpersonal (OPTIONAL) Be a Light, p. 61 Multiple Intelligence: Visual/Spatial	
Share Your Faith: Think, Share, Act, p. 63 Multiple Intelligence: Visual/Spatial (OPTIONAL) Lion and Mouse, p. 62 Multiple Intelligence: Bodily/Kinesthetic	• **Quick Tip:** Meaning in Literature, p. 62 • **Reaching All Learners:** Interpreting Stories, p. 63 • **Justice and Peace:** Remembering Older People, p. 63
Connect Your Faith: God's Love, p. 65 Multiple Intelligence: Visual/Spatial	• **Teacher Background:** The Eternal Trinity, p. 64 • **Quick Tip:** Graphic Organizer, p. 65 • **Teacher Background:** Holy Spirit, p. 65
Live Your Faith: Name the Person, p. 67 Multiple Intelligence: Verbal/Linguistic (OPTIONAL) Cross-Curricular: Math, p. 66 Multiple Intelligence: Logical/Mathematical (OPTIONAL) Cross-Curricular: Reading, p. 67 Multiple Intelligence: Verbal/Linguistic	• **Teacher Background:** The Trinity, p. 66 • **Christian Living Skills:** Recognizing God's Presence, p. 67
	• **Liturgy Link:** Repeated Actions, p. 68 • **Lectionary Link:** Break Open the Word, p. 68

BOOK

Rock, Lois. *A First Look: God.* Lion Publishing. 2001. Children learn about God's love through biblical images.

VIDEO

Prayer of Praise (10 min). Ikonographics. Invites children to practice prayer that praises the Holy Trinity.

 Teacher Resources
www.harcourtreligion.com

• **For interactive lesson planner, chapter resources, and activities**
• **For free materials and information**

Home Connection

Chapter 4 Family Faith, p. 70
Take-home activities, chapter content review, saint features and prayer

 For more family activities
www.harcourtreligion.com

(A) **Work with Words**   Write the word from the Word Bank that best completes the sentence.

I. The three Persons in the Holy Trinity are

_____

God the _____ ,

WORD BANK
Son
Father
Holy Spirit

God the _____ ,

_____

and God the _____ .

(B) **Check Understanding**   Your teacher will help you read the sentences. Circle the answer that best completes each sentence.

2. The Holy Trinity is _____ Persons in one God.

two    **three**

3. The Holy Spirit helps you know and love _____ and the Father.

books    **Jesus**

Answers can be found in the back of the Teacher Manual.

©Harcourt Religion

ASSESSMENT

Chapter 4 The Trinity

Let Us Pray

Leader: God, help us to tell the story of your love.

"Tell God's glory among the nations; among all peoples, God's marvelous deeds."
Psalm 96:3

All: God, help us to tell the story of your love. Amen.

Activity — Let's Begin

A Light

This lamp in my window
Glows warmly, shines bright.
It guides friends and strangers
Who travel at night.
Arnold Lobel

• How does the lamp help people?

_____

- - - - - - - - - - - - - - - - - - -

_____

Talk with a Partner Think of the ways you help people and people help you. Tell a partner one way you help and one way you are helped.

61

OPTIONAL ACTIVITY

Be a Light Give children a strip of heavy paper and colored pencils to draw with.

- Tell them to select some object that gives light (a candle, a lamp, the sun) and draw it on the paper.
- Suggest they use the bookmark to remind them to be a light for others.

Multiple Intelligence: Visual/Spatial

DAY 1

Objective: To explore the idea of lighting other people's way

Open

Prayer Space You may wish to have children move to your classroom prayer space. In the space, have a crucifix and a Bible opened to *Psalm 96:3*.

Let Us Pray Pray the psalm aloud. Have boys pray the first line of the psalm and girls pray the second. Have all pray the response.

Build

Activity

- Read aloud "A Light." Explain to children that the poem is about being a "light" for other people.
- Ask children which words in the poem are the most important clues to what the poem means. Ask them what the lamp does. Responses will vary. Ask children how they could be a "light" for others, like the lamp in the poem. Responses will vary.
- Have children read and answer the question. Write a few responses on the board or on chart paper.

Extension Activity

- Organize children in groups of two.
- Have the groups share and discuss the ways they help people and the ways people help them.
- Ask each group to share their responses.

Close

Have children tell what they learned about helping others.

Objective: To consider the value of having friends

Open

 Let Us Pray Invite children to pray the psalm verse on page 61 with you.

Focus **What did Lion learn about being nice to others?** List children's answers on the board or on chart paper.

Build

Help Others
Read the introductory paragraph and ask children to listen for how the lion and the mouse solve their problem.

The Lion and the Mouse
Read aloud The Lion and the Mouse.

• Cue children to roar whenever Lion roars.

❓ **Why do you think Lion let Mouse go?** Allow children to discuss the question with a partner.

Explore

Help Others

Focus **What did Lion learn about being nice to others?**

God always wants you to be nice to other people. Lion and Mouse have a problem. Read to find out how they solve the problem.

A STORY

THE LION AND THE MOUSE

A mighty lion was fast asleep in the woods. Mouse thought Lion was a rock. She ran up his back. Lion woke at once.

He grabbed poor Mouse's tail.

"How dare you wake me up?" he roared. "I am going to eat you!"

"Oh, please," Mouse said. "Let me go. Someday I will repay you."

"Don't be silly!" Lion roared. "How will you repay me? You are just a little mouse." Then he laughed. "All right. Go on," he said.

He put Mouse down. She ran into the woods.

❓ **Why do you think Lion let Mouse go?**
Possible responses: He was nice; he really didn't want to hurt Mouse.

62

QUICK TIP

Meaning in Literature Focus children on learning a new skill—interpreting the message of a story or poem.

• As you read a piece of literature, ask questions to see that children are looking for clues to the meaning of the story or poem on their own.

OPTIONAL ACTIVITY

Lion and Mouse Have one or more pairs of children act out the story for the rest of the group.

Multiple Intelligence: Bodily/Kinesthic

Many days had passed. Mouse ran
y that same place. Mouse heard an
wful roar. She soon found Lion.

Lion was caught in a net. Quickly
ouse ran to the net. She took the
pe in her teeth and chewed and
ewed. She chewed right through
e rope. She set Lion free!

"Thank you," roared Lion.

"You are welcome," said Mouse.
Now I hope that you can see what
big help small friends can be!"

What did Lion learn?
ossible responses: Anybody can be
ur friend; friends care
r each other.

Activity

Share Your Faith

Think: Think about things you can do to be a
good friend.

Share: Talk with a partner about being a
good friend.

Act: On a piece of paper draw a picture of
one way you can be a good friend.

63

- Ask children why Lion thought that
Mouse could never repay him for
letting her go. Possible response:
because the mouse was too small to be
any help to a big lion

- Finish reading the story.

❷ What did Lion learn? Write
responses on the board or on chart
paper.

Activity

- Tell children to think about their
friends. Ask them what being a
friend really means.

- Encourage them to talk with a
partner about what friends do for
each other.

- Give children a few minutes to think
and talk about what they will draw.

Close

Remind children that good friends
care for each other.

★ REACHING ALL LEARNERS

Interpreting Stories Some children display a
natural flair for interpreting stories. Others find this skill
more difficult to acquire.

- Make sure children understand that they must wait
to be called on to answer questions about a poem
or a story. This will help you avoid a situation
where the same one or two children always
interpret the poems or stories you read.

- Call on different children each time.

✚ JUSTICE AND PEACE

Remembering Older People Have children make
a greeting card for a grandparent or
someone in a care center.

- Suggest that children mail the card or
deliver it with their family.

- Explain that older people are
sometimes lonely. You can make
them happy by writing to them.

Catholic Social Teaching: Solidarity

Objective: To discover what Jesus reveals about his Father

Open

Let Us Pray Invite children to pray the psalm verse on page 61 with you.

Focus Who is God? List children's answers on the board or on chart paper.

Build

God's Love

Read aloud the first two paragraphs.

- Tell children that there is another way to know God. Read the next paragraph.
- Explain to children that God's Son is Jesus. Hold up an index card with the word *Jesus* on it.
- Tell children that Jesus liked to talk about God, his Father.

God the Father

- Proclaim the scripture story.

❷ **How does Jesus show you God the Father's love?** Write all responses on the board or on chart paper.

Explore

God's Love

Focus Who is God?

Mouse taught Lion about being a good friend and caring for others. God cares for you like a good friend does. He loves you like a loving parent or grandparent does.

You can call God "Father." You can see God's love in creation. You learn about God's love from Jesus.

Jesus is the Son of God. God the Father sent his Son to earth to show people his love.

✝ SCRIPTURE John 14:7

Read to Me

God the Father

One of Jesus' Apostles said to Jesus, "Show us the Father." Jesus replied, "Whoever has seen me has seen the Father."

Based on John 14:7–9

❷ **How does Jesus show you God the Father's love?**

Possible responses: He cares about me; he wants me to know more about him; he makes me strong.

64

The Eternal Trinity God has always been a Trinity. The Son and the Holy Spirit are eternal, just as the Father is. There was never a time when the Father alone existed. But Jesus Christ is both God and man. At a particular point in history, God the Son took on a human nature. The Son will remain united with this human nature forever.

✝ SCRIPTURE BACKGROUND

"Show Us the Father" We know that our God is a God of love because of Jesus.

- Jesus' whole life—his words and his actions, what he said and didn't say—revealed the Father.
- Jesus' whole life was an expression of love for sinful humans. Since the Son became man in order to do his Father's will, the depth of the Father's love for us is unmistakably manifested in Jesus.

he Holy Trinity

Jesus is God the Son. He showed od's love by loving others. God the oly Spirit helps you know and love esus and the Father.

God the Father, God the Son, and od the Holy Spirit are called the **Holy Trinity**. The Holy Trinity is the hree Persons in one God.

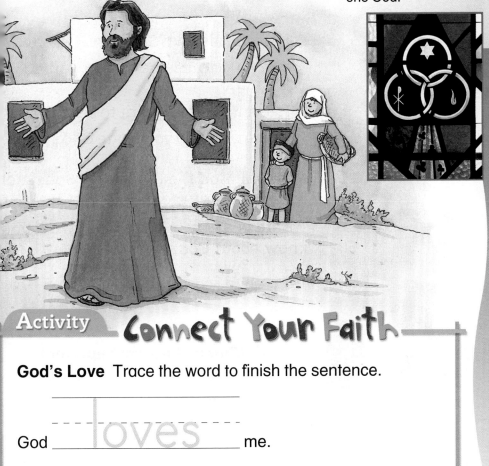

Words of Faith

Jesus is the Son of God. Jesus is also human.

God the Father, God the Son, and God the Holy Spirit are the **Holy Trinity**, the three Persons in one God.

Activity Connect Your Faith

God's Love Trace the word to finish the sentence.

God ____loves____ me.

65

The Holy Trinity

Read aloud The Holy Trinity.

- Draw the graphic organizer on the board or on chart paper. Then use the organizer to explain what is meant by the Holy Trinity.

- Have children sing the following words to the melody of "London Bridge":

  God the Father, be with us, be with us, be with us. God the Father, be with us. You are our Creator.

  Dear sweet Jesus, be with us . . . . You show us the Father.

  Holy Spirit, be with us . . . . You are God's love.

- Explain the Words of Faith by making index cards for *Jesus* and *Holy Trinity*.

Activity

- Have children trace the word in pencil.

Close

Review with children that the Holy Trinity is three Persons in one God— the Father, the Son, and the Holy Spirit.

QUICK TIP

Graphic Organizer

```
        ( Father )
  ( Son )   ( Holy
              Spirit )
        God
```

Holy Trinity

TEACHER BACKGROUND

Holy Spirit   The Holy Spirit is eternally joined with the Father and the Son.

- After his Resurrection, Jesus sent down the Holy Spirit on the Church he had founded, to empower and unite his disciples and to bring them into unity.

- Tell children that whenever they see people show love and care, they see the work of the Holy Spirit on earth.

DAY 4

Objective: To name the Persons of the Trinity

Open

 Let Us Pray Invite children to repeat after you the psalm verse from page 61.

◎ **Focus** **What do we know about God?** List children's responses on the board or on chart paper.

Build

Three in One

Read aloud the first sentence.

• Invite children to follow along as you read aloud the bulleted text.

• Note that each word printed in a red heart is a reference to love.

• Read aloud the rest of the text, using the words *plus* and *equals* when you read aloud the "equation."

❷ **What is the most important thing to remember about God?** Lead children in discussing the question.

Three in One

◎ **Focus** **What do we know about God?**

Jesus taught some important things about God. The most important thing he taught is that God loves everyone.

■ God made all things, and cares for creation like a **loving** Father.

■ He sent his own Son, Jesus, to save people, because he **loves** you.

■ He sent his Holy Spirit to be with you always, to help you share God's **love**

We call God the Father, the Son, and the Holy Spirit the Holy Trinity.

Here is a way to remember what you know about God.

Father + Son + Holy Spirit = 1 God = Love

❷ **What is the most important thing to remember about God?**

God loves us.

66

OPTIONAL ACTIVITY

Cross-Curricular: Mathematics Help children visualize the concept of "three in one."

• Draw on the board or show children a three-leafed clover, which Saint Patrick, according to tradition, used to illustrate the Trinity in his mission to Ireland.

• Invite children to suggest other things that are "three in one" that can be signs of the Holy Trinity.

Multiple Intelligence: Mathematical/Logical

TEACHER BACKGROUND

The Trinity The doctrine of the Trinity is a mystery of faith, not intended to be comprehended literally by anyone, let alone first graders, for whom this brief introduction will be sufficient. To further your own reflection on this mystery, see the *Catechism*, 232–260.

Live Your Faith

✎ **Name the Person** Read each description. Write the name of the correct Person of the Trinity in each blank.

My name is Jesus. I came into the world to save people. I taught people about God, my Father. _____

I am God the _____ Son _____.

I am with you always to help you share God's love. _____

I am God the _____ Holy Spirit _____.

I made the whole world, and I care for you like a parent. Jesus is my Son. _____

I am God the _____ Father _____.

67

- Read aloud the directions for the activity.
- Have children work in pairs to complete the exercise.
- Review the responses by having volunteers share their answers.
- Direct attention to the illustrations, and discuss with children why each was chosen to represent a Person of the Trinity.

Close

Lead children in praying the Sign of the Cross slowly and reverently.

CHRISTIAN LIVING SKILLS

Recognizing God's Presence Help children understand that although they cannot see God, they experience his presence whenever they love and are loved.

- Ask children to think about the ways in which they showed love or were shown love today.
- Remind children that they can recognize his presence in these loving moments.

OPTIONAL ACTIVITY

Cross-Curricular: Reading Share with children *God Is Like: Three Parables for Children* by Julie Walters (Waterbrook, 2002), which illuminates biblical images for the Persons of the Trinity.

- Invite children to work together to make up their own "God is like . . ." stories.

Multiple Intelligence: Verbal/Linguistic

Objective: To pray to the Holy Trinity

Prepare

Tell children that this prayer is a short prayer of praise to all three persons of the Holy Trinity—Father, Son, and Holy Spirit.

 Use the *Call to Faith 1* CD, track 4, to rehearse the song.

Gather

Invite children to assemble in the prayer space. Check to be sure children know how to make the Sign of the Cross correctly.

Pray

A Prayer of Praise

 Let Us Pray   Follow the order of prayer on page 56.

• Lead children in praying the "Glory to the Father," making the Sign of the Cross as they salute each of the persons of the Trinity.

Celebrate

A Prayer of Praise

 Let Us Pray

Gather and begin with the Sign of the Cross.

Leader: Glory to the Father,

All: Glory to the Father,

Leader: and to the Son,

All: and to the Son,

Leader: and to the Holy Spirit:

All: and to the Holy Spirit:

Leader: as it was in the beginning, is now, and will be forever.

All: Amen.

Sing together.

Blessed be the name
  of the Lord
forever and ever.

"Psalm 113: Blessed Be the Name" © 1969, 1981, and 1997, ICEL.

68

 LITURGY LINK

Repeated Actions   Children will come to know and love the traditional prayers and hymns of the Catholic Church by praying or singing them over and over again.

• Six-year-old children love repetition. To have them repeat a prayer or a song more than once can be both prayerful and enjoyable.

LECTIONARY LINK

Break Open the Word   Read last week's Sunday Gospel. Invite children to think about what the reading means to them as they try to follow Christ's example. For questions related to the weekly Gospel reading, visit our Web site at **www.harcourtreligion.com.**

 GO ONLINE Visit www.harcourtreligion.com for weekly scripture readings and seasonal resources.

A **Work with Words** Circle the correct answers.

1. Jesus is the ___(p. 64)___ of God.

   (Son)   **Father**

2. Who are the three Persons in the Holy Trinity?

   (Father)   (Son) (p. 65)

   Grandma   (Holy Spirit)

3. You can call God ___(p. 64)___.

   (Father)   **Mother**

B **Check Understanding** Trace the letters to complete the sentence. There are three Persons in the ___(p. 65)___.

69

Review

A **Work with Words** Direct children to circle the correct answer.

B **Check Understanding** Have children trace the letters to complete the sentence.

Assessment

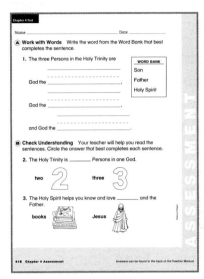

▲ **Chapter 4 Test**
  page 61E

Answers to the Chapter Test can be found in the back of the Teacher Manual.

TEACHER BACKGROUND

Symbol of the Holy Trinity Point out to children that Saint Patrick used a shamrock to try to explain the nature of the Trinity to the Irish people.

- As the one God has made himself known to humans in three Persons, so a shamrock is one leaf forming three separate lobes.

OPTIONAL ACTIVITY

Activity Master 4: The Holy Trinity Distribute copies of the activity found on teacher page 70A.

- Tell children the illustration will remind them of the Holy Trinity.
- As an alternative, you may wish to send this activity home with children.

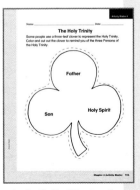

▲ **Activity Master 4**
  page 70A

The Trinity 69

Family Faith

Remind children to discuss the Family Faith page at home. Encourage children to read the scripture passage from the Gospel according to Luke.

Activity

• Encourage children to copy the Bible verse, decorate it, and post it on their home refrigerator.

People of Faith

Tell children about Saint Patrick.

• Patrick and his disciples preached and converted thousands of people in Ireland and built churches all over the country. Many people converted to Christianity when they heard Patrick's message.

• Remind children to add Saint Patrick to their People of Faith albums.

• Encourage them to pray the prayer at home with their families.

  Visit **www.harcourtreligion.com** for weekly scripture readings and seasonal resources.

Unit 2: CHAPTER 4
Family Faith

Catholics Believe

■ The Holy Trinity is God the Father, God the Son, and God the Holy Spirit.

■ Jesus is the Son of God.

SCRIPTURE

Read Luke 6:27–36 as a family. Talk about how Jesus wants us to treat others.

GO ONLINE www.harcourtreligion.com
For weekly Scripture readings and seasonal resources

Activity
Live Your Faith

Decorate a Bible Verse Work together to copy the following Bible verse on art paper. Use colorful markers or crayons. Post the verse on your refrigerator. Read the verse every day this week.

"Whoever has seen me has seen the Father."
John 14:9

▲ Saint Patrick, 387–493

People of Faith

Once pirates in England kidnapped a boy named **Patrick**. They took him to Ireland to be a slave. Often Patrick was hungry or sick. He was very courageous. After six years, Patrick escaped. Years later, Patrick returned to Ireland, but this time he was a priest. He used a shamrock to teach people about the Trinity. Saint Patrick's feast day is March 17.

Family Prayer

Saint Patrick, pray for us that we may be like Jesus and show our love of the Holy Trinity by loving others. Amen.

In Unit 2 your child is learning about the TRINITY.
70 **CCC** *See Catechism of the Catholic Church 261–264 for further reading on chapter content.*

HOW DID I DO?

This week my religion classes were

☐ *some of the best ever!* ☐ *pretty good.* ☐ *in need of improvement.*

In what discussions and activities were children most interested?

_____

What activity did I most enjoy teaching?

_____

In what area do I need to improve?

_____

Name _____ Date _____

The Holy Trinity

Some people use a three-leaf clover to represent the Holy Trinity. Color and cut out the clover to remind you of the three Persons of the Holy Trinity.

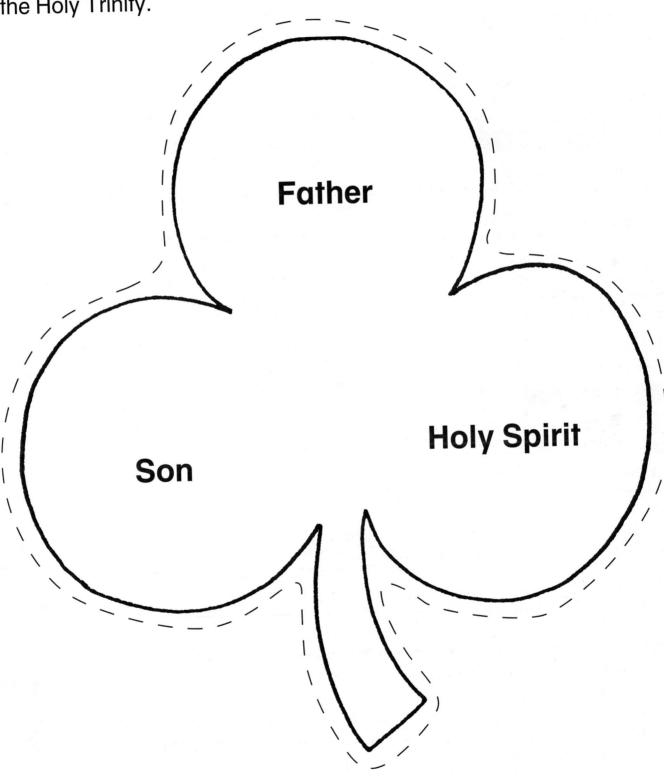

Father

Son

Holy Spirit

The Holy Family

CHAPTER BACKGROUND

Faith Focus

- **Jesus Christ is both true God and true man.** *(CCC 461, 464, 469–478)*
- **Jesus was an obedient son to his mother Mary and his legal father Joseph.** *(CCC 531–532)*

Catechism Connection

The *Catechism* points out that Jesus, for most of his life, "shared the condition of the vast majority of human beings." He lived as a member of a family that supported itself by manual work. People can therefore imitate Jesus while performing the everyday duties of an ordinary life. *(CCC 531–533)*

GDC Link

The *Directory* calls communion with Jesus the primary objective of catechesis. *(GDC 80–81, 98)*

 He went down with them and came to Nazareth, and was obedient to them; and his mother kept all these things in her heart. And Jesus advanced [in] wisdom and age and favor before God and man.

Luke 2:51–52

Family Life

As he grew to adulthood in Nazareth, Jesus encountered most of the challenges that children you teach will encounter in growing up. Like anyone else, Jesus had to learn how to bear his responsibilities as a member of a family, and how to make the small adjustments and compromises that were assuredly necessary to preserve harmony even within a family as extraordinary as his. The *Catechism* suggests that Jesus' perfect obedience to his earthly parents can be seen as an image of his perfect obedience to his Father in heaven (*CCC 532*).

Living in a family requires mutual respect, a willingness to work together, and self-sacrifice. In his letter to the Colossians, Paul told the early Christians, "Put on then . . . heartfelt compassion, kindness, humility, gentleness, and patience, bearing with one another and forgiving one another, if one has a grievance against another" (*Colossians 3:12–13*). Paul's advice will never become outdated; these same principles must be followed today to produce a happy Christian family.

Reaping the Rewards

In his letter, Paul goes on to remind the Colossians of the fourth commandment: "Children, obey your parents in everything, for this is pleasing to the Lord" (*Colossians 3:20*). Growing up in a family isn't exactly painless, but it is rewarding. Loving your family sometimes takes effort. Most people would agree, however, that the effort is worth it. The rewards of belonging to a loving family are great.

Reflect   *Who in your family has been a particular blessing for you recently?*

Family Life Experiences

The focus on Jesus as a member of the Holy Family can be directly connected with children's own experiences. To have them contemplate the life of the Holy Family is a way of helping children develop a personal relationship with Jesus, a relationship that is the only possible foundation of a Christian life.

Every child in your class has a family, but children's experiences of family life differ greatly. Because of the high divorce rate among parents, many children divide their time between two different households, which may require a lot of adjusting.

- At times, children may appear tired, confused, or moody. Their behavior may be inspired by other events in their lives.

- Remember that teaching is most successful when the catechist creates a family-like environment, one that expresses God's love.

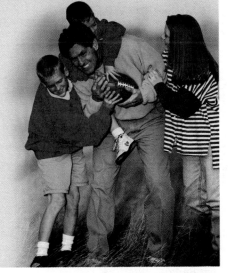

Dealing with Adults

- I am eager to please you and other significant adults.

- I can be very emotional. Gentleness and humor work best to head off any outbursts I may have.

- My family is important to me. I like to tell stories about what we do.

Multiple Belonging

People who are comfortable belonging to groups of people possess a wealth of resources. Sustaining the spirit to teach is easier for those who have been raised in one core group of people but have now learned how to move smoothly within another group. The second group may have a different economic or educational level, value system, or ethnicity.

Living within just one core group can lead to a narrow sense of what is important, a poor sense of what is needed, and limited ways of coping with tough times. Belonging to multiple groups can help sustain your spirit by broadening your ability to handle difficulties, communicate, and appreciate what others cherish.

Reflect **How has belonging to multiple groups helped you sustain the spirit to teach?**

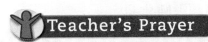

Teacher's Prayer

Jesus, Mary, and Joseph, help me to make a family of children in my care, united by the spirit of love that united you as a family. Amen.

Weekly Planner

		Objective	Materials	Prayer & Scripture
DAY 1 Invite	**The Holy Family** Page 71	**Objective:** *To discuss family life*	☐ Pencils	🙌 Let Us Pray *Psalm 36:8*
DAY 2 Explore	**Hello, Families** Pages 72–73	**Objective:** *To explain how families can show God's love*	☐ Board or chart paper ☐ Art supplies	🙌 Let Us Pray *Psalm 36:8*
DAY 3 Explore	**The Son of God** Pages 74–75	**Objective:** *To describe Jesus' relationship with his earthly family*	☐ Board or chart paper ☐ Index card ☐ Copies of Activity Master 5, p. 80A ☐ Images of the Holy Family ☐ Art supplies	🙌 Let Us Pray *Psalm 36:8* ✝ **Scripture:** *Luke 2:51–52* ✝ **Scripture Background:** Family Life, p. 75
DAY 4 Explore	**Jesus' Family, Your Family** Pages 76–77	**Objective:** *To see how Jesus' family is like our families*	☐ Board or chart paper ☐ Art supplies	🙌 Let Us Pray *Psalm 36:8*
DAY 5 Celebrate	**Pray with God's Word** Page 78	**Objective:** *To pray with Scripture*	☐ Bible ☐ Hymnals ☐ Music CD	🙌 Let Us Pray **Pray with God's Word** ✝ **Scripture:** *John 5:20* 🎵 **Hymn:** "Alleluia"

Chapter 5 Wrap-Up: Review and Apply p. 79 • Chapter 5 Assessment p. 71E

Words of Faith

Holy Family

Activities	Enrichment
Let's Begin: My Family, p. 71 Multiple Intelligence: Bodily/Kinesthetic	• **Teacher Background:** Take Refuge, p. 71
Share Your Faith: Think, Share, Act, p. 73 Multiple Intelligence: Interpersonal OPTIONAL Family Names, p. 72 Multiple Intelligence: Verbal/Linguistic	• **Reaching All Learners:** Including Everyone, p. 72 • **Cultural Awareness:** Family Customs, p. 73 • **Justice and Peace:** Acceptance, p. 73
Connect Your Faith: Act Out Family Life, p. 75 Multiple Intelligence: Bodily/Kinesthetic OPTIONAL The Holy Family, p. 74 Multiple Intelligence: Visual/Spatial OPTIONAL Activity Master 5, p. 75 Multiple Intelligence: Bodily/Kinesthetic	• **Quick Tip:** Enhance the Lesson, p. 74
Live Your Faith: Color the Picture, p. 77 Multiple Intelligence: Visual/Spatial OPTIONAL Cross-Curricular: Art, p. 77 Multiple Intelligence: Visual/Spatial	• **Teacher Background:** Jesus' Life, p. 76 • **Christian Living Skills:** Using Religious Imagination, p. 76 • **Quick Tip:** Family Composition, p. 77
	• **Liturgy Link:** Crossing Forehead, Lips, and Heart, p. 78 • **Lectionary Link:** Break Open the Word, p. 78

Multimedia Resources

 BOOK
Boadt, Lawrence. *Stations of the Nativity.* Paulist Press. 2002. A journey in story and prayer through the events surrounding Jesus' birth.

 VIDEO
The Beginner's Bible: The Story of the Nativity (30 min). SONY Wonder. Animated account of Jesus' birth.

 Teacher Resources
www.harcourtreligion.com
• For interactive lesson planner, chapter resources, and activities
• For free materials and information

Home Connection

Chapter 5 Family Faith, p. 80
Take-home activities, chapter content review, saint features and prayer

 For more family activities
www.harcourtreligion.com

Name _____ Date _____

(A) Work with Words Unscramble the words to name the three people in the Holy Family.

1. essJu _____

2. yMra _____

3. Jpesho _____

(B) Check Understanding Draw a line to the best ending for each sentence.

4. Jesus is a man and

a. God.

5. The Holy Family is

b. the name for the human family of Jesus.

Answers can be found in the back of the Teacher Manual.

ASSESSMENT

©Harcourt Religion

Chapter 5
The Holy Family

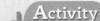 **Let Us Pray**

Leader: Loving Father, teach us to be thankful for the love of our families.

"How precious is your love, O God! We take refuge in the shadow of your wings." *Psalm 36:8*

All: Loving Father, teach us to be thankful for the love of our families. Amen.

Activity Let's Begin

● **My Family**

When you need someone to talk to
If you're feeling kind of low,
When you need some help or comfort
There's somewhere you can go!
Now where in the world
Will that special place be?
It's with your family!

• What is one way your family cheers you up?

_____

_ _ _ _ _ _ _ _ _ _ _ _ _ _ _ _ _ _ _

_____

Act It Out Show something you and your family like to do together.

71

TEACHER BACKGROUND

Take Refuge The expression "take refuge," found in today's psalm, might not be familiar to children.

• Explain that the word *refuge* means a place that you go to find protection from danger. In Psalm 36, the protection that God gives his people is compared to the shelter a mother bird provides for her chicks.

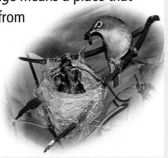

Objective: To discuss family life

Open

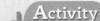 **Let Us Pray** Invite children to move into the prayer space. Pray the psalm verse aloud and have children pray the response with you.

Build

Activity

• Read aloud the first six lines of the poem to children.

• Ask them where they might go for help or comfort. Possible responses: to parents or siblings

• Read the rest of the poem to the children and compare their responses to it.

• Give children time to write down their answers to the question in the text.

Extension Activity

• Divide children into small groups.

• Have children take turns acting out something they like to do with their family.

• Ask other children to guess what the activity is.

Close

Have children tell why family is important.

Objective: To explain how families can show God's love

Open

Let Us Pray Invite children to pray the psalm verse on page 71 with you.

Focus **How can families show love?** List children's answers on the board or on chart paper.

Build

Hello, Families

Talk to children about families. Tell children that some families are large and some are small. Tell them that some children live with their grandparents.

- Tell children that God loves all families.
- Introduce Mr. Grant, who delivers the mail on Elm Street.
- Read aloud the poems Jimmy's Family, My-Ling's Family, and Jorge's Family. Then invite three children to reread one poem each to the group.

Explore

Hello, Families

Focus How can families show love?

God the Father loves all families. Meet the families who live on Elm Street. Walk along with Mr. Grant as he delivers the mail.

Jimmy's Family

Jimmy's Dad moved away, and Jimmy is sad.

Having Uncle to talk to makes Jimmy feel glad.

My-Ling's Family

"Let's pray for your Gram," says Dad to My-Ling.

"She hurt her right hand, and it's in a sling."

72

REACHING ALL LEARNERS

Including Everyone Some children may never raise their hands to volunteer, even though they wish to take part.

- To include these children, ask them to represent the family members in the poems. Invite another child to be Mr. Grant and deliver the mail while the poems are read.

OPTIONAL ACTIVITY

Family Names Have children help you list on the board or on chart paper all of their family names. Invite children to determine

- who has the shortest last name.
- who has the longest last name.
- whose name contains the most occurrences of a single letter.

Multiple Intelligence: Verbal/Linguistic

Jorge's Family

There's Jorge and Mama and Papa, too, on a picnic in the park.

"Fetch the tennis ball, Scamp," Jorge says.

"I'll do it right now!" says Scamp with a bark.

❓ How is each family showing love?
Possible responses: talking to each other; praying for each other; spending time together

Activity — **Share Your Faith**

Think: How does your family show love?

Share: Tell one way your family shares love.

✏️ **Act:** Draw a picture of your family sharing God's love.

73

- Talk with children about ways the families in the stories differ.

❓ How is each family showing love?
Write all responses on the board or on chart paper.

Activity

- Give children time to draw their families sharing God's love.
- Walk around the room, and give positive feedback to each child about his or her family.

Close

Remind children that family members care for one another and share God's love.

 CULTURAL AWARENESS

Family Customs   Families have varied traditions. Some family traditions are the product of a family's cultural background.

- Vietnamese families celebrate the Chinese/ Vietnamese new year with foods such as coconut jam, rice cake, pork, fish, and eggs.
- They decorate their homes with colorful balloons and flowers for this holiday.

 JUSTICE AND PEACE

Acceptance   First graders have a strong sense of right and wrong. However, this may make them too quick to judge.

- Children may criticize other children whose families differ from their own.
- The poems illustrate that there are all kinds of families. All good families show love. Stress that God loves all families.

Catholic Social Teaching: Life and Dignity

DAY 3

Objective: To describe Jesus' relationship with his earthly family

Open

Let Us Pray Invite children to pray the psalm verse on page 71 with you.

Focus **What was Jesus' family like?** List children's answers on the board or on chart paper.

Build

The Son of God

Read aloud the introductory paragraph.

The Holy Family

Read aloud The Holy Family.

- Tell them we call Jesus' family the Holy Family. Hold up an index card with *Holy Family* written on it.
- Tell children that Jesus' family shared God's love with each other just like their families do.

What do you know about the Holy Family? Ask volunteers to share their responses.

Explore

The Son of God

Focus **What was Jesus' family like?**

Jesus is the Son of God. Jesus is also human. He is like you in almost every way. Jesus shows you how to live. He teaches you about God's love

The Holy Family

Long ago, Jesus was born into a family. Jesus lived with his mother and his foster father, Joseph. They lived in a town called Nazareth. Jesus, Mary, and Joseph are called the **Holy Family**.

What do you know about the Holy Family? Responses will vary.

74

QUICK TIP

Enhance the Lesson To help teach about Jesus' life in a family, work with your school librarian or media specialist to find paintings or other images of the Holy Family.

Place the images in the prayer space or another central location for children to observe throughout the lesson.

OPTIONAL ACTIVITY

The Holy Family Many churches are adorned with statues of Mary and Joseph.

- The Mary statue is usually found at the head of the left aisle, the Joseph statue at the head of the right aisle.
- Visit the parish church to let the children look at the statues. Note that Mary often carries lilies; Joseph, cherry blossoms.

Multiple Intelligence: Visual/Spatial

The Boy Jesus

...sus obeyed his family. He became
...ise and good. Jesus grew strong. God
...as pleased with him and so were
...e people.

Based on Luke 2:51–52

Day in Nazareth

All families can share God's love.
...hen Jesus was your age, he showed
...od's love in his family. This
...s what could have happened
...hen Jesus was young.

...The family begins the day with
...a prayer.
...Mary bakes bread for breakfast.
...oseph makes a chair for neighbors.
...esus helps his dad carry it to them.

Words of Faith

The **Holy Family** is the name for the human family of Jesus, Mary, and Joseph.

Activity — Connect Your Faith

Act Out Family Life With a partner, role-play other things the Holy Family might have done together. Then role-play something families can do to show God's love.

75

The Boy Jesus
Proclaim the scripture story.

- Ask children to raise their hands every time they hear a word that describes, or tells about, Jesus. obeyed, wise, good, strong

- Explain to children that Jesus passed through the same stages of growth as they are doing.

A Day in Nazareth
Have children read what Jesus and his family did on an ordinary day at home.

- Write the following on the board or on chart paper to summarize each activity mentioned in the text: pray, cook, work, help.

- Point to the words you have printed, and ask children what they have learned about Jesus' family. Responses will vary.

Activity

- Allow enough time for children to role-play family life situations.

Close

Remind children that Catholics call Jesus' human family the Holy Family. The three members of the Holy Family are Jesus, Mary, and Joseph.

SCRIPTURE BACKGROUND

Family Life The Gospels according to Matthew, Mark, Luke, and John all acknowledge Joseph's role as foster father to Jesus, which can open the door to discussions with the children about what makes a family. Families can be made up of a mother and her child, or may include such extended family members as grandparents, cousins, and half-siblings all living under one roof. Point out to children that the common denominator is the love shared among family members.

OPTIONAL ACTIVITY

Activity Master 5: Finger Puppets Distribute copies of the activity found on teacher page 80A.

- Tell children they can use the stories in the chapter for their puppet plays.

- As an alternative, you may wish to send this activity home with children.

▲ Activity Master 5 page 80A

DAY 4

Objective: To see how Jesus' family is like our families

Open

Let Us Pray Invite children to repeat after you the psalm verse from page 71.

Focus **How is your family like Jesus' family?** List children's responses on the board or on chart paper.

Build

Jesus' Family, Your Family

Invite children to listen as you read aloud the first paragraph. Ask children to name the members of Jesus' human family.

• Draw attention to the chart. Have children follow along as you read aloud each entry.

• Pause after each entry, and invite children to compare the illustrations of Jesus' family and a family of today.

❷ **What are some other things your family and Jesus' family might have in common?** Have children form small groups to discuss the question.

Explore

Jesus' Family, Your Family

Focus How is your family like Jesus' family?

Jesus grew up in a human family. He and his family did many of the same things together that you and your family do.

Here are some things that your family and Jesus' family may share.

Doing Chores

Traveling

Celebratin Holidays

76

❷ What are some other things your family and Jesus' family might have in common?
Responses will vary.

★ **TEACHER BACKGROUND**

Jesus' Life To help give children a better sense of the time and place in which Jesus grew up, share with them pictures from *The Land and People Jesus Knew: A Visual Tour of First-Century Palestine,* by J. Robert Teringo (Bethany House, 1985). This book can help address children's questions about everyday life in Jesus' time.

✋ **CHRISTIAN LIVING SKILLS**

Using Religious Imagination Children use their religious imagination when they project themselves into the past to learn more about Jesus' life. Some ways to foster this skill include:

• asking children to put themselves into the story when they read or hear Scripture.

• having children draw their ideas about abstract religious concepts such as God and heaven.

Live Your Faith

 Color the Picture Color the picture of the Holy Family in the top frame. Then draw or glue a picture of your family in the bottom frame.

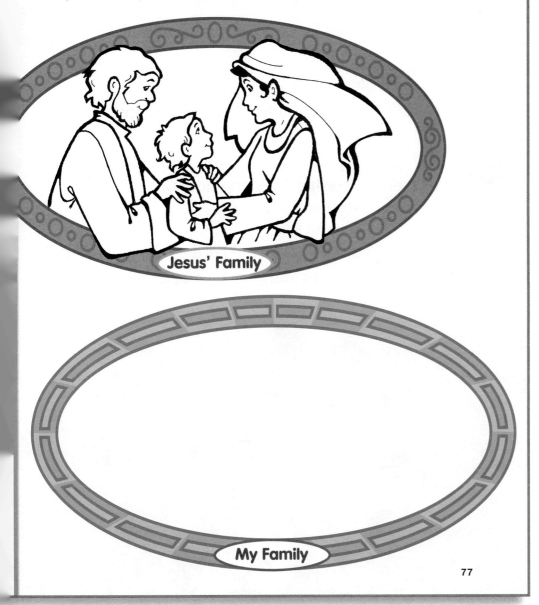

Jesus' Family

My Family

77

- Review with children the directions for the activity, reading aloud the labels for the two frames.

- Provide art materials, and allow time for children to work independently on their art work. (If children wish to glue family photos into their frames, but have not brought pictures from home, this part of the activity may be assigned as homework.)

- Encourage children to share their art work with family members.

Close

Ask children to name one activity they will do with their families this week that Jesus would have done with his family.

QUICK TIP

Family Composition Children come from families of varying composition. When discussing comparisons between Jesus' family and the children's families, be sensitive to the fact that some children do not live with both parents (or either parent). Allow children to discuss their families without overemphasizing generalizations about family structure or asking personal questions.

OPTIONAL ACTIVITY

Cross-Curricular: Art Show children some examples of fine art or folk art depicting the Holy Family.

- If possible, share examples that reflect diverse ethnic representations, as a way of reminding children that families all over the world identify with Jesus' family.

Multiple Intelligence: Visual/Spatial

DAY 5

Objective: To pray with Scripture

Prepare

Review the gestures and responses that Catholics make when the Gospel is read at Mass. Have children repeat several times the response, "Praise to you, Lord Jesus Christ."

 Use the *Call to Faith 1* CD, track 5, to rehearse the song.

Gather

Invite children to gather in the prayer space, ideally facing a lectern from which you can proclaim the Gospel.

Pray

Pray with God's Word

 Let Us Pray Follow the order of prayer on page 78.

• Optional songs from *Singing Our Faith:* "We Sing of the Saints," #274, "Jesus in the Morning," #168, "He Came Down," #111.

Celebrate

Pray with God's Word

 Let Us Pray

Gather and begin with the Sign of the Cross.

Leader: Let us listen to the word of God.

 Sing together.

Alleluia, alleluia, Alleluia, allelu!

"Alleluia," Traditional

Leader: A reading from the holy Gospel according to John.
Read John 5:20.
The Gospel of the Lord.

All: Praise to you, Lord Jesus Christ.

78

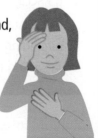 **LITURGY LINK**

Crossing Forehead, Lips, and Heart Ask children what gesture they are supposed to make after the priest at Mass announces which Gospel he is going to read.

• Show them how to sign their forehead, lips, and heart with a small sign of the cross. Explain that they should say aloud "Glory to you, Lord" as they do this.

 LECTIONARY LINK

Break Open the Word Read last week's Sunday Gospel. Invite children to think about what the reading means to them as they try to follow Christ's example. For questions related to the weekly Gospel reading, visit our Web site at **www.harcourtreligion.com**.

 Visit www.harcourtreligion.com for weekly scripture readings and seasonal resources.

CHAPTER 5
Review

A Check Understanding Answer the following questions.

1. Mark an X next to the things Jesus might have done with his family. **(p. 75)**

   __X__ pray   __X__ talk   __X__ eat

   __X__ play   __X__ visit   __X__ help

2. Who are the three people in the Holy Family? **(p. 74)**

   Jesus

   Mary

   Joseph

B Make Connections Jesus helped his mother and father. Circle ways you can help.

79

CHAPTER WRAP-UP

Review

A Check Understanding Instruct children to mark the things Jesus might have done with his family. Then have them write the answer to the question in the lines provided.

B Make Connections Have children circle the ways they can help.

Assessment

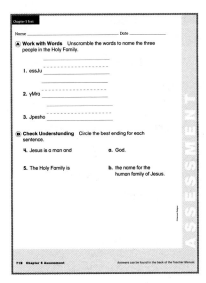

▲ **Chapter 5 Test page 71E**

Answers to the Chapter Test can be found in the back of the Teacher Manual.

QUICK TIP

The Christ Child First graders are likely familiar with the "WWJD"—What Would Jesus Do?—slogan that appears on items such as bracelets and bumper stickers.

- Ask children to pose that question regarding everyday situations, reminding them that Jesus was a child just like them once, facing the same types of daily chores and challenges that they do.

OPTIONAL ACTIVITY

Review Catch List the words from question 1 on the board or on chart paper. Add the word *obey*.

- Have children sit in a circle and toss a ball. After they have tossed it a few times, read a word from the list.
- Whichever child catches the ball next must suggest a way of performing the action with their family.

Multiple Intelligence: Bodily/Kinesthetic

The Holy Family 79

Family Faith

Remind children to discuss the Family Faith page at home. Encourage children to read the scripture passage from the Gospel according to Mark.

Activity

• Show children a picture or statue of the Holy Family and encourage them to display one in their homes.

People of Faith

Tell children about Jesus' relatives—Saints Zechariah, Elizabeth, and John.

• John preached on the banks of the Jordan River against the evils of the times and called men to penance. He baptized Jesus. He inspired many of his followers to follow Jesus when he called him "the Lamb of God."

• Remind children to add Saints Zechariah, Elizabeth, and John to their People of Faith albums.

• Encourage them to pray the prayer at home with their families.

Visit **www.harcourtreligion.com** for weekly scripture readings and seasonal resources.

Unit 2: CHAPTER 5

Family Faith

◎ Catholics Believe

■ Jesus is both God and man.

■ Jesus, Mary, and Joseph are the Holy Family.

✝ SCRIPTURE

Read Mark 10:13–16 to see how Jesus wanted us to care for children and families.

GO ONLINE www.harcourtreligion.com
For weekly Scripture readings and seasonal resources

Activity
Live Your Faith

Honor the Holy Family Every family can be like the Holy Family. Display a statue, a picture of the Holy Family, or a picture of Mary in your home. Pray to ask Mary, Jesus' mother, to ask her Son to bless your family.

People of Faith

Elizabeth was Mary's cousin. Zechariah and Elizabeth were married and loved God very much. They did not have children. One day an angel appeared to Zechariah when he was praying in the temple. The angel told him that his wife would have a son named John. He would be filled with the Holy Spirit. Elizabeth and Zechariah were filled with joy. When John grew up, he was known as John the Baptist. He taught people how to turn their hearts to God.

▲ Zechariah, Elizabeth, and John, first century

🙏 Family Pray

Dear Elizabeth, Zechariah, and John, pray for us that God will bless our family with happiness. Amen.

In Unit 2 your child is learning about the TRINITY.
80 **CCC** *See Catechism of the Catholic Church 531–534 for further reading on chapter content.*

❓ HOW DID I DO?

This week my religion classes were

☐ *some of the best ever!* ☐ *pretty good.* ☐ *in need of improvement.*

In what discussions and activities were children most interested?

_____

What activity did I most enjoy teaching?

_____

In what area do I need to improve?

_____

Name _____ Date _____

Hand Puppets

Color the figures of the Holy Family.

Cut out the puppets.

Fold back the tabs and tape them together.

Tell stories about the Holy Family.

Jesus

Mary

Joseph

Overview

Jesus the Storyteller

CHAPTER BACKGROUND

Faith Focus

- Jesus told parables to convey his message about God, his kingdom, and his love for the poor and for sinners. *(CCC 543–546)*
- The Bible is God's Word. The books of the Bible were inspired by the Holy Spirit and written down in human words. *(CCC 102, 105–110)*

Catechism Connection

The *Catechism* affirms that God is the author of the Bible. The Church can be sure that it teaches his saving truth without error. *(CCC 119, 136)*

GDC Link

The *Directory* describes God's word and its role in the Church. "All God's children, animated by the Spirit, are nourished by this treasure of the Word." *(GDC 94)*

 With many such parables he spoke the word to them as they were able to understand it. Without parables he did not speak to them, but to his own disciples he explained everything in private.

Mark 4:33–34

A Great Storyteller

All the Gospels agree that much of Jesus' public teaching took the form of parables, brief stories about incidents of everyday life that contained a profound religious message. *Parable* comes from the Greek word *parabolé*, which conveys the idea of putting two things side by side in order to compare them. Jesus intended that his audience relate the parables to their own experiences as members of the community that worshiped the God of Israel. In the process, they were to discover surprising truths about God, his love, and the demands that he made of his people.

A Great Story

In the parable of the lost sheep, for example, Jesus compared God to a shepherd who temporarily abandons the rest of the flock to seek out the one sheep that has become lost. The message is that, to him, every member of his flock is precious, even those who have strayed farthest into sin. Jesus hoped his parables would lead his hearers to faith, to conversion of heart. No matter how many times we read the parables or hear them proclaimed, they are always new, because through them, the voice of God addresses each one of us directly.

Reflect **How can you share the word with others today?**

Jesus as Storyteller

The parables of Jesus are a literary form that is particularly accessible to young children. First graders like to hear stories, and they appreciate a good storyteller. They can relate to Jesus as a storyteller.

Children are mature enough to practice active reading and active listening. When asking children questions about the stories, they become involved in learning a new skill—story interpretation—that requires them to listen carefully to the new stories you tell them.

- Telling stories well is a gift; but if you are not a natural storyteller, you can improve your performance considerably by careful preparation.

- Try to tell the story, rather than simply read it. Plan what tone of voice you will use for each section of the story, and what you will emphasize.

- Now and then add a layer of interest by making simple puppets or props for a story.

Learning Through Stories

- I learn through stories.

- I learn the most from them when I hear stories over and over again.

- I really like to be read to. I also like retelling the stories I have heard with gestures.

Marginality

Many who sustain a life committed to the good of others can describe times in which they were ignored or marginalized. As a catechist, you may also feel marginalized. You may find that others push you to the margins because of your values, your convictions, your educational level, your financial status, or even your geographic roots.

Marginality, that lonesome place of exclusion and insignificance within a school or parish program, does not have to hamper your ability to sustain the spirit to teach. Resilient people have used occasional experiences of marginalization to reexamine and reaffirm their core values.

Reflect **When have you been marginalized, and has it helped or hindered your ability to sustain the spirit to teach?**

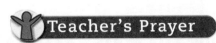
Teacher's Prayer

Lord Jesus, you taught how to love God and neighbor through your parables. Though the stories are simple, they are not always easy to live by. Help me follow the example you have given me. Amen.

Weekly Planner

		Objective	Materials	Prayer & Scripture
DAY 1 Invite	**Jesus the Storyteller** Page 81	**Objective:** *To practice interpreting stories*	☐ Pencils	🙏 Let Us Pray *Psalm 23:1*
DAY 2 Explore	**The Shepherd and the Sheep** Pages 82–83	**Objective:** *To explain how God loves everyone*	☐ Board or chart paper ☐ Copies of Activity Master 6, p. 90 A ☐ Crayons or markers ☐ Scissors	🙏 Let Us Pray *Psalm 23:1* ✝ **Scripture:** *Luke 15:3–6* ✝ **Scripture Background:** Shepherds, p. 82
DAY 3 Explore	**Stories About God** Pages 84–85	**Objective:** *To identify the Bible as the Church's holy book*	☐ Board or chart paper ☐ Pencils ☐ Bible ☐ Index card ☐ Art supplies ☐ *The Little Shepherd by Heidi Bratton* (Paulist Press, 2000)	🙏 Let Us Pray *Psalm 23:1* ✝ **Scripture:** *John 10:14–15* ✝ **Scripture Background:** Ancient Scrolls, p. 85
DAY 4 Explore	**The Bible** Pages 86–87	**Objective:** *To identify the contents of the Bible*	☐ Board or chart paper ☐ Shower curtain and rod ☐ Pencils ☐ Crayons ☐ Blocks ☐ Finger Puppets ☐ Stuffed animals	🙏 Let Us Pray *Psalm 23:1*
DAY 5 Celebrate	**Prayer of Thanks** Page 88	**Objective:** *To pray to the Good Shepherd in words and song*	☐ Hymnals ☐ Music CD	🙏 Let Us Pray **Prayer of Thanks** 🎵 **Hymn:** "The Lord, the Lord, the Lord Is My Shepherd" African-American spiritual

Chapter 6 Wrap-Up: Review and Apply p. 89 • Chapter 6 Assessment p. 81E

Words of Faith

parable

Activities	Enrichment
Let's Begin: A True Friend, p. 81 Multiple Intelligence: Interpersonal (OPTIONAL) Friends, p. 81 Multiple Intelligence: Musical	
Share Your Faith: Think, Share, Act, p. 83 Multiple Intelligence: Bodily/Kinesthetic (OPTIONAL) Activity Master 6: A Story About God, p. 83 Multiple Intelligence: Visual/Spatial	• Reaching All Learners: Highly Verbal Children, p. 82 • Justice and Peace: Jesus' Love for the Poor, p. 83
Connect Your Faith: Write About the Bible, p. 85 Multiple Intelligence: Verbal/Linguistic (OPTIONAL) The Good Shepherd, p. 84 Multiple Intelligence: Visual/Spatial (OPTIONAL) Cross-Curricular: Reading, p. 84 Multiple Intelligence: Visual/Spatial	• Teacher Background Books of the Bible, p. 85
Live Your Faith: Follow the Maze, p. 87 Multiple Intelligence: Visual/Spatial (OPTIONAL) Cross-Curricular: Music, p. 86 Multiple Intelligence: Musical	• Christian Living Skills: Applying the Bible Message, p. 86 • Reaching All Learners: Vision Impaired, p. 87 • Quick Tip: Instant Puppet Theater, p. 87
	• Liturgy Link: The Bible at Mass, p. 88 • Lectionary Link: Break Open the Word, p. 88

Multimedia Resources

 BOOK
My First Catholic Bible. Nelson Bibles. 2001. Favorite scripture texts and commentaries for young children.

 VIDEO
Veggie Tales: Heros of the Bible—Stand Up, Stand Tall, Stand Strong! (45 min). Warner Home Video. The characters enact three Bible stories.

 Teacher Resources
www.harcourtreligion.com
• For interactive lesson planner, chapter resources, and activities
• For free materials and information

Home Connection

Chapter 6 Family Faith, p. 90
Take-home activities, chapter content review, saint features and prayer

 For more family activities
www.harcourtreligion.com

Name _____ Date _____

Work with Words Draw a line to a good title for each sentence.

1. It tells about times
   before Jesus was born.   New Testament

2. Jesus loves and cares
   for all people.   Bible

3. A kind of story that
   teaches something
   important.   Parable

4. It tells about Jesus'
   life and teachings.   Old Testament

5. God's word was written
   down by humans.   The Good Shepherd

ASSESSMENT

Chapter 6 Jesus the Storyteller

Invite

 **Let Us Pray**

Leader: God, help me learn from the stories of your Son.

"The LORD is my shepherd . . ."
Psalm 23:1

All: God, help me learn from the stories of your Son. Amen.

Activity *Let's Begin*

● **A True Friend** One day Bear saw Squirrel in a tree. Bear thought Squirrel would be a tasty lunch. He grabbed Squirrel by the tail. Bug saw what Bear did. Bug would not let Bear hurt her friend! So Bug flew right into Bear's face. Bear was so mad that he dropped Squirrel. Squirrel and Bug quickly ran away!

• Bug was a good friend to Squirrel. Write the name of one of your friends here.

_____

- -

_____

Tell a Story Share a time when someone was a good friend to you.

81

Objective: To practice interpreting stories

Open

 Let Us Pray Ask children to gather in the classroom prayer space. Pray aloud the psalm verse and invite children to pray the response.

Build

Activity

• Read aloud A True Friend.
• Ask children why Bug helped Squirrel. Possible responses: Bug was Squirrel's friend. Bug didn't want anything bad to happen to Squirrel.
• Give children time to write their response to the question.

Extension Activity

• Divide children into several small groups.
• Ask children to think of a time when someone was a good friend to them.
• Have them share their story with the group.
• Ask for volunteers to share their story with the whole class.

Close

Remind children that friends help each other.

OPTIONAL ACTIVITY

Friends This lesson teaches a folktale about friendship. Have children learn to sing the following song to the tune of "Mary Had a Little Lamb." Have each child insert the name of a friend into the song.

• (Name) is a friend of mine, friend of mine, friend of mine.

(Name) is a friend of mine, who (insert action) around with me.

Multiple Intelligence: Musical

DAY 2

Objective: To explain how God loves everyone

Open

 Let Us Pray Invite children to pray the psalm verse on page 81 with you.

Focus **How is God like a shepherd?** List children's answers on the board or on chart paper.

Build

The Shepherd and the Sheep

Read aloud the introductory paragraph.

- Tell children that Jesus used stories about everyday life to teach lessons about God and his love for people.

The Lost Sheep

Gather children in the story circle to hear the scripture story.

- Proclaim the scripture story.

❷ **Have you ever lost something? How did you feel when you found it?** Encourage children to give specific responses.

Explore

The Shepherd and the Sheep

Focus **How is God like a shepherd?**

Jesus was a wonderful storyteller. His stories tell about God's love. Jesus told this story about a shepherd.

✝ **SCRIPTURE** Luke 15:3–

The Lost Sheep

There was a shepherd. He cared for 100 sheep. One sheep ran away. The shepherd was very worried. The shepherd left all his other sheep. He had to find the sheep that ran away.

The shepherd found the lost sheep. He was very happy. He told all his friends and neighbors that he had found his sheep.

Based on Luke 15:3–6

❷ **Have you ever lost something? How did you feel when you found it?**
Responses will vary.

82

✝ **SCRIPTURE BACKGROUND**

Shepherds The work of a shepherd involves watchfulness, caring, and courage. In the Old Testament, the image of the shepherd defending his flock was used as a symbol both for God and for Israel's king.

- Jesus called himself the Good Shepherd, ready to lay down his life for the sheep. The Church refers to herself as God's flock.

⭐ **REACHING ALL LEARNERS**

Highly Verbal Children You could invite children with strong verbal-linguistic skills to invent their own stories about someone who helped a friend.

- Ask children to illustrate their story at home.
- At the next session, have them tell it to the others with the aid of the illustration.

82 Chapter 6

God Loves You

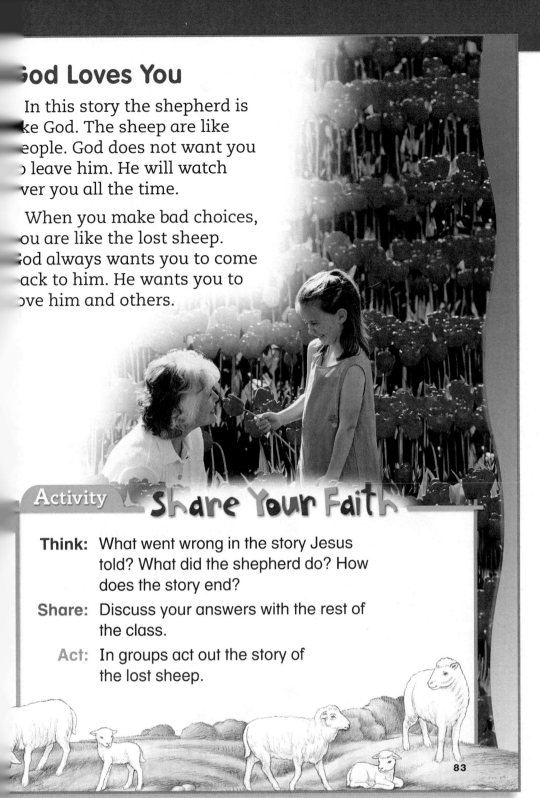

In this story the shepherd is like God. The sheep are like people. God does not want you to leave him. He will watch over you all the time.

When you make bad choices, you are like the lost sheep. God always wants you to come back to him. He wants you to love him and others.

Activity

Share Your Faith

Think: What went wrong in the story Jesus told? What did the shepherd do? How does the story end?

Share: Discuss your answers with the rest of the class.

Act: In groups act out the story of the lost sheep.

83

God Loves You

Ask children what lesson Jesus is teaching about God's love in the story of the lost sheep.

- Retell the story with God as the shepherd if children can't answer. Let children interject when they catch on.
- Read God Loves You. Tell children that God's love is great and that he is happy when people come back to him.

Activity

- Have children retell the scripture story in small groups. Tell them they can tell the original parable and then retell the story with God as the shepherd.
- Have groups of children act out the story. Tell children they can be talking sheep, making up conversations with one another and with the shepherd.

Close

Tell children that God is like a shepherd because he watches over people and cares for them.

JUSTICE AND PEACE

Jesus' Love for the Poor   People who are poor are often left behind or abandoned by other people, like the one lost sheep in the story Jesus told.

- But the Church teaches that Jesus had a special love for people who are "left behind."
- Jesus wants his friends to show special love to such people, too.

Catholic Social Teaching: Option for the Poor

OPTIONAL ACTIVITY

Activity Master 6: A Story About God   Distribute copies of the activity found on teacher page 90A.

- As an alternative, you may wish to send this activity home with children.

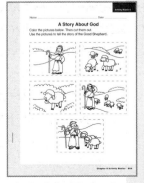

▲ Activity Master 6 page 90A

DAY 3

Open

Let Us Pray Invite children to pray the psalm verse on page 81 with you.

Focus **What is the Bible?** List children's answers on the board or on chart paper.

Build

Stories About God

Read aloud Stories About God.

- Hold up an index card with the word *parable* written on it. Explain that the story Jesus told about the lost sheep is an example of a parable.

The Good Shepherd

Proclaim the scripture story.

- Explain that when Jesus says, "I will lay down my life for the sheep," he means he will do everything for them.

❷ **What does Jesus want you to know?** Write responses on the board or on chart paper.

Stories About God

Focus **What is the Bible?**

A parable is a story that teaches something important. The story you just read about the lost sheep is a **parable**. Jesus told parables to teach people about God.

Jesus is like a shepherd. He loves all God's people. He always cares for them. Read this parable that Jesus told

Faith Fact

Jesus told more than 25 parables to his followers.

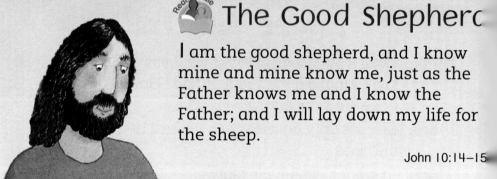

✝ SCRIPTURE   John 10:14–1

The Good Shepherd

I am the good shepherd, and I know mine and mine know me, just as the Father knows me and I know the Father; and I will lay down my life for the sheep.

John 10:14–15

❷ **What does Jesus want you to know?**

Possible response: He loves me; he knows me; he takes care of me.

84

The Good Shepherd Jesus as the Good Shepherd carrying his one lost sheep was one of the most popular subjects of early Christian art.

- Have children draw a picture of Jesus as the Good Shepherd with his sheep.
- When children have finished their drawings, post them around the prayer space.

Multiple Intelligence: Visual/Spatial

Cross-Curricular: Reading *The Little Shepherd* with photography by Heidi Bratton and words by Sally Anne Conan (Paulist Press, 2000), is a retelling of the parable of the Good Shepherd that uses a simple text and black-and-white photos to convey the message that each of us is special and worthy of being found.

THE LITTLE SHEPHERD
Heidi Bratton · Sally Anne Conan

Multiple Intelligence: Visual/Spatial

The Holy Book

The parable of the Good Shepherd is the Bible. The Bible is God's word written down by humans. The Bible is the Church's holy book.

There are two parts to the Bible. The first part is the Old Testament. It is about times before Jesus was born.

The second part is the New Testament. It tells about Jesus and his followers. The stories and parables that Jesus told are part of the New Testament.

Words of Faith

A **parable** is a story Jesus told that teaches something about God.

Activity

Connect Your Faith

 Write About the Bible Find the first book in the Old Testament. Write the name of the book on the first line below. Find the first book of the New Testament. Write the name of it on the second line below.

_____

_____ Genesis _____

_____

_____ Matthew _____

85

The Holy Book

Read aloud The Holy Book.

- Show children the Bible. Tell them that the Bible contains many smaller books. Point out the Old Testament and the New Testament.
- Explain that the Bible is different from every book in the world. It is a holy book.
- Tell children that God speaks to us through the words in the Bible.
- Pass around the Bible so each child has a chance to see it.

Activity

- Show children the Bible's table of contents.
- Have them find the titles of the first book of the Old Testament and the first book of the New Testament. Write them out on the board or on chart paper.
- Have children copy down the titles on the lines in their books.

Close

Review with children that the Church's holy book is called the Bible. It is made up of the Old Testament and the New Testament.

TEACHER BACKGROUND

Books of the Bible The Old Testament contains forty-six books, written in various literary forms, including stories, poems, proverbs, law, and history. Twenty-seven books, most written in the first century A.D., form the New Testament.

- The four Gospels recount the public life of Jesus.
- Acts describes the early development of the Church.
- The rest of the New Testament consists of letters composed by early Church leaders and the Book of Revelation.

SCRIPTURE BACKGROUND

Ancient Scrolls After looking at the Bible during the activity, young children may assume that the Bible has always been in book form.

- Explain to children that the books of the Bible were originally written on rolled-up pieces of parchment called scrolls.
- You may wish to show children a sheet of paper rolled into a scroll shape to illustrate the point.

DAY 4

> **Objective:** To identify the contents of the Bible

Open

Let Us Pray Invite children to repeat after you the psalm verse from page 81.

 Focus **What can you find in the Bible?** List children's responses on the board or on chart paper.

Build

The Bible

Write the word *Bible* on the board or on chart paper. Show children the Bible.

- Invite children to listen carefully as you read aloud the first two paragraphs.
- Direct attention to the chart, and have children follow along as you read aloud the contents of the chart.

❷ What are some of your favorite stories from the Bible? List children's responses on the board or on chart paper.

Explore

The Bible

 Focus **What can you find in the Bible?**

The Bible is the book of God's word. It is full of stories about his love. The words of the Bible tell us how to show love for him and others.

You hear stories from the Bible at church, in school, and at home. You may have seen stories from the Bible made into books or videos.

The Two Parts of the Bible

The Old Testament

The stories of holy men and women like Noah, Moses, Ruth, Jonah, and Daniel come from the Old Testament.

The New Testament

You will find the parables, or teaching stories, Jesus told here. The New Testament also tells about the coming of the Holy Spirit and the work of the first followers of Jesus.

❷ What are some of your favorite stories from the Bible? Responses will vary.

86

OPTIONAL ACTIVITY

Cross-Curricular: Music Share with children some favorite songs based on Bible stories. Play recordings of or teach children to sing one or more of these songs:

- "Rise and Shine" (Noah's Ark)
- "The Battle of Jericho" (Joshua)
- "Away in a Manger" and other Christmas carols (the Nativity)

Multiple Intelligence: Musical

♥ CHRISTIAN LIVING SKILLS

Applying the Bible Message When sharing Bible stories with children, make a point of asking the following questions:

- What does this story mean to you?
- What can you learn from this story?
- How can you live the message of this story in your own life?

Live Your Faith

 Follow the Maze Use a pencil or crayon to find the right path through the maze so the shepherd can find the lost sheep.

87

- Read aloud the directions for the activity.
- Suggest that children use their fingers to trace the maze paths before using a pencil or crayon.
- Allow time for children to work independently on the activity.
- Ask children to explain in their own words the point of the parable of the lost sheep.

Close

Have children act out the story of the lost sheep or another favorite Bible story. Allow them to use props such as finger puppets and stuffed animals.

★ REACHING ALL LEARNERS

Vision Impaired Children with impaired vision may have difficulty with the maze activity, as will children whose hand-eye coordination has not yet matured.

- Construct a maze from blocks, and have children use their sense of touch to find the correct path.
- Ask children to think of other clues the shepherd could rely on to find the sheep (sound, scent, touch).

QUICK TIP

Instant Puppet Theater Give children a "stage" where they can perform the puppet play. Simply take an inexpensive vinyl shower curtain and cut its length to 36 inches. Then, add shower hooks and place it on a tension rod that will fit the width of a doorway in the room. Place the rod with curtain in a doorway, and allow the puppeteers to stand behind it to perform their play. If no doorway is available, the rod may be placed across two chair backs or desks.

DAY 5

Objective: To pray to the Good Shepherd in words and song

Prepare

Teach children the response "Thank you, Jesus."

 Use the *Call to Faith 1* CD, track 6, to rehearse the song.

Gather

Lead children in procession to the classroom prayer space.

Pray

A Prayer of Thanks

 Let Us Pray Follow the order of prayer on page 88.

• Optional music from *Singing Our Faith:* "With a Shepherd's Care," #225.

Celebrate

Prayer of Thanks

 Let Us Pray

Gather and begin with the Sign of the Cross.

Leader: Thank you, Jesus, for loving us.

All: Thank you, Jesus.

Leader: Thank you, Jesus, for taking care of us.

All: Thank you, Jesus. Amen.

Sing together the refrain.

The Lord, the Lord, the Lord
  is my shepherd,
The Lord, the Lord, the Lord
  is my shepherd,
The Lord, the Lord, the Lord
  is my shepherd,
The Lord is my shepherd
  and I shall not want.

African-American spiritual

88

 LITURGY LINK

The Bible at Mass Pretend to be the reader at Mass.

• Explain to children that the first of the three readings at Mass is usually taken from the Old Testament. The second is taken from the New Testament, and the third from one of the Gospels.

• Everyone stands when the Gospel is read, to honor the Lord Jesus.

 LECTIONARY LINK

Break Open the Word Read last week's Sunday Gospel. Invite children to think about what the reading means to them as they try to follow Christ's example. For questions related to the weekly Gospel reading, visit our Web site at **www.harcourtreligion.com**.

GO ONLINE **Visit www.harcourtreligion.com for weekly scripture readings and seasonal resources.**

CHAPTER 6
Review

A **Work with Words** Circle the right answer for each sentence.

1. The __(p. 85)__ is God's word written in human words.

   (**Bible**)   **prayer**

2. The __(p. 85)__ is about Jesus' life and stories.

   Old Testament   (**New Testament**)

3. A __(p. 84)__ is a story that teaches about God and his love.

   prayer   (**parable**)

4. The __(p. 85)__ is about time before Jesus.

   (**Old Testament**)   **New Testament**

5. You are like a __(p. 83)__ when you make bad choices.

   (**lost sheep**)   **shepherd**

B **Check Understanding** How is God like the shepherd? Draw a heart around the answer. (p.83)

He is lost.   **He loves us.**

89

Review

A **Work with Words** Have children circle the right answer for each sentence.

B **Check Understanding** Have children read the question and draw a heart around the right answer.

Assessment

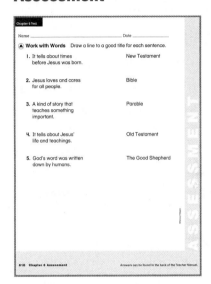

▲ **Chapter 6 Test page 81E**

Answers to the Chapter Test can be found in the back of the Teacher Manual.

TEACHER BACKGROUND

Vocabulary: Bible The word *Bible* comes from the Greek words *ta biblia,* meaning "a collection of writings."

- The Bible, also known as Holy Scripture, is the message of God written in human words.

OPTIONAL ACTIVITY

Make Bookmarks Have children make bookmarks to use at home in their family Bibles.

- Supply blank bookmarks or index cards and art materials.

- Write *The Bible Is God's Word* on the board or on chart paper, and have children copy this phrase onto their bookmarks and decorate.

Multiple Intelligence: Visual/Spatial

Jesus the Storyteller   89

Family Faith

Remind children to discuss the Family Faith page at home. Encourage children to read the scripture passage from the Gospel according to Matthew.

Activity

• Tell children that the family project encourages their family to share more parables of Jesus.

People of Faith

Tell children about Pope John XXIII.

• The pope is the highest leader of the Catholic Church. The *X's* and *I's* after John's name are roman numerals, the numbers that the ancient Romans used. *XXIII* means 23. Pope John XXIII was the twenty-third pope named John.

• Remind children to add Pope John XXIII to their People of Faith albums.

• Encourage them to pray the prayer at home with their families.

Visit **www.harcourtreligion.com** for weekly scripture readings and seasonal resources.

Unit 2: CHAPTER 6
Family Faith

Catholics Believe

■ Jesus told stories, or parables, to teach about God's love.

■ The Bible is God's word written in human words.

✝ **SCRIPTURE**

Read Matthew 13:10–15 to find out why Jesus used parables to teach.

GO ONLINE www.harcourtreligion.com
For weekly Scripture readings and seasonal resources

Activity
Live Your Faith

Retell Parables As a family, read and about some of the parables that Jesus The Gospel of Matthew is a good place look. Retell the parables in your own words. Go to the library or a bookstore and find picture books with parables.

▲ Pope John XXIII (Angelo Roncalli), 1881–1963

People of Faith

Pope John XXIII called a meeting of all the world's bishops. He wanted everyone to talk together to find ways to live the way God asks of us. Pope John showed people how to get along. He knew that people could find ways to live in peace and friendship. In 2000 Pope John was named Blessed.

Family Pray

Dear God, help us be like Pope John and find ways to get along with other people at school and work and home. Amen.

In Unit 2 your child is learning about the TRINITY.
90 **CCC** *See Catechism of the Catholic Church 134–139 for further reading on chapter content.*

? HOW DID I DO?

This week my religion classes were

☐ *some of the best ever!* ☐ *pretty good.* ☐ *in need of improvement.*

In what discussions and activities were children most interested?

_____

What activity did I most enjoy teaching?

_____

In what area do I need to improve?

_____

Name _____ Date _____

A Story About God

Color the pictures below. Then cut them out.
Use the pictures to tell the story of the Good Shepherd.

Care for God's Creation

Life and Dignity of the Human Person

Rights and Responsibilities of the Human Person

Dignity of Work and the Rights of Workers

Solidarity of the Human Family

Call to Family, Community, and Participation

Option for the Poor and Vulnerable

Faith in Action!
CATHOLIC SOCIAL TEACHING

Connect to Unit 2

This unit's Faith in Action feature teaches first graders the principle of defending the life and dignity of the human person. It connects to topics covered in this unit.

Children learned that
- Jesus is the Son of God who became human.
- Jesus grew up in a human family.
- Jesus taught us that God loves everyone.

Discover Catholic Social Teaching

Principle: Life and Dignity of the Human Person

The principle of the dignity of the human person is rooted in our belief that every person is created in God's image. It is this participation in divine life—not the circumstances of the person's physical or mental abilities, ethnic origins, age, gender, or social status—that confers dignity. The Church's efforts to protect and defend all human life at every stage and in every condition are inseparable from its belief in the dignity of the human person.

Catholic tradition calls us
- to realize that all people are worthy of dignity and respect.
- to treat all people with kindness.
- to work tirelessly for the protection of human life in all its diversity.

Reflect   ***How do you reinforce the lesson of respect for human life in your interactions with the children?***

Catholic Social Teaching Document

"The basis for all that the Church believes about the moral dimensions of economic life is its vision of the transcendent worth—the sacredness—of human beings . . . Human personhood must be respected with a reverence that is religious. When we deal with each other, we should do so with the sense of awe that arises in the presence of something holy and sacred. For that is what human beings are: we are created in the image of God (Gn 1:27)."

From *Economic Justice for All*, U.S. Catholic Bishops, 1981

Faith in Action!
CATHOLIC SOCIAL TEACHING

In this unit you learned that Jesus is the Son of God. He became human like us. He grew up in a family and had many friends.

The Gift of Life

People live in many different countries. They speak different languages. They have different colors of skin, hair, and eyes.

All people are the same in one important way. God made each one of us. God gave us the gift of his own life and love. God wants us to respect his life in others.

❷ How can you take care of other people?

Possible responses: be kind, help when you can, visit older people

91

DISCOVER

Catholic Social Teaching

Let Us Pray God our Father, help us to see you in every person we meet.

Faith in Action
Summarize the content of this unit by reading aloud the first paragraph.

The Gift of Life
Read aloud the two paragraphs.

- Invite children to name other ways in which all people are alike.
- Direct attention to the photograph, and tell children how the people depicted show respect for one another.

❷ How can you take care of other people? Invite children to respond to the question aloud or by drawing or writing in their faith journals or notebooks.

QUICK TIP

Population Facts To help children gain some understanding of the diversity of the Earth's population, explain to them that the United States is only the third most populous country. China is the most populous, and India is the second most populous.

OPTIONAL ACTIVITY

Notice Others' Gifts Have children choose partners.

- Supply art materials, and invite children to draw one special thing about their partners.
- Ask volunteers to share their work. Have children give drawings to their partners to take home.

Multiple Intelligence: Interpersonal

CONNECT

With the Call to Justice

With the Call to Justice

All Together

Direct attention to the pictures, and ask children to guess what the story on this page is about.

- Read aloud the first three paragraphs.

- Ask children to think about how these very different people might become friends. Then read aloud the last paragraph.

❷ **How does the St. Ann Center help people show respect for everyone?** Discuss the question as a class.

All Together

Every person deserves respect. Let's look at how people of different ages and abilities are getting to know one another.

Billy and Joe are best friends.

Billy is six years old. He lives with his mom. He needs a place to stay after school while his mom is at work. Billy loves music.

Joe is seventy-six. He has trouble remembering some things. But he remembers all the words to the songs he likes to sing.

People like Billy and Joe come together every afternoon in a special place called the St. Ann Center in Wisconsin. The center offers day care for people of all ages and abilities. Everyone at St. Ann's spends time together. Joe and Billy sing the songs Joe likes best. No one feels lonely or left out.

❷ **How does the St. Ann Center help people show respect for everyone?**

Possible responses: They invite all different kinds of people to come; the people all help each other.

92

TEACHER BACKGROUND

St. Ann Center The St. Ann Center for Intergenerational Care in Milwaukee, Wisconsin, is a ministry of the Sisters of St. Francis of Assisi.

- The people in the story are fictionalized representatives of those served by the center.

JUSTICE AND PEACE

Building Bridges The St. Ann Center was cited in testimony given by the Vatican to the UN General Assembly on Aging in 2002. "We must create an inclusive society for all ages," Msgr. Renato Martini told the assembly. "One way to accomplish this is to strive toward the development of programs that help to expand understanding among and between generations."

Catholic Social Teaching: Life and Dignity

What Can You Learn?

You can learn a lot from people who are different from you. Everyone has gifts to share. With a partner, talk about these questions.

What could you learn from

- someone who comes from another country?
- someone who has trouble seeing or hearing?

What could you share with

- someone who is younger than you?
- someone who uses a wheelchair?

You're Invited!

Make a Difference

Have a "Grandparents" Day Invite older people from your parish to come to your school and share time with your class. You can invite your own grandparents, too, if they live nearby. With your teacher's help, plan some games, songs, and food to share with your older visitors.

93

Your Community

Reach Out!

What Can You Learn?

Activity

- Read aloud the directions for the discussion activity.
- Have children choose partners. Read aloud the questions, and allow time for the pairs to discuss them.
- Invite volunteers to share their responses.

Make a Difference

Activity

- Read aloud the directions.
- Work with your parish pastoral ministry to identify older parishioners who will be invited.
- Help children plan and carry out the visit.

Encourage children to share what they have learned with friends, family members, and other classes.

TEACHER BACKGROUND

Adopt a Grandparent Many dioceses sponsor Adopt-a-Grandparent or Foster Grandparent programs that match children with elderly people for correspondence and activities. Check with your diocesan Catholic Charities office to find out what programs are offered in your area.

OPTIONAL ACTIVITY

Cross-Curricular: Reading Invite children to read these or similar books about the relationship between children and grandparents:

- *My Most Favorite Thing* by Nicola Moon (Dutton, 2001)
- *My Grandma, My Pen Pal* by Jan Dale Koutsky (Boyds Mills Press, 2002)

Multiple Intelligence: Verbal/Linguistic

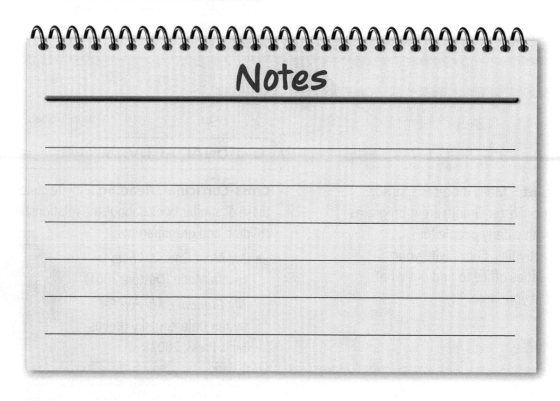

1. Who are the three Persons in the Holy Trinity?

Father (p. 65)

Son (p. 65)

Holy Spirit (p. 65)

2. Who is the Son of God?

Jesus

3. What can you find in the Bible?

Responses will vary.

4. What can you call God? (p. 64)

Mother   Adam   (Father)

5. Who are Jesus, Mary, and Joseph? (p. 74)

Trinity   (Holy Family)   Church

6. What stories did Jesus tell? (p. 84)

prayer   sheep   (parables)

C Make Connections   Write what God does.

God _____ (p. 66) loves _____ me!

© Harcourt Religion

© Harcourt Religion

94

95

Unit Review

The Unit Review is designed to prepare children for the Unit Assessment. Have children complete the Review pages. Then discuss the answers as a class. You may wish to review any concepts with which children are having difficulty before the Unit Assessment.

Notes

Name ______________________ Date ______________

(A) Work with Words Write the word from the Word Bank that completes the sentence.

WORD BANK		
Holy Family	love	Bible
New	Jesus	

1. Jesus, Mary, and Joseph are called the ______________________.

2. The ______________ Testament tells stories about Jesus.

3. Jesus' stories tell about God's ______________.

4. In the parable in this chapter, ______________ is the Good Shepherd.

5. Stories about God's love are in the ______________.

ASSESSMENT

Name _____ Date _____

6. The Bible is the Church's holy _____.

building   **book**

7. The Old Testament is the _____ part of the Bible.

first   **second**

Draw a line to the best ending for the sentence.

8. Jesus used parables   a parable.

9. Jesus is the Good   cares for all
Shepherd. He   God's people.

10. The Good Shepherd story is   to teach people
about God.

ASSESSMENT

UNIT 3
God's Son

Chapter 7
Jesus Heals
How did Jesus help people?

Chapter 8
Jesus Teaches Love
What is Jesus' command?

Chapter 9
Pray to God
How do you pray?

Faith in Action!

**Catholic Social Teaching Principle:
Rights and Responsibilities of
the Human Person**

96

UNIT 3 OPENER

Preview Unit Content

Tell children that Unit 3 is about God's son.

- Invite a volunteer to read aloud the chapter title and question for Chapter 7. Ask children what they think they will learn in this chapter.

- Repeat this for Chapters 8 and 9.

- Tell children that at the end of the unit they will learn how children at one school helped protect children's rights.

Overview

Faith Focus

- Jesus' healing signs manifest God's power and love. (CCC 547–550)
- Faith is the gift of trusting in God and assenting to his revelation. (CCC 153, 155, 1814)

Catechism Connection

The *Catechism* points out that Jesus' works of healing serve as testimonies that he was the Son of God. *(CCC 548)*

GDC Link

People tell about themselves through their actions. The *Directory* notes that Jesus' words and deeds show him as "'the Way' that leads to the innermost mystery of God." *(GDC 99)*

Jesus Heals

CHAPTER BACKGROUND

[T]hen he looked up to heaven and groaned, and said to him, "Ephphatha!" (that is, "Be opened!") And [immediately] the man's ears were opened, his speech impediment was removed, and he spoke plainly.

Mark 7:34–35

Jesus the Healer

Anyone reading the Gospels for the first time must be struck by the amount of attention that is devoted to Jesus' acts of healing. Jesus healed many people—people who were blind and deaf and lame, people who were possessed by devils, and people suffering from leprosy and other debilitating diseases for which there was, at the time, no cure. Jesus lived amidst sickness, suffering, and early death in a society that believed that these things were punishments for sin. Jesus healed those who were sick to end their physical suffering, but also to convey a message about God's universal love and compassion.

A Vocation to Heal

Disciples who follow in Jesus' footsteps can become signs, as he is, of God's loving compassion. But in order to do this, Christians must learn to see Jesus in those who suffer. Mother Teresa became a sign of his presence for the people of Calcutta because she saw the face of Jesus in the faces of Calcutta's poor. You, too, can be a sign of God for others.

Reflect ***How are you a healing presence for others?***

Jesus the Healer

The word *healing* is probably familiar to children. Yet they may not understand when the word is used metaphorically to describe the healing of the mind or spirit. Introduce children to the extended meanings of the word to promote a deeper understanding of Jesus' miracles.

Jesus' compassion for people who were hurting marked him as a unique agent of God the Father's power and love.

No other person and no object can heal as Jesus did. Why? Because Jesus is the Son of God, and his healing miracles were signs of the Father's love and of the imminent arrival of his kingdom.

- Emphasize that while some methods of healing can make people feel better, Jesus' healing actually made people well.

- Help children to perceive the uniqueness of Jesus' works of healing.

The Child and Illness

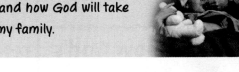

- I get a sore throat and earaches often. When this happens, I like being cared for.

- I worry about being separated from family members when they are sick or in the hospital.

- Help me understand how God will take care of me and my family.

Habits of Mind

Blessed assurance and constructive engagement with others can help you develop good critical thinking habits. Solid thinking skills allow you to think beyond the obvious and to realize what contributes to difficult problems.

Those who sustain their spirit seek different views to enhance, but not compromise, their own. Others seek feedback from anyone familiar with their work, not just from friends. Practicing this kind of thinking—these habits of mind—allows you to harvest richer resources for sustaining your spirit.

Reflect **Check the habit(s) of mind you would like to cultivate or improve:**

situational analysis   dialogue   seeking feedback

Teacher's Prayer

Jesus, teacher and healer, thank you for entrusting these children to me. Bless me with a generous heart that sees each child as your image. Amen.

Weekly Planner

		Objective	Materials	Prayer & Scripture
DAY 1 Invite	**Jesus Heals** Page 97	**Objective:** *To relate experiences of being sick*	☐ Art supplies ☐ Pencils	🙏 Let Us Pray *Psalm 4:4*
DAY 2 Explore	**Show God's Love** Pages 98–99	**Objective:** *To discuss how caring for those who are sick is a way to show God's love*	☐ Board or chart paper ☐ Art supplies ☐ Empty paper towel tube	🙏 Let Us Pray *Psalm 4:4*
DAY 3 Explore	**God's Power** Pages 100–101	**Objective:** *To discuss Jesus' acts of healing*	☐ Board or chart paper ☐ Index card ☐ Pencils ☐ Copies of Activity Master 7, p. 106A	🙏 Let Us Pray *tPsalm 4:4* ✝ **Scripture:** *Luke 8:40–56* ✝ **Scripture Background:** Jairus, p. 101
DAY 4 Explore	**Sharing God's Love** Pages 102–103	**Objective:** *To practice reaching out to others*	☐ Board or chart paper ☐ Art supplies	🙏 Let Us Pray *Psalm 4:4*
DAY 5 Celebrate	**Prayer for Healing** Page 104	**Objective:** *To pray for those who are sick*	☐ Hymnals ☐ Music CD	🙏 Let Us Pray **Prayer for Healing** 🔥 **Hymn:** "When Jesus the Healer"

Chapter 7 Wrap-Up: Review and Apply p. 105 • Chapter 7 Assessment p. 97E

Words of Faith

faith

Activities	Enrichment
Let's Begin: How Are You?, p. 97 **Multiple Intelligence:** Visual/Spatial	• **Reaching All Learners:** Verbal-Linguistic Learners, p. 97
Share Your Faith: Think, Share, Act, p. 99 **Multiple Intelligence:** Visual/Spatial OPTIONAL Circle Time, p. 99 **Multiple Intelligence:** Intrapersonal	• **Quick Tip:** Prayer, p. 98 • **Teacher Background:** Mother Teresa of Calcutta, p. 98 • **Quick Tip:** A Sensitive Topic, p. 99
Connect Your Faith: Tell the Story, p. 101 **Multiple Intelligence:** Verbal/Linguistic OPTIONAL Activity Master 7: Jesus' Life, p. 100 **Multiple Intelligence:** Visual/Spatial	• **Teacher Background:** Jesus the Healer, p. 100 • **Teacher Background:** Faith, p. 101
Live Your Faith: Draw Pictures of Healing, p. 103 **Multiple Intelligence:** Visual/Spatial OPTIONAL Role-Play Reaching Out, p. 102 **Multiple Intelligence:** Bodily/Kinesthetic OPTIONAL Cross-Curricular: Health, p. 103 **Multiple Intelligence:** Verbal/Linguistic	• **Quick Tip:** Emotional Illness, p. 102 • **Christian Living Skills:** Practicing Empathy, p. 103
	• **Liturgy Link:** Praying for Those Who Are Sick, p. 104 • **Lectionary Link:** Break Open the Word, p. 104

Multimedia Resources

 BOOK

Humble-Jackson, Sally. *The Miracle Maker: A Child's Story of Jesus.* Fleming H. Revell. 2001. Jesus' story is told by Darcas, the centurion's daughter who was healed.

 VIDEO

The Beginner's Bible: The Story of Jesus and His Miracles (30 min). SONY Wonder. Animated accounts of Jesus' healing actions.

 Teacher Resources
www.harcourtreligion.com
• **For interactive lesson planner, chapter resources, and activities**
• **For free materials and information**

Home Connection

Chapter 7 Family Faith, p. 106
Take-home activities, chapter content review, saint features and prayer

 For more family activities
www.harcourtreligion.com

Jesus Heals 97D

Name _____

Date _____

Ⓐ Work with Words   Write the word from the Word Bank that best completes each sentence.

1. Mother Teresa knew that God's

_____

- - - - - - - - - - - - - - - -

_____

   is in all people.

┌─────────────────────┐
│   **WORD BANK**   │
│   │
│ goodness   │
│   │
│ faith   │
│   │
│ power   │
└─────────────────────┘

_____

- - - - - - - - - - - - - - - -

2. _____ is the gift of believing in God.

3. Jesus' healing actions show God's

_____

- - - - - - - - - - - - - - - -

_____ and love.

Ⓑ Check Understanding   Trace the line to the best way to complete the sentence.

4. Jesus healed people.

   This was a sign of ⋯⋯⋯⋯⋯ God's love.

   ⋯⋯⋯⋯⋯ bad things.

5. Jesus told Jairus to have ⋯⋯⋯⋯⋯ food.

   ⋯⋯⋯⋯⋯ faith.

ASSESSMENT

Answers can be found in the back of the Teacher Manual.

Chapter 7 Jesus Heals

Invite

 Let Us Pray

Leader: God of mercy, help us to care for the sick.
"Know that the LORD works wonders for the faithful."

Psalm 4:4

All: God of mercy, help us to care for the sick. Amen.

 Activity **Let's Begin**

● **How Are You?** "Ooh," said Jordan. "I feel sick. It feels like hundreds of fish are doing flips in my tummy! A thousand worms are dancing a jig inside of me! My tummy really hurts!"

• Write one thing that makes you feel better when you feel sick.

_____

– – – – – – – – – – – – – – – – – –

_____

✏ **Draw How You Feel** Draw two circles. On one circle, draw a face that shows how you feel when you are sick. On the other, draw a face that shows how you feel when you get better.

97

★ REACHING ALL LEARNERS

Verbal/Linguistic Learners Children may prefer to write about feeling sick rather than draw.

• Have children read their descriptions to the class. Invite discussion.

Objective: To relate experiences of being sick

Open

Prayer Space Have children move to your classroom prayer space. In the space, have a crucifix and a Bible opened to the psalm verse.

 Let Us Pray Pray together the psalm verse and the response.

Build

Activity

• Read aloud the story.
• Ask children why Jordan feels sick. Possible responses: He ate too much. He has the flu.
• Have children write the answer to the question in the text.

Extension Activity

• Tell children they will be drawing.
• Distribute art supplies and ask them to draw a face that shows how they feel when they are sick and another face that shows how they feel when they get better.
• Ask children to share their drawings with the class.

Close

Have children tell what they learned about healing.

Objective: To discuss how caring for those who are sick is a way to show God's love

Open

Let Us Pray Invite children to pray the psalm verse on page 97 with you.

Focus **How did Mother Teresa help people?** List children's answers on the board or on chart paper.

Build

Show God's Love

Show children the picture of Mother Teresa to introduce the story.

- Tell children that the story takes place in Calcutta, India, where many poor people live in the streets.

Care for the Sick

Read aloud Care for the Sick.

- Have children circle Mother Teresa's loving actions. She smiled, held people's hands, prayed with them and for them.

- ❷ **What prayer can you say for someone who is sick?** Ask volunteers to share their responses with the class.

Explore

Show God's Love

Focus How did Mother Teresa help people?

Mother Teresa cared for the poor and sick in India. Read about how Mother Teresa showed God's love.

A BIOGRAPHY

Care for the Sick

The streets of Calcutta, India, were very crowded with people. Many people were sick. They lived on the streets.

Mother Teresa saw a sick man. His clothes were dirty. He was covered with mud and very thin. The man was dying.

Mother Teresa smiled at him. No one ever smiled at him. She and another nun took him to their hospital.

Mother Teresa had a hospital for the dying. There she and other women cared for people who were very sick. They held hands with dying people. They prayed with them and for them.

❷ **What prayer can you say for someone who is sick?**
Responses will vary.

98

QUICK TIP

Prayer Children may think that prayer is a kind of magic, and that prayers for the sick that don't produce physical healing have not been heard.

- In writing prayers for people who are sick, lead children to ask for other graces in addition to healing—relief from pain, feeling brave, knowing that people care.

TEACHER BACKGROUND

Mother Teresa of Calcutta Agnes Gonxha Bojaxhiu (1910–1997) was only 18 when she was sent by her community, the Sisters of Loretto in Ireland, to teach in Calcutta, India. In Calcutta, thousands of people are homeless, living on its streets.

- Mother Teresa, as she came to be known, left her religious order and founded a new one, the Missionaries of Charity.

od's Goodness

Mother Teresa knew that od's goodness is in all eople. The people she elped could hear love her voice. They could e love in her sweet mile. They could feel od's love in her touch.

Share Your Faith

Think: Think about what Mother Teresa might have said to a sick child.

Share: Talk about your ideas in small groups.

Act: Make your own card for a sick child. Mail it or deliver it yourself.

Get Well

99

God's Goodness

Read aloud God's Goodness. Ask children to recall some of the things Mother Teresa did for people. Possible responses: kind words, her smile, caring touch

- Tell children that people experience God's love through the loving actions of other people. Tell them God the Father wants them to treat everyone as lovingly as they would treat his Son, Jesus.

Activity

- Provide materials for making cards.
- Ask children for suggestions for appropriate messages.
- Print the good suggestions on the board or on chart paper for children to copy.
- Explain to children that they don't have to use the suggestions; they can use their own words if they prefer.

Close

Tell children that Mother Teresa showed people God's love by caring for very poor people in India who were sick or dying.

QUICK TIP

A Sensitive Topic   When you talk about those who are sick and dying, remember that some children you teach may be grieving the death of someone close.

- Be ready to provide these children with assurance that death is not the end.
- Tell them the Church encourages them to hope that loved ones are happy with God.

OPTIONAL ACTIVITY

Circle Time   Ask the children to sit in a circle. Hand one child the cardboard tube from a roll of paper towels upon which you have drawn lines and numbers to resemble a thermometer.

- Have the child describe a time when he or she was sick and what made him or her feel better—a hug, a popsicle for a sore throat, and so on—and then pass the tube along to the next child until all have responded.

Multiple Intelligence: Intrapersonal

DAY 3

Objective: To discuss Jesus' acts of healing

Open

Let Us Pray Invite children to pray the psalm verse on page 97 with you.

Focus **Why did Jesus heal people?** List children's answers on the board or on chart paper.

Build

God's Power

Read aloud God's Power.

- Explain to children how Jesus' acts of healing brought about bigger results than the simple restoration of bodily health.

❓ **Why do you think Jesus could heal people?** Help children understand that Jesus is God's son.

Explore

God's Power

Focus **Why did Jesus heal people?**

Mother Teresa followed Jesus' example. She loved and cared for the sick.

When Jesus saw sick people, he was sad. He did whatever he could to help people who needed him.

Jesus healed people. He made them well. When Jesus healed people, it was a sign of God's power and love. When Jesus healed people, they often changed their hearts, too. They saw God's love and power in Jesus. They came to believe in Jesus.

❓ **Why do you think Jesus could heal people?**
Possible response: He is the Son of God; he is God; he had God's power.

Words of Faith

Faith is the gift of believing in God and all that he has told about himself.

100

OPTIONAL ACTIVITY

Activity Master 7: Jesus' Life
Distribute copies of the activity found on teacher page 106A.

- Tell children that they will learn how to tell people about Jesus in a new way—without words.

- As an alternative, you may wish to send this activity home with children.

▲ Activity Master 7 page 106A

TEACHER BACKGROUND

Jesus the Healer Explain that Jesus did more than make the bodies of people who were sick healthy again, the way doctors try to do. Jesus made the whole person better.

- Jesus' healing was a powerful sign of God's power and love. The people Jesus healed in body were also brought closer to God. Having recovered their health, they went and did good things for others.

100 Chapter 7

Have Faith

One day a man named Jairus came to Jesus. Jairus said, "My daughter is very sick. I know you can help her."

Jesus agreed. On the way to Jairus's house, a servant came. "It is too late," he said to Jairus. "Your daughter is dead."

Jesus told Jairus, "Do not be afraid; just have **faith** and she will be saved."

Then Jesus went into the house and took the daughter's hand. Jesus said, "Child, arise!" The girl's breath returned, and she got up. Her parents were full of joy.

Based on Luke 8:40–56

❓ **What did Jesus do? Why did Jesus do it?** Jesus saved the girl because the father had faith.

Activity Connect Your Faith

🖊 **Tell the Story** Retell the story in your own words. Write one thing you learned from it.

_____

- - - - - - - - - - - - - - - - - - - -

_____

101

Have Faith

Gather children in a story circle. Tell them that they will hear a story about Jesus' power to heal.

- Proclaim the scripture story. When you have read the first two paragraphs, pause and ask children what they think Jesus will do now.

- Finish proclaiming the scripture story. Hold up an index card with the word *faith* written on it. Ask children why they think Jairus asked Jesus to heal his daughter.

- Tell children that Jesus is God's Son, and when Jesus healed people, they felt God's power and love.

❓ **What did Jesus do? Why did Jesus do it?** Write responses on the board or on chart paper.

Activity

- Have children retell the scripture story in their own words and write one thing that they learned from it.

Close

Emphasize to children that Jesus was able to heal people because he was God. He healed them in order to show his Father's power and love.

 TEACHER BACKGROUND

Faith   Before Jesus healed someone, he often asked whether the person had faith. Confidence in God's power and mercy seems to have been almost a condition for individuals to receive healing from Jesus.

- Note how the story of Jairus stresses that Jairus came to Jesus full of confidence that Jesus could help his daughter.

 SCRIPTURE BACKGROUND

Jairus   The father of the girl whom Jesus raised from the dead in *Luke 8:40–56* was an important man in the community. He was the ruler of a synagogue near Capernaum.

Objective: To practice reaching out to others

Open

 Let Us Pray Invite children to repeat after you the psalm verse from page 97.

Focus **How can you help people feel better?** List children's responses on the board or on chart paper.

Build

Sharing God's Love

Read aloud the first paragraph.

- Invite children to give examples of how Jesus helped people who were sick, lonely, or sad.

- Introduce the chart by reading aloud the second paragraph.

- Direct attention to the pictures, and ask children to explain how they show ways to help others.

- **?** **What are some other ways you can help people feel better?** Have children discuss the question in small groups.

Explore

Sharing God's Love

Focus How can you help people feel better?

Jesus healed people who were sick. He gave hope and friendship to people who were lonely. He did these things as signs of God's love.

You can share signs of God's love, too. You cannot heal people the way Jesus did. You cannot care for them the way family members and doctor can. There are still things you can d to help people feel better.

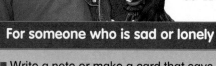

For someone who is sad or lonely

- Write a note or make a card that says you are thinking of the person.
- Tell some jokes to cheer the person up.
- Do a chore to help the person.
- Pray for the person.

For someone who is sick

- Draw a colorful picture for the person to look at.
- Sing a song on a tape for the person to listen to.
- Help make a treat for the person eat when he or she feels better.
- Pray for the person.

? What are some other ways you can help people feel better?

Responses will vary.

102

OPTIONAL ACTIVITY

Role-Play Reaching Out Have children act out ways to reach out to people who are sick, lonely, or sad.

- Ask children to work in small groups. Have them choose examples from the chart or from the list on the board or have them come up with their own.

- Allow time for groups to act out their situations.

Multiple Intelligence: Bodily/Kinesthetic

QUICK TIP

Emotional Illness Childhood depression is rare, but does occur. Be alert to these signs:

- sadness or listlessness that lasts for a long time and appears unrelated to external events.

- marked negative changes in behavior, hygiene, or academic performance.

- prolonged episodes of anger, aggression, or hyperactivity, which may mask depression.

Live Your Faith

Draw Pictures of Healing In the blue box, draw a picture of a time when someone made you feel better. In the red box, draw a picture of a time when you made someone else feel better.

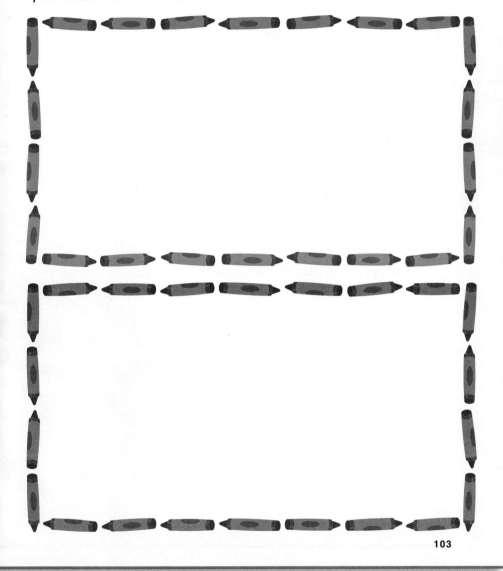

103

- Read aloud the directions for the activity.
- Provide art supplies, and give children time to complete their individual illustrations.
- Have children share their work by passing their books around the room.

Close

Lead children in spontaneous prayers for people who are sick, lonely, or sad.

CHRISTIAN LIVING SKILLS

Practicing Empathy Young children may not know the meaning of the word *empathy*, but they can use their imaginations to put themselves in another's place.

- Reinforce lessons on empathy by asking children to ask themselves, "How would I feel if this were happening to me?"
- Remind children of the Golden Rule: Treat others as you want them to treat you.

OPTIONAL ACTIVITY

Cross-Curricular: Health Have children make posters promoting good health practices when they are sick or when they visit people who are sick.

- Brainstorm a list of good health practices, such as washing hands, and covering the mouth when coughing.
- Have children work in groups to make their posters.

Multiple Intelligence: Verbal/Linguistic

Objective: To pray for those who are sick

Prepare

Tell children that people who are sick need our prayers. Ask children to name people they know who are sick, so that the group can pray for them.

 Use the *Call to Faith 1* CD, track 7, to rehearse the song.

Gather

Invite children to assemble quietly in the prayer space.

Pray

A Prayer for Healing

 Let Us Pray Ask children to quietly think of the people who are sick.

- Pray together, following the order of prayer on page 104.
- Optional music from *Singing Our Faith:* "Jesus' Hands Were Kind Hands," #170.

Celebrate

Prayer for Healing

 **Let Us Pray**

Gather and begin with the Sign of the Cross.

 Sing together the refrain.

Heal us, heal us today.
Heal us, Lord Jesus.

"When Jesus the Healer," Peter D. Smith © 1978, Stainer & Bell, Ltd. (administered by Hope Publishing Co.)

Leader: Jesus, Son of God,
we pray for those who are sick.
For children who are sick, we pray.

All: Help them be strong
and well again.

Leader: For all people who are
sick, we pray.

All: Help them be strong
and well again.
Amen!

104

 LITURGY LINK

Praying for Those Who Are Sick Remind children that prayer is a wonderful gift to give anyone who is sick.

- Prepare a big cardboard flower with a stiff stem and room for several construction paper petals. Have children print the name of each person for whom they want to pray on a petal, and attach it to the flower.

 LECTIONARY LINK

Break Open the Word Read last week's Sunday Gospel. Invite children to think about what the reading means to them as they try to follow Christ's example. For questions related to the weekly Gospel reading, visit our Web site at **www.harcourtreligion.com**.

GO ONLINE Visit www.harcourtreligion.com for weekly scripture readings and seasonal resources.

CHAPTER 7

Review

A Check Understanding

1. Name one thing Mother Teresa did to show God's love to people.

_____

- - - - - - - - - - - - - - - - - - -

Responses will vary.

_____

2. What did Jesus do to show God's power and love?

- - - - - - - - - - - - - - - - - - -

Responses will vary.

_____

3. What is faith?

_____

- - - - - - - - - - - - - - - - - - -

Responses will vary.

_____

- - - - - - - - - - - - - - - - - - -

B Make Connections Circle the right answer.

4. How can you help a sick person?

   play   **fight**   (**pray**)

5. How can you help a sad person?

   swim   (**visit**)   **sleep**

105

Review

A Check Understanding Have children respond on the lines provided.

B Make Connections Have children circle the right answer.

Assessment

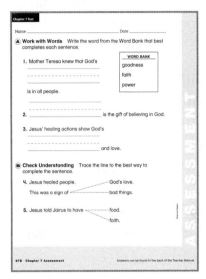

▲ Chapter 7 Test
page 97E

Answers to the Chapter Test can be found in the back of the Teacher Manual.

 JUSTICE AND PEACE

Compassion for the Sick After the prayer activity is completed, choose as a class one way to do the healing work of Jesus in the community.

- Children could make a sign with a smiling face and "Get Well Soon" on it for a child in a children's hospital or Pediatric Department of a nearby hospital.

Catholic Social Teaching: Call to Community

 CULTURAL AWARENESS

Mother Teresa In *Mother Teresa: A Simple Path*, compiled by Lucinda Vardey (Ballantine Books, 1995), Mother Teresa is quoted as saying, "I'm only a little wire—God is the power." This "little wire" touched the lives of countless people around the world before her death in 1997.

Family Faith

Remind children to discuss the Family Faith page at home. Encourage children to read the scripture passage from the Gospel according to Matthew.

Activity

- Suggest that each child should make the list and post it in a place where all family members can see it.

People of Faith

Tell children about Saint Louise de Marillac.

- Louise traveled all over France establishing the Daughters of Charity in hospitals, orphanages, and other institutions. She was declared Patroness of Social Workers by Pope John XXIII.
- Remind children to add Saint Louise de Marillac to their People of Faith albums.
- Encourage them to pray the prayer at home with their families.

Visit **www.harcourtreligion.com** for weekly scripture readings and seasonal resources.

Unit 3: CHAPTER 7
Family Faith

Catholics Believe

- Jesus' healing actions show God's power and love.
- Faith is the gift of believing in God.

✝ SCRIPTURE

Read Matthew 8:5–13 about another person Jesus healed.

GO ONLINE www.harcourtreligion.com
For weekly Scripture readings and seasonal resources

Activity
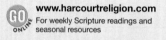
Live Your Faith

Make Family Lists Have each family member make a list of "comfort items" that help him or her feel good. You might choose a stuffed animal, a special pillow, a pair of slippers, or a religious symbol, such as a cross. When one family member is sick, the others can bring the comfort items to help the person feel better.

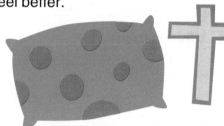

People of Faith

As a child, Saint Louise had a difficult life. She cared about the poor and the sick. Louise wanted to share God's love by helping others. After her husband died, Louise met Saint Vincent de Paul. They started the Daughters of Charity. These women worked in hospitals, homes, prisons, and during wars. There are still over 25,000 Daughters of Charity helping others. The Church celebrates her feast day on March 15.

▲ Saint Louise de Marillac, 1591–1660

🙌 Family Prayer

Dear Saint Louise, pray for us that we may bring cheer to those who are feeling sad or sick. Amen.

In Unit 3 your child is learning about JESUS CHRIST.
106 **CCC** *See Catechism of the Catholic Church 547–550 for further reading on chapter content.*

❓ HOW DID I DO?

This week my religion classes were

☐ *some of the best ever!* ☐ *pretty good.* ☐ *in need of improvement.*

In what discussions and activities were children most interested?

_____

What activity did I most enjoy teaching?

_____

In what area do I need to improve?

_____

Name _____ Date _____

Jesus' Life

Use words and pictures to tell about one part of Jesus' life.

Overview

Faith Focus

- The Great Commandment is one of God's laws. *(CCC 2052)*
- You are to love God above all else and to love others as you love yourself. *(CCC 2196)*

Catechism Connection

The *Catechism* explains that the full meaning of the Ten Commandments is revealed in Jesus. All the commandments of the Decalogue must be read in light of Jesus' law of love. *(CCC 2055–2056)*

GDC Link

The *Directory* describes the Great Commandment as the summation of the Ten Commandments and charter of the Christian life preached by Jesus. *(GDC 115)*

Jesus Teaches Love

CHAPTER BACKGROUND

 Owe nothing to anyone, except to love one another; for the one who loves another has fulfilled the law.

Romans 13:8

Your Neighbor

One of Jesus' followers, a scholar of the law, questioned him about inheriting eternal life. Instead of telling him, Jesus asked the scholar how he read the law, and the scholar responded with what is referred to as the Great Commandment. Jesus affirmed his answer. Love for God is the greatest commandment, and love for neighbor is like it.

Who is your neighbor? Jesus died for all people out of love. He died even for those who were his enemies. The Lord asks you to love as he does, loving even those who are the most difficult to love.

Loving Your Enemy

The crazy driver, the bad-mouthed child around the block, the ornery grandparent, the grumpy grocery store checker, the beggar on the street—on a daily basis there are many people with whom you may have a difficult time. The command to love them is a great test of faith, yet that challenge comes from Jesus. Catholics are called to see those who are sick, poor, and disadvantaged as neighbors. Catholics are called to love the child who disrespects them, the parent who grieves them, and the co-worker who antagonizes them.

Reflect **Who is your "neighbor"?**

The Great Commandment

Unit 3 asks, "How Do You Love God?" Chapter 8 answers: the Great Commandment. In its simplest form, the Great Commandment is love God, love others.

- Show children that the two directives interrelate through strong visuals, activities, and song.

- Young children are easily impressed. Ask a parent or student volunteer to make a striking poster that reads "Love God. Love others." Keep the Great Commandment poster on display so that you can refer to it throughout the year.

- Repetition and recognition work well with young children. Find different ways to show them that kindness, care, and forgiveness of others are signs of their love for God.

- You may want to add stars to the Great Commandment poster at the end of each session to praise children for their actions.

Keep Moving

- I like to sing, dance, and move around. Teach me some songs about God.

- I can solve problems. Give me some puzzles and situations that I can try to figure out.

- I like to act out stories. It helps me remember the stories better.

Vocational Seasons

In *The Courage to Teach,* Parker Palmer suggests that the teaching vocation consists of seasons. In some seasons we may be full of hope and new initiatives. At other times we may be "on low maintenance" and relaxed. Some people may be in a season of deep introspection even as others are experiencing a season of excitement or transitions.

The image of vocational seasons can be of great help in sustaining your spirit. If you are in a season that you don't enjoy, take consolation—the season will pass. Your catechetical vocation isn't over. On the other hand, if you are in a glorious vocational season, enjoy it to the full.

Reflect **Which vocational season are you in at this time: spring, summer, fall, or winter? Explain.**

 Teacher's Prayer

God of many blessings, I cherish the gifts you have given me. I promise to use these gifts to help children know you. Amen.

Weekly Planner

		Objective	Materials	Prayer & Scripture
DAY 1 Invite	**Jesus Teaches Love** Page 107	**Objective:** To reflect on how to express love for a person	☐ *Ask Mr. Bear* by Marjorie Flack (Aladdin Library, 1971.) ☐ Pencils	**Let Us Pray** *Psalm 119:44*
DAY 2 Explore	**Gifts of Love** Pages 108–109	**Objective:** To describe signs of love	☐ Board or chart paper ☐ Crayons	**Let Us Pray** *Psalm 119:44*
DAY 3 Explore	**Jesus Teaches** Pages 110–111	**Objective:** To identify ways to love God	☐ Board or chart paper ☐ Art supplies ☐ Copies of Activity Master 8, p. 116A ☐ Index card	**Let Us Pray** *Psalm 119:44* ✝ **Scripture:** *Luke 10:25–28* ✝ **Scripture Background:** The Great Commandment, p. 110
DAY 4 Explore	**Showing Love** Pages 112–113	**Objective:** To practice showing love for God and others	☐ Board or chart paper ☐ Art supplies ☐ Pencils ☐ Paper	**Let Us Pray** *Psalm 119:44*
DAY 5 Celebrate	**Pray with God's Word** Page 114	**Objective:** To celebrate loving God and others in song and in prayer	☐ Bible ☐ Hymnals ☐ Music CD ☐ Great Commandment chain from Day 3	**Let Us Pray** **Pray with God's Word** 🔔 **Hymn:** "This Little Light of Mine"

Chapter 8 Wrap-Up: Review and Apply p. 115 • Chapter 8 Assessment p. 107E

Words of Faith

Great Commandment

Activities	Enrichment
Let's Begin: Favorite Gifts, p. 107 Multiple Intelligence: Interpersonal OPTIONAL Cross Curricular: Reading, p. 107 Multiple Intelligence: Verbal/Linguistic	
Share Your Faith: Think, Share, Act, p. 109 Multiple Intelligence: Verbal/Linguistic OPTIONAL Acting, p. 108 Multiple Intelligence: Bodily/Kinesthetic OPTIONAL Chores Can Be Gifts, p. 109 Multiple Intelligence: Verbal/Linguistic	• Reaching All Learners: Critical Thinking, p. 108 • Quick Tip: Acting, p. 109
Connect Your Faith: Make a Great Commandment Chain, p. 111 Multiple Intelligence: Visual/Spatial OPTIONAL Activity Master 8: Love God and Others, p. 110 Multiple Intelligence: Verbal/Linguistic	• Quick Tip: Graphic Organizer, p. 111 • Justice and Peace: Unjust Behavior, p. 111
Live Your Faith: Show Your Love, p. 113 Multiple Intelligence: Visual/Spatial OPTIONAL Cross-Curricular: Language Arts, p. 112 Multiple Intelligence: Verbal/Linguistic OPTIONAL Act It Out, p. 113 Multiple Intelligence: Bodily/Kinesthetic	• Reaching All Learners: Gifted, p. 112 • Christian Living Skills: Expressing Affection, p. 113
	• Liturgy Link: Procession, p. 114 • Lectionary Link: Break Open the Word, p. 114

Multimedia Resources

 BOOK
Vollbracht, James. *Small Acts of Kindness.* Paulist Press. 1995. A boy's hug starts a chain of kind and loving actions.

 VIDEO
The Gospel with a Smile: Charity (18 min). Ikonographics. Stories and songs teach the meaning of loving as Jesus did.

 Teacher Resources
www.harcourtreligion.com
• For interactive lesson planner, chapter resources, and activities
• For free materials and information

Home Connection

Chapter 8 Family Faith, p. 116
Take-home activities, chapter content review, saint features and prayer

 For more family activities
www.harcourtreligion.com

Name _____ Date _____

Ⓐ Work with Words Write the word from the Word Bank that best completes the sentence.

```
                        WORD BANK
          Great         others          love
```

1. The _____ Commandment

   teaches you to _____ God and

   to love _____ .

Ⓑ Check Understanding Circle the word that best completes each sentence.

2. You show love for God when you _____ .

   talk    **pray**

3. A commandment is a law that God made for _____ to obey.

   plants    **people**

©Harcourt Religion

ASSESSMENT

Chapter 8 Jesus Teaches Love

Let Us Pray

Leader: God, we want to follow your teachings.
"I will keep your teachings always,
for all time and forever." *Psalm 119:44*

All: God, we want to follow your teachings.
Amen.

Activity Let's Begin

● **Favorite Gifts**
What are some gifts
you really like?
A doll, a game, a bike?

• What is a special gift someone has
given you?

_____

_____

_____

_____

Act It Out Show yourself giving a friend or
family member a special gift.

107

Objective: To reflect on how to express
love for a person

Open

Let Us Pray
Tell children to move
to the classroom prayer space. Pray
together the psalm verse.

Build

Activity

• Read aloud Favorite Gifts.
• Ask children what kinds of gifts they
  like to receive. Possible responses:
  games, toys.
• Allow children time to write their
  responses to the text question.

Extension Activity

• Divide children into small groups.
• Ask each child to act out giving a
  friend or family member a special
  gift.
• Have the other children try to guess
  what the gift is.

Close

Have children tell you what they
learned about gifts.

OPTIONAL ACTIVITY

Cross-Curricular: Reading You might
want to ead the story, *Ask Mr. Bear* by
Marjorie Flack (Aladdin Library, 1971).
This is about a little boy who was trying
to think of the best birthday present he
could give to his mother. Mr. Bear suggested
that Danny give his mother what only he
could give—a big hug.

ASK MR. BEAR
By Marjorie Flack

Multiple Intelligence: Verbal/Linguistic

Objective: To describe signs of love

Open

 Let Us Pray Invite children to pray the psalm verse on page 107 with you.

Focus **What gift can you give?** List children's answers on the board or on chart paper.

Build

Gifts of Love

Gather children in a circle.

• Read The Gift. Involve children in the story by asking one child to pretend to be Timmy and other to be Timmy's mom.

• Give the actors simplified lines of what is in the text on this page.

• As you read, give children a cue, such as pointing a finger, for when to say their lines.

❷ **What do you think Timmy will give Grandpa?** Ask volunteers to share responses.

Gifts of Love

Focus **What gift can you give?**

A STORY

The Gift

Timmy asked, "Mom, what can I do for Grandpa's birthday?"

Mom said, "Let's think. What do you and Grandpa like to do?"

"We like to build things. He plays ball with me, too," said Timmy.

Mom asked, "Is there anything else?"

"Yes!" Timmy said. "He likes my drawings. He always saves them. I've got it! Thanks, Mom!"

❷ **What do you think Timmy will give Grandpa?** Possible response: a drawing

108

★ REACHING ALL LEARNERS

Critical Thinking A question on this page asks children to suggest what Timmy will give his grandpa. Children need to use the clues in the story to figure out a logical answer.

• Some children may give a general answer, such as "candy."

• These children need direction in thinking back to what they heard. If needed, reread those story sections.

OPTIONAL ACTIVITY

Acting Children love to play different roles, especially the role of grown-ups.

• Allow various volunteers to act out the story of Timmy and his mother by making up their own conversation.

• Suggest other types of situations for them to role-play, such as picking up toys or helping with jobs around the house.

Multiple Intelligence: Bodily/Kinesthetic

On Grandpa's birthday, Timmy gave him a gift.

It was a drawing of Timmy and Grandpa playing ball and riding bikes. Timmy also drew the birdhouse they made together. The picture said "I love you, Grandpa."

"Thank you, Timmy," said Grandpa. "This is the best gift! I will hang it up for everyone to see."

"Great!" Timmy said happily. "Let's go play catch!"

Faith Fact

God gives you the gifts of faith, hope, and love.

Activity

Share Your Faith

Think: How did Timmy show love with his gift?

Share: How can you show love for others? Talk about your answer with a partner.

 Act: Mark an X next to the ways to show that you love God and others.

   x   Share your toys.

   x   Help do the dishes.

          Fight about your place in line.

   x   Pray every day.

109

- Finish the story and ask children to imagine Timmy's picture.
- Discuss with children how Timmy showed his love for his grandpa. Ask children to name other gifts that don't cost money and show love. Possible answers: a smile, a hug, some help, something you make

Activity

- Direct children to identify ways they can show love for God and for other people.

Close

Remind children that the best gift to give someone is love.

OPTIONAL ACTIVITY

Chores Can Be Gifts Discuss with children how family chores can be seen as gifts to the whole family.

- Have children ask family members about what they do to help the family. Explain that families do these chores out of love.

Multiple Intelligence: Verbal/Linguistic

QUICK TIP

Giving Gifts Invite children to tell about a gift or another item made by a family member. This could be as simple as a birthday cake for a special celebration or a craft that an older child helped a child make.

- Emphasize that these gifts are gifts of knowledge, time, and talent that family members give each other out of love.

DAY 3

Objective: To identify ways to love God

Open

Let Us Pray Invite children to pray the psalm verse on page 107 with you.

Focus **What did Jesus say about love?** List children's answers on the board or on chart paper.

Build

Jesus Teaches
Read aloud Jesus Teaches.

- Explain that people have always argued about the best way to please God.

Loving Others
Proclaim the scripture story.

- Have children point to the man who asked Jesus the question. Have them say the question he asked. Then have them say aloud the answer the man gave to Jesus' question.

❓ **How much should you love God and others?** Write children's responses on the board or on chart paper.

Jesus Teaches

Focus What did Jesus say about love?

Timmy's drawing was a sign of his love for his Grandpa. Listen to this Bible story about love.

✝ SCRIPTURE   Luke 10:25–28

Loving Others

One day a man said, "I want to be happy with God forever. What should I do?"

Jesus asked, "What is written in the law?"

The man replied, "You shall love the LORD, your God, with all your heart, with all your being, with all your strength, and with all your mind, and your neighbor as yourself."

Jesus said, "You have answered correctly."

From Luke 10:25–28

❓ **How much should you love God and others?** Love God above all else, and others as yourself.

110

OPTIONAL ACTIVITY

Activity Master 8: Love God and Others Distribute copies of the activity on teacher page 116A.

- Tell children that they will create a checklist of ways to show love.
- As an alternative, you may wish to send the activity home with children.

▲ Activity Master 8 page 116A

✝ SCRIPTURE BACKGROUND

The Great Commandment For the author of the Gospel according to Luke, there is nothing particularly complicated or mysterious about the path to salvation.

- Jesus simply tells the man who came to him with the question about salvation to do what he himself already knows he should do: love God above everything else, and love others as he loves himself.
- These two instructions constitute what is often called the Great Commandment.

The Great Commandment

A commandment is a law that God made for people to obey. Loving God and others is the most important commandment. This law is called the **Great Commandment**.

The Great Commandment teaches you to love God more than anything. It also tells you to love others as you love yourself.

❓ **What are some ways parents show love to their children?**

Possible responses: spend time with them, take care of them, protect them

 Activity

Connect Your Faith

Make a Great Commandment Chain Draw pictures on strips of colored paper. The pictures should show your love for God and others. Work in groups to put the links together. Hang the chain across the classroom.

111

Words of Faith

The **Great Commandment** is to love God above all else and to love others the way you love yourself.

The Great Commandment

Read aloud The Great Commandment.

- Hold up an index card with *Great Commandment* written on it.
- Explain to children that the main way you show your love for God is by obeying his command to love other people.
- On the board or on chart paper, draw the graphic organizer. Use the drawing to explain to children the connection between love of God and love of neighbor.

❓ **What are some ways parents show love to their children?** Encourage children to give specific examples.

 Activity

- Tell children to look at the hearts that were drawn. Tell them they are linked together because loving God requires loving others. Loving others deepens love for God.
- Help children make a Great Commandment chain.

Close

Emphasize that the Great Commandment tells people to love God and love others.

💡 **QUICK TIP**

Graphic Organizer

```
   Love God.    Love others.
```

✝ **JUSTICE AND PEACE**

Unjust Behavior Perhaps you are noticing that some children are being ignored, teased, or even bullied.

- Call attention to this unacceptable behavior without calling attention to those who are at fault.
- Use the Great Commandment to lead the children to correct the behavior.

Catholic Social Teaching: Rights and Responsibilities

Objective: To practice showing love for God and others

Explore

Open

Let Us Pray Invite children to pray the psalm verse from page 107.

Focus **How can you show love for God and others?** List responses on the board or on chart paper.

Build

Showing Love

Ask children to recall the Great Commandment.

- Read aloud the first sentence.
- Draw attention to the chart by reading aloud the second sentence.
- Read aloud the heading *Love God.*
- Invite children to follow along as four volunteers take turns reading aloud the suggestions.
- Repeat this process for the column headed *Love Others.*

❷ **What are some ways to show love for God and others?** List responses on the board or on chart paper.

Showing Love

Focus **How can you show love for God and others?**

There are many ways to keep the Great Commandment. Here are some ways that you can show love for God and for others.

Love God	Love Others
■ Pray every day. ■ Learn about God at home, at church, and in school. ■ Get to know the stories in the Bible. ■ Take care of God's creation.	■ Do what parents and family members ask of you without grumbling. ■ Share what you have. ■ Be kind. Don't tease or fight. ■ Help younger children.

❷ **What are some other ways to show love for God and others?** Responses will vary.

112

OPTIONAL ACTIVITY

Cross-Curricular: Language Arts Have children write or tell short stories about showing love for God and others.

- Ask children to choose a picture on page 112 as a prompt. Have children imagine that the picture they choose is an illustration for their story.

Multiple Intelligence: Verbal/Linguistic

★ **REACHING ALL LEARNERS**

Gifted First graders who are gifted in reading and writing may feel held back by the slower pace of the rest of the class. Engage gifted students by inviting them to assist you in reading aloud or writing on the board, and by encouraging them to serve as mentors to other children.

Live Your Faith

Show Your Love On the candle that says **Love God,** write or draw one way you show love for God. On the candle that says **Love Others,** write or draw one way you show love for others.

† Love God ♡

† Love Others ♡

113

- Read aloud the directions for the activity.
- Help children brainstorm actions they might draw. Refer to the list on the board if necessary.
- Supply art materials, and have children work independently on their drawings.
- Invite volunteers to share their art work.

Close

Ask children to think of one way they can show love for God and for their family members at home today.

CHRISTIAN LIVING SKILLS

Expressing Affection People have different ways of expressing affection, often related to family history and cultural customs. Help children see that love, affection, and friendship can be expressed in a variety of ways, from kind words to comforting gestures.

- Remind children that expressions of affection may be appropriate or inappropriate depending on the people and circumstances involved.

OPTIONAL ACTIVITY

Act It Out Have children role-play ways to show love for God and others.

- Ask children to choose partners to prepare their role-plays.
- Challenge children to include nonverbal as well as verbal signs of love.

Multiple Intelligence: Bodily/Kinesthetic

DAY 5

Objective: To celebrate loving God and others in song and in prayer

Prepare

Introduce the song. Explain to children that "letting your light shine" means letting other people see your goodness and love.

 Use the *Call to Faith 1* CD, track 8, to rehearse the song.

Gather

Have children form a long line at the opposite end of the room from the prayer space. Have everyone hold part of the Great Commandment chain. Invite them to sing the song as they process to the prayer space.

Pray

Pray with God's Word

 Let Us Pray Follow the order of prayer on page 114.

• Optional reading: *Luke 8:16*.

• Additional verses to the song can be found in *Singing Our Faith*, #208.

Celebrate

Pray with God's Word

 Let Us Pray

Gather and begin with the Sign of the Cross.

Leader: Blessed be God.

All: Blessed be God forever.

Leader: A reading from the holy Gospel according to Matthew.

        Read Matthew 5:14–16.
        The Gospel of the Lord.

All: Praise to you,
             Lord Jesus Christ.

Sing together.

This little light of mine,
I'm gonna let it shine;
This little light of mine,
I'm gonna let it shine;
This little light of mine,
I'm gonna let it shine,
Let it shine, let it
shine, let it shine.

"This Little Light of Mine," African-American spiritual

114

 LITURGY LINK

Procession Tell children that the way they walked to the prayer space is called a procession.

• Have groups of children recall times they have seen processions during Mass.

• Appoint children to pretend to be the cross-bearer, the servers, the reader, and the priest in an entrance procession.

 LECTIONARY LINK

Break Open the Word Read last week's Sunday Gospel. Invite children to think about what the reading means to them as they try to follow Christ's example. For questions related to the weekly Gospel reading, visit our Web site at **www.harcourtreligion.com**.

 Visit **www.harcourtreligion.com** for weekly scripture readings and seasonal resources.

A **Work with Words** Circle the correct word to complete each sentence.

1. A commandment is a __(p. 111)__ God made for people to obey.

   parable ⬭**law**

2. __(p. 110)__ taught the Great Commandment.

   ⬭**Jesus** **Jairus**

3. The Great Commandment begins with __(p. 111)__ God.

   ⬭**loving** **knowing**

4. You can love God by __(p. 112)__.

   ⬭**praying** **pushing**

5. A __(p. 111)__ is a law God made.

   gift ⬭**commandment**

B **Check Understanding** Name a way to love others. Draw a picture to show the way to love others.

_____

- -
_____

Responses will vary. (p. 112)

115

Review

A **Work with Words** Have children circle the correct word to complete the sentence.

B **Check Understanding** Have children name a way to love others in the space provided. Then have them draw a picture showing the way to love others.

Assessment

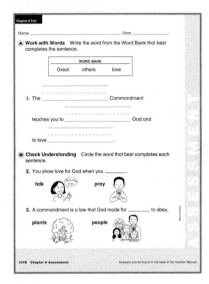

▲ **Chapter 8 Test page 107E**

Answers to the Chapter Test can be found in the back of the Teacher Manual.

QUICK TIP

Make a Joyful Noise You may wish to supply simple musical instruments such as two blocks to clap together, bells, or similar items for the children to accompany the song.

OPTIONAL ACTIVITY

Learn by Singing Research has shown that people learn material better when it is set to music.

- Because children need to think about ways they can show love, the song they sing is a learning experience.

- Encourage children to make up gestures to accompany the song. They can do this in class or at home.

Multiple Intelligence: Musical

Family Faith

Remind children to discuss the Family Faith page at home. Encourage children to read the scripture passage from the Book of Exodus.

Activity

- Describe the activity as a fun game to play.

People of Faith

Tell children about Saint Thomas of Villanova.

- Thomas worried about the poor. He founded colleges for the children of new converts and the poor. He organized priests for service among foreign people and was known for his personal saintliness.

- Remind children to add Saint Thomas of Villanova to their People of Faith albums.

- Encourage them to pray the prayer at home with their families.

Visit **www.harcourtreligion.com** for weekly scripture readings and seasonal resources.

Unit 3: CHAPTER 8
Family Faith

Catholics Believe

- The Great Commandment is one of God's laws.

- You are to love God above all else and love others as you love yourself.

✝ **SCRIPTURE**

Read about the Ten Commandments in Exodus 20:1–17.

GO ONLINE www.harcourtreligion.com
For weekly Scripture readings and seasonal resources

Activity
Live Your Faith

Make a Heart Cut out a large paper heart, and put it where all can see it. When you see someone show love for God or others, draw a red heart on the large heart. Count the hearts at the end of the week. Say a prayer thanking God for the love in your family.

▲ **Saint Thomas of Villanova, 1486–1555**

People of Faith

Thomas was a teacher, a monk, and a bishop in Spain. He was known as the "almsgiver." He gave his money to people who had nothing. People who were poor heard about Thomas. They lined up outside his house to receive food and money. Thomas found homes for many orphaned children. He paid to free many slaves. The Catholic Church celebrates Saint Thomas's special day on September 8.

Family Prayer

Saint Thomas, pray for us that we may care for people who have little money and people who are hungry. Amen.

In Unit 3 your child is learning about JESUS CHRIST.
116 **CCC** *See Catechism of the Catholic Church 2052–2055 for further reading on chapter content.*

? **HOW DID I DO?**

This week my religion classes were

☐ *some of the best ever!* ☐ *pretty good.* ☐ *in need of improvement.*

In what discussions and activities were children most interested?

_____

What activity did I most enjoy teaching?

_____

In what area do I need to improve?

_____

Name _____ Date _____

Love God and Others

Listen to each sentence.

Draw a happy face next to some ways to love God and others.

_____ 1.   Say "I'm sorry."

_____ 2.   Pick up your toys.

_____ 3.   Tell a little lie.

_____ 4.   Pray.

_____ 5.   Make your brother or sister cry.

_____ 6.   Help at home.

_____ 7.   Go to Mass.

_____ 8.   Help a classmate who is sad.

_____ 9.   Take something that does not belong to you.

_____ 10.   Start a fight.

Overview

Pray to God

CHAPTER BACKGROUND

 "And I tell you, ask and you will receive; seek and you will find; knock and the door will be opened to you."

Luke 11:9

A Man of Prayer

Jesus was a man of prayer. He prayed alone on a mountaintop; he prayed as he was baptized; he prayed before choosing his Apostles; and he prayed during his agony in the garden before his arrest. Jesus prayed often, and eventually his disciples asked him to teach them how to pray. Jesus responded by teaching his disciples the Lord's Prayer.

Jesus not only prayed often, but he prayed with confidence of being heard. His example is one of serenity and trust. Yet most people find it difficult to pray as Jesus prayed. A busy life, unfruitful liturgical experiences, or spiritual emptiness can be obstacles to prayer. The question may arise in the human heart, "What good does it do to pray?"

Learning to Pray

"Prayer is the raising of one's mind and heart to God" *(CCC 2559)*. In sadness, emptiness, and great need, find the humility to turn to the Father, who is always ready to meet you. Whatever your faults or grievances, "God tirelessly calls [you] to that mysterious encounter known as prayer" *(CCC 2567)*. So persevere in prayer. Go with your family or friends to worship together at Mass. Willingly surrender your struggles to God. The next time you take a moment to have a cup of tea or coffee, invite him along for a short visit.

Reflect **Is prayer a part of your daily life right now?**

Pray

Prayer is a way to cultivate friendship with God. For most young children, praying is as natural as talking and listening to their family and friends. This characteristic of six-year-olds helps them develop their own spirituality through prayer.

- New experiences have a powerful impact on children. Take note of major events in children's lives—the birth of a sibling, the death of a pet—by praying about them.

- Six-year-olds see you as a model to be imitated. Let them hear you pray. Offer an example of joy and reverence in prayer.

- Young children possess a strong sense of right and wrong. Prayer is one means for them to address the injustices that they feel so acutely. Many problems are too big for children to solve, but prayer can help them combat feelings of powerlessness.

Kids at Prayer

- I am verbal and like to talk.

- I think prayers are important. Give me some quiet time to pray by myself and with others.

- I may expect God to answer my prayers immediately.

Living with Complexity

Most of us require clarity and consistency from the people around us. However, those who are comfortable with paradox, ambiguity, and complexity are better equipped to sustain the spirit to teach.

None of us should compromise our deepest principles of integrity. To do so would put our vocational spirit at risk. We can work at holding the contradictions in balance and living with the complexity of human imperfection. This will help us sustain the spirit to teach.

Reflect   **How would you rate your ability to live with complexity and hold the contradictions in balance?**

Teacher's Prayer

God the Father, I praise you. God the Son, I love you. God the Holy Spirit, I welcome you. Infuse my life with your presence. Amen.

Weekly Planner

		Objective	Materials	Prayer & Scripture
DAY 1 Invite	**Pray to God** Page 117	**Objective:** To explore different types of prayer	☐ Pencils	Let Us Pray *Psalm 145:2*
DAY 2 Explore	**Stay Close to God** Pages 118–119	**Objective:** To recognize that prayer is a way of coming close to God	☐ Board or chart paper ☐ Art supplies ☐ Copies of Activity Master 9, p. 126A ☐ Index cards	Let Us Pray *Psalm 145:2*
DAY 3 Explore	**Learn to Pray** Pages 120–121	**Objective:** To conclude that prayer is a way to love God	☐ Board or chart paper ☐ Pencils	Let Us Pray *Psalm 145:2* ✝ **Scripture:** *Ephesians 5:18–20* ✝ **Scripture Background:** Ephesians 5, p. 120
DAY 4 Explore	**The Lord's Prayer** Pages 122–123	**Objective:** To practice praying the Lord's Prayer	☐ Board or chart paper ☐ Pencils ☐ Index cards ☐ Musical selections of the Lord's Prayer	Let Us Pray *Psalm 145:2* ✝ **Scripture Background:** Abba, p. 122
DAY 5 Celebrate	**Prayer of Thanks** Page 124	**Objective:** To praise God in prayer with happy hearts	☐ Music CD	Let Us Pray **Prayer of Thanks** 🎵 **Hymn:** "Psalm 89: For Ever I Will Sing"

Chapter 9 Wrap-Up: Review and Apply p. 125 • Chapter 9 Assessment p. 117E

Words of Faith

prayer

Lord's Prayer

Activities	Enrichment
Let's Begin: Talk to God, p. 117 Multiple Intelligence: Interpersonal	• **Cultural Awareness:** Celebrations, p. 117
Share Your Faith: Think, Share, Act, p. 119 Multiple Intelligence: Verbal/Linguistic (OPTIONAL) Activity Master 9: A Prayer Card, p. 118 Multiple Intelligence: Visual/Spatial (OPTIONAL) A Blessing, p. 118 Multiple Intelligence: Verbal/Linguistic (OPTIONAL) Spontaneous Prayer, p. 119 Multiple Intelligence: Verbal/Linguistic	• **Justice and Peace** Sharing with Others, p. 119
Connect Your Faith: Pray Together, p. 121 Multiple Intelligence: Verbal/Linguistic	• **Quick Tip:** Offering Blessings, p. 120 • **Reaching All Learners:** Understanding the Lord's Prayer, p. 121 • **Teacher Background:** The Lord's Prayer, p. 121
Live Your Faith: Trace the Words, p. 123 Multiple Intelligence: Visual/Spatial (OPTIONAL) Cross-Curricular: Music, p. 122 Multiple Intelligence: Musical (OPTIONAL) Prayer Puzzle, p. 123 Multiple Intelligence: Verbal/Linguistic	• **Teacher Background:** Abba, p. 122 • **Christian Living Skills:** How to Pray, p. 123
	• **Liturgy Link:** Lifting Hearts, p. 124 • **Lectionary Link:** Break Open the Word, p. 124

Multimedia Resources

 BOOK

Grimes, Nikki. *When Daddy Prays.*
Wm. B. Eerdmans. 2002. A boy observes
his father incorporating prayer into
every part of his day.

 VIDEO

The Angel's Prayer Lesson (12 min).
Twenty-Third Publications. Guardian
angels teach children about prayer.

 Teacher Resources
www.harcourtreligion.com

• For interactive lesson planner, chapter
resources, and activities
• For free materials and information

Home Connection

Chapter 9 Family Faith, p. 126
Take-home activities, chapter content
review, saint features and prayer

 For more family activities
www.harcourtreligion.com

Name _____ Date _____

Ⓐ Work with Words   Write the word from the Word Bank to complete the first part of the Lord's Prayer.

```
      WORD BANK
  heaven        name
```

1. Our father, who art in _____ ,

hallowed be thy _____ .

Ⓑ Check Understanding   Draw a line to the best ending for each sentence.

2. Prayer is   a. two ways to pray.

3. The Lord's Prayer is   b. listening and talking to God.

4. Ask and thank are   c. the prayer Jesus taught.

©Harcourt Religion

ASSESSMENT

Chapter 9 Pray to God

Let Us Pray

Leader: God, we praise you always.
"Every day I will bless you;
I will praise your name forever."
Psalm 145:2

All: God, we praise you always. Amen.

Activity Let's Begin

● **Talk to God** Dad placed his hand on Lamont's head. He prayed, "May God be with you today and always."

Dad lit the candles on the cake.

Lamont said quietly, "Dear God, thank you for making me. Help me to be kind, happy, and good this year."

• What do you think Lamont's family was celebrating?

_____

– – – – – – – – – – – – – – – – –

Tell a Friend Choose a partner. Tell the partner one thing you say to God when you pray.

117

DAY 1

Objective: To explore different types of prayer

Open

Let Us Pray   Invite children to move into the prayer space. Pray the psalm verse and have them pray the response.

Build

Activity

• Read aloud Talk to God.

• Ask children why they think Lamont's dad was praying. Possible responses: He loves Lamont. He's asking God to watch over Lamont.

• Allow children time to write their response to the text question.

Extension Activity

• Tell children to pick a partner.

• Have them tell their partner one thing they say to God while praying.

• Ask for volunteers to share their answers with the whole class.

Close

Have children tell what they learned about prayer.

🌐 CULTURAL AWARENESS

Celebrations   Cultures have different ways of observing birthdays.

• Catholics in European countries may celebrate their "name days" as well as their birthdays. Birthday and name day celebrations are ways to show thanks for the life God has given you.

• Ask volunteers to share any special customs they observe on birthdays.

Objective: To recognize that prayer is a way of coming close to God

Open

Let Us Pray Invite children to pray the psalm verse on page 117 with you.

Focus **What are some ways to pray?** List children's answers on the board or on chart paper.

Build

Stay Close to God

Read aloud Stay Close to God.

- Show children the word *prayer* written on an index card.

- Explain that prayer is the way to have a friendship with God.

- Ask if there is anyone who knows the words of a prayer in a language other than English.

- ❷ **When have you heard blessing prayers?** Encourage children to give specific examples.

Explore

Stay Close to God

Focus **What are some ways to pray?**

Talking with family and friends helps you feel close to them. Talking with and listening to God is called **prayer**.

God wants you to be his friend. God wants you to pray to him. You feel close to God when you pray.

Blessing prayers thank God for the good things he gives you. They ask God to keep caring for you and others.

❷ **When have you heard blessing prayers?** Possible responses: before and after meals; at beginning of day

118

Activity Master 9: A Prayer Card Distribute copies of the activity found on teacher page 126A.

- Tell children they will be making a prayer card of their own.

- As an alternative, you may wish to send this activity home with children.

▲ Activity Master 9 page 126A

A Blessing To help children understand what a blessing is, teach them the words of this traditional blessing at meals: "Bless us O Lord, and these your gifts which we are about to receive from your goodness through Christ our Lord. Amen."

- Explain that in this blessing we thank God for the food he has given us from his generous store of gifts.

Multiple Intelligence: Verbal/Linguistic

Pray Anywhere

You can pray wherever you are. You can talk to God at home or in church. You can pray in your classroom or on the playground.

Wherever you are, God will hear you. You can say your own prayer. You can say prayers of the Church. You can pray silently or out loud.

Begin your prayer by thanking God the Father for all that he gives you.

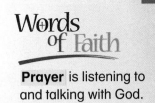

Words of Faith

Prayer is listening to and talking with God.

Activity

Share Your Faith

Think: Think of gifts that God gives you that make you happy.

Share: Discuss things to be thankful for.

Act: Draw a picture of something that makes you happy, and say a prayer of thanks to God.

Mom

Dad

119

Pray Anywhere

Ask children about places they pray. Then read aloud Pray Anywhere. Tell children that they can talk to God wherever they are.

• Have children make an index card with a Y on one side and an N on the other side. Call out places, such as "in school," "in church," "in your bedroom," "on a bus," "on your bike," or "at a playground." Tell children to hold up the side with the Y if the place is a place where you can pray, and the side with the N if it isn't. The Y should be held toward you each time. This reinforces the concept that prayer can take place anywhere.

Activity

• Have children discuss things they are thankful for.

• Allow children time to do their drawings and say their prayers.

Close

Remind children that you can talk to God anywhere and about anything. He will always hear your prayers.

✚ JUSTICE AND PEACE

Sharing with Others   Point out to children that one way they can pray to God in thanksgiving for the gifts they have received is by sharing what they have with others.

• Suggest that children perform an act of kindness during the coming week, such as calling a grandparent or a relative who lives far away.

Catholic Social Teaching: Solidarity

OPTIONAL ACTIVITY

Spontaneous Prayer   Children of this age are able to memorize formal prayers, but can also pray in their own words.

• Give children a few quiet moments to talk with God. Ask them to pray for their own needs, or for other people who need help.

Multiple Intelligence: Verbal/Linguistic

DAY 3

Learn to Pray

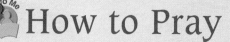

 Focus What special prayer did Jesus give his followers

You can learn songs, words, and actions to talk with God. You can use them to pray any time you wish.

The Church family can learn from the Bible to pray together.

Objective: To conclude that prayer is a way to love God

Open

 Let Us Pray Invite children to pray the psalm verse on page 117 with you.

Focus **What special prayer did Jesus give his followers?** List children's answers on the board or on chart paper.

Build

Learn to Pray
Read aloud Learn to Pray.

- Explain that every generation of Catholics learns certain prayers.

How to Pray
Tell children that the writer of this scripture story tells us about different ways we should pray.

- Proclaim the scripture story.

❓ **What are some ways you pray?** Ask volunteers to share their responses.

✝ **SCRIPTURE** Ephesians 5:18–

How to Pray

Be filled with the Holy Spirit. Sing psalms, hymns, and holy songs. Sing and pray in your hearts. Give thanks always and for everything. Pray to the Father in the name of Jesus Christ.

Based on Ephesians 5:18–20

❓ **What are some ways you pray to God?** Responses will vary.

✝ **SCRIPTURE BACKGROUND**

Ephesians 5 This part of the letter to the Ephesians instructs Christian converts on how to live as followers of Christ.

- The writer stresses that the converts' lives should be filled with prayer.
- They should pray together—and sing together—as a group, but they should also pray individually, in their hearts.

💡 **QUICK TIP**

Offering Blessings Explain to children that when they ask God to bless someone, they are asking him to place that person under his divine care.

- In other words, they are saying, "God, please watch over this person."

The Lord's Prayer

At Mass, you pray a very important prayer called the **Lord's Prayer**.

Jesus taught his friends to pray this way.

The Lord's Prayer

Our Father
who art in heaven,
hallowed be thy name;
thy kingdom come;
thy will be done on earth
   as it is in heaven.
Give us this day our daily bread;
and forgive us our trespasses
as we forgive those who trespass
   against us;
and lead us not into temptation,
but deliver us from evil. Amen.

Activity

Connect Your Faith

Pray Together Who do you pray with?

_____

- -

_____

_____

- -

_____

121

The Lord's Prayer

Read the first paragraph of The Lord's Prayer. Ask children to raise their hands if they have heard of the Lord's Prayer. Explain that the Lord Jesus taught the first Christians this prayer.

- Read the second paragraph and then read the first part of the Lord's Prayer (to "as it is in heaven"). Tell children that since they are friends of Jesus, the Lord's Prayer is for them, too.

- Explain that at every Mass, the Church family stands and prays this prayer aloud.

- Help children understand the words of the prayer by suggesting simple synonyms for any words they do not understand.

Activity

- Discuss praying with other people. Ask children to write who they pray with.

Close

Tell children that Jesus taught his friends how to pray to his Father. The prayer he taught them is called the Lord's Prayer. Christians still say it today.

REACHING ALL LEARNERS

Understanding the Lord's Prayer Explain to the children the difficult words in the first part of the prayer.

- who art—you who are (addressed to God)
- hallowed—called or treated as holy
- thy kingdom—God's rule on the earth
- thy will—what God wants people to do

TEACHER BACKGROUND

The Lord's Prayer This prayer has its roots in Scripture in the Gospels according to Matthew *(Matthew 6:9–13)* and Luke *(Luke 11:2–4)*.

- Jesus teaches a form of this prayer to his disciples. Catholics sometimes refer to this prayer as the Our Father, from its first words. The Lord's Prayer is prayed at Mass and in the Rosary.

Objective: To practice praying the Lord's Prayer

Open

Let Us Pray Invite children to repeat after you the psalm verse from page 117.

Focus **What do we ask for in the Lord's Prayer?** List children's responses on the board or on chart paper.

Build

The Lord's Prayer

Invite children to name some prayers they know by heart.

- Introduce the chart by reading aloud the first paragraph.

- Ask children to follow along as you read aloud the chart, pausing after each phrase of the prayer to read the simplified translation.

- Have children read aloud the text of the Lord's Prayer from the first column of the chart.

❷ **When do you pray the Lord's Prayer?** Discuss the question as a class.

Explore

The Lord's Prayer

Focus **What do we ask for the Lord's Prayer?**

You have learned the first part of the prayer Jesus taught us. Here are the words of the whole prayer. The chart tells what we ask God for when we pray the Lord's Prayer.

Words of the Prayer	What We Ask
Our Father, who art in heaven, hallowed be thy name.	God our Father, may everyone praise your holy name.
Thy kingdom come, thy will be done on earth as it is in heaven.	May the whole world be full of your love. May people do what you ask here on earth as the angels and saints do in heaven.
Give us this day our daily bread;	May we have the things we need today.
and forgive us our trespasses as we forgive those who trespass against us;	Please forgive us for the things we do wrong, and help us forgive those who hurt us.
and lead us not into temptation, but deliver us from evil.	Keep us safe from anything that would harm us or lead us away from you.
Amen!	May it be so!

❷ **When do you pray the Lord's Prayer?**
Responses will vary.

122

Cross-Curricular: Music Play for the children several musical selections of the Lord's Prayer.

- Invite children to develop gestures or dance movements to accompany their favorite musical selection.

Multiple Intelligence: Musical

TEACHER BACKGROUND

Abba Remind children that Jesus called on God the Father, and asked us to do so, too.

- The title Jesus uses in the Gospels is the Aramaic *Abba*, an affectionate nickname similar to "Daddy" or "Papa." This usage demonstrates the close, loving relationship between God the Father and God the Son—a relationship we are called to emulate.

Live Your Faith

Trace the Words Trace the words to complete the Lord's Prayer. See how much of the prayer you can learn by heart.

The Lord's Prayer

Our Father, who art in heaven,

hallowed be thy name.

Thy kingdom come, thy will be

done on earth as it is in heaven.

Give us this day our daily bread; and

forgive us our trespasses as

we forgive those who trespass against us;

and lead us not into temptation, but deliver

us from evil. Amen.

123

- Read aloud the directions to the activity.
- Invite children to join you in reading aloud the prayer before they begin the tracing activity.
- Allow time for children to work independently on the tracing.
- Read aloud the prayer, inviting children to supply the traced words.

Close

Lead children in praying the simplified explanation of the Lord's Prayer, reading aloud from the right column of the chart on page 122.

CHRISTIAN LIVING SKILLS

How to Pray Memorization, or learning by heart, is one of the first prayer skills children learn.

- Committing short traditional prayers and liturgical responses to memory helps children feel a part of the worshiping community, and gives them models for their own spontaneous or self-composed prayers.
- Children's comprehension of memorized prayers will mature as they do.

OPTIONAL ACTIVITY

Prayer Puzzle Have children work together to put the phrases of the Lord's Prayer in order.

- Print each phrase of the prayer on an index card. Shuffle the cards.
- Invite children to put the phrases of the prayer in order by laying the cards out on a desk or table.

and lead us not into temptation

but deliver us from evil

Multiple Intelligence: Verbal/Linguistic

Objective: To praise God in prayer with happy hearts

Prepare

Tell children to think back to the scripture story they heard earlier, in which Christians were told to "give thanks always and for everything." Tell them that they will use the prayer time today to offer God thanks.

• Choose a leader.

 Use the *Call to Faith 1* CD, track 9, to rehearse the song.

Gather

Have children spend a few quiet moments thinking about why they have happy hearts.

Pray

A Prayer of Thanks

 Let Us Pray Follow the order of prayer on page 124.

• Tell children that the opening words of this prayer are said at every Mass.

Celebrate

Prayer of Thanks

 Let Us Pray

Gather and begin with the Sign of the Cross.

Leader: We lift our hearts to the Lord.

All: It is right to give him thanks and praise.

Leader: Take turns telling God why you have a happy heart. We will sing this refrain after each child has prayed.

Sing together the refrain.

For ever I will sing
the goodness of the Lord.

"Psalm 89: For Ever I Will Sing," *Lectionary for Mass* © 1969, 1981, ICEL.

124

 LITURGY LINK

Lifting Hearts Children this age often move when they sing.

• You may have them begin the prayer by putting their hands over their hearts.

• Once the leader has said, "We lift our hearts to the Lord," have children mime "lifting up their hearts" by raising their clasped hands to God as they say the response.

LECTIONARY LINK

Break Open the Word Read last week's Sunday Gospel. Invite children to think about what the reading means to them as they try to follow Christ's example. For questions related to the weekly Gospel reading, visit our Web site at **www.harcourtreligion.com**.

 Visit www.harcourtreligion.com for weekly scripture readings and seasonal resources.

Review

A Work with Words
Fill in each blank with a word from the Word Bank.

WORD BANK

Prayer
Lord's
Father
singing

1. _____ Prayer (p. 117) _____ is talking and listening to God.

2. One name to call God when you pray

   is _____ Father (p. 119) _____ .

3. Jesus taught his friends to pray the

   _____ Lord's (p.121) _____ Prayer.

4. You can pray by

   _____ singing (p. 120) _____ .

B Check Understanding
Circle ways to pray.

125

Review

A Work with Words
Ask children to fill in the blanks with words from the Word Bank.

B Check Understanding
Have children circle the correct answers.

Assessment

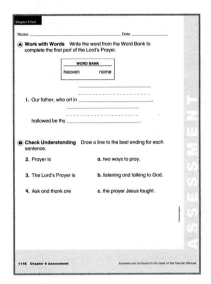

▲ **Chapter 9 Test**
page 117E

Answers to the Chapter Test can be found in the back of the Teacher Manual.

TEACHER BACKGROUND

Different Gestures Children will be familiar with clasping their hands together in prayer, but may not realize that other gestures may be used. Holding one's hands up towards the heavens while praying, as is often done during the recitation of the Our Father at Mass, is another method you may wish to describe to the class.

OPTIONAL ACTIVITY

Blessings Asking God to bless is a wonderful form of prayer. You might want to have children write their own book of blessing prayers.

- You could have them make up daily blessings such as brushing their teeth or playing with their friends. In this way, they are offering what they do during the day to God.

Multiple Intelligence: Verbal/Linguistic

HOME CONNECTION

Family Faith

Remind children to discuss the Family Faith page at home. Encourage children to read the scripture passage from the Gospel according to John.

- Tell children that the activity calls for them to write a family prayer with the help of the rest of their family.

People of Faith

Tell children about Father Frederick William Faber.

- Frederick was a wonderful preacher. It is mainly as a hymn-writer that he is remembered. He wrote many pamphlets and translations, and published many books.

- Remind children to add Father Frederick William Faber to their People of Faith albums.

- Encourage them to pray the prayer at home with their families.

 Visit **www.harcourtreligion.com** for weekly scripture readings and seasonal resources.

Unit 3: CHAPTER 9
Family Faith

Catholics Believe

- Prayer is talking and listening to God.
- Jesus taught his friends how to pray the Lord's Prayer.

SCRIPTURE

Read John 17:1–25 to see how Jesus prayed to the Father.

www.harcourtreligion.com For weekly Scripture readings and seasonal resources

Activity
Live Your Faith

Write Prayers Choose a time to pray each day as a family. Always pray the Lord's Prayer. Write another prayer that you can say together. Here is an example.

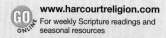

Dear _____, (Add name for God.)
Thank you for _____.
We ask you to _____.
We ask you in the name of Jesus, your Son.
Amen

People of Faith

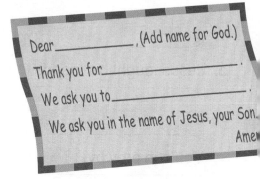

▲ Frederick William Faber, 1814–1863

Frederick was born in Yorkshire, England. After reading and listening to others about the Catholic Church, he became a Catholic. He wrote books about prayers. He gave the Church many hymns by writing the words for music that others wrote. His most famous hymn is "Faith of Our Fathers." Frederick began a religious community of men and was ordained as a Catholic priest.

Family Pray

God our Father, help us sing our praises to you daily. Help us love you as Frederick did. Amen.

In Unit 3 your child is learning about JESUS CHRIST.
126 **CCC** *See Catechism of the Catholic Church 2607–2612 for further reading on chapter content.*

? HOW DID I DO?

This week my religion classes were

☐ *some of the best ever!* ☐ *pretty good.* ☐ *in need of improvement.*

In what discussions and activities were children most interested?

_____

What activity did I most enjoy teaching?

_____

In what area do I need to improve?

_____

Name _____ Date _____

A Prayer Card

Draw a picture of something you are thankful for.

Trace the words of thanks to God.

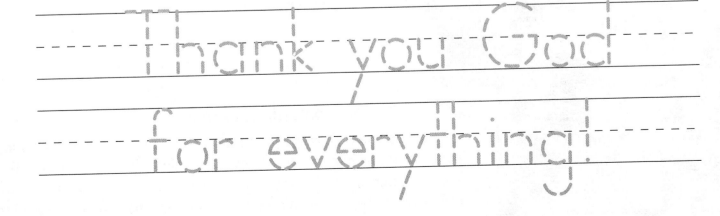

Thank you God
for everything!

Seven Principles of CATHOLIC SOCIAL TEACHING

- Care for God's Creation
- Life and Dignity of the Human Person
- **Rights and Responsibilities of the Human Person**
- Dignity of Work and the Rights of Workers
- Solidarity of the Human Family
- Call to Family, Community, and Participation
- Option for the Poor and Vulnerable

Faith in Action!
CATHOLIC SOCIAL TEACHING

Connect to Unit 3

This unit's Faith in Action feature teaches first graders the principle of peaceful conflict resolution as a tool for protecting human rights. It connects to topics covered in this unit.

Children learned that
- Jesus healed people.
- they are called to show love for God and others.
- they can help work for God's kingdom of peace and love.

Discover Catholic Social Teaching

Principle: Rights and Responsibilities of the Human Person

An American legal aphorism notes that "your individual rights stop at my nose." That's a simple way of summarizing the problems that occur when rights and responsibilities conflict. The rights we have as humans created in God's image are universal but not absolute, because we are also created to live in community, honoring one another's rights and working for the common good. When conflicts arise—as they inevitably will—we are called to use peaceful means to resolve them.

Catholic tradition calls us
- to recognize and respect the rights of each person.
- to take responsibility for protecting others' rights.
- to resolve conflicts peacefully whenever possible.

Reflect *How can you model for children a commitment to peaceful conflict resolution?*

Catholic Social Teaching Document

" . . . duties find their source, their sustenance and their inviolability in the natural law which grants or enjoins them. Those, therefore, who claim their own rights, yet altogether forget or neglect to carry out their respective duties, are people who build with one hand and destroy with the other. . . "

From *Pacem in Terris (Peace on Earth)*, Encyclical Letter of Pope John XXIII, 1963

DISCOVER

Catholic Social
ing:
s and
nsibilities of
uman Person

Faith in Action!
CATHOLIC SOCIAL TEACHING

In this unit you learned that Jesus cared for all people. He called people to work for God's kingdom of peace and love.

Rights and Responsibilities

Have you ever listened to a choir sing? Some people sing high notes. Some people sing low notes. When they sing together in the right way, they make harmony. Harmony is a beautiful blend of different sounds.

People are like singers in a choir. Each person has rights, things that he or she can do freely. Each person also has to protect other people's rights. When everyone's rights are protected, we live in peace. We make the beautiful harmony of God's kingdom.

❷ **What are some things that keep people from living in harmony?**

Possible responses: fighting, stealing, war

127

DISCOVER

Catholic Social Teaching

Let Us Pray Jesus, you are the Prince of Peace. Help us live with one another peaceably and respect one another's rights.

Faith in Action
Read aloud the first paragraph.

• Ask children to describe God's kingdom in their own words.

Rights and Responsibilities
Write the word *harmony* on the board or on chart paper, and have children speculate about its meaning.

• Ask children to listen carefully as you read these two paragraphs aloud.

• Review briefly the comparison between singers in a choir and people in society, making sure children understand the similarities.

❷ **What are some things that keep people from living in harmony?**
Discuss the question as a class.

TEACHER BACKGROUND

Pacem in Terris In 1963, Pope John XXIII wrote an encyclical on world peace called *Pacem in Terris* (*Peace on Earth*). The pope's letter summed up the essential rights of every person, and called on governments and individuals to take responsibility for securing these rights. Only when people's needs are met, Pope John XXIII argued, will peace truly be possible.

OPTIONAL ACTIVITY

Cross-Curricular: Music Play for children recordings of choirs or choruses singing in harmony.

• Ask children to listen for the different musical parts working together.

• As an alternative, invite the parish music minister or choir director to teach the class a hymn with simple harmony.

Multiple Intelligence: Musical

CONNECT

With the Call to Justice

Kelly Steps In

Direct attention to the pictures, and ask children to predict what they think will happen in the story.

• Invite children to listen carefully as you read aloud the story.

❷ **How do you think Kelly helped Paul and Alex?** Discuss the question as a class. You may wish to have children role-play the story as a way of brainstorming possible resolutions.

CONNECT

With the Call to Justice

Jesus calls us to live in harmony with all people. Let's look at how the students at one school are working to build harmony.

Kelly Steps In

Paul and Alex are fighting over who is first in line. It starts with words. Then Alex pushes Paul. Paul pushes back.

Mr. Lin quickly breaks up the fight. He asks the boys to sit at a table. Then he calls Kelly, an eighth grader.

Kelly sits with Paul and Alex. She listens to both boys. She lets Paul and Alex work things out. After talking, they shake hands.

Kelly and other students at Cohoes Catholic School in New York help other students. They teach students to work out problems. This is a way to protect the rights of students to a peaceful day.

❷ **How do you think Kelly helped Paul and Alex?** Possible responses: She gave them time to think about their problem. She taught them to find different ways to get along.

128

TEACHER BACKGROUND

Conflict Resolution The story on this page is a fictionalized presentation of a typical situation addressed by the peer mediation program at Cohoes Catholic School in New York.

QUICK TIP

Peacemaking Share with children ideas from these books on conflict resolution:

• *Peacefulness* by Lucia Raatma (Bridgestone Books, 2000)

• *How to Turn War into Peace: A Child's Guide to Conflict Resolution* by Louise Armstrong (Harcourt Brace Jovanovich, 1979)

Reach Out!

Bring Harmony

Pretend that you are like Kelly. Read about the following problem. With a partner, talk about how you could help bring harmony.

The Problem

Emma brought a new game to school. She played against Jai at lunch, and Jai won. After lunch, Emma couldn't find her game. She told the teacher that Jai must have taken her game. Jai says he didn't steal it.

Make a Difference

Protect Rights Think about your class. What rights do first graders have? Make a list on a separate sheet of paper. Then talk about ways you can protect the rights of everyone in your class.

1.

2.

3.

129

SERVE

Your Community
Reach Out!

Bring Harmony

> **Activity**

- Read aloud the directions.
- Have children choose partners, and read aloud the problem.
- Give pairs time to develop their ideas on resolving the conflict.
- Invite volunteers to share their ideas. Have the class vote on the best resolution.

Make a Difference

> **Activity**

- Read aloud the directions.
- Brainstorm rights and how to protect them, listing children's ideas on the board or on chart paper.

Encourage children to share what they have learned with friends, family members, and other classes.

QUICK TIP

Classroom Connections Put ideas about conflict resolution into practice in the classroom.

- See *Tired of Yelling: Teaching Our Children to Resolve Conflict* by Lyndon D. Waugh (Longstreet, 1999) for practical suggestions.
- Invite peer counselors from diocesan or parish programs to visit the class and answer questions.

OPTIONAL ACTIVITY

Make Posters Have children make posters promoting respect for others' rights.

- Provide children with art materials.
- Have children choose rights and how to protect them from the list on the board or on chart paper to feature in their posters.

Multiple Intelligence: Visual/Spatial

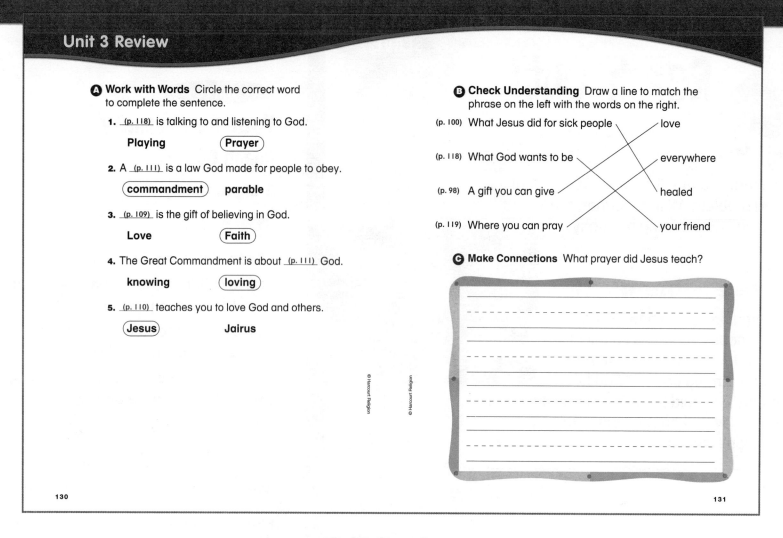

A Work with Words Circle the correct word to complete the sentence.

1. _(p. 118)_ is talking to and listening to God.

   Playing   (Prayer)

2. A _(p. 111)_ is a law God made for people to obey.

   (commandment)   parable

3. _(p. 109)_ is the gift of believing in God.

   Love   (Faith)

4. The Great Commandment is about _(p. 111)_ God.

   knowing   (loving)

5. _(p. 110)_ teaches you to love God and others.

   (Jesus)   Jairus

© Harcourt Religion

B Check Understanding Draw a line to match the phrase on the left with the words on the right.

(p. 100) What Jesus did for sick people ———— love

(p. 118) What God wants to be ———— everywhere

(p. 98) A gift you can give ———— healed

(p. 119) Where you can pray ———— your friend

C Make Connections What prayer did Jesus teach?

© Harcourt Religion

130

131

Unit Review

The Unit Review is designed to prepare children for the Unit Assessment. Have children complete the Review pages. Then discuss the answers as a class. You may wish to review any concepts with which children are having difficulty before the Unit Assessment.

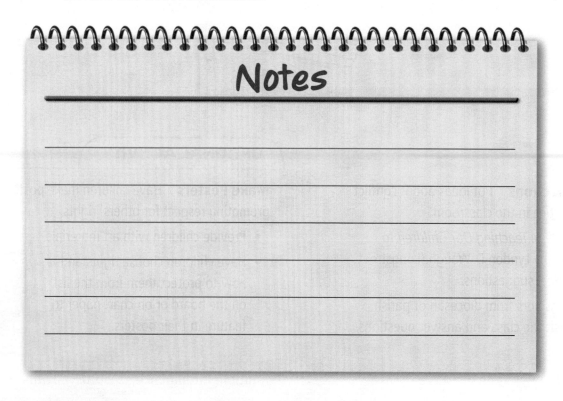

Notes

Name _____ Date _____

Ⓐ Work with Words   Write the word from the Word Bank that best completes the sentence.

WORD BANK
Great
Our Father
law

1. The _____
Commandment tells you to love God
and other people.

2. The Lord's Prayer is also called the _____.

3. A commandment is a _____ that God made.

Ⓑ Check Understanding   Draw a line from each picture to the best title.

4. talking and listening to God

Jesus

5. the one who taught the Lord's Prayer

prayer

6. Jesus' healing actions

God's power and love

©Harcourt Religion

Name _____ Date _____

ⓒ Make Connections   Trace the words to answer the questions.

7. What is one way to show love for others?

8. How should you love God?

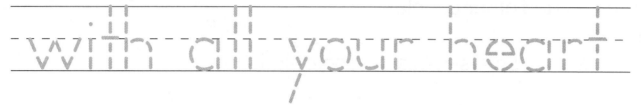

9. How should you love others?

10. What is the gift of believing in God?

©Harcourt Religion

ASSESSMENT

Answers can be found in the back of the Teacher Manual.

UNIT 4
The Church

Chapter 10 **Say "Yes" to God**
What is God's kingdom?

Chapter 11 **The Holy Spirit**
What does the Spirit do?

Chapter 12 **Holy People**
Who are the saints?

Faith in Action! Catholic Social Teaching Principle:
Dignity of Work and Rights
of Workers

132

© Harcourt Religion

UNIT 4 OPENER

Preview Unit Content

Tell children that Unit 4 is about the Catholic Church.

- Invite a volunteer to read aloud the chapter title and question for Chapter 10. Ask children what they think they will learn in this chapter.

- Repeat this for Chapters 11 and 12.

- Tell children that at the end of the unit they will learn how the parishes in one town showed respect for workers.

Say "Yes" to God

CHAPTER BACKGROUND

Faith Focus

- Through Jesus, God invites everyone into his kingdom. *(CCC 541–545, 551)*
- The Church is made up of those people who say "yes" to God's gracious offer of salvation in Jesus. *(CCC 781–782, 837)*

Catechism Connection

The *Catechism* repeatedly asserts that the Church is "the seed and beginning" of the kingdom of God on earth. *(CCC 541, 768–769, 778)*

GDC Link

As the *Directory* notes, Jesus proclaimed that the kingdom of God is for everyone. Jesus sent forth his disciples to preach the Gospel "to all nations." *(GDC 163)*

 By faith Noah, warned about what was not yet seen, with reverence built an ark for the salvation of his household.

Hebrews 11:7

Believing

Trust and loyalty are the crucial virtues of many great figures of Scripture. Despite being surrounded by great animosity and disbelief, Noah trusted the Lord and built an ark as he had been commanded. Abraham's fierce loyalty and faith in God led him to the point where he was about to sacrifice his son, because he had been told by an angel that God wanted him to. Despite his bodily weaknesses, Moses led the Israelites out of Egypt in response to God's call. Mary, the mother of Jesus, said "yes" when God called on her. Jesus himself gave his life to reconcile all people with God.

An Invitation

Open up the newspaper and you may feel like burying your head in the sand. The world isn't exactly a picture of peace. When you stand alone, the society mirrored in the media is frightening. However, God does not ask you to wade through troubled times by yourself. Instead, he invites you to be a part of a community that says "yes"—yes to faith, yes to sharing his love with one another. With the support of the faith community, you can live in the peace of the kingdom of God.

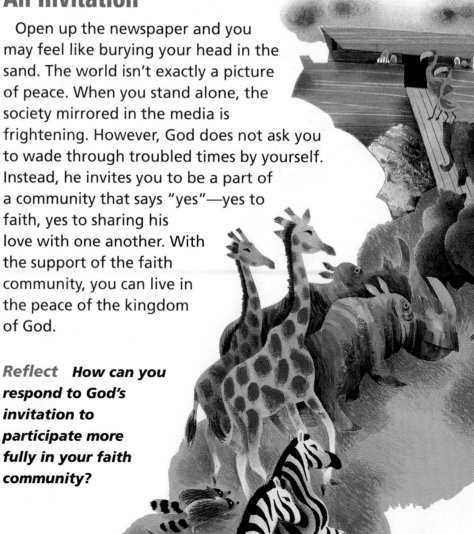

Reflect **How can you respond to God's invitation to participate more fully in your faith community?**

Discipleship

Introduce children to their discipleship—saying "yes" to living as Jesus did.

- Young children like the word *yes* and want to hear it all the time. But saying "yes" to God differs from Mom saying, "Yes, you can have an extra cookie." Saying "yes" to God does not even involve using the word *yes* —it means making the choice to act as God wills us to.

- Analogies will help children understand the concept. You may say, "Your dad wants you to make your bed every day. You make your bed without your dad asking you. You don't complain. Making your bed is like saying, 'Yes, Dad, I love you. I will obey you.'"

- Use the metaphor of saying "yes" to affirm children and to reinforce the concept of discipleship. For example, you may say, "Working nicely with your partner is a good way to say 'yes' to God."

Willingness

- I learn best when I'm actively involved.

- I enjoy helping people. Show me how helping others is a way of following Jesus.

- I want to be good, although there are times when my first impulse is to say "no" to a request.

Motivations

Many things probably motivated you to enter into the catechetical ministry. At the center of all ministry is a call from God to love and serve him and his Church. The love for Christ and others drives and motivates you to share the good news and work for the kingdom. Take time to think about what else motivated you to become a catechist. The process of naming and claiming the authentic motivations behind your commitment as a catechist can deepen your understanding of your role. Even motivations that may not seem ideal are important to examine.

Reflect **What motivations fuel your spirit to teach?**

Teacher's Prayer

Yes, Lord, yes! I welcome the opportunity to share your love with the children you have entrusted to me. Amen.

Weekly Planner

		Objective	Materials	Prayer & Scripture
DAY 1 Invite	**Say "Yes" to God** Page 133	**Objective:** *To enumerate experiences of saying "yes"*	☐ Pencils	🙌 Let Us Pray *Psalm 57:11*
DAY 2 Explore	**A Promise** Pages 134–135	**Objective:** *To examine one example of a person who said "yes" to God*	☐ Board or chart paper ☐ Art supplies ☐ CD of soothing music ☐ Simple musical instruments	🙌 Let Us Pray *Psalm 57:11* ✝ **Scripture:** *Genesis 6:14–22, 7:1–23* ✝ **Scripture Background:** Covenant, p. 134
DAY 3 Explore	**The Invitation** Pages 136–137	**Objective:** *To explain what it means to say "yes" to God*	☐ Board or chart paper ☐ Crayons ☐ Copies of Activity Master 10, p. 142A ☐ Index cards ☐ Pencils	🙌 Let Us Pray *Psalm 57:11* ✝ **Scripture:** *Luke 14:16–23* ✝ **Scripture Background:** Kingdom of God, p.136
DAY 4 Explore	**Mary's Story** Pages 138–139	**Objective:** *To identify Mary as a model of faith*	☐ Board or chart paper ☐ Art supplies ☐ Art resources ☐ Music CD	🙌 Let Us Pray *Psalm 57:11*
DAY 5 Celebrate	**"Yes" Prayer** Page 140	**Objective:** *To say "yes" to God in prayer*	☐ Tambourines ☐ Hymnals ☐ Music CD	🙌 Let Us Pray **"Yes" Prayer** 🎵 **Hymn:** "I Say 'Yes,' Lord/Digo 'Sí,' Señor"

Chapter 10 Wrap-Up: Review and Apply p. 141 • Chapter 10 Assessment p. 133E

Words of Faith

kingdom of God

Church

Activities	Enrichment
Let's Begin: Saying "Yes," p. 133 Multiple Intelligence: Interpersonal	• **Quick Tip:** Vocabulary: Faithfulness, p. 133
Share Your Faith: Think, Share, Act, p. 135 Multiple Intelligence: Verbal/Linguistic (OPTIONAL) Many Ways to Say "Yes," p. 134 Multiple Intelligence: Verbal/Linguistic (OPTIONAL) Rainbow of Friends, p. 135 Multiple Intelligence: Interpersonal (OPTIONAL) Noah Lyrics, p. 135 Multiple Intelligence: Musical	
Connect Your Faith: God Calls You, p. 137 Multiple Intelligence: Visual/Spatial (OPTIONAL) Activity Master 10: Kingdom of God, p. 136 Multiple Intelligence: Visual/Spatial	• **Reaching All Learners:** Whom Does God Love?, p. 137 • **Quick Tip:** Graphic Organizer, p. 137
Live Your Faith: Draw Pictures, p. 139 Multiple Intelligence: Visual/Spatial (OPTIONAL) Cross-Curricular: Art, p. 138 Multiple Intelligence: Visual/Spatial	• **Teacher Background:** The Annunciation, p. 138 • **Christian Living Skills:** Keeping Promises, p. 139 • **Quick Tip:** The Hail Mary, p. 139
	• **Liturgy Link:** Praying as One, p. 140 • **Lectionary Link:** Break Open the Word, p. 140

Multimedia Resources

 BOOK
Magliano, Tony. *The Moonlight Miracle.*
Paulist Press. 2000. All people are part
of one human family.

 VIDEO
*Sealed with God's Spirit: A Child's View
of Community* (30 min). Catholic
Update Video. The community of faith
as seen through children's eyes.

 GO ONLINE Teacher Resources
www.harcourtreligion.com
• **For interactive lesson planner, chapter
resources, and activities**
• **For free materials and information**

Home Connection
Chapter 10 Family Faith, p. 142
Take-home activities, chapter content
review, saint features and prayer

 GO ONLINE For more family activities
www.harcourtreligion.com

Name _____ Date _____

(A) Work with Words   Circle the word that best completes each sentence.

1. Noah said _____ to God's invitation.

no   **yes**

2. Sharing _____ is a way to say yes to God.

sadness   **love**

3. The _____ tells people about God and his kingdom.

Church   **ark**

(B) Check Understanding   Draw a line to the best ending for each sentence.

4. The kingdom of God is

   a. the world of love, peace, and justice that God wants.

5. God invites all people

   b. into his kingdom.

©Harcourt Religion

Answers can be found in the back of the Teacher Manual.

ASSESSMENT

Chapter 10 Say "Yes" to God

 Let Us Pray

Leader: God help us say yes to your invitation.
"For your love towers to the heavens;
your faithfulness, to the skies."
Psalm 57:11

All: God help us say yes to your invitation.
Amen.

Activity — Let's Begin

● **Saying "Yes"** We have many choices to make every day.

Mark an X beside the questions to which you can answer "yes."

_____ Would you like to bake a cake?

_____ Would you help rake the leaves?

_____ Would you please pass out the papers?

_____ Have you fed the dog?

_____ Did you clean your room?

Talk About It In a small group, talk about times when it is hard to say "yes."

133

QUICK TIP

Vocabulary: Faithfulness Children may not be familiar with the word *faithfulness* that appears in the psalm verse. This is not a difficult word for children to pronounce, but you can explain its meaning in simple terms.

- To say that God shows faithfulness means that his love for them is constant and lasting. He continues to love them, even when they do wrong.

Objective: To enumerate experiences of saying "yes"

Open

Prayer Space Invite children to move to your classroom prayer space. In the prayer space, have a crucifix and a Bible opened to the psalm

Let Us Pray Pray the psalm verse and ask children to pray the response.

Build

Activity

- Read aloud Saying "Yes."
- Ask children for examples of other questions. Possible responses: Did you finish your homework? Would you like a cookie?
- Allow children time to mark the questions.

Extension Activity

- Divide children into small groups.
- Ask them to discuss when it is hard to say "yes."

Close

Have children tell what they learned about saying "yes."

Objective: To examine one example of a person who said "yes" to God

Open

 Let Us Pray Invite children to pray the psalm verse found on page 133 with you.

Focus **What did God promise Noah?** List children's answers on the board or on chart paper.

Build

A Promise

Tell children that God wants us to choose to say "yes" to him.

• Ask children to gather and to listen for what God asked Noah to do.

Noah Says "Yes"

Proclaim the scripture story.

• Instruct children to say "Yes, I will!" during the reading whenever you point to them.

❷ **What did God ask Noah to do?** Write all responses on the board or on chart paper.

Explore

A Promise

Focus **What did God promise Noah?**

The story of Noah is in the Old Testament. Noah said "yes" when God asked him a very big question.

✝ S C R I P T U R E   Genesis 6:14–22, 7:1–

📖 Noah Says "Yes"

Noah was a good man. God told Noah to build an ark, or very large boat.

God said it was going to rain for forty days and forty nights. There would be a flood. God wanted Noah to be safe.

Noah said, "Yes, I will!" He built the ark even though he saw no rain anywhere.

God told Noah to take his family and two of each kind of animal into the ark. Noah, his family, and all the animals said, "Yes, we will!" and went into the ark.

❷ **What did God ask Noah to do?**
Possible responses: to build the ark; to stay on the ark with his family and the animals

134

OPTIONAL ACTIVITY

Many Ways to Say "Yes" If you have bilingual students or children for whom English is their secondary language, let them teach everyone how to say "yes" in their language.

• Teach the class how to say "yes" in Spanish, *sí* (see) or French, *oui* (we).

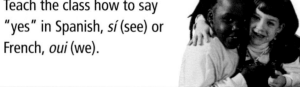

Multiple Intelligence: Verbal/Linguistic

✝ S C R I P T U R E   B A C K G R O U N D

Covenant The story of Noah is the story of God's first covenant with humans. In making a covenant, he binds himself by a promise to his people.

• After the great flood, God promises Noah and his family never again to destroy creation by a flood.

• God put the rainbow in the sky as a sign of his covenant.

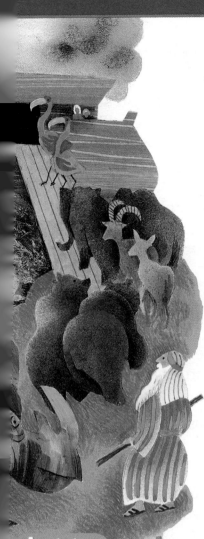

The Flood

Then the rains came. The streams and the rivers swelled until they flooded all the earth. Noah, his family, and all the animals stayed dry in the ark.

After forty days, the rain stopped. God promised that water would never flood the whole earth again.

God gave Noah and his family a sign of his promise. God put a rainbow in the sky.

Based on Genesis 6:14–22, 7:1–23

❷ Why were Noah, his family, and the animals safe?

Possible responses: They were in the ark; God was taking care of them.

Activity
Share Your Faith

Think: Think about how Noah felt when he saw God's rainbow.

Share: Talk with a partner about God's promise.

Act: Color a beautiful rainbow. Write "God's Promise" on the page. Work together to plan a class bulletin board. Use your rainbow pictures.

135

The Flood

Proclaim the conclusion of the scripture story. Then ask the question at the end of the story. Possible responses: because they said "yes" to God; they trusted him to care for them; they knew he loved them wherever they are.

- Ask children what they will think of when they see a rainbow in the sky. Answers will vary.

❷ Why were Noah, his family, and the animals safe? Ask volunteers to share their responses.

Activity

- Play soothing music if possible while the activity is being completed. Allow children time to color.

Close

Explain that God promised Noah he would never again destroy the earth by a flood. The rainbow was a sign of that promise.

OPTIONAL ACTIVITY

Rainbow of Friends Use the image of the rainbow to teach the goodness of diversity. Using mural paper, have children paint a large rainbow together. Have each child paint a self-portrait on a small paper plate. Hang the rainbow mural, and have children add their portraits to it.

Multiple Intelligence: Interpersonal

OPTIONAL ACTIVITY

Noah Lyrics Have children devise lyrics about Noah to fit the familiar tune "Old MacDonald Had a Farm."

- Provide simple instruments to accompany the lyrics.
- You may want to begin with "God told Noah, 'build an ark' . . ."

Multiple Intelligence: Musical

Say "Yes" to God   135

Objective: To explain what it means to say "yes" to God

Open

 Let Us Pray Invite children to pray the psalm verse found on page 133 with you.

Focus **How do you say "yes" to God?** List children's answers on the board or on chart paper.

Build

The Invitation

Read the paragraph aloud.

• Have one child read the definition of *kingdom of God* under Words of Faith. Hold up an index card of the words *kingdom of God*.

Come Join Me

Proclaim the scripture story.

❷ **Who is the rich man in the story like?** Invite volunteers to share their answers.

Explore

The Invitation

Focus **How do you say "yes" to God?**

Jesus told a story about God's care for all people. In the story, everyone is invited into the **kingdom of God**.

 SCRIPTURE Luke 14:16

Come Join Me

A rich man gave a big party. He invited many people. No one came.

The rich man spoke to his servants. "Go out and invite those who are poor, blind, and lame."

The servants did as the man asked. Soon the house was filled with happy people. There still was room for more people.

The rich man said, "Go and find people anywhere you can. Ask them to come to my party."

Based on Luke 14:16–23

❷ **Who is the rich man in this story like?** Possible response: God the Father

136

OPTIONAL ACTIVITY

Activity Master 10: Kingdom of God Distribute copies of the activity on teacher page 142A.

• As an alternative, you may wish to send this activity home with children.

▲ **Activity Master 10 page 142A**

SCRIPTURE BACKGROUND

Kingdom of God Explain that the kingdom of God is not the name of a place or country.

• God's kingdom exists wherever people recognize him as their king by doing what is right and just, and by loving others.

• When they act as God wants them to, they are signs that his kingdom is starting to arrive.

The Church

The **Church** shares Jesus' message about God's kingdom.

You became a member of the Church when you were baptized. Your parents said "yes" to God for you. Now you can say "yes" for yourself.

You share love as a member of the Church. You help the kingdom of God to grow.

You can invite others into God's kingdom. You can ask them to say "yes" to God, too.

Activity

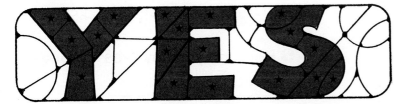

 God Calls You God calls you into his kingdom. What do you say? Color the spaces that have stars to find the answer.

137

The Church

Tell children that there were servants, or helpers, in the story Jesus told. Tell them the rich man asked the servants to go gather everyone in.

- Explain to children that the members of the Church are like the servants in the story. Tell them God sends out the people who make up the Church to invite everyone to his kingdom.
- Read aloud The Church.
- Hold up the *Church* index card.
- Draw the graphic organizer on the board or on chart paper.
- Ask children to name specific ways in which they can share God's love.
- Write children's answers around the graphic organizer.

Activity

- Read the instructions to children and provide crayons.
- Allow them time to complete the activity.

Close

Tell children that God invites everyone into his kingdom. The job of the Church is to carry this invitation to all people.

★ REACHING ALL LEARNERS

Whom Does God Love? Your group may include children who have not yet been baptized, or who have a non-Catholic parent.

- You should make it clear that God loves everyone, including the many people who do not belong to the Catholic Church.

QUICK TIP

Graphic Organizer

Say "Yes" to God

Objective: To identify Mary as a model of faith

Open

Let Us Pray Invite children to repeat after you the psalm verse from page 133.

Focus **How did Mary answer God's question?** List children's responses on the board or on chart paper.

Build

Mary's Story

Help children recall that Mary is the mother of Jesus.

- Read aloud the first sentence, and help children connect the picture of Mary with her name.

- Read aloud the picture story through the next-to-last line, pausing at each picture to allow children to supply the appropriate word.

- Read aloud the last line, inviting children to read aloud the word *Yes*.

❓ **How can you say "yes" to God?** Allow time for children to respond.

Explore

Mary's Story

Focus **How did Mary answer God's question?**

KEY

angel

baby

Mary

question ❓

God asked Mary to do something hard, just as God had asked Noah. Here is Mary's story.

One day was praying.

An came to see her.

The was God's messenger.

The told that God had a ❓ for her.

He wanted to have a .

This would be very special.

This would be God's Son.

 loved God very much.

The asked what he should tell God.

And said, "Tell God YES!"

❓ **How can you say "yes" to God?**
Responses will vary.

138

OPTIONAL ACTIVITY

Cross-Curricular: Art Show children examples of art depicting the Annunciation from various historical periods and cultural traditions.

- Use art books, slides, or Web sites to share examples with children.

- Invite children to create their own artistic interpretations of this incident in Mary's life.

Multiple Intelligence: Visual/Spatial

✝ **SCRIPTURE BACKGROUND**

The Annunciation The story on this page is based on the account in Luke 1:26–38.

- The archangel Gabriel is mentioned in the Old Testament Book of Daniel, where he appears in a vision to announce the coming of the One who will bring the kingdom.

- The Church celebrates the Feast of the Annunciation on March 25, nine months before Christmas.

✏️ **Draw Pictures** In the top box, draw a scene from the story of Noah or the story of Mary. In the bottom box, draw a picture of a way you say "yes" to God.

They Said "Yes"

I Say "Yes"

139

-134• ead aloud the directions for the drawing activity.

• Ask volunteers to read aloud the titles for the two picture boxes.

• Distribute art materials, and allow time for children to work independently on their drawings.

• Invite volunteers to share and explain their drawings.

Close

Lead the class in singing "I Say Yes, My Lord/Digo Sí, Señor."

-130### ✋ CHRISTIAN LIVING SKILLS

Keeping Promises The Church honors Mary not simply because she said "yes" to God at the Annunciation, but because she remained true to that commitment throughout her life. Help children see the importance of keeping good promises.

• Remind children that their families helped them say "yes" to God in Baptism, and they can continue to say "yes" to God every day.

💡 QUICK TIP

The Hail Mary Use the story of the Annunciation as an opportunity to reinforce the children's learning of the Hail Mary.

• Explain that the first line of the prayer ("Hail, Mary, full of grace, the Lord is with you") is based on the archangel Gabriel's greeting to Mary.

-124Say "Yes" to God   **139**

Prepare

Choose four leaders, one to say each of the lines labeled Leader. Allow time for children to practice.

 Use the *Call to Faith 1* CD, track 10, to rehearse the song.

Gather

Gather in the prayer space. Have everyone hold hands except for the leaders, who will hold their books.

Pray

"Yes" Prayer

 Let Us Pray Follow the order of prayer on page 140.

- Invite children to add their own prayers.

- Leader's prayer: **Heavenly Father, help us follow the examples of Noah and Mary, so that we may always say "yes" to you.**

- Optional music from *Singing Our Faith:* "You Are My Shepherd," #197.

Yes Prayer

 Let Us Pray

Gather and begin with the Sign of the Cross.

Leader: Lord, you ask us to be kind to our families.

All: We say "yes!"

Leader: You ask us to share what we have.

All: We say "yes!"

Leader: You want us to ask everyone to play.

All: We say "yes!"

Leader Let us pray.
  Bow your heads as the leader prays.

All: Amen.

Sing together the refrain.

I say "Yes," my Lord.
I say "Yes," my Lord,
in all the good times,
through all the bad times,
I say "Yes," my Lord,
to ev'ry word you speak.

"I Say 'Yes,' Lord/Digo 'Sí,' Señor," Donna Peña ©1989, GIA Publications, Inc.

140

LITURGY LINK

Praying as One It can be a powerful experience when a group prays with one voice.

- Have children practice saying the response together.

- You may want to have children beat tambourines after each response.

LECTIONARY LINK

Break Open the Word Read last week's Sunday Gospel. Invite children to think about what the reading means to them as they try to follow Christ's example. For questions related to the weekly Gospel reading, visit our Web site at **www.harcourtreligion.com**.

 Visit www.harcourtreligion.com for weekly scripture readings and seasonal resources.

Ⓐ Work with Words Circle the correct word to complete each sentence.

1. God wants you to say "__(p. 133)__" to him.

   no   **(yes)**

2. Noah said "__(p. 134)__" to God's invitation.

   (yes)   **no**

3. God invites __(p. 136)__ people into his kingdom.

   (all)   **some**

4. Being __(p. 137)__ is a way of saying "yes" to God.

   (kind)   **unfair**

5. The story of the rich man was told by __(p. 136)__.

   Noah   **(Jesus)**

6. God put a __(p. 135)__ in the sky as a sign to Noah.

   bird   **(rainbow)**

Ⓑ Make Connections Choose ways to say "yes" to God. Mark an X in front of your choices.

__X__ Pray with your family.

__X__ Take care of a brother or sister.

_____ Fight with your parents.

__X__ Take the newspaper to a neighbor.

__X__ Care for a neighbor's pet.

_____ Tease a younger child.

141

Review

Ⓐ Work with Words Ask children to complete the sentences by circling the correct words.

Ⓑ Make Connections Ask children to choose ways to say "yes" to God by marking an X in front of their choices.

Assessment

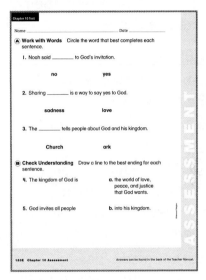

▲ **Chapter 10 Test page 133E**

Answers to the Chapter Test can be found in the back of the Teacher Manual.

✚ JUSTICE AND PEACE

Participation God calls everyone to help make the world a better place. People have a duty to act together in society to make life better for everyone, especially the poor. A "yes" response to God begins in the home. It is here that children first learn to cooperate with others to achieve the common good.

Catholic Social Teaching: Call to Community

OPTIONAL ACTIVITY

Silence Is Golden The children have learned many ways to say "yes" in this chapter; you may wish to lead them in a discussion of how people can communicate that response without speaking.

• Ask them if they can think of ways to say "yes" silently—by nodding, giving a thumbs-up or OK sign with their hands, even by smiling.

Multiple Intelligence: Bodily/Kinesthetic

Family Faith

Remind children to discuss the Family Faith page at home. Encourage children to read the scripture passage from the Gospel according to Matthew.

Activity

• Explain that children's families get to choose a way to say "yes" to God. Remind children to encourage their families to make a choice.

People of Faith

Tell children about Blessed Mother Theresa of the Child Jesus.

• Mother Theresa's order started their work in the United States in Pennsylvania. They educated girls in elementary schools and also in orphanages. The sisters also trained future teachers.

• Remind children to add Blessed Mother Theresa of the Child Jesus to their People of Faith albums.

• Encourage them to pray the prayer at home with their families.

 Visit **www.harcourtreligion.com** for weekly scripture readings and seasonal resources.

 Unit 4: CHAPTER 10

Family Faith

◉ Catholics Believe

■ God invites everyone into his kingdom.

■ The Church is people who follow Jesus and say "yes" to God's call.

✝ SCRIPTURE

Read Matthew 4:18–22 to find out about ways the first Apostles said "yes" to God.

 www.harcourtreligion.com For weekly Scripture readings and seasonal resources

Activity

Live Your Faith

Say "Yes" As a family, say "yes" to God. Here are some ideas.
• Volunteer to present the gifts at Mass.
• Introduce yourselves to a new family at Sunday Mass.
• Greet workers by name at the supermarket, restaurants, or at a park.

People of Faith

Caroline was born in Germany. During college she studied to be a teacher. Later she founded an order of nuns. They taught young girls in Germany. The new order of nuns was called the School Sisters of Notre Dame. Caroline's name as a sister was Mother Theresa of the Child Jesus. The sisters started kindergartens and schools in Germany and the United States. Theresa is a patron of Catholic education. The Church celebrates her feast day on May 9.

▲ **Blessed Mother Theresa of the Child Jesus 1797–1879**

🙌 Family Pray

Dear God, help us appreciate our parish workers and teachers. Thank you for the love they show. Amen.

In Unit 4 your child is learning about the CHURCH.
142 **CCC** *See Catechism of the Catholic Church 541–546 for further reading on chapter content.*

❓ HOW DID I DO?

This week my religion classes were

☐ *some of the best ever!* ☐ *pretty good.* ☐ *in need of improvement.*

In what discussions and activities were children most interested?

_____

What activity did I most enjoy teaching?

_____

In what area do I need to improve?

_____

Name _____ Date _____

Kingdom of God

You belong to the Catholic Church.

The Church invites people to God's kingdom.

The Church shares God's love.

Draw a line from the person coming out of church to the picture of that same person sharing God's love.

The Holy Spirit

CHAPTER BACKGROUND

 The Advocate, the holy Spirit that the Father will send in my name—he will teach you everything and remind you of all that [I] told you.

John 14:26

A Great Guide

In Catholic Tradition, the Holy Spirit is recognized as the third Person of the Holy Trinity. The Holy Spirit was given to Jesus' followers after his Ascension and has continued to be poured out to strengthen disciples on their journey of life. Today he remains with the Body of Christ, forever guiding the Church to God the Father.

In the depths of anxiety and worry, the Holy Spirit can guide you to the light. Think about a time you were in need of God's love and guidance. Dealing with a difficult child, facing a hostile person, or living with ambiguity can present challenges. The Holy Spirit was at work in the kind words, the love of another, or loving actions that helped get you through this tough period.

Always with Us

Jesus breathed the Holy Spirit on his disciples on the day of Pentecost. He sent forth his disciples to share his message. The Holy Spirit strengthens his followers to do the same—leading them to the truth and encouraging them to bear witness to the good news of Jesus. He is active in the Church. He continues to minister through you and others.

Reflect *How has the Holy Spirit strengthened you this day?*

Faith Focus

- The third Person of the Holy Trinity is God the Holy Spirit. *(CCC 243, 685, 687)*
- The Holy Spirit inspires the faithful with love and guides the Church to all truth. *(CCC 684, 688, 731–733, 747)*

Catechism Connection

The *Catechism* reminds us that Christ communicates the Holy Spirit to his followers above all through the sacraments of the Church. *(CCC 739)*

GDC Link

According to the *Directory*, when you catechize you convey the faith of the whole people of God as it has been transmitted and lived throughout the history of the Church. "There is present in catechesis the faith of all those who believe and allow themselves to be guided by the Holy Spirit." *(GDC 105)*

The Holy Spirit

This chapter describes the Holy Spirit as the Church's guide. The chapter begins with children acting as guides or helpers. Then they will think about people in their lives who help them be the best people they can be.

- Children most likely will think of family members, teachers, and team managers as those who fill physical and emotional needs. This may be the first time children see larger roles for the helpers in their lives.

- Young children don't hesitate to admit they need help. Lead children to see that the Holy Spirit gives them the spiritual help that they need. He helps them do good, and by doing good, to stay close to the Holy Trinity.

- Children will read that the Holy Spirit is the third Person of the Holy Trinity, a concept that may be too abstract for them. There is value, however, in being exposed to a faith mystery at a young age.

Community

- I don't like to make mistakes. Help me understand that I can learn from my mistakes.

- I like doing things by myself. Help me learn that sometimes things get done better in a group.

Growing from Pain

Catechesis, like all endeavors, can bring you rejection, apathy, ridicule, and even betrayal. Catechists must know that great things are often achieved as a result of painful events.

- Painfulness is the practice of turning pain into a learning experience. As a catechist, you may allow pain to touch you, but you should not get lost in it.

- You can learn to recognize pain in others.

- Pain can help you sustain the spirit to teach if you can predict when your words may cause pain to yourself or others and when some of your past patterns need to be changed.

Reflect **What painful experience has actually improved your ability to sustain your spirit?**

Teacher's Prayer

Holy Spirit, come dwell in me. Shower me with your life so that I may carry out the work that Jesus began. Help me be a sign of your presence to others. Amen.

Weekly Planner

	Objective	Materials	Prayer & Scripture
DAY 1 Invite	**The Holy Spirit** Page 143	**Objective:** *To recall experiences of being guided*	☐ Pencils	Let Us Pray *Psalm 143:10*
DAY 2 Explore	**Be My Guide** Pages 144–145	**Objective:** *To introduce the concept of the Holy Spirit as guide*	☐ Board or chart paper ☐ *Little Polar Bear* by Hans de Beer (North-South Books, 1999) ☐ Index card	Let Us Pray *Psalm 143:10*
DAY 3 Explore	**The Church's Guide** Pages 146–147	**Objective:** *To describe how the Holy Spirit guides the Church*	☐ Copies of Activity Master 11, p. 152A ☐ Pencils ☐ Board or chart paper ☐ Art Supplies	Let Us Pray *Psalm 143:10* ✛ **Scripture:** *John 14:26* ✛ **Scripture Background:** Coming of the Holy Spirit, p. 146
DAY 4 Explore	**The Holy Spirit Helps** Pages 148–149	**Objective:** *To identify the gifts of the Holy Spirit*	☐ Board or chart paper ☐ Crayons or colored pencils ☐ Pencils ☐ Paper	Let Us Pray *Psalm 143:10*
DAY 5 Celebrate	**Asking Prayer** Page 150	**Objective:** *To pray to the Holy Spirit for guidance*	☐ Bible ☐ Hymnals ☐ Music CD ☐ Scarves or streamers	Let Us Pray **Asking Prayer** 🎵 **Hymn:** "Love One Another"

Chapter 11 Wrap-Up: Review and Apply p. 151 • Chapter 11 Assessment p. 143E

Words of Faith

Holy Spirit

Activities	Enrichment
Let's Begin: Who Can Help?, p. 143 Multiple Intelligence: Interpersonal OPTIONAL Guide Game, p. 143 Multiple Intelligence: Bodily/Kinesthetic	
Share Your Faith: Think, Share, Act, p. 145 Multiple Intelligence: Verbal/Linguistic OPTIONAL Sing and Learn, p. 144 Multiple Intelligence: Musical OPTIONAL Cross-Curricular: Reading, p. 145 Multiple Intelligence: Verbal/Linguistic	• Quick Tip: Animal Guides, p. 144 • Reaching All Learners: Readers, p. 145
Connect Your Faith: Solve the Code, p. 147 Multiple Intelligence: Visual/Spatial OPTIONAL Helpers, p. 146 Multiple Intelligence: Verbal/Linguistic OPTIONAL Activity Master 11: A Sign of the Holy Spirit, p. 147 Multiple Intelligence: Visual/Spatial	• Teacher Background: Symbols and Titles, p. 147
Live Your Faith: Follow the Holy Spirit, p. 149 Multiple Intelligence: Visual/Spatial OPTIONAL Cross-Curricular: Language Arts, p. 148 Multiple Intelligence: Verbal/Linguistic	• Christian Living Skills: Dealing with Anxiety, p. 148 • Reaching All Learners: Vision Impaired, p. 149 • Quick Tip: Sin or Mistake?, p. 149
	• Liturgy Link: A Round, p. 150 • Lectionary Link: Break Open the Word, p. 150

Multimedia Resources

 BOOK
Bratton, Heidi. *Spirit!* Paulist Press. 1997. Photos capture the fruit of the Spirit in children's everyday lives.

 VIDEO
Who Is the Spirit? (14 min). St. Anthony Messenger Press. Children identify the presence of the Holy Spirit.

 Teacher Resources
www.harcourtreligion.com
• For interactive lesson planner, chapter resources, and activities
• For free materials and information

Home Connection
Chapter 11 Family Faith, p. 152
Take-home activities, chapter content review, saint features and prayer

 For more family activities
www.harcourtreligion.com

Name _____ Date _____

A **Work with Words**   Circle the word that best completes each
sentence.

I. Jesus promised to send the _____.

Church

Holy Spirit

2. The Holy Spirit guides the _____.

Church

bears

B **Check Understanding**   Draw a line to the best ending for each
sentence.

3. The Holy Spirit

a. your heart with God's love.

4. The Holy Spirit will help you

b. make good choices.

5. The Holy Spirit fills

c. will guide you.

©Harcourt Religion

Chapter 11 The Holy Spirit

Invite

 **Let Us Pray**

Leader: God, teach me to follow the Holy Spirit.
"May your kind spirit guide me
on ground that is level."
Psalm 143:10

All: God, teach me to follow the Holy Spirit. Amen.

Activity

● **Who Can Help?** A ranger guides people who visit a park.

A guide shows children interesting things at the science center.

Guides help lead us and teach us.

• Write the name of someone who is a guide for you.

_____

— — — — — — — — — — — — — — — — — —

_____

Act It Out With a small group, act out one of the ways a guide helps lead and teach children.

143

Objective: To recall experiences of being guided

Open

 **Let Us Pray** Ask children to gather in the prayer space. Pray aloud the psalm verse and invite them to pray the response.

Build

Activity

• Tell children to look at the picture as you read aloud the story.

• Ask children what the man in the picture does. Possible responses: Guides children across the street; makes cars stop.

• Have children write the name of a guide on the page.

Extension Activity

• Divide the class into small groups.

• Have each group act out one of the ways a guide helps lead and teach children.

Close

Have children tell what they learned about people who guide.

OPTIONAL ACTIVITY

Guide Game Arrange the room so that there are no broad paths from one side of the room to the other.

• Group children in pairs. When their turn comes, the children in each pair should go to opposite sides of the room. Have one child cover his or her eyes, and have the other child call out directions to help the first child get across the room.

_____

Multiple Intelligence: Bodily/Kinesthetic

Objective: To introduce the concept of the Holy Spirit as guide

Open

 **Let Us Pray** Invite children to pray the psalm verse on page 143 with you.

Focus Who will show you the way to God? List children's answers on the board or on chart paper.

Build

Be My Guide

Have children look at the illustrations of Brandon the Hippo and of the bird Dylan.

- Gather children around you. Read aloud Brandon the Hippo.
- Ask children about Brandon's problem.
- Ask children what Dylan did to guide Brandon.

Explore

Be My Guide

Focus Who will show you the way to God?

A STORY

Brandon the Hippo

Brandon the hippo's mom just yelled at him for not picking up his toys. Brandon was very sad so he stomped off into the jungle. He stomped until he was so deep in the jungle that he was lost!

He sat down and began to cry. All he wanted to do was go home and be with his parents. A little bird swooped down and perched on his shoulder saying, "I'm Dylan, I heard you crying. Can I help you?"

Brandon dried his tears. He told Dylan he was lost. Then he said, "I just want to be home with my parents."

144

OPTIONAL ACTIVITY

Sing and Learn After the second and third paragraphs, invite children to sing the words below to the tune of "Here We Go 'Round the Mulberry Bush."

- Brandon, Brandon, you need a guide,
  need a guide, need a guide.
  Brandon, Brandon, you need a guide
  to get you home to your family.

Multiple Intelligence: Musical

QUICK TIP

Animal Guides Tell children that animals can also be guides for people.

- Specially trained guide dogs help those who are visually or hearing impaired.
- Tell children that these dogs are more than pets. Explain that they should not interfere when these dogs are working.

Dylan showed Brandon how to get home through the jungle. When they finally arrived, Brandon told his parents he was sorry.

Brandon said, "I wouldn't have made it home if it weren't for my guide!"

Who are some safe guides who could help you if you were lost?
Responses will vary.

A Guide for You

Brandon needed a guide to find his way home. You need a guide to stay close to God the Father and to Jesus, God the Son. God the **Holy Spirit** will guide you.

Words of Faith

The **Holy Spirit** is the third Person of the Holy Trinity.

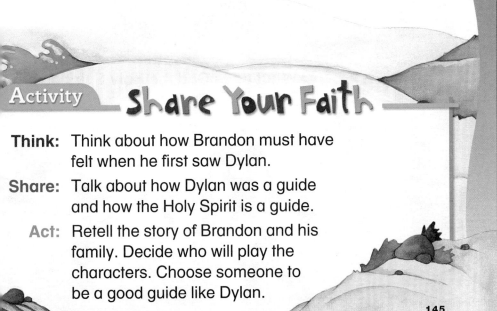

Activity

Share Your Faith

Think: Think about how Brandon must have felt when he first saw Dylan.

Share: Talk about how Dylan was a guide and how the Holy Spirit is a guide.

Act: Retell the story of Brandon and his family. Decide who will play the characters. Choose someone to be a good guide like Dylan.

145

A Guide for You

Read aloud A Guide for You.

• Hold up an index card with *Holy Spirit* written on it, and discuss the definition.

❓ **Who are some safe guides who could help you if you were lost?** Write the responses on the board or on chart paper.

Activity

• Have children role-play the activity. Or you might choose to have children act out other situations in which children their age would need a guide.

Close

Tell children that the Holy Spirit is a guide who helps people stay close to God the Father.

★ **REACHING ALL LEARNERS**

Readers The story of Brandon the Hippo is written in very simple language.

• If you want to experiment with having some of the better readers in your group read a story to the other children, this might be the one to try.

OPTIONAL ACTIVITY

Cross-Curricular: Reading You may wish to read *Little Polar Bear* by Hans de Beer. It is the story of Lars, a small polar bear, who needs a guide to get home, just as people continually need a guide to help them stay close to God. (North-South Books, 1999)

Multiple Intelligence: Verbal/Linguistic

DAY 3

Objective: To describe how the Holy Spirit guides the Church

Open

 Let Us Pray Invite children to pray the psalm verse on page 143 with you.

Focus **Whom does the Holy Spirit help?** List children's answers on the board or on chart paper.

Build

The Church's Guide

Tell children that Jesus knew he would leave his followers one day to return to God his Father. Tell them he promised his followers a guide to be with them always.

Jesus Promises the Holy Spirit

Proclaim the Scripture. Discuss with children how Jesus' followers would have felt after hearing Jesus' words.

❷ **What does God the Holy Spirit do?** Ask volunteers to share their responses.

The Church's Guide

Focus Whom does the Holy Spirit help?

Jesus would soon be going back to God the Father. He promised his followers a helper. The guide who came to them is the Holy Spirit.

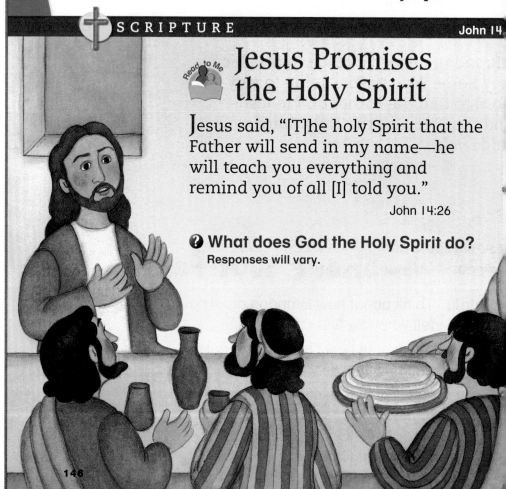

SCRIPTURE John 14

Jesus Promises the Holy Spirit

Jesus said, "[T]he holy Spirit that the Father will send in my name—he will teach you everything and remind you of all [I] told you."

John 14:26

❷ **What does God the Holy Spirit do?**
Responses will vary.

146

Helpers The Holy Spirit is described here as a helper and teacher.

- Ask children to name different types of helpers and teachers, such as fire fighters, medical professionals, their teachers at school, and so on.
- Tell children that the Holy Spirit inspires such people to help and teach others.

Multiple Intelligence: Verbal/Linguistic

SCRIPTURE BACKGROUND

Coming of the Holy Spirit The Gospel according to John depicts a Jesus who is very open about his heavenly origin and his mission.

- The passage on this page comes from the longest of these discourses, delivered at the Last Supper.
- In his sermon, Jesus foretells the coming of the Holy Spirit as an advocate and teacher of truth for the disciples.

146 Chapter 11

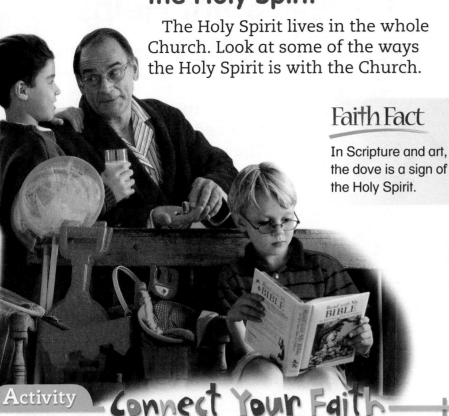

The Work of the Holy Spirit

The Holy Spirit lives in the whole Church. Look at some of the ways the Holy Spirit is with the Church.

Faith Fact

In Scripture and art, the dove is a sign of the Holy Spirit.

Connect Your Faith

Solve the Code Use this code to learn who guides the Church. Write the letter that matches each number.

1	2	3	4	5	6	7	8	9
H	I	L	O	P	R	S	T	Y

God the   H   O   L   Y
           1   4   3   9

            S   P   I   R   I   T
            7   5   2   6   2   8

147

The Work of the Holy Spirit

Have children look at the picture on the page.

- Ask children how the Holy Spirit is guiding the people of the Church in the picture. Possible responses: The Holy Spirit helps children to understand the Word of God; he inspires children to help others.

Activity

- Direct children to work alone to solve the code.
- Encourage children to make up their own short codes for others to solve using sentences from the chapter.

Close

Remind children that Jesus promised to send to his followers the Holy Spirit to guide them into truth.

Activity Master 11: A Sign of the Holy Spirit Distribute copies of the activity found on teacher page 152A.

- Tell children that they will cut out a dove which represents the Holy Spirit.
- You may wish to send this activity home with children.

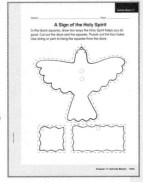

▲ Activity Master 11 page 152A

Symbols and Titles Besides the dove, symbols of the Holy Spirit include water, anointing, fire, cloud and light, the hand of God, and the finger of God *(CCC 694–701).*

- Other titles of the Holy Spirit are Paraclete, the Spirit of Truth, and the Spirit of Christ *(CCC 692–693).*

Objective: To identify the gifts of the Holy Spirit

Open

 Let Us Pray Invite children to repeat after you the psalm verse from page 143.

Focus **How does the Holy Spirit help you?** List children's responses on the board or on chart paper.

Build

The Holy Spirit Helps

Ask volunteers to review what they know about the Holy Spirit.

- Read aloud the first two paragraphs.
- Ask children to pay careful attention as you read aloud the descriptions of the gifts of the Holy Spirit.
- Read aloud the first part of each line, and invite children to join you in reading aloud the second part (beginning with "to help you").

❷ **When can you ask the Holy Spirit to help you?** Invite children to choose partners to discuss the question.

Explore

The Holy Spirit Helps

Focus How does the Holy Spirit help you?

Jesus' friends felt sad after he returned to his Father in heaven. They thought they were alone. Th the Holy Spirit came to them. He helped Jesus' friends. He gave the gifts like courage and hope.

Here are some of the gifts the Holy Spirit gives you.

- **wisdom** to help you **make good choices**
- **understanding** to help you **get along with others**
- **courage** to help you **act bravely when you feel afraid**
- **knowledge** to help you **know God better**
- **reverence** to help you **pray every day**
- **wonder and awe** to help you enjoy **God's wonderful wo**

❷ **When can you ask the Holy Spirit to help you?** Responses will vary.

148

OPTIONAL ACTIVITY

Cross-Curricular: Language Arts Have children write acrostic poems based on the gifts of the Holy Spirit.

- Show children how to write the name of the gift vertically down the left margin of a sheet of paper. Ask children to write poems about the gifts, beginning each line of the poem with one of the letters in the name of the gift.

Multiple Intelligence: Verbal/Linguistic

CHRISTIAN LIVING SKILLS

Dealing with Anxiety Young children sometimes experience anxiety or phobias such as fear of the dark. Remind children that God is always with them. Help children compose brief prayers asking for the Holy Spirit's help in time of anxiety. Explain that he often helps us through other people, such as family members and teachers, who help us overcome our fears.

Live Your Faith

 Follow the Holy Spirit Read each action. If you think the action shows love for God and others, color the dove of the Spirit. If you think the action does not show love, cross out the dove.

 Share your new toy with a friend.

 Listen to your teacher.

 Hit someone.

 Pray.

 Throw trash on the playground.

 Visit someone who is sick.

 Call someone a bad name.

 Help fold the laundry.

Loving Actions Pick one of the choices that does not show love. With a partner, act out how you can change the action to one that shows love.

149

- Read aloud the directions for Follow the Holy Spirit. If necessary, read aloud each of the statements.
- Provide crayons or colored pencils, and allow time for children to work independently on the activity.
- Invite volunteers to share their responses.
- Read aloud the directions for Loving Actions.
- Have children choose partners, and allow time for pairs to prepare their dramatizations.
- Invite pairs to share their role-plays.

Close

Lead children in a litany of spontaneous prayers for the Holy Spirit's help, responding to each petition with "Come, Holy Spirit!"

REACHING ALL LEARNERS

Vision Impaired Offer these alternatives to children with impaired vision or reading difficulties:

- Have children work with partners who read aloud each statement and invite an oral response, such as "shows love" or "does not show love."
- Invite children to brainstorm their own lists of actions that show love and actions that do not show love.

QUICK TIP

Sin or Mistake? Help children develop their ability to discern right from wrong by reviewing the difference between sins—deliberate wrong choices—and mistakes or accidents.

- Tell children that each of the actions that do not show love from the list on page 149 are sins.
- Remind children that they are still responsible for apologizing and offering to make up for harm they cause mistakenly or accidentally.

DAY 5

Objective: To pray to the Holy Spirit for guidance

Prepare

Teach children the spoken prayer response, "Come, Holy Spirit, guide me."

 Use the *Call to Faith 1* CD, track 11, to rehearse the song.

Gather

Assemble children in the prayer space.

Pray

An Asking Prayer

 Let Us Pray Follow the order of prayer on page 150.

- Direct children to gently wave scarves or streamers as they sing the verses.
- Optional reading: Philippians 4:4–7.
- Optional music from *Singing Our Faith:* "We Are Walking in the Light," #262.

An Asking Prayer

 Let Us Pray

Gather and begin with the Sign of the Cross.

Leader: When I ask others to play,

All: Come, Holy Spirit, guide me.

Leader: When I am afraid to do what is right,

All: Come, Holy Spirit, guide me.

Leader: When I need to help others,

All: Come, Holy Spirit, guide me.

Sing together the refrain.

Love one another.
Love one another,
as I have loved you.

"Love One Another," Rob Glover © 2000, GIA Publications, Inc.

150

 LITURGY LINK

A Round If you think children are capable of it, divide them into two groups and have them sing the refrain of "Love One Another" as a round, following the directions in *Singing Our Faith*.

- Explain that each group should start singing the refrain all over again as soon as they reach the end of it.

LECTIONARY LINK

Break Open the Word Read last week's Sunday Gospel. Invite children to think about what the reading means to them as they try to follow Christ's example. For questions related to the weekly Gospel reading, visit our Web site at **www.harcourtreligion.com**.

 Visit **www.harcourtreligion.com** for weekly scripture readings and seasonal resources.

A Work with Words Circle the correct answer to complete each sentence.

1. Jesus promised to send the (p. 146) .

   Church   (Holy Spirit)

2. The Holy Spirit guides the (p. 147) .

   (Church)   animals

3. The Holy Spirit is the (p. 145) Person of the Holy Trinity.

   first   (third)

4. The Holy Spirit is with (p. 147) .

   (the Church)   the animals

B Check Understanding Answer the question.

How can the Holy Spirit help you?

_____

- - - - - - - - - - - - - - - - - -

Responses will vary. (p. 148)

_____

Write two ways you can follow the Holy Spirit.

_____

- - - - - - - - - - - - - - - - - -

Responses will vary. (p. 149)

_____

- - - - - - - - - - - - - - - - - -

Responses will vary.

151

Review

A Work with Words Ask children to circle the correct word or words to fill each blank.

B Check Understanding Have children write the answers to the questions.

Assessment

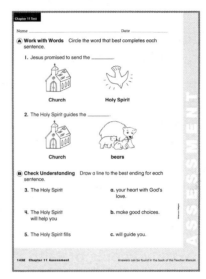

▲ **Chapter 11 Test page 143E**

Answers to the Chapter Test can be found in the back of the Teacher Manual.

TEACHER BACKGROUND

The Advocate In *John 14:26*, Jesus refers to the Holy Spirit as "The Advocate," which means, "one that pleads the cause of another." Jesus wanted to reassure his disciples that his cause would not end when his life on earth ended.

OPTIONAL ACTIVITY

Showing Solidarity Organize an age-appropriate charity drive.

- Hold a bake sale or a book sale in the parish, and donate the proceeds to a sister parish.

- If the parish does not have a sister parish, help children write a letter to the pastoral council suggesting that they adopt one.

Family Faith

Remind children to discuss the Family Faith page at home. Encourage children to read the scripture passage from the Acts of the Apostles.

Activity

- Encourage children to ask members of their families about people who have been good guides for them.

People of Faith

Tell children about Saint Pedro de San Jose.

- Pedro built chapels and shrines in the poor sections of Guatemala. He started the tradition of the Christmas Eve procession in which people representing Mary and Joseph seek a night's lodging from their neighbors.
- Remind children to add Saint Pedro de San Jose to their People of Faith albums.
- Encourage them to pray the prayer at home with their families.

Visit **www.harcourtreligion.com** for weekly scripture readings and seasonal resources.

Unit 4: CHAPTER 11
Family Faith

Catholics Believe

- God the Holy Spirit is the third Person of the Holy Trinity.
- The Holy Spirit fills people's hearts with love and guides the Church.

✝ SCRIPTURE

Read about the coming of the Holy Spirit in the Acts of the Apostles 2:1–13.

GO ONLINE www.harcourtreligion.com
For weekly Scripture readings and seasonal resources

Activity

Live Your Faith

Gather as a Family Talk about someone who has been a good guide for you. Who has helped you to show God's love to others? People need to be good guides for each other. At the end of your conversation, pray a short prayer to the Holy Spirit.

People of Faith

Pedro de San Jose (Peter of Saint Joseph) Betancur was born in the Canary Islands. Pedro loved Jesus so much that he told everyone about him. Pedro traveled to Guatemala, where he spent the rest of his life helping people. He especially helped those who were sick and homeless. Pedro opened a hospital and a school. In 2002 Pedro became the first Guatemalan named as a saint. The Church celebrates his feast day of April 18.

▲ Saint Pedro de San Jose Betancur, 1619–1667

Family Prayer

Saint Pedro, pray for us that we may not be afraid to do what is right and good. Amen.

In Unit 4 your child is learning about the CHURCH.

152 **CCC** *See Catechism of the Catholic Church 737–741 for further reading on chapter content.*

❓ HOW DID I DO?

This week my religion classes were

☐ *some of the best ever!* ☐ *pretty good.* ☐ *in need of improvement.*

In what discussions and activities were children most interested?

_____

What activity did I most enjoy teaching?

_____

In what area do I need to improve?

_____

Name _____ Date _____

A Sign of the Holy Spirit

In the blank boxes, draw two ways the Holy Spirit helps you do good. Cut out the dove and the squares. Punch out the four holes. Use string or yarn to hang the squares from the dove.

Holy People
CHAPTER BACKGROUND

Faith Focus

- Saints are friends of God who provide other Christians with the helpful example of their holy lives. *(CCC 828, 829, 1023)*
- All members of the Church are called to lead holy lives, as the saints did. *(CCC 825)*

Catechism Connection

The *Catechism* affirms that the saints in heaven continually intercede with God the Father for those Christians who are still pilgrims on earth. *(CCC 956, 2683)*

GDC Link

The *Directory* points out that the saints are one of the Church's sources of the message of catechesis. *(GDC 83, 95)*

 Let love be sincere; hate what is evil, hold on to what is good; love one another with mutual affection; anticipate one another in showing honor.

Romans 12:9–10

Holy People

The Church has long held the practice of canonizing some of its members who have heroically lived faithful lives. These men and women serve as mentors and models of faith for the Church, whose members continue to strive to live as Jesus taught. By calling attention to the lives of the faithful of the past, the Church of today helps people act with faith and conviction.

Along your journey of life, certain people have been your guides, encouraging you. In the same way, the saints of the Church inspire loving faith and perseverance. Their lives are a living testimony to the gifts of the Holy Spirit. Reflect on how as a catechist, teacher, parent, or friend, you are a living testimony and an inspiration of faith to others.

Communion of Saints

As a baptized Catholic, you are a part of a holy people, the communion of saints. As a member of the Body of Christ, you are called to nourish and sustain faith—your own and that of others. The saints in heaven are intercessors for you, bringing your needs to God.

Reflect   Of the many canonized saints, whom might you choose to be your intercessor or model?

The Saints

Children have heard the word *holy* used to describe God's love. Broaden their understanding of holiness to include those people who are filled with the Holy Spirit.

- To help children understand the concept of sainthood and holiness, use a concrete object—a paper halo. Share with children that a saint or a holy person does not really wear a halo. A halo is a sign of holiness just like a heart is a sign of love. A halo is used in art as a sign of being close to God.

- Through a discovery method, lead children to a wonderful conclusion—they can be saints. Children can discover that saints are ordinary people who served God with all their hearts—an extraordinary task.

- There are various ways you can help children develop devotion to the saints. Pray at times for the intercession of the patron saint of the parish. Decorate your room with pictures of Mary and other saints. Lend age-appropriate saint books to children to take home and share with their families.

Example and Praise

- I like to be praised for good work and good behavior.
- Stories help me learn what to do. Tell me stories of holy people.
- I like to help in the classroom. Give me some jobs to do.

Holy Urgency

Sometimes advice to wait your turn, calm down, and be patient decreases the passion fueling your catechetical commitment. Sustaining your spirit seems to require a mixture of perspective, passion, humility, and self-importance.

Those who sustain their commitments know that their contribution may not compare to other great works, but that it is their most important contribution. They will stop at nothing to do it well, and they will not lower their expectations. In maintaining this holy urgency about their work, they protect themselves from the kind of passivity that extinguishes the fire of the spirit to teach.

Reflect **How much passion do you have for your catechetical efforts? What fuels it? What weakens it?**

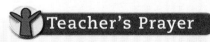
Teacher's Prayer

Saints of God, you have given me wonderful examples of holiness. Pray that I have the strength and courage to love God and others as you did. Amen.

Weekly Planner

		Objective	Materials	Prayer & Scripture
DAY 1 Invite	**Holy People** Page 153	**Objective:** To explore the concept of friendship	☐ Pencils ☐ Art supplies ☐ Paper ☐ Board or chart paper	🎁 Let Us Pray *Psalm 40:5*
DAY 2 Explore	**Friends of God** Pages 154–155	**Objective:** To explain how the Catholic Church celebrates saints	☐ Board or chart paper ☐ Pencils ☐ Index cards ☐ Rulers	🎁 Let Us Pray *Psalm 40:5* ✝ **Scripture:** Romans 12:10–13 ✝ **Scripture Background:** Some Good Advice, p. 154
DAY 3 Explore	**All Kinds of Saints** Pages 156–157	**Objective:** To describe how some saints showed love for God	☐ Board or chart paper ☐ Pencils ☐ Copies of Activity Master 12, p. 162A ☐ Art Supplies	🎁 Let Us Pray *Psalm 40:5*
DAY 4 Explore	**Being Saints** Pages 158–159	**Objective:** To identify the qualities of saintliness	☐ Board or chart paper ☐ Art supplies ☐ Poster board ☐ Pencils	🎁 Let Us Pray *Psalm 40:5*
DAY 5 Celebrate	**Prayer of Saints** Page 160	**Objective:** To pray a litany	☐ Hymnals ☐ Music CD	🎁 Let Us Pray **Prayer of Saints** 🎵 **Hymn:** "Psalm 119: Happy Are They"

Chapter 12 Wrap-Up: Review and Apply p. 161 • Chapter 12 Assessment p. 153E

Words of Faith

saints
holy

Activities	Enrichment
Let's Begin: Friends, p. 153 Multiple Intelligence: Interpersonal (OPTIONAL) Friendship Book, p. 153 Multiple Intelligence: Visual/Spatial	
Share Your Faith: Think, Share, Act, p. 155 Multiple Intelligence: Interpersonal (OPTIONAL) Friendship Day, p. 154 Multiple Intelligence: Interpersonal (OPTIONAL) Saints' Days, p. 155 Multiple Intelligence: Logical/Mathematical	• **Reaching All Learners:** For Math Wizards, p. 155
Connect Your Faith: Matching, p. 157 Multiple Intelligence: Verbal/Linguistic (OPTIONAL) Activity Master 12: Make a Halo, p. 156 Multiple Intelligence: Visual/Spatial (OPTIONAL) Tour the Church, p. 157 Multiple Intelligence: Visual/Spatial	• **Quick Tip:** Ordinary People, p. 156 • **Cultural Awareness:** Saints Around the World, p. 157
Live Your Faith: Being a Saint, p. 159 Multiple Intelligence: Visual/Spatial (OPTIONAL) Chart Patron Saints, p. 158 Multiple Intelligence: Verbal/Linguistic (OPTIONAL) Cross-Curricular: Art, p. 159 Multiple Intelligence: Visual/Spatial	• **Christian Living Skills:** Choosing Good Friends, p. 158 • **Reaching All Learners:** Color Blindness, p. 159
	• **Liturgy Link:** A Litany, p. 160 • **Lectionary Link:** Break Open the Word, p. 160

Multimedia Resources

 BOOK
Armstrong, Carole. *Lives and Legends of the Saints.* Simon & Schuster. 1995. Favorite saint stories illustrated by the works of great artists.

 VIDEO
Heroes and Heroines: People of Prayer (15 min). Ikonographics. Profiles of four people of faith: Kateri Tekakwitha, Thomas Merton, Saint Teresa of Avila, and Saint Francis of Assisi.

 Teacher Resources
www.harcourtreligion.com
• For interactive lesson planner, chapter resources, and activities
• For free materials and information

Home Connection

Chapter 12 Family Faith, p. 162
Take-home activities, chapter content review, saint features and prayer

 For more family activities
www.harcourtreligion.com

Check Understanding Draw a line from the saint to something
about that person.

1. Blessed Kateri   **a.** opened schools for girls.

2. Saint Elizabeth Ann   **b.** was a Native American.

Trace the line to the best ending for each sentence.

3. Saints are ------------------------ sad people.

                                    ------ holy people.

4. Those who are holy ------------ serve God with all their hearts.

                                    ---- do whatever they feel like doing.

5. Saints are filled with ---------- themselves.

                                    ---- the Holy Spirit.

Answers can be found in the back of the Teacher Manual.

©Harcourt Religion

ASSESSMENT

Chapter 12 Holy People

🎁 Let Us Pray

Leader: We trust you always, O Lord.
"Happy those whose trust is the LORD."
Psalm 40:5

All: We trust in you always, O Lord. Amen.

Activity — Let's Begin

● **Friends**

Wherever I am, you are there.
You and I are quite a pair.
We talk and play,
We laugh all day.
You and I are quite a pair.

• Write two words that describe
a good friend.

_____

– – – – – – – – – – – – – – – –

_____

_____

– – – – – – – – – – – – – – – –

_____

🖍 **Draw a Picture** Draw a picture of
something that is more fun to do with a
friend than by yourself.

153

Objective: To explore the concept of friendship

Open

🎁 **Let Us Pray** Ask children to move into the prayer space. Pray the psalm verse aloud, and have children pray the response.

Build

Activity

• Have children look at the picture as you read aloud the poem.
• Ask children what the poem is about. Possible response: friends
• Give them time to write their responses to the question in the text.

Extension Activity

• Distribute art supplies.
• Tell children to draw a picture of something that is more fun to do with a friend.
• Ask volunteers to share their drawings with the class.

Close

Have children tell why it is good to have friends.

OPTIONAL ACTIVITY

Friendship Book Write the following song lyrics on the board or on chart paper: "Make new friends, but keep the old. One is silver but the other is gold."

• Have children make a friendship book of the friends in their new class. Supply paper to make a booklet, and have children decorate it and draw pictures of friendship to each other.

Multiple Intelligence: Visual/Spatial

Objective: To explain how the Catholic Church celebrates saints

Open

 Let Us Pray Invite children to pray the psalm verse on page 153 with you.

Focus **How do people become holy?** List children's answers on the board or on chart paper.

Build

Friends of God

Show children an index card with the word *saint*. Read the first paragraph aloud. Tell children that everyone is called to be a saint by loving God and others.

- Explain to children that they will listen to some wise advice Saint Paul gave about how to become a saint.

- Proclaim the scripture story. Tell children to listen for things people can do to help them become saints.

❓ **What good things does Jesus ask you to do?** Write responses on the board or on chart paper.

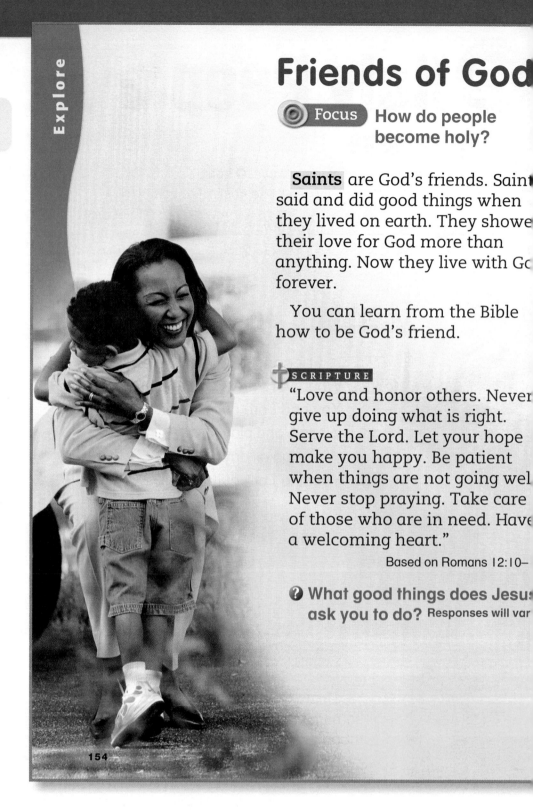

Explore

Friends of God

Focus **How do people become holy?**

Saints are God's friends. Saint said and did good things when they lived on earth. They showe their love for God more than anything. Now they live with Go forever.

You can learn from the Bible how to be God's friend.

✝ SCRIPTURE

"Love and honor others. Never give up doing what is right. Serve the Lord. Let your hope make you happy. Be patient when things are not going wel Never stop praying. Take care of those who are in need. Have a welcoming heart."

Based on Romans 12:10–

❓ **What good things does Jesus ask you to do?** Responses will var

154

✝ SCRIPTURE BACKGROUND

Some Good Advice Saint Paul, in his letter to the Romans (*Romans 12:10–13*), explained how to live as a good Christian.

- He told the faithful of the Church living in Rome that they should do their "best to live at peace with everyone" and "defeat evil with good."

- He called these followers saints because he knew that all members of the Church are called to be holy.

OPTIONAL ACTIVITY

Friendship Day Tell children that the first Sunday in August every year is celebrated as Friendship Day.

- Tell children they can make any day Friendship Day.

- Tell them they could invite their friends to a picnic, or give them a call on the phone.

Multiple Intelligence: Interpersonal

Family of Saints

Saints are **holy** people. They are filled with the Holy Spirit. Holy people serve God with love.

Catholics celebrate many saints. You are part of the family of saints! You are connected to the saints who have lived before. You are also connected to holy people who live now.

Words of Faith

Saints are people who lived a good life and loved God.

To be **holy** means to be filled with the Holy Spirit and to serve God with all your heart.

Activity

Share Your Faith

Think: Who is someone who serves God?

Share: Tell a partner about this person. Talk about ways you can serve God.

Act: Write the letter that matches each number. You'll learn a way to serve God.

1	2	3	4	5	6	7	8	9	10	11	12	13	14	15
A	B	C	D	E	F	G	H	I	J	K	L	M	N	O

B ___ E ___ K ___ I ___ N ___ D ___ .
2   5   11   9   14   4

155

Family of Saints

Read aloud the first paragraph. Hold up an index card with the word *holy*, and then add the card to the vocabulary display.

- Explain to children what the word *holy* means. (See Words of Faith.)
- Tell children that Catholic artists often indicate which of the figures in their pictures are saints by painting haloes above their heads. Have children find haloes in the portraits of saints in this chapter.
- Read aloud the second paragraph and tell children they are all part of the family of saints.

Activity

- Have children work with a partner to find a way to be holy and to serve God.

Close

Remind children that saints are holy people who are friends of God and live with him forever.

REACHING ALL LEARNERS

For Math Wizards Making a neat calendar of saints' days is an activity that involves measurement and counting.

- Assign a leading role in this activity to children with mathematical proficiency.

OPTIONAL ACTIVITY

Saints' Days Use a book of saints to draw a calendar of children's saints' days.

- Children who were not named after a saint can choose a saint from a People of Faith page.
- Pick a date when the group can celebrate saints' days that have already passed or will occur in the summer.

Multiple Intelligence: Mathematical/Logical

Open

Objective: To describe how some saints showed love for God

Let Us Pray Invite children to pray the psalm verse on page 153 with you.

Focus **How do saints show their love?** List children's answers on the board or on chart paper.

Build

All Kinds of Saints

Tell children that stories about saints help them learn how to be holy. Ask children to put their fingers next to the description of each saint as you read aloud All Kinds of Saints.

• Read to children about each saint. Have children circle a word or words that tell how that saint showed love for God. For example, Mary took care of Jesus; Benedict served others; Martin shared his coat; Philip showed how to pray and do good; Kateri told children about God's love; Elizabeth Ann opened schools for girls.

All Kinds of Saints

Focus **How do saints show their love?**

Stories about the saints help you learn how to be holy. Saints have loved God and others.

Mary

A Mother Mary, the mother of Jesus, is the greatest of the saints. Mary is the Mother of God. She too care of Jesus.

Saint Benedict

A Cook Saint Benedict was the son of African slaves. He used his talent for cooking to serve others.

Saint Martin

A Soldier Saint Martin was a soldier. He shared his coat with a homeless person.

A Happy Spirit Saint Philip liked to laugh and make others laugh, too. He was a good listener. He showed young people how to pray and do good things.

Saint Philip

156

QUICK TIP

Ordinary People Point out to children that these saints were real people who achieved extraordinary results by doing ordinary things, such as parenting, cooking, sharing, teaching, and laughing.

OPTIONAL ACTIVITY

Activity Master 12: Make a Halo Distribute copies of the activity found on teacher page 162A.

• Tell children that they will cut out a halo and decorate it.

• As an alternative, you may wish to send this activity home with children.

▲ Activity Master 12 page 162A

Young Woman Blessed Kateri was Mohawk Indian. She told Native American children about God's wonderful love.

Blessed Kateri

Saint Elizabeth Ann Seton

A Teacher Saint Elizabeth Ann Seton is an American saint. She opened schools for girls. She taught many young people about God.

❷ **Which of these people would you want to be like?** Responses will vary.

❷ **How can you be a holy person?** Responses will vary.

Activity **Connect Your Faith**

Matching Read the descriptions below. Match each description with a holy person on these pages. Write the number in the box next to the person's picture.

1. Used his talents to serve others as a cook
2. Opened schools and taught children about God
3. Mother of Jesus
4. Listened to people and made them laugh
5. Shared his coat
6. Told children about God's love

157

❷ **Which of these people would you want to be like? How can you be a holy person?** Invite volunteers to respond.

Activity

- Ask children to locate the boxes found at the lower corner of each saint's picture. Tell children that they are going to write a number in each box.
- Read each numbered phrase with children. Allow time for them to identify which saint the phrase describes.
- Ask volunteers to share their answers.

Close

Tell children that the saints showed their love for God and for other people in many different ways.

🌐 **CULTURAL AWARENESS**

Saints Around the World Your class may come from a variety of cultural backgrounds.

- Use the study of saints to develop their appreciation for cultural diversity.
- Take a survey of the country of origin of children's families.
- Find pictures of the patron saints of these countries and show them to the children at a later session.

OPTIONAL ACTIVITY

Tour the Church If time allows, go to the church and look at various artistic depictions of saints.

- Guide children to look for clues in the art that tell about the saints—a halo or an item that reveals the saint's background.

Multiple Intelligence: Visual/Spatial

Objective: To identify the qualities of saintliness

Open

![Let Us Pray] **Let Us Pray** Invite children to pray the psalm verse from page 153 with you.

![Focus] **Focus** **How can you be a saint?** List children's responses on the board or on chart paper.

Build

Being Saints

Invite children to listen carefully as you read aloud the first paragraph.

• Draw attention to the list by reading aloud the introductory sentence.

• Invite seven children to take turns reading aloud the bulleted entries.

❷ **What is one way you can show that you are a saint today?** Discuss the question as a class. Encourage practical suggestions.

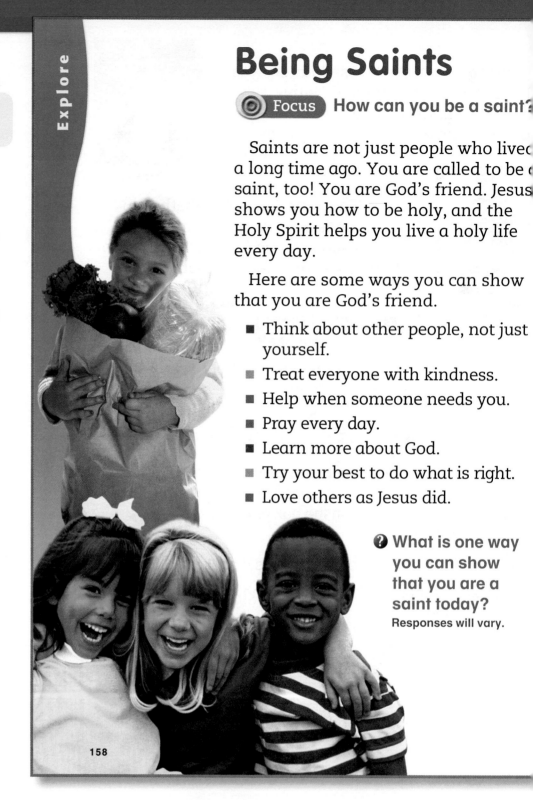

Explore

Being Saints

![Focus] **Focus** **How can you be a saint?**

Saints are not just people who lived a long time ago. You are called to be a saint, too! You are God's friend. Jesus shows you how to be holy, and the Holy Spirit helps you live a holy life every day.

Here are some ways you can show that you are God's friend.

■ Think about other people, not just yourself.

■ Treat everyone with kindness.

■ Help when someone needs you.

■ Pray every day.

■ Learn more about God.

■ Try your best to do what is right.

■ Love others as Jesus did.

❷ **What is one way you can show that you are a saint today?**
Responses will vary.

158

Chart Patron Saints Help children make a class chart listing each child's patron saint.

• Supply poster board and markers, and help children list their names in one column of a two-column chart.

• Help children list their patron saints in the second column of the chart.

Multiple Intelligence: Verbal/Linguistic

 CHRISTIAN LIVING SKILLS

Choosing Good Friends Remind children that being and choosing good friends can help them grow in their friendship with God.

• Ask children to think about what makes a good friend.

• Help children see that their choice of companions can contribute to or distract from their ability to show love for God and others.

Live Your Faith

 Being a Saint Solve the puzzles to find clues. Color all the spaces with an X in them red. Color the other spaces any other colors you want. Then copy the red words on the lines below.

1. _____ love _____

2. _____ God _____

3. _____ love _____

4. _____ others _____

159

- Read aloud the directions for the activity.
- Supply children with markers, crayons, or colored pencils. Each child should have a red and a mix of other colors.
- Allow time for children to work independently on the activity.
- Invite volunteers to read aloud their solutions.

Close

Lead children in praying a simplified version of the Litany of the Saints. Include the names of children's patron saints.

★ REACHING ALL LEARNERS

Color Blindness Children who have difficulty distinguishing colors or who have other visual impairments may be unable to complete the puzzle independently. Ask these children to color only the shapes marked with an X, or to work with partners who can help them distinguish colors.

OPTIONAL ACTIVITY

Cross-Curricular: Art Show children examples of artwork depicting the saints from various eras and cultures.

- Invite children to make holy cards of their patron saints, using a favorite style or medium from the examples shown.

Multiple Intelligence: Visual/Spatial

DAY 5

Objective: To pray a litany

Prepare

Explain to children what a litany is. Tell children they will walk in procession to the prayer space as they say the litany.

- Explain that they will ask for the prayers of the saints they just read about.

 Use the *Call to Faith 1* CD, track 12, to rehearse the song.

Gather

Line up children on the opposite side of the room from the usual prayer space. Stand at the head of the line.

Pray

A Prayer of Saints

 Let Us Pray Follow the order of prayer on page 160.

- Process to the prayer space while praying the litany.
- Conclude with the song.

Celebrate

Prayer of Saints

 Let Us Pray

Gather and begin with the Sign of the Cross.

Leader: Holy Mary,

All: pray for us.

Leader: Saint Benedict,

All: pray for us.

Leader: Saint Martin,

All: pray for us.

Leader: Saint Philip,

All: pray for us.

Leader: Blessed Kateri,

All: pray for us.

Leader: Saint Elizabeth Ann,

All: pray for us.

Sing together the refrain.

Happy are they
who follow the law of
the Lord.

"Psalm 119: Happy are They," *Lectionary for Mass*
© 1969, 1981, and 1997, ICEL.

160

 LITURGY LINK

A Litany A litany is any prayer in which certain short phrases are said over and over again.

- Litanies are often prayed as people are walking in processions in church. The litany most commonly heard is the litany of the saints, used at the Easter Vigil. This litany is based on it.

 LECTIONARY LINK

Break Open the Word Read last week's Sunday Gospel. Invite children to think about what the reading means to them as they try to follow Christ's example. For questions related to the weekly Gospel reading, visit our Web site at **www.harcourtreligion.com**.

 Visit www.harcourtreligion.com for weekly scripture readings and seasonal resources.

CHAPTER 12
Review

A Check Understanding Answer the questions.

1. Who are the saints?

_____

Possible responses: friends of God; people who loved God and

others; people who served God and followed Jesus (p. 154)

2. Name a saint. Tell a good thing the saint did.

_____

– –

Responses will vary. (p. 156)

_____

– –

3. Name a way that you can be like a saint.

_____

– –

Responses will vary. (p. 158)

_____

_____

B Make Connections Circle the correct answer.

4. The greatest saint is _(p. 156)_ .

   Saint Benedict   **(Mary)**

5. To be holy means to be filled with _(p. 155)_ .

   (the Holy Spirit)   **life**

6. You are _(p. 158)_ .

   God's father   **(God's friend)**

161

Review

A Check Understanding Have children answer the questions on the lines provided.

B Make Connections Have children circle the correct answers.

Assessment

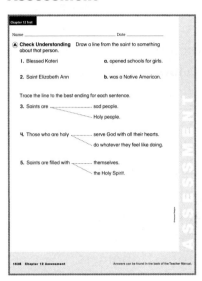

▲ **Chapter 12 Test**
   page 153E

Answers to the Chapter Test can be found in the back of the Teacher Manual.

JUSTICE AND PEACE

Christian Living In Saint Paul's letter to the Romans, he says that Christians must take care of those in need. Involve children in a food drive.

- Children can volunteer to write the note that tells their families about the food drive or decorate baskets to hold the food.

- Include prayer cards with the baskets.

_____

Catholic Social Teaching: Option for the Poor

OPTIONAL ACTIVITY

Paper Hearts Give each child crayons and a large heart cut out of construction paper.

- Ask children to draw a picture that shows their welcoming hearts.

_____

Multiple Intelligence: Visual/Spatial

Family Faith

Remind children to discuss the Family Faith page at home. Encourage children to read the scripture passage from the Acts of the Apostles with their families.

Activity

• Tell children that the family project is a looking activity—to search in church for pictures and statues of saints and to look on the Internet, if possible, to find information about a saint.

People of Faith

Tell children about Saint Dominic.

• Dominic was born in Spain. He traveled and preached in Italy, Spain, and France. He is known as the patron saint of astronomers.

• Remind children to add Saint Dominic to their People of Faith albums.

• Encourage them to pray the prayer at home with their families.

  Visit **www.harcourtreligion.com** for weekly scripture readings and seasonal resources.

Unit 4: CHAPTER 12

Family Faith

 Catholics Believe

■ Saints are friends of God who can show us how to live.

■ People in the Church are called to live holy lives, as the saints did.

✝ SCRIPTURE

Read the Acts of the Apostles 5:12–16 to find out more about Jesus' followers.

GO ONLINE www.harcourtreligion.com For weekly Scripture readings and seasonal resources

Activity

Live Your Faith

Work together as a family to learn about one saint. Use a computer and the Internet, if you can. Choose one thing that saint did that your family can also do. For example, Saint Francis of Assisi cared for animals. What could your family do to care for animals?

▲ **Saint Dominic, 1170–1221**

People of Faith

People in the back of the crowd were trying to see **Dominic**. The people were confused. They wanted him to tell them right from wrong. The crowd hushed as Dominic spoke. He held his Bible high. Dominic said, "The answers you are looking for are in the Holy Book." Dominic went from village to village telling people how to love God. The Catholic Church celebrates Saint Dominic's feast day on August 8.

 Family Prayer

Saint Dominic, pray for us that we may be good listeners when people tell us about God. Amen

In Unit 4 your child is learning about the CHURCH.
162 CCC *See Catechism of the Catholic Church 956–958 for further reading on chapter content.*

 ? HOW DID I DO?

This week my religion classes were

☐ *some of the best ever!* ☐ *pretty good.* ☐ *in need of improvement.*

In what discussions and activities were children most interested?

_____

What activity did I most enjoy teaching?

_____

In what area do I need to improve?

_____

Name _____ Date _____

Make a Halo

Color the halo and decorate it, too. Cut out the halo.
Let the halo remind you to live as a friend of God.

Seven Principles of CATHOLIC SOCIAL TEACHING

Care for God's Creation

Life and Dignity of the Human Person

Rights and Responsibilities of the Human Person

Dignity of Work and the Rights of Workers

Solidarity of the Human Family

Call to Family, Community, and Participation

Option for the Poor and Vulnerable

Faith in Action!
CATHOLIC SOCIAL TEACHING

Connect to Unit 4

This unit's Faith in Action feature teaches first graders the principle that workers deserve to be treated with dignity. It connects to topics covered in this unit.

Children learned that
- they can say "Yes" to God as Noah and Mary did.
- the Holy Spirit helps us do what is right.
- everyone is called to be a saint.

Discover Catholic Social Teaching

Principle: Dignity of Work and the Rights of Workers

In our society, people are often distanced from the workers who make their lives comfortable and convenient. The farm workers who harvest the produce we eat every day are often migrants, workers who travel from field to field following the seasons. Migrant farm workers face a number of challenges that flow from their transient status. Many come from other countries and are not fluent in English. Pay rates and working conditions for migrant laborers are often substandard. Many people are working to improve conditions for migrant workers.

Catholic tradition calls us
- to respect the dignity of all labor.
- to help secure adequate employment for all.
- to reach out to the migrant workers and their families.

Reflect   How can you learn more about, and show appreciation for, the workers who supply the food you eat?

Catholic Social Teaching Document

"We commend church communities that have established migrant shelters that provide appropriate pastoral and social services to migrants. We encourage Catholics and all people of good will to work with the community to address the causes of undocumented migration and to protect the human rights of all migrants . . . ."

From *Strangers No Longer: Together on the Journey of Hope*, A Pastoral Letter of the Catholic Bishops of Mexico and the United States, 2003

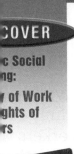

Faith in Action!
CATHOLIC SOCIAL TEACHING

In this unit you learned that you are called to say "yes" to God. The Holy Spirit helps you do what is right at home and at work.

Respect for Workers

People work in all kinds of jobs. People work to earn money so they can live and care for their families. They also work so they can use the gifts and talents God gave them.

Every kind of work is important. Every worker is needed. All workers are not treated the same. Some workers do jobs that are not pleasant. Some workers do not earn enough money. Some workers become ill or injured and cannot work at all. Some people cannot find work.

The Church teaches that work and workers should be treated well. It should not matter who the workers are or what they do.

❷ **What kind of work would you like to do when you grow up?**

163

DISCOVER
Catholic Social Teaching

 Let Us Pray God our Creator, teach us to celebrate all kinds of work and to respect all workers.

Faith in Action
Read aloud the first paragraph. Explain to children that work is one of the ways in which humans say "Yes" to God.

Respect for Workers
Read aloud the first paragraph.

• Invite children to name various jobs with which they are familiar.

• Read aloud the rest of the text.

• Direct attention to the photographs, and ask children to explain how these workers are saying "Yes" to God.

❷ **What kind of work would you like to do when you grow up?** Have children respond to the question in small groups. Ask volunteers from each group to list on the board or on chart paper ideas about future jobs.

 QUICK TIP

Families and Work Children's attitudes toward the Church's teachings on work may depend on family experiences.

• Be aware that children whose families are farmers or business owners may have different perspectives than those whose families are union members, or who have had experience with unemployment.

• Remind children to listen to one another with openness and respect.

OPTIONAL ACTIVITY

Draw Your Work Invite children to draw themselves as adults carrying out a job or profession that interests them.

• Have children write on their drawings a one-sentence description of how their work will help them say "Yes" to God.

• Display the completed art work.

Multiple Intelligence: Visual/Spatial

CONNECT

With the
Call to Justice

CONNECT

With the Call to Justice

A Harvest of Hope

Read aloud the introduction in the margin.

- Invite children to think about what it would be like to move with their families from place to place every few weeks.

- Write the word *migrant* on the board or on chart paper. Explain to children that this word means "moving from place to place."

- Invite children to listen carefully as you read aloud the text on this page.

- Refer to the photograph to enhance the children's understanding of the text.

❷ **How are the Catholics of Rochester showing respect for migrant workers?** Discuss the question as a class.

Farm workers who move from field to field face special difficulties in their jobs. Let's look at how some Catholic parishes are reaching out to these workers.

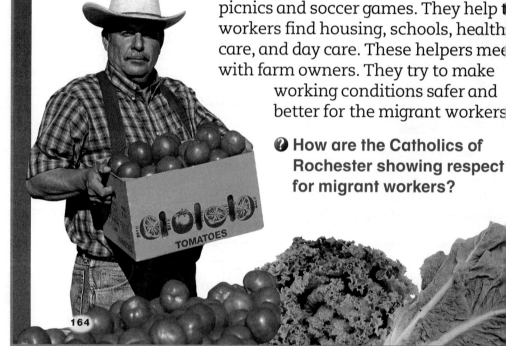

A Harvest of Hope

Who picks the lettuce, tomatoes, grapes, and peaches your family eat? Many crops are picked by workers who move from field to field. These **migrant** workers work hard, often for little money. Many come from other countries. They may not speak English. It is hard for children of migrant workers to keep up with school work or make friends because they move so often.

There are more than 18,000 migrant workers on the farms outside Rochester, New York. The Catholic parishes of Rochester help these migrant workers. They invite them to Mass. They share picnics and soccer games. They help the workers find housing, schools, health care, and day care. These helpers meet with farm owners. They try to make working conditions safer and better for the migrant workers.

❷ **How are the Catholics of Rochester showing respect for migrant workers?**

TEACHER BACKGROUND

Outreach to Migrants Parish outreach to migrant workers is part of the Diocese of Albany's Project Unity program, which is designed to bring together groups of people with different cultural experiences to promote mutual understanding.

- For a better understanding of the challenges facing migrant workers, you may wish to view the video *A Treasure Revealed: Migrant Farm Workers in Our Midst,* available from the Diocese of Rochester.

OPTIONAL ACTIVITY

Cross-Curricular: Reading Share with children one or both of these fictionalized treatments of migrant life:

- *Working Cotton* by Sherley Anne Williams (Harcourt, 1992)

- *Going Home* by Eve Bunting (HarperCollins, 1996)

Multiple Intelligence: Verbal/Linguistic

Reach Out!

SERVE

Do Your Part

[Y]ou are a worker, too. You do [ch]ores to help your family. You [wo]rk at school. You study and [do] your homework.

[Th]ink about the ways you [wo]rk. Read each sentence. [If i]t is true for you, circle the [ha]ppy face. If it is not, circle [the] sad face. If it is true [so]metimes, and you need to [do] better, circle the question [m]ark.

1. I do my best school work.

2. I do my chores at home as soon as I am asked.

3. I am proud of the work I do.

4. I try not to be lazy.

5. I thank my family for the work they do.

[M]ake a Difference

[Le]arn About Work Invite family members [an]d parishioners to talk to your class about [th]eir work. Before you meet, [ma]ke a list of questions for the [wo]rkers. Share a snack as a way [to] say thank you.

165

UNIT 4

SERVE

Your Community
Reach Out!
Do Your Part

Activity

- Read aloud the first paragraph.
- Ask children to suggest other ways in which they are workers.
- Share with children the directions for the activity. If necessary, read aloud the numbered statements and point out the individual icons.
- Allow time for children to complete the activity independently. Tell children they may keep their responses private.

Make a Difference

Activity

- Read aloud the directions.
- Help children identify possible speakers and plan and execute the activity.

Encourage children to share what they have learned with friends, family members, and other classes.

QUICK TIP

Model Respect for Workers When planning visits from children's family members and parishioners to discuss various careers, be sure to model attitudes of respect for the dignity of all jobs and all workers. Encourage children to invite guests who are stay-at-home parents, retired workers, and people training for jobs as well as those employed outside the home.

OPTIONAL ACTIVITY

Make Job Jars Have children decorate job jars in which family members can leave notes about chores that need to be done.

- Give each child an empty, clean lidded jar.
- Supply art materials for children to decorate their jars before taking home.

Multiple Intelligence: Bodily/Kinesthetic

A **Work with Words** Fill in each blank with a word from the Word Bank.

WORD BANK

Saints

Holy Spirit

kingdom

1. The _____ kingdom (p. 136) _____ of God is the world of love, peace, and justice that God wants.

2. The _____ Holy Spirit (p. 145) _____ guides the Church.

3. _____ Saints (p. 154) _____ are people who lived a good life and loved God.

B **Check Understanding** Answer the questions.

4. How can you say "yes" to God?

_____

Responses will vary.

5. What did Jesus promise his followers?

_____

Responses will vary.

6. How did Noah say "yes" to God?

_____

Responses will vary.

7. How does the Holy Spirit help you?

_____

Responses will vary.

8. Why are saints called holy?

_____

Responses will vary.

C **Make Connections** Draw one way to show a welcoming heart.

© Harcourt Religion

166

167

Unit Review

The Unit Review is designed to prepare children for the Unit Assessment. Have children complete the Review pages. Then discuss the answers as a class. You may wish to review any concepts with which children are having difficulty before the Unit Assessment.

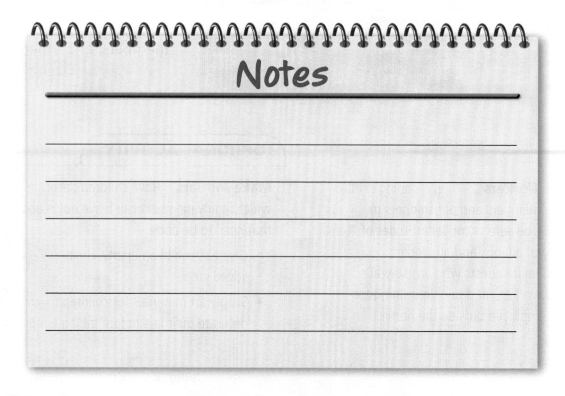

Notes

Name ______________________ Date ____________

(A) Work with Words Write the words from the Word Bank that best complete the sentences.

WORD BANK
peace
Holy Spirit
Church

1. The ____________ is made up of people who follow Jesus.

2. The kingdom of God is the world of love, ____________, and justice.

3. The ____________ is your guide and helper to follow God.

(B) Check Understanding Draw a line to the best ending for the sentence.

4. When you were baptized,	loved God.
5. Saints lived good lives and	you became a member of the Church.
6. The sign of God's promise to Noah was	Jesus.
7. The people of the Church believe in God and follow	a rainbow.

ASSESSMENT

Answers can be found in the back of the Teacher Manual.

Name _____ Date _____

Circle the best answer.

8. Jesus told the story of the rich man's _____.

party

bed

9. Those who are holy love God with all their _____.

hearts

hands

10. The Son of God is _____.

Noah

Jesus

Answers can be found in the back of the Teacher Manual.

©Harcourt Religion

A S S E S S M E N T

UNIT 5
Following Jesus

Chapter 13 Love and Serve
What do followers of Jesus do?

Chapter 14 Making Choices
What can help you choose?

Chapter 15 Say "I'm Sorry"
How can you obey God?

Faith in Action! Catholic Social Teaching Principle:
Solidarity of the Human Family

168

UNIT 5 OPENER

Preview Unit Content

Tell children that Unit 5 is about following Jesus.

- Invite a volunteer to read aloud the chapter title and question for Chapter 13. Ask children what they think they will learn in this chapter.

- Repeat this for Chapters 14 and 15.

- Tell children that at the end of the unit they will learn how friends shared with their neighbors on the other side of the globe.

Overview

Faith Focus

- Jesus came among humans as a servant. *(CCC 565, 608)*
- Jesus taught his followers to serve others as he served them. *(CCC 459, 852)*

Catechism Connection

The *Catechism* says that praying that the Father's "will be done" means asking the Father "to unite [your] will to his Son's," in order that with Jesus' help you may achieve what you could never achieve by yourself: "to do what is pleasing to the Father." *(CCC 2825)*

GDC Link

The *Directory* lists four fundamental objectives of catechesis: (1) knowledge of and adherence to the faith; (2) awareness of the liturgical presence of Christ in the Church; (3) prayer; and (4) moral formation. *(GDC 85)*

"If I, therefore, the master and teacher, have washed your feet, you ought to wash one another's feet. I have given you a model to follow, so that as I have done for you, you should also do."

John 13:14–15

Jesus the Servant

During the Passover celebration with his disciples, Jesus—teacher, master, and honored guest—washed the feet of his disciples. Having astonished his followers with his humble service, he then turned and commissioned them to go and do the same. This command still challenges even the most fervent Christians.

Think for a moment about a person you have helped or served—a child, a parent, your spouse, or your boss. Now, imagine the roles being reversed, and the person serving you. This can be a humbling experience. Christ's love is similar. When Jesus washed his disciples' feet, it foreshadowed his greatest act of service—an act that would come only hours after the Last Supper. Jesus gave his life for all people, and all were undeserving. Jesus humbled himself for you out of love. You are called to do the same for others.

Humble Action

Think about those who are sometimes considered the lowliest in society—those who are poor, ill, or in prison. Imagine what it would be like to wash their feet. Find in Jesus' message the challenge to do the unthinkable. Serve those who are marginalized in your neighborhood and your parish, honoring their God-given dignity.

Reflect **Whom does the Lord call you to serve?**

Morality

The goal of Christian moral formation is to inspire children to follow Jesus by living a life of service to God and to others.

Teaching about service begins with the familiar concept of helping others. Young children are eager to help but they aren't likely to initiate. Be prepared to guide them in serving others.

- Give opportunities for children to serve through helping in the classroom. Establish routines, such as setting up the room, watering the plants, and passing out supplies. Reserve some tasks for children who are shy or hesitant to volunteer.

- Guide children to see that Christian service begins with a willing heart. Help them meet others' needs, using prompts such as, "If you see someone who's sad today, share a smile," or "Someone may like a little help doing the word game. Who will be a kind helper?"

- Model happy, willing service. Holding a door for children or helping them put on their coats are ways to teach service.

Loving Actions

- I like helping others. Give me some jobs to do.

- I like caring for and playing with younger children. Provide me with some time to do this.

- I want to be a follower of Jesus. Share with me some ways to do that.

Keeping Company

Sustaining your spirit requires a community of voices. Some voices cheer you on and unconditionally support you. Other voices ask you to reevaluate and extend your thinking.

We tend to let our relationships and networks develop naturally. If instead you intentionally keep company with colleagues, friends, and family who provide challenging and supportive voices, you gain the confidence to sustain your spirit.

Keeping company with prophets and cheer-leaders, mystics and managers, sergeants and social workers allows you to create and maintain a kind of invisible community that is pulsating instead of passive.

Reflect *Does the company you keep comfort and challenge you? If so, list three voices and the roles they play in sustaining your spirit.*

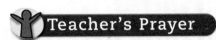

Teacher's Prayer

Lord Jesus, help me to recognize moments of grace and to share this ability with the children. Amen.

Weekly Planner

		Objective	Materials	Prayer & Scripture
DAY 1 Invite	**Love and Serve** Page 169	**Objective:** To describe what service means	☐ Pencils ☐ Paper	🙏 Let Us Pray *Psalm 101:1*
DAY 2 Explore	**Jesus the Servant** Pages 170–171	**Objective:** To discuss how Jesus served others	☐ Board or chart paper ☐ Art supplies ☐ Copies of Activity Master 13, p. 178A ☐ Index card ☐ Pencils	🙏 Let Us Pray *Psalm 101:1* ✝ **Scripture:** John 13:4–17 ✝ **Scripture Background:** Feet Washing, p. 170
DAY 3 Explore	**Follow Jesus** Pages 172–173	**Objective:** To describe how being a follower of Jesus means serving others joyfully	☐ Board or chart paper ☐ Index card ☐ Pencils	🙏 Let Us Pray *Psalm 101:1*
DAY 4 Explore	**Following Jesus** Pages 174–175	**Objective:** To practice following Jesus	☐ Board or chart paper ☐ Art supplies ☐ Outstanding Service certificates or ribbons	🙏 Let Us Pray *Psalm 101:1*
DAY 5 Celebrate	**Pray with God's Word** Page 176	**Objective:** To pray with God's word	☐ Bible ☐ Music CD	🙏 Let Us Pray **Pray with God's Word** 🎵 **Hymn:** "This Is My Commandment"

Chapter 13 Wrap-Up: Review and Apply p. 177 • Chapter 13 Assessment p. 169E

Words of Faith

serve

follower

Activities	Enrichment
Let's Begin: At Your Service, p. 169 Multiple Intelligence: Intrapersonal OPTIONAL Parish Family, p. 169 Multiple Intelligence: Verbal/Linguistic	
Share Your Faith: Think, Share, Act, p. 171 Multiple Intelligence: Visual/Spatial OPTIONAL Activity Master 13: Watch Me Serve, p. 171 Multiple Intelligence: Interpersonal	• **Reaching All Learners:** Increasing Comprehension, p. 170 • **Quick Tip:** Picking Partners, p. 171
Connect Your Faith: Do the Puzzle, p. 173 Multiple Intelligence: Visual/Spatial OPTIONAL Follow the Leader, p. 172 Multiple Intelligence: Bodily/Kinesthetic OPTIONAL Following Jesus, p. 173 Multiple Intelligence: Bodily/Kinesthetic	• **Quick Tip:** Helpful Hints, p. 172 • **Quick Tip:** Word Searches, p. 173
Live Your Faith: Picture Yourself Serving, p. 175 Multiple Intelligence: Visual/Spatial OPTIONAL Cross-Curricular: Citizenship, p. 174 Multiple Intelligence: Visual/Spatial OPTIONAL Act It Out, p. 175 Multiple Intelligence: Bodily/Kinesthetic	• **Christian Living Skills:** Offering Solidarity, p. 174 • **Quick Tip:** Involve Children, p. 175
	• **Liturgy Link:** Praise to You, Lord Jesus Christ, p. 176 • **Lectionary Link:** Break Open the Word, p. 176

Multimedia Resources

 BOOK
Morneau, Robert F. *The Gift.* Paulist Press. 2000. A parable of service.

 VIDEO
Works of Mercy (15 min). Paulist Press. Traditional gestures of service brought to life.

 Teacher Resources
www.harcourtreligion.com
• **For interactive lesson planner, chapter resources, and activities**
• **For free materials and information**

Home Connection

Chapter 13 Family Faith, p. 178
Take-home activities, chapter content review, saint features and prayer

 For more family activities
www.harcourtreligion.com

Name _____ Date _____

A **Work with Words** Circle the word that best completes each
sentence.

1. Jesus washed his friends' feet. He showed them how to
   _____.

   serve   **play**

2. When you serve others, you show your _____ for God.

   hope   **love**

3. To serve is to help give others what they need in a _____
   way.

   loving   **selfish**

B **Check Understanding** Put an **S** on the line if the person is
serving.

_____ 4. Elena sees her teacher carrying books. Elena walks
away.

_____ 5. A child is hurt on the playground. Trevor leads the
crying child to a teacher.

_____ 6. It snowed all night. Cassie sleeps in while her dad
cleans the sidewalk.

_____ 7. Kyle carries groceries for a neighbor who uses a
cane.

©Harcourt Religion

ASSESSMENT

Answers can be found in the back of the Teacher Manual.

Chapter 13 Love and Serve

Let Us Pray

Leader: O Lord, teach me how to help others.
"I sing of love and justice;
to you, LORD, I sing praise."

Psalm 101:1

All: O Lord, teach me how to help others. Amen.

Activity — Let's Begin

At Your Service

"Help me get my shoes on,"
Felipe whined quite loud.

"I'll help you, little brother,"
Rosa smiled and bowed.

"I'll slip a shoe on your foot
And I'll tug, tug, tug!
Now push, push, push
While I shove, shove, shove!"

• How did Rosa help Felipe?

_____

- - - - - - - - - - - - - - - - - -

_____

✎ **Write About Helping** Write about a time when you were a good helper.

169

OPTIONAL ACTIVITY

Parish Family Many people serve the parish.

- Help children make a list of people who serve during Mass (ushers, greeters, gift bearers, readers, altar servers).
- Ask one person to visit and describe how they serve the parish.

Multiple Intelligence: Verbal/Linguistic

Objective: To describe what service means

Open

Prayer Space Invite children to gather in the prayer space. In the space, have a crucifix and a Bible opened to the psalm verse.

Let Us Pray Pray aloud the psalm verse and ask children to pray the response.

Build

Activity

- Tell children to look at the picture while you read the poem.
- Ask each child to find a partner and act out the parts of Rosa and Felipe.
- Ask them why Rosa helped Felipe. Possible responses: because he is too little to tie his shoes, because she's older and wants to help
- Give children time to write their responses.

Extension Activity

- Tell children they will be doing a writing exercise.
- Have them write their response to the text question.
- Ask for volunteers to share their stories with the class.

Close

Have children tell what they learned about helping others.

Objective: To discuss how Jesus served others

Open

 Let Us Pray Invite children to pray the psalm verse on page 169 with you.

 Focus **What does it mean to serve others?** List children's answers on the board or on chart paper.

Build

Jesus the Servant

Tell children that God sent his Son, Jesus, to show people how to love. Then introduce the word *serve* written on an index card.

Jesus Serves

- Tell children to imagine that they are characters in the Bible story along with Jesus. Ask them to imagine what their feet would look like after a very long journey.
- Proclaim the scripture story.

❷ **What did Jesus do to teach his followers?** Write responses on the board or on chart paper.

Explore

Jesus the Servant

 **Focus** **What does it mean to serve others?**

Jesus taught people to **serve**. Sometimes this surprised them.

 SCRIPTURE John 13:4–1

✝ Jesus Serves

One night Jesus shared a special meal with his followers. During supper Jesus got up and tied a towe around his waist. He poured water into a basin. Jesus washed and drie his disciples' feet. His followers wer surprised to see their teacher do th work of a servant.

"Yes, I am your teacher," Jesus said. "If I wash your feet, you should do the same. Serve others."

Based on John 13:4–17

❷ **What did Jesus do to teach his followers?** Possible response: He washed their feet, a sign of service.

170

⭐ **REACHING ALL LEARNERS**

Increasing Comprehension Before you proclaim the scripture story, set the scene for the children and give them whatever help you can to visualize the story. By taking these two steps, you will increase their comprehension of an unfamiliar situation.

- Studies show that the more background information people are given in advance, the better they will understand a story. The production of mental images also greatly aids comprehension.

✝ **SCRIPTURE BACKGROUND**

Foot Washing In biblical times, hosts provided towels and water for their guests to wash the dust from their feet, or had a slave wash their feet.

- In the scripture story, Jesus himself washes the feet of his followers to demonstrate in a dramatic way that they must be prepared to serve each other.

erve Like Jesus

Jesus served his followers. He taught em to serve others. Rosa helped her rother Felipe. Good helpers serve ith love in their hearts. You can rve others in many ways.

How can you serve others?

ssible responses: help rents and teachers; ve food or clothing the needy; help ke care of someone o is sick or hurt

Words of Faith

To **serve** is to help others in a loving way with what they need.

Activity — Share Your Faith

Think: How did Jesus help his followers?

Share: With a partner, talk about ways you can help, or serve, people in your school.

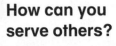 **Act:** Draw a picture of something you can do.

Serve Like Jesus

Tell children that good helpers serve others.

- Read aloud Serve Like Jesus.
- Have children look at the poem on page 169 and discuss the ways that Rosa served her brother Felipe.
- Tell children to look at the picture on this page, and describe what is happening. Discuss how this shows service.

❷ How can you serve others?
Encourage children to give specific examples.

Activity

- Have students pair up with a partner to discuss the question.
- Distribute crayons.
- Invite children to draw what they will do to serve others.

Close

Remind children that good servers give people what they need. By washing their feet, Jesus taught his followers to take the role of a servant.

💡 QUICK TIP

Picking Partners Assign partners rather than have children choose because some of them may not have a close friend. Try pairing children by lot.

- Use small objects that come in varied colors (marbles, candies). You will need one object per child, two of each color. Put the objects in a bag, and have everyone pick one. Children who pick objects of the same color then pair up.

OPTIONAL ACTIVITY

Activity Master 13: Watch Me Serve Distribute copies of the activity found on teacher page 178A.

- Tell children that they will give coupons to people they would like to serve.
- As an alternative, you may wish to send this activity home with children.

▲ Activity Master 13 page 178A

DAY 3

Objective: To describe how being a follower of Jesus means serving others joyfully

Open

Let Us Pray Invite children to pray the psalm verse on page 169 with you.

Focus How can you be a follower of Jesus? List children's answers on the board or on chart paper.

Build

Follow Jesus

Read aloud Follow Jesus. Hold up an index card of the word *follower* to introduce the term.

• Draw a gift box on the board or on chart paper. Tell children that serving others is like giving someone a gift. Let volunteers suggest "gifts" that they can give by serving.

• Write their suggestions in the gift box.

• Draw children's attention to the pictures.

❷ **How are the people in these pictures helping others?** Ask volunteers to share their responses.

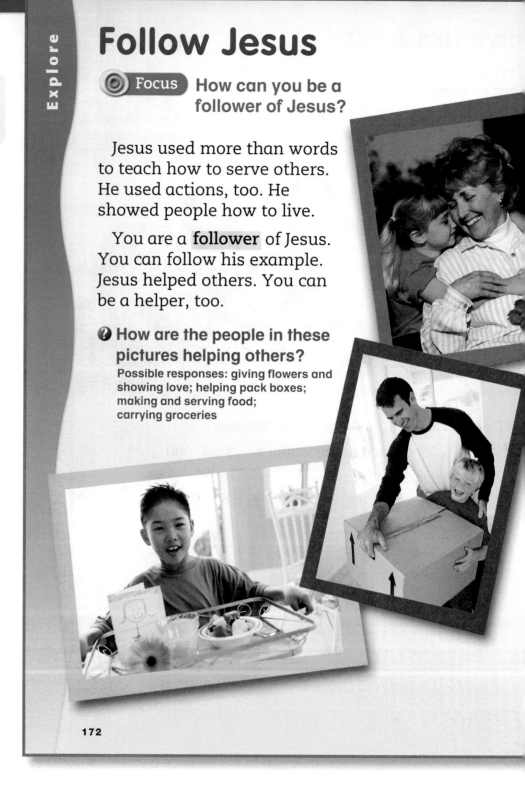

Follow Jesus

Focus How can you be a follower of Jesus?

Jesus used more than words to teach how to serve others. He used actions, too. He showed people how to live.

You are a **follower** of Jesus. You can follow his example. Jesus helped others. You can be a helper, too.

❷ **How are the people in these pictures helping others?**
Possible responses: giving flowers and showing love; helping pack boxes; making and serving food; carrying groceries

172

QUICK TIP

Helpful Hints Children may run out of ideas on how to become a better server.

• They should be able to list concrete actions, such as making their beds at home or helping the teacher pass out papers in the classroom, but may miss more subtle ways.

• Help them by letting children know that they also can become better servers through such actions as listening attentively in class and being cooperative at home.

OPTIONAL ACTIVITY

Follow the Leader Children this age will be familiar with the game of "Follow the Leader."

• If possible, take children outside to play the game.

• Point out that just as the followers in the game depend on the leader not to lead them astray, Christians rely on Jesus' teachings to lead faith-filled lives.

Multiple Intelligence: Bodily/Kinesthetic

Happy to Serve

Serving others made Jesus happy. Jesus served others with a kind heart. Some people serve others but don't seem happy about it. They serve because others tell them to.

God wants you to love and serve others. By serving others, you serve God. He wants you to be the best you can be. Your actions can make others happy. Try to be a happy server like Jesus!

Words of Faith

A **follower** of Jesus is someone who believes in Jesus and lives by his teachings.

Activity

Connect Your Faith

Do the Puzzle Circle these words in the word puzzle: **help, smile, love, serve, God.**

T	G	O	D	T	O	A	A
S	M	I	L	E	C	G	W
E	G	R	S	E	R	V	E
T	F	L	O	V	E	Y	O
V	A	F	K	H	E	L	P

173

Happy to Serve

Tell children to make a grumpy face, and then ask them if that is the way to help others.

- Read aloud Happy to Serve.
- Ask children to show what their faces might look like when they serve others in a loving way.
- Ask children to tell you when it might be hard to serve others with a smile.

Activity

- Read children the directions and the list of words that they are to search for.
- Give children time to find the words. Note that some children may find the activity difficult to do and may work better with a partner.

Close

Tell children that to be a follower of Jesus means to serve others joyfully as Jesus did.

Name _____ Date _____

Make Good Choices

Look carefully at the pictures below. They tell a story. Help the children in the story make a good choice. Draw a picture of the good choice they make.

Overview

Faith Focus

- God always forgives those who sin if they are truly sorry and resolve to avoid future sin. *(CCC 982, 1431, 1443)*
- God commands humans to forgive others. *(CCC 2840, 2844)*

Catechism Connection

The *Catechism* notes that Christ instituted the sacrament of Penance for the forgiveness of sins committed after Baptism. *(CCC 1446–1450)*

GDC Link

According to the *Directory*, conversion is a profound change of heart, arising from deep within a person. It includes repentance and the desire to follow Christ. Conversion is an ongoing process that lasts throughout life. *(GDC 53, 56)*

Saying "I'm Sorry"

CHAPTER BACKGROUND

 "Be on your guard! If your brother sins, rebuke him; and if he repents, forgive him. And if he wrongs you seven times in one day and returns to you seven times saying, 'I am sorry,' you should forgive him."

Luke 17:3–4

Sin and Forgiveness

Sin can cause harm and alienate one from God and others. Jesus knew the human condition. Jesus himself faced the temptation to sin, but he chose not to give in. Jesus reached out to those who had sinned. He forgave them and called them to change their ways. Through his own life, death, and Resurrection, Jesus overcame the power of sin.

Christians are called to be signs of Christ's forgiveness and compassion. Jesus forgave sins and then welcomed sinners to sit at his table. Christians are called to follow the example of Jesus—a difficult challenge, indeed.

To Forgive and to Be Forgiven

Think about someone whom you have a difficult time forgiving. Put aside your own hurt and walk in that person's shoes for a moment. What is the experience of that person? What is his or her loneliness and pain? Occasionally, a hurt is so deep that forgiving the offender doesn't seem to be an option. Yet your own anguish can cause a deeper wound if it is allowed to fester. Lighten your burden. God's love is abundant. Pray for the strength to forgive and the grace to be forgiven.

Reflect *Whom do you need to forgive?*

Forgiveness

The theme of the final chapter on moral living is the Christian's need to forgive in imitation of the God who forgives.

Because they are eager to please, young children may be quick to apologize, at times without an awareness of why the apology is needed. Children know the power of an apology. The words "I'm sorry" can stave off punishment; they can cause a smile; they can make things better. An apology is not the same as experiencing forgiveness, however.

- Spend time helping children forgive each other. Teaching forgiveness is teaching them how to love God.

- When apologies are needed, take children involved to a quiet space, such as a corner in the room. Model care and kindness. Lead the one who is apologizing to say specifically what he or she is sorry for doing. Ask the child to think of a way to make up for the wrong.

- Remind the child who is forgiving that forgiving is more than words. The child needs to show forgiveness by not holding a grudge or seeking revenge.

- Praise children for showing love for God and for each other.

Correction

- When I act inappropriately, correct my behavior but tell me you still care about me.

- Teach me the words and actions that help me ask forgiveness.

- Teach me why I should be sorry.

Challenges and Practices

Some challenges in catechesis are adaptive challenges in which changes are required to sustain your spirit. Some adaptive challenges are obvious, while others erode the ability to sustain your spirit.

The best way to respond to adaptive challenges is with specific practices that

- are intentional ways of doing something instead of simply trying to hold on.

- are proactive responses instead of reactive responses.

- require discipline or courage.

Reflect **What is the greatest challenge you face in sustaining your spirit, and how do you deal with it?**

Teacher's Prayer

Heavenly Father, help me instill in children the willingness to ask forgiveness and the desire to forgive others freely. Amen.

Weekly Planner

		Objective	Materials	Prayer & Scripture
DAY 1 Invite	**Say "I'm Sorry"** Page 189	**Objective:** *To identify the need for forgiveness*	☐ Pencils	**Let Us Pray** *Psalm 51:12*
DAY 2 Explore	**Obey God** Pages 190–191	**Objective:** *To explore the concepts of sin and forgiveness*	☐ Board or chart paper ☐ Art supplies ☐ Index Card	**Let Us Pray** *Psalm 51:12* ✝ **Scripture:** *Luke 18:9–13* ✝ **Scripture Background:** Parables, p. 191
DAY 3 Explore	**Ask for Forgiveness** Pages 192–193	**Objective:** *To explain ways to receive God's forgiveness*	☐ Board or chart paper ☐ Art supplies ☐ Paper Plates	**Let Us Pray** *Psalm 51:12*
DAY 4 Explore	**Making It Better** Pages 194–195	**Objective:** *To practice forgiving and asking forgiveness*	☐ Board or chart paper ☐ Art supplies ☐ Index Cards	**Let Us Pray** *Psalm 51:12*
DAY 5 Celebrate	**Prayer for Help** Page 196	**Objective:** *Ask God's help in forgiving others*	☐ Bible ☐ Hymnals ☐ Music CD ☐ Battery-powered candles	**Let Us Pray** **Prayer for Help** ♫ **Hymn:** "Guide My Feet"

Chapter 15 Wrap-Up: Review and Apply p. 197 • Chapter 15 Assessment p. 189E

Words of Faith

sin

forgive

Activities	Enrichment
Let's Begin: Forgiveness, p. 189 Multiple Intelligence: Verbal/Linguistic	• **Quick Tip:** Clarifying Concepts, p. 189
Share Your Faith: Think, Share, Act, p. 191 Multiple Intelligence: Bodily/Kinesthetic OPTIONAL Family Ties, p. 191 Multiple Intelligence: Visual/Spatial	• **Teacher Background:** Forgiveness, p. 190 • **Cultural Awareness:** Rosh Hashanah, p. 190
Connect Your Faith: Draw an Ending, p. 193 Multiple Intelligence: Visual/Spatial OPTIONAL Feelings, p. 192 Multiple Intelligence: Verbal/Linguistic OPTIONAL God's Love, p. 193 Multiple Intelligence: Visual/Spatial	• **Reaching All Learners:** Early Readers, p. 193
Live Your Faith: Draw a Storyboard, p. 195 Multiple Intelligence: Visual/Spatial OPTIONAL Cross-Curricular: Language Arts, p. 194 Multiple Intelligence: Verbal/Linguistic	• **Christian Living Skills:** Reconciling, p. 194 • **Quick Tip:** Share a Video, p. 195 • **Reaching All Learners:** Vision Impaired, p. 195
	• **Liturgy Link:** Rite of Penance, p. 196 • **Lectionary Link:** Break Open the Word, p. 196

Multimedia Resources

 BOOK
Sjaz, Kathleen C. *Elizabeth, Who is Not a Saint.* Paulist Press. Mahwah, NJ. 1997. A young girl learns about forgiveness.

 VIDEO
The Candy Store (15 min). Ikonographics. Cincinnati, OH. 1978. Overcoming peer pressure and learning to make good choices.

 **Teacher Resources**
www.harcourtreligion.com
• For interactive lesson planner, chapter resources, and activities
• For free materials and information

Home Connection

Chapter 15 Family Faith, p. 198
Take-home activities, chapter content review, saint features and prayer

 For more family activities
www.harcourtreligion.com

Name _____ Date _____

(A) Work with Words   Write the word from the Word Bank that best completes each sentence.

WORD BANK
sin
forgive

1. To _____ is to choose to disobey God and

   do wrong.

2. To _____ is to put aside what someone has

   done to hurt you.

(B) Check Understanding   Circle the word that best completes each sentence.

3. When you sin, you hurt your _____ with God.

   friendship   **neighbor**

4. You can start over with God by saying, "_____."

   I'm sorry   **Thank you**

5. God _____ gives you another chance to change.

   never   **always**

©Harcourt Religion

Answers can be found in the back of the Teacher Manual.

Chapter 15 — Say "I'm Sorry"

Let Us Pray

Leader: Thank you for your forgiveness, O God.
"A clean heart create for me, God;
renew in me a steadfast spirit."

Psalm 51:12

All: Thank you for your forgiveness, O God. Amen.

Activity — Let's Begin

● **Forgiveness** Sometimes you do things that you shouldn't do. Then you need to say you are sorry. You might hurt a friend's feelings. You might not listen to your parents. You might fight with your sister. You might ask her to forgive you.

• How do you show you are sorry?

_____

_ _ _ _ _ _ _ _ _ _ _ _ _ _ _ _ _ _ _

_____

_ _ _ _ _ _ _ _ _ _ _ _ _ _ _ _ _ _ _

_____

✎ **Write About Forgiveness** Write about a time when you said you were sorry.

189

QUICK TIP

Clarifying Concepts Help children learn to distinguish between deliberate sins and accidents.

• Sin always involves an awareness that an act is wrong and a choice to do it anyway.

• Give children an example of a sin and an accident.

DAY 1

Objective: To identify the need for forgiveness

Open

🙌 **Let Us Pray** Have children move into the classroom prayer space. Pray aloud the psalm verse and invite children to pray the response.

Build

Activity

• Read aloud Forgiveness.

• Ask children for some other examples of things they shouldn't do. Possible responses: not listen to the teacher, take something that is not theirs

• Allow children time to answer the text question.

Extension Activity

• Tell children they will be doing a writing exercise.

• Allow time for children to write their answers.

• Ask for volunteers to share their answers with the class.

Close

Have children tell what they learned about forgiveness.

Objective: To explore the concepts of sin and forgiveness

Open

 Let Us Pray Invite children to pray the psalm verse on page 189 with you.

Focus **How do you help your friendship with God grow?** List children's answers on the board or on chart paper.

Build

Obey God

Read aloud Obey God.

- Read to children the definition of *sin* in the Words of Faith box on page 191.

- Hold up an index card with the word *sin* written on it. Tell children that every time you sin, you disobey God. Reassure them that God forgives sinners when they are sorry and promise to do better.

❷ **When may it be hard to obey God?**
❷ **How can you make the right choices?** Encourage children to give specific examples.

Explore

Obey God

 **Focus** How do you help your friendship with God grow?

Sometimes when you make bad choices, you disobey God. When you disobey God, you **sin**.

When you sin, it hurts your friendship with God. You also hurt yourself and others.

God wants you to obey him. He wants you to love him and others with your whole heart. When you do this, your friendship with God grows stronger.

❓ **When may it be hard to obey God?**
Responses will vary.

❓ **How can you make the right choices?**
Responses will vary.

190

 TEACHER BACKGROUND

Forgiveness Remind children about the words of the Lord's Prayer.

- Have them pay close attention to the phrase "forgive us our trespasses as we forgive those who trespass against us." Tell them that God wants us to forgive others as well as ask forgiveness for what we have done.

CULTURAL AWARENESS

Rosh Hashanah The Jewish people celebrate this special holiday by demonstrating that they are sorry for things they have done.

- They observe a custom called *tashlikh*, or "throwing away your sins."

- Give children strips of paper, and have them write bad habits they would like to throw away.

how Sorrow

esus told a story about how God
ants you to act when you are sorry.

Words of Faith

To **sin** is to choose
to disobey God and
do wrong.

✝ SCRIPTURE   Luke 18:9–13

Two Men Who Prayed

Two people went to the temple to
pray. The first man talked about
how bad others were and how
great he was. The second man
had cheated many people. He
was very sorry for what he had
done. He asked God to forgive him.

When Jesus finished this story, he
said, "It was the second man's
prayer that pleased God."

Based on Luke 18:9–13

❓ **When can you be like the
second man in the story?**
Possible responses: When I pray and
mean it; when I tell God I'm truly sorry

Activity

Share Your Faith

Think: Think about a problem that friends might have
with each other.

Share: Talk with your group about some problems that
friends might have.

Act: Choose one problem and act out a way to solve it.

191

Show Sorrow

Invite children to listen to a story Jesus
told. Ask them to listen carefully to see
how God wants us to pray.

Two Men Who Prayed

Proclaim the scripture story.

• Have children look at the illustration
of the man praying. Ask them which
character in the story is pictured.

• Discuss with children the story's
message. Ask them what they can
learn from the story about saying
you're sorry to God and others.
Possible response: Don't be too proud to
say you are wrong.

❓ **When can you be like the second
man in the story?** List children's
responses on the board or on chart
paper.

Activity

• Have children brainstorm problems.

• Give children time to act out a
solution to their problems.

Close

Emphasize to children that sin is the
choice to disobey God. God always
gives people who sin another chance if
they are sorry.

OPTIONAL ACTIVITY

Family Ties   Have children draw a picture of a
smiling face or a sunny day to demonstrate their happy
feelings when they have been forgiven.

• Send the pictures home with a note
thanking families for being an
example of God's mercy when
they forgive.

Multiple Intelligence: Visual/Spatial

✝ SCRIPTURE BACKGROUND

Parables   The story in the text is based on a parable
in the Gospel according to Luke usually known as "The
Pharisee and the Tax Collector." The Pharisee reflects
with self-satisfaction on his own righteousness, while
the tax collector—despised by everyone in Judea as an
agent of the Romans—admits his sinfulness and need
for God's mercy.

Objective: To explain ways to receive God's forgiveness

Open

Let Us Pray Invite children to pray the psalm verse on page 189 with you.

Focus **How do you receive God's forgiveness?** List children's answers on the board or on chart paper.

Build

Ask for Forgiveness

Read aloud Ask for Forgiveness.

• Introduce children to the word *forgive*.

• Tell children that saying "I'm sorry" and "I forgive you" go together like two pieces in a puzzle—they mend a friendship, whether the friendship is between two people or between a person and God.

❓ **How does God know if you are sorry for doing wrong?** Ask volunteers to share their responses.

Explore

Faith Fact

Kneeling is a way to show sorrow for sins.

Ask for Forgiveness

Focus How do you receive God's forgiveness?

Jesus said that God forgives sinners.

God wants you to forgive, too. G[o] wants all people to be friends.

When people forgive, they show love for God and others. When you ask someone to forgive you, you hope the person will say "Yes!"

❓ **How does God know if you are sorry for doing wrong?** Responses

192

OPTIONAL ACTIVITY

Activity Master 15: Show Love
Distribute copies of the activity found on teacher page 198A.

• As an alternative, you may want to send this activity home with children.

▲ Activity Master 16 page 198A

OPTIONAL ACTIVITY

Feelings Teach children how to express their feelings in helpful ways.

• Draw two columns on the board. Label one Sorry and the other Forgive. Have children list phrases they can use to express sorrow and forgiveness.

Multiple Intelligence: Verbal/Linguistic

Make Things Better

God wants you to be close to him.
When you sin, you can say "I'm
sorry. Please forgive me. I will try to
make better choices."

God will always say "I forgive you!"
God is always ready to forgive you.
God's love for you never ends.

Words of Faith

To **forgive** is to agree to put aside what someone has done and not hold it against him or her.

Activity

Connect Your Faith

✏ **Draw an Ending** Work with a partner.
Imagine that you have hurt someone's feelings.
Draw a way to make things better.

193

Make Things Better

Read aloud the first paragraph of Make Things Better.

- Read aloud the second paragraph. Read the first sentence and omit the word *always*. Ask children how often they can try harder to make good choices and lead them to the word *always*.

- Do the same with the reading of the second sentence; omit the word *always* and make it a game for them to guess how often God forgives.

- Read the final sentence, and then ask each child to turn to someone who sits nearby and share the statement.

Activity

- Ask children to suggest examples of wrong moral choices. Write the children's suggestions on the board or on chart paper.

Close

Remind children that God is always ready to forgive.

OPTIONAL ACTIVITY

God's Love To concretize the children's understanding that God is always ready to forgive, give each child a small paper plate.

- Have children write along the outer edge: I am sorry. God forgives.

- Have children cut out the center of the plates and string them into a chain.

Multiple Intelligence: Visual/Spatial

★ **REACHING ALL LEARNERS**

Early Readers Children with reading proficiency may benefit from a more challenging activity.

- Invite these children to write words on their drawings.

- Ask volunteers to read their words or sentences to the group.

Objective: To practice forgiving and asking forgiveness

Open

Let Us Pray   Invite children to repeat after you the psalm verse from page 189.

Focus   How can you make up for doing something wrong? List children's responses on the board or on chart paper.

Build

Making It Better

Read aloud the introductory paragraph.

• Draw attention to the numbered steps and their accompanying pictures.

• Ask four children to read aloud the numbered steps.

❷ **Why should you ask for the Holy Spirit's help when you do something wrong?** Discuss the question as a class.

Making It Better

Focus How can you make up f doing something wrong

When you make the wrong choic you hurt others and yourself. It might seem hard to make things better. The Holy Spirit will help yo Here are some steps to follow.

Think about what you have done. Tell God you are sorry.

Tell the person you hurt that yo are sorry and ask for forgivene

Do whatever you can to make up for what you did wrong.

Ask the Holy Spirit to help you do better in the future.

❷ **Why should you ask for the Holy Spirit's help when you do something wrong?** Responses wi

194

Cross-Curricular: Language Arts   Have children make up short stories about forgiveness.

• Ask children to work in pairs to write or to tell their stories.

• Encourage children to incorporate the numbered steps on page 194 into their stories.

Multiple Intelligence: Verbal/Linguistic

 CHRISTIAN LIVING SKILLS

Reconciling   Help children see that forgiveness is an important part of bringing peace, not only to relationships with family and friends, but also to the world.

• Remind the children to look for peaceful, nonviolent resolutions to conflicts.

• Ask children to serve as mediators when their friends or siblings quarrel.

Live Your Faith

 Draw a Storyboard Think of a wrong choice that first graders sometimes make. Draw pictures of the steps you should follow if you made that wrong choice.

Think about what you have done.

Ask the person you hurt to forgive you.

Do whatever you can to make up for what you did wrong.

Ask the Holy Spirit to help you do better in the future.

195

Activity

- Read aloud the directions for the activity.
- To help children understand the sequence of the storyboard, remind them of other panel stories, such as Sunday comics and comic books.
- Distribute art materials, and allow time for children to work independently on their drawings.
- Have children share their work by passing around their books.

Close

Give each child an index card with *I'm sorry* written on one side and *I forgive you* on the other side. Tell children to use these cards as reminders at home.

QUICK TIP

Share a Video Children may enjoy watching *Larryboy: The Angry Eyebrows* (VHS, 30 min., Big Idea). This *VeggieTales* cartoon uses gentle humor to convey the importance of asking God's help in overcoming wrong choices.

REACHING ALL LEARNERS

Vision Impaired Allow children with visual impairments to complete the drawing activity using one of these alternatives:

- Have children speak their ideas into a tape recorder.
- Invite children to act out their ideas.

DAY 5

Objective: Ask God's help in forgiving others

Prepare

Have children rehearse the response to the prayer.

 Use the *Call to Faith 1* CD, track 15, to rehearse the song.

Gather

Invite children to gather in the prayer space. Remind them that they are praying to God for help in forgiving others.

Pray

A Prayer for Help

 Follow the order of prayer on page 196.

Leader's prayer: **God, help us to forgive others as you have forgiven us.**

• Sing the song together.

Celebrate

Prayer for Help

 **Let Us Pray**

Gather and begin with the Sign of the Cross.

Leader: Let us pray.
Bow your heads as the leader prays.

All: Amen.

Leader: Jesus, help us forgive others.

All: Help us, Jesus.

Leader: Jesus, help us to follow your example.

All: Help us, Jesus. Amen.

Sing together.

Guide my feet while I run this race.
Guide my feet while I run this race.
Guide my feet while I run this race,
For I don't want to run this race in vain!

"Guide My Feet" African-American Traditional

196

 LITURGY LINK

Rite of Penance   Explain to children that the prayer of sorrow for sin is from the Sacrament of Reconciliation, which they will celebrate for the first time next year.

• **Through the absolution of a priest, God forgives people for their sins.**

LECTIONARY LINK

Break Open the Word   Read last week's Sunday Gospel. Invite children to think about what the reading means to them as they try to follow Christ's example. For questions related to the weekly Gospel reading, visit our Web site at **www.harcourtreligion.com**.

 Visit www.harcourtreligion.com for weekly scripture readings and seasonal resources.

CHAPTER 15
Review

A Work with Words
Write the letter of a word from the Word Bank to complete each sentence.

WORD BANK
a. obey
b. sin
c. always
d. friendship
e. sorry
f. forgive

1. Disobeying God's law is called <u>b (p. 190)</u>.

2. When you sin, you hurt your <u>d (p. 190)</u> with God.

3. You can start over with God by saying "I'm <u>e (p. 193)</u>."

4. God <u>c (p. 193)</u> gives you another chance to change.

5. When you <u>a (p. 190)</u> God, you show your love.

6. God will always <u>f (p. 193)</u> you.

B Check Understanding
You can make up for doing something wrong. Number the steps to saying, "I'm sorry."(p. 194)

_____3_____ Ask the Holy Spirit to help you do better in the future.

_____1_____ Think about what you have done.

_____2_____ Ask the person you hurt to forgive you.

197

Review

A Work with Words
Tell children to write the letter of the correct word from the Word Bank to complete the sentence.

B Check Understanding
Ask children to number the steps to saying "I'm sorry" in the correct order.

Assessment

▲ Chapter 15 Test page 189E

Answers to the Chapter Test can be found in the back of the Teacher Manual.

 JUSTICE AND PEACE

The Sacredness of Life The sacredness of human life has always been a fundamental principle of Catholic ethics.

• In recent years, the pope and many bishops have suggested that this principle applies even to people who have committed grave crimes.

Catholic Social Teaching: Life and Dignity

QUICK TIP

Keeping Order In their excitement, children sometimes can become disruptive during games that require spontaneous responses. Instead of allowing children to call out their answers at will, introduce a "talking stick" or other object that signals that only the child who has possession of the object is permitted to speak.

• Be sure the object gets passed around frequently so that all children have an opportunity to contribute.

Family Faith

Remind children to discuss the Family Faith page at home. Encourage children to read the scripture passage from the Gospel according to Luke.

- Encourage interest in the family project by briefly explaining the game.

People of Faith

Tell children about Saint Teresa of Jesus of the Andes.

- Teresa is considered a model for young people because she dedicated her life to God at a very young age.
- Remind children to add Saint Teresa of Jesus of the Andes to their People of Faith albums.
- Encourage them to pray the prayer at home with their families.

Visit **www.harcourtreligion.com** for weekly scripture readings and seasonal resources.

Unit 5: CHAPTER 15
Family Faith

Catholics Believe

- God always forgives those who are truly sorry and want to do better.
- God asks that we forgive others and ourselves.

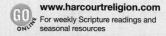

SCRIPTURE

Read Luke 19:1–10 about a time Jesus forgave someone.

GO ONLINE www.harcourtreligion.com
For weekly Scripture readings and seasonal resources

Activity
Live Your Faith

Play a Penny Game Talk with your family about words and actions you can use to show forgiveness. You will need some rolls of pennies and a bowl. Drop a penny into the bowl whenever someone asks for or offers forgiveness. When the bowl is full, offer the money to your paris...

Pennies

▲ Saint Teresa of Jesus of the Andes, 1900–1920

People of Faith

Saint Teresa of Jesus is the first canonized saint of Chile. At the age of nineteen, she entered the Carmelites of Los Andes. She is known for her loving relationship with God. Much of her day was spent praying and writing down her conversations with God. Many of her letters inspire people to love God more each day. She died when she was only twenty years old. Saint Teresa's feast day is April 12. She is the patron of those who are sick.

Family Pray

Saint Teresa, pra
for us that we ma
have a wonderfu
friendship with
God. Amen.

In Unit 5 your child is learning about MORALITY.

198 **CCC** *See Catechism of the Catholic Church 1846–1850 for further reading on chapter content.*

? HOW DID I DO?

This week my religion classes were

☐ *some of the best ever!* ☐ *pretty good.* ☐ *in need of improvement.*

In what discussions and activities were children most interested?

_____

What activity did I most enjoy teaching?

_____

In what area do I need to improve?

_____

Name _____   Date _____

Show Love

Cut out the puzzle pieces. Then put the pieces together to discover what God says when we are sorry.

Care for God's Creation

Life and Dignity of the
Human Person

Rights and Responsibilities
of the Human Person

Dignity of Work and the
Rights of Workers

Solidarity of the
Human Family

Call to Family, Community,
and Participation

Option for the Poor
and Vulnerable

Faith in Action!
CATHOLIC SOCIAL TEACHING

Connect to Unit 5

This unit's Faith in Action feature teaches first graders the principle of seeing themselves as part of the human family. It connects to topics covered in this unit.

Children learned that

- the followers of Jesus are called to serve others.
- we show love by keeping the commandments.
- when we do wrong, the Holy Spirit helps us ask forgiveness and do better.

Discover Catholic Social Teaching

Principle: Solidarity of the Human Family

First graders have a fairly strong sense of themselves as members of their families and their school class. They may know many of their neighbors, and are beginning to take a stronger role in the parish and in the community. But it is still difficult for six year olds to understand the concept of solidarity—the understanding that all people are our neighbors, part of one human family.

Catholic tradition calls us

- to recognize that we are all children of God.
- to share fully in the joys and sorrows of the human condition.
- to do what we can to extend God's healing love to all.

Reflect **How can I set a strong example of solidarity for the children?**

Catholic Social Teaching Document

"Perhaps the most pressing question of our day concerns the relationship between economically advanced commonwealths and those that are in process of development. The former enjoy the conveniences of life; the latter experience dire poverty . . . . Therefore, the nations that enjoy a sufficiency and abundance of everything may not overlook the plight of other nations whose citizens experience such domestic problems . . . ."

From *Mater et Magistra (Mother and Teacher)*, Encyclical Letter of Pope John XXIII, 1961

Faith in Action!
CATHOLIC SOCIAL TEACHING

In this unit you learned to serve others and to love like Jesus did.

One Big Neighborhood

Who are your neighbors? People who live close to you are neighbors. So are the people who live in your city or town.

Jesus taught that all people are our neighbors. All humans are part of God's family.

Families and neighbors share good times and bad times. Neighbors can live close by or far away.

❷ **How can you get to know your neighbors around the world?**
Possible responses: You can send letters, e-mail, collect food.

199

DISCOVER

Catholic Social Teaching

🙌 **Let Us Pray** Jesus, you taught us to love our neighbors. Remind us that all people, everywhere, are part of our family and our neighborhood.

Faith in Action
Ask children to recall the Great Commandment.

One Big Neighborhood
Invite children to listen as you read aloud the text on this page.

• Ask children for their reaction to the idea that all people are neighbors.

❷ **How can you get to know your neighbors around the world?** Discuss the question as a class, listing children's responses on the board or on chart paper.

💡 **QUICK TIP**

Draw on Children's Experience Invite children who have lived in or visited other countries to talk about that experience.

• Ask the children to identify similarities and differences in the places they have lived and the people they have encountered.

• Mark a wall map to show the various countries in which children have lived or spent time.

✴ **TEACHER BACKGROUND**

Vocabulary: Solidarity To help children understand the term *solidarity*, use the following strategies.

• Write the term on the board, and underline the word *solid*. Tell children that *solidarity* is standing firmly with others.

• Have one group of children scatter themselves around the classroom, while another group stands close together. Ask which group is stronger.

CONNECT

With Catholics Around the World

Kids Helping Kids

Share the first paragraph with children, noting the locator map that shows Kosovo.

• Ask children to listen as you read aloud the text.

❷ **Why do you think Erin and her friends wanted to help the children of Kosovo?** Discuss the question as a class. Help children see that Erin and her friends felt love and care for the children of Kosovo, who were their neighbors even though they had never met them.

CONNECT

With the Call to Justice

We are called to love and care for our neighbors. Let's look at how some young people found a way to help neighbors they had never met.

Kids Helping Kids

Neighbors don't always treat one another with love. In a place called Kosovo, neighbors once fought neighbors in a war. Many people were killed. Many families lost their homes.

Erin was an American teenager. Her dad worked in Kosovo. He saw how hard life was for the children. They were cold and hungry. They had few toys or school supplies. When Erin read about them in letters from her dad, she wanted to help.

Erin started a project called Kosovo Kids. She asked everyone she knew to help collect warm clothing and other supplies. Soon people all over the state of Virginia joined in. Erin's project sent 65 boxes full of friendship and care to the children of Kosovo.

CLOTHING DRIVE

200

❷ **Why do you think Erin and her friends wanted to help the children of Kosovo?** Possible response: They knew the children were cold and hungry.

⬥ TEACHER BACKGROUND

Kosovo Kids Other Kosovo Kids projects have been developed independently in many parts of the country, often inspired by U.S. military and civilian workers stationed in Kosovo. Check the Internet for similar programs in your area.

OPTIONAL ACTIVITY

Cross-Curricular: Social Studies Share with children the following resources to help them learn more about the conflict in Kosovo:

• *Girl of Kosovo* by Alice Mead (Farrar Straus Giroux, 2001)

• *One Boy from Kosovo* by Trish Marks (Lothrop, Lee, and Shepherd, 2000)

Multiple Intelligence: Verbal/Linguistic

Reach Out!

lelp Your Neighbor

'hat can you do to help your neighbors?
olve the word puzzle. You will read one thing
ou can do for your neighbors everywhere.

Write the letter that is in PAT but not in HAT.

Write the letter that is in RAN but not in PAN.

Write the letter that is in DAN but not in DEN.

Write the letter that is in MAY but not in MAN.

P

R

A

Y

lake a Difference

leet Your Neighbors Find out more
bout your neighbors in another
ountry. Make a poster or bulletin board
rith pictures and words about these
eighbors. Remember to pray for them.

201

SERVE

Your Community
Reach Out!
Help Your Neighbor

Activity

- Read aloud the introductory paragraph.
- Have children choose partners and work in pairs to solve the word puzzle.

Make a Difference

Activity

- Share with children the directions.
- Work with the class to choose a country, conduct research, and prepare the poster or bulletin board.
- Include the people of the chosen country in class prayer.
- Encourage children to share what they have learned with friends, family members, and other classes.

QUICK TIP

Children's Literature   To help children remember to welcome new neighbors at home and in school, share one or more of these books:

- *The Brand New Kid* by Katie Couric (Doubleday, 2000)
- *The Berenstain Bears' New Neighbors* by Stan and Jan Berenstain (Random House, 1994)

OPTIONAL ACTIVITY

Write a Prayer   Invite children to compose prayers for neighbors around the world.

- Have children write their prayers on cards.
- Choose a card each day and invite the child to lead the class in his or her prayer.

Multiple Intelligence: Visual/Spatial

A Work with Words Circle the correct word to complete each sentence.

1. Jesus taught his followers to _(p. 170)_ others.

   (serve)   have fun with

2. The _(p. 181)_ Commandments tell how to love God and others.

   Five   (Ten)

3. _(p. 183)_ choices help you show love and respect for God and others.

   Wrong   (Right)

4. When you _(p. 188)_ God, you sin.

   (disobey)   obey

5. Jesus taught that God _(p. 190)_.

   forgets   (forgives)

B Check Understanding

6. Name one way to serve others.

   _____
   - - - - - - - - - - - - - - - - -
   Responses will vary.

7. Tell about one commandment.

   _____
   - - - - - - - - - - - - - - - - -
   Responses will vary.

8. Who forgives you when you say, "I'm sorry"?

   _____
   - - - - - - - - - - - - - - - - -
   Responses will vary.

C Make Connections Circle the pictures that show how to follow Jesus.

202

203

Unit Review

The Unit Review is designed to prepare children for the Unit Assessment. Have children complete the Review pages. Then discuss the answers as a class. You may wish to review any concepts with which children are having difficulty before the Unit Assessment.

Notes

_____

_____

_____

_____

_____

Name _____ Date _____

(A) Work with Words   Write the word from the Word Bank that best completes the sentence.

WORD BANK
good
God
forgives
choice
serve

_____
_ _ _ _ _ _ _ _ _ _ _ _ _ _

1. Jesus shows you how to _____ others.

2. The Ten Commandments help you make
_____
_ _ _ _ _ _ _ _ _ _ _ _ _ _ _
_____ choices.

_____
_ _ _ _ _ _ _ _ _ _ _ _ _ _ _ _

3. Every _____ has a consequence.

_____
_ _ _ _ _ _ _ _ _ _ _ _ _ _ _

4. God _____ you when you are sorry.

_____
_ _ _ _ _ _ _ _ _ _ _ _ _ _ _ _

5. When you serve others, you serve _____.

©Harcourt Religion

Name _____ Date _____

B **Check Understanding**   Choose the best ending for each sentence.

6. God's love for you   to be free.

7. A consequence can be   good or bad.

8. God created you   never ends.

9. A follower of Jesus treats people   God's laws.

10. The Ten Commandments are   the way Jesus did.

Answers can be found in the back of the Teacher Manual.

©Harcourt Religion

ASSESSMENT

UNIT 6

Signs of Love

Chapter 16 Jesus the Savior
How does Jesus save people?

Chapter 17 Sacraments
How is Jesus with the Church?

Chapter 18 Baptism
How do you become a member of the Church?

Faith in Action!

**Catholic Social Teaching Principle:
Call to Family, Community,
and Participation**

204

UNIT 6 OPENER

Preview Unit Content

Tell children that Unit 6 is about signs of God's love.

- Invite a volunteer to read aloud the chapter title and question for Chapter 16. Ask children what they think they will learn in this chapter.

- Repeat this for Chapters 17 and 18.

- Tell children that at the end of the unit they will learn how one parish made life better for the people in their community.

Faith Focus

- God so loved humankind that he sent his Son to be its Savior. *(CCC 416–418, 422, 457–458)*

- Jesus died to free us from our sins, and rose from the dead to give us new life in him. *(CCC 601, 613–614, 654–655)*

Catechism Connection

In the words of the *Catechism*, "The Resurrection of Jesus is the crowning truth of our faith in Christ." *(CCC 638)*

GDC Link

Catechesis is centered on Christ, according to the *Directory*. The mystery of Christ "is not another element alongside others, it is rather the center from which all the other elements are structured and illuminated." *(GDC 40–41)*

 "Do not be afraid! I know that you are seeking Jesus the crucified. He is not here, for he has been raised just as he said."

Matthew 28:5–6

Be Not Afraid

Do not be afraid. Do not let your hearts be troubled. Do not fear. God the Father continually assures his people that there is no reason to fear, because he is with them. Yet it is human nature to be afraid—of the unknown or a new situation, of being alone, of what is to come. The shepherds who stood watch in the fields of Bethlehem were afraid. The women at the empty tomb were afraid. The Apostles were afraid when the resurrected Jesus first appeared to them and again as they huddled in an upstairs room awaiting the Holy Spirit.

Recall a time when you felt real fear. It might have been a fear about a physical or emotional pain, a family member being ill, or a relationship that ended. Think about your reaction. Did you ask anyone for help? Did you turn to God in prayer?

Jesus the Savior

Throughout his ministry Jesus listened and heard his followers' cries for help. Those who believe in him have no reason to fear. Jesus is the savior whose loving gift of himself saved people. God knows all there is to know about you, even the number of hairs on your head, and loves you unconditionally. There is nothing to fear *(Matthew 10:26, 30)*.

Reflect **From what fear has God rescued you?**

Jesus the Savior

God's love is so great and so desiring of a relationship with his people that he sent his Son to save them from the power of sin and death.

- Children, through personal experiences or through public events, know about acts of saving. Help connect children's experiences with God's salvation.

- This chapter involves a simple teaching process that encompasses two factors that help children learn—the use of repetition, and the use of celebration.

- You may need to give a simple introduction to the idea of original sin. Young children need not master the theology of original sin. Instead, inspire them by describing God's loving response to the sin of humans.

The Joy of Salvation

- Tell me how Christmas and Easter connect with Jesus' life.

- Spring and summer are my favorite seasons. Let's talk about all the signs of new life.

- Sometimes I am afraid. Help me know that God will keep me safe.

Moments of Grace

Catechesis puts you in touch with the longings and dreams of those around you. It is an important spiritual task to listen to and truly hear the inner voices of students and their parents. You may see the unspoken pain in someone's eyes. You may hear important questions that shy souls are afraid to ask.

The practice of collecting moments of grace is a way to stay in touch with the spiritual nature of your work by deliberately paying attention. You can collect moments of grace by noticing when people invite you to come to know them better or let you get a glimpse of their vulnerability. Moments of grace are collected when you realize that the present is sacred and the ordinary is holy.

Reflect **What moments of grace have sustained your spirit in the past?**

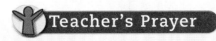 Teacher's Prayer

Jesus, in all you said and did, you showed how to love. Help me live by your example. When I feel in need of comfort, may I trust in your everlasting love. Amen.

Weekly Planner

		Objective	**Materials**	**Prayer & Scripture**
DAY 1 Invite	**Jesus the Savior** Page 205	**Objective:** *To reflect on the experience of being rescued*	☐ Pencils	🙌 Let Us Pray *Psalm 141:1*
DAY 2 Explore	**The First Humans** Pages 206–207	**Objective:** *To explain the need for a Savior*	☐ Board or chart paper ☐ Art supplies	🙌 Let Us Pray *Psalm 141:1*
DAY 3 Explore	**Jesus Saves** Pages 208–209	**Objective:** *To identify Jesus as Savior*	☐ Board or chart paper ☐ Art supplies ☐ Copies of Activity Master 16, p. 214A ☐ Pencils	🙌 Let Us Pray *Psalm 141:1* ✝ **Scripture:** *Luke 23–24* ✝ **Scripture Background:** Resurrection, p. 209
DAY 4 Explore	**Sharing Good News** Pages 210–211	**Objective:** *To practice sharing the good news*	☐ Board or chart paper ☐ Pencils	🙌 Let Us Pray *Psalm 141:1*
DAY 5 Celebrate	**Prayer of Praise** Page 212	**Objective:** *To praise Jesus the Savior through one of the memorial acclamations*	☐ Bible ☐ Hymnals ☐ Music CD	🙌 Let Us Pray **Prayer of Praise** 🎵 **Hymn:** "Alleluia"

Chapter 16 Wrap-Up: Review and Apply p. 213 • Chapter 16 Assessment p. 205E

Words of Faith

Savior
Resurrection

Let's Begin: The Rescue, p. 205 Multiple Intelligence: Interpersonal OPTIONAL Exodus, p. 205 Multiple Intelligence: Verbal/Linguistic	
Share Your Faith: Think, Share, Act, p. 207 Multiple Intelligence: Visual/Spatial OPTIONAL Alleluia, p. 207 Multiple Intelligence: Musical	• Reaching All Learners: Being Rescued, p. 206 • Teacher Background: Original Sin, p. 206 • Teacher Background: Savior, p. 207
Connect Your Faith: Good News, p. 209 Multiple Intelligence: Visual/Spatial OPTIONAL Activity Master 16: p. 208 Multiple Intelligence: Visual/Spatial OPTIONAL Good News p. 209 Multiple Intelligence: Visual/Spatial	• Quick Tip: Graphic Organizer, p. 209
Live Your Faith: Write About Jesus, p. 211 Multiple Intelligence: Verbal/Linguistic OPTIONAL Act It Out, p. 210 Multiple Intelligence: Interpersonal OPTIONAL Cross-Curricular: Music, p. 211 Multiple Intelligence: Musical	• Christian Living Skills: Confronting, p. 210 • Quick Tip: Make a Good News Board, p. 211
	• Liturgy Link: Memorial Acclamation, p. 212 • Lectionary Link: Break Open the Word, p. 212

Multimedia Resources

 BOOK
Greene, Carol. *Amazing Grace! Lord Jesus Lives!* Paulist Press. Mahwah, NJ. 1997. The Easter story in verses that may be sung to the familiar hymn tune.

 VIDEO
Jesus Promises (15 min). Ikonographics. Cincinnati, OH. 1999. Jesus' death and Resurrection reveal God's saving love.

 Teacher Resources
www.harcourtreligion.com
• For interactive lesson planner, chapter resources, and activities
• For free materials and information

 Home Connection
Chapter 16 Family Faith, p. 214
Take-home activities, chapter content review, saint features and prayer

 For more family activities
www.harcourtreligion.com

Name _____ Date _____

(A) Work with Words   Write the word from the Word Bank that best completes each sentence.

> **WORD BANK**
>
> mysteries   life

1. Jesus gave his life so that people could have new

_____

_ _

_____ with God.

2. Jesus' death and being raised to new life are holy

_____

_ _

_____.

(B) Check Understanding   Circle the best title for the topic.

3. He was sent to bring people back to God the Father.

    Savior   **Creator**

4. They brought sin into the world.

    The First People   **The Holy Trinity**

5. This is the name for being raised from the dead to new life.

    Saved   **Resurrection**

©Harcourt Religion

ASSESSMENT

Jesus the Savior

Let Us Pray

Leader: Thank you for saving us, Jesus.
"LORD, I call to you;
come quickly to help me . . ."
Psalm 141:1

All: Thank you for saving us, Jesus. Amen.

Activity — Let's Begin

● The Rescue

"Help, help," cried Tanya.

The harder she pulled, the more her foot became twisted under the tree trunk. Tanya hoped someone would hear her.

"Help, help," she cried again.

Finally, Tanya's father heard her cries. He ran quickly to help her. He had to work hard to get her foot out.

"Thank you, Dad. I was afraid you would never hear me."

• Who saved Tanya?

_____

- - - - - - - - - - - - - - - - - -

_____

Share a Story Think of a story or a movie you know about someone who is saved from danger. Share the story.

205

Objective:
To reflect on the experience of being rescued

Open

Prayer Space You may wish to have children move to your classroom prayer space. In the space, have a crucifix and a Bible opened to *Psalm 141:1*.

Let Us Pray
Invite children to stand and pray together the psalm verse.

Build

Activity

• Read aloud The Rescue.

• Ask children to imagine ways in which Tanya might have gotten her foot caught. Responses will vary.

• Tell children Tanya did something that put her in need of help, and as a result, she needed to be saved or rescued.

• Have children write their response to the question.

Extension Activity

• Ask children to think of a story or a movie about someone who is saved from danger.

• Allow time for children to share the stories.

Close

Have children tell what they have learned about being saved.

OPTIONAL ACTIVITY

Exodus Another way to introduce children to the concept of being rescued or "saved" is to review with them the story of Moses and the Exodus.

• Some children might have seen the movie *Prince of Egypt.* If they have, ask them to describe the plight of the Hebrews in Egypt and how God saved them by bringing them out of Egypt.

Multiple Intelligence: Verbal/Linguistic

DAY 2

Objective:
To explain the need for a Savior

Open

 Let Us Pray Invite children to pray the psalm verse on page 205 with you.

Focus **Why did God's people need to be saved?** List children's answers on the board or on chart paper.

Build

The First Humans

Read aloud The First Humans and invite children to look at the illustration.

• Ask children to retell the story in just a few words. On the board or on chart paper, write "First, Adam and Eve sinned."

God Loves

Read aloud God Loves.

• Ask children how God reacted to Adam and Eve's sin. He continued to love them.

❓ **How do you show love for God?** Write all responses on the board or on chart paper.

The First Humans

Focus **Why did God's people need to be saved?**

God created the first people to be like him. He made them happy and gave them a garden to care for. Adam and Eve made a bad choice. They brought sin into the world.

God Loves

Adam and Eve were no longer the kind of people God wanted them to be.

They broke their friendship with God. They suffered, and they missed God.

But God did not stop loving them. He wanted them to love him.

❓ **How do you show love for God?**
Responses will vary.

206

⭐ **REACHING ALL LEARNERS**

Being Rescued Some children may need some additional information to answer the question after the story. Tell them that sometimes children need to be rescued when they get lost.

• Explain the concept by referring to the plots of TV shows or stories.

✳ **TEACHER BACKGROUND**

Original Sin The sin of Adam and Eve destroyed their descendants' friendship with God as well as their own.

• The doctrine of original sin is a difficult idea for first graders to understand. Explain that once sin came into the world, it became hard for people to be God's friends and to avoid sin.

od's Promise

God said, "I love you always. I will ow you how much I love you. I will nd a **Savior** to bring you back to me."

Activity — Share Your Faith

Think: How does Jesus bring you closer to God the Father?

Share: Talk with a partner about Jesus.

Act: Color the X's red and the O's blue to find a name for Jesus.

207

God's Promise

Have a volunteer read aloud the sentence you wrote on the board or on chart paper: "First, Adam and Eve sinned."

- Explain that God was unhappy that the first people had broken their friendship with him. Tell children he wanted the children and grandchildren of Adam and Eve to be his friends again.
- Read aloud God's Promise.
- On the board or on chart paper, write in big letters "Then God sent people a savior." Explain that this is what he did to rescue people.
- Have children look at the picture.
- Introduce the word *Alleluia* as meaning, "Praise God!"

Activity

- Ask children to work in pairs to find the hidden name in the puzzle.

Close

Tell children that after humans sinned, God promised to send a Savior, his own Son, to rescue them from their sin.

TEACHER BACKGROUND

Savior Have children pronounce the word Savior. Ask them to say aloud what little word they hear at the beginning of the word *Savior*—save. Say that a Savior saves people.

- Jesus is the Savior who saved people from the sin that broke their friendship with God the Father. Jesus brought people back to him.

OPTIONAL ACTIVITY

Alleluia The word *alleluia*, a word of praise that has been used in the Hebrew, Greek, and Latin languages, is used throughout the psalms and in prayers at Mass.

- If your parish uses a musical version of this word, teach children the melody so that when they hear it at Mass, they will be able to join in saying "Praise God."

Multiple Intelligence: Musical

Objective: To identify Jesus as Savior

Open

 Let Us Pray   Invite children to pray the psalm verse on page 205 with you.

Focus   What did Jesus do to save people? List children's answers on the board or on chart paper.

Build

Jesus Saves

Hold up an index card of the word *Savior* as you read the paragraph.

Jesus Lives

Proclaim the first paragraph of the scripture story. Point to the crucifix in the room to show how Jesus died.

- Ask children to listen to what happened after Jesus died as you proclaim the second paragraph.

❷ **What would you have thought about the empty cave if you had been there with the women?** Invite children to respond to the question.

Explore

Jesus Saves

 Focus **What did Jesus do to save people?**

Jesus saved people from the power of sin. He also brought them back to God. Jesus is the Savior.

SCRIPTURE
Luke 23

Jesus Lives

Some people did not believe that Jesus was God's Son. He was arrested and nailed to a cross, where he died. His friends laid his body in a cave and blocked it with a large stone.

Some holy women went to visit the cave where Jesus was laid. The large stone was rolled away. The cave was empty. Two angels said, "Jesus is not here. He is risen from the dead!"

Then Jesus appeared to his followers. He ate with them. He showed them his wounds.

Based on Luke 23–24

❷ **What would you have thought about the empty cave if you had been there with the women?**
Responses will vary.

208

SCRIPTURE BACKGROUND

Resurrection   The word *resurrection* means "the act of rising from the dead." In the Gospel according to Matthew an angel said to the women looking for Jesus after his death, "Do not be afraid! I know that you are seeking Jesus the crucified. He is not here, for he has been raised just as he said" (Matthew 28:5–6). It is through Jesus' Resurrection that we are shown that all who love God will have new life in heaven with him.

OPTIONAL ACTIVITY

Activity Master 16: Jesus the Savior   Distribute copies of the activity on teacher page 214A.

- Tell children that by cutting out the figure of Jesus, they can act out the scenes in the text.

- As an alternative, you may wish to send this activity home with children.

▲ Activity Master 16 page 214A

ew Life with God

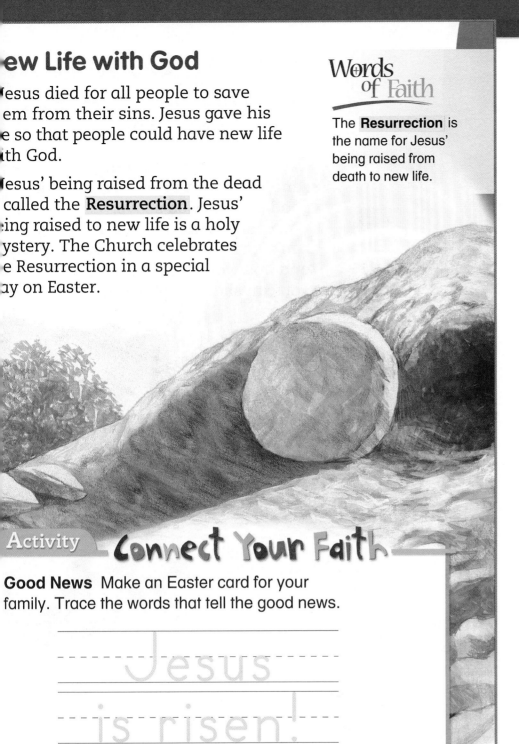

esus died for all people to save
em from their sins. Jesus gave his
e so that people could have new life
th God.

'esus' being raised from the dead
called the **Resurrection**. Jesus'
ing raised to new life is a holy
ystery. The Church celebrates
e Resurrection in a special
ay on Easter.

Activity · Connect Your Faith

Good News Make an Easter card for your
family. Trace the words that tell the good news.

Jesus
is risen!

209

New Life with God

Read aloud New Life with God. Have
children listen to learn what the
Church calls Jesus being raised from
the dead.

- Hold up an index card to introduce
  the word *Resurrection.* Review the
  definition with children.
- Draw the graphic organizer on the
  board or on chart paper. Use the
  organizer to help summarize the
  Resurrection story.

Activity

- Explain to children how to make an
  Easter card. Tell them to trace the
  message in the activity box on their
  card.
- Walk around the room as children
  color, commenting on their work.

Close

Remind children that Jesus is called the
Savior because he saved people from
their sins and brought them back to
God. Jesus' being raised from the dead
is called the Resurrection.

QUICK TIP

Graphic Organizer

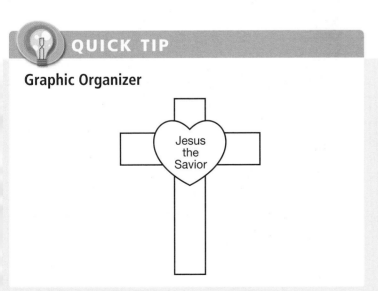

Jesus
the
Savior

OPTIONAL ACTIVITY

Good News Have children make Easter cards for
another class.

- Obtain a list of names, and assign each child a
  recipient.
- Have children deliver their cards to the other class.

Multiple Intelligence: Visual/Spatial

Objective: To practice sharing the good news

Open

Let Us Pray Invite children to pray the psalm verse from page 205 with you.

Focus **How can you share the good news of God's love?** List children's responses on the board or on chart paper.

Build

Sharing Good News

Read aloud the first paragraph.

• Draw attention to the bulleted list of ways to share good news.

• Invite volunteers to read aloud the suggestions.

• Point out the pictures, and ask children to explain how the children depicted are helping to share Jesus' good news.

❷ **What are some other ways you can share good news?** Invite children to discuss the question in small groups.

Explore

Sharing Good New

Focus How can you share the good news of God's love?

After Jesus rose from the dead, he sent his friends to tell everyone the good news of God's love. Jesus wants you to share the good news, too. You can share good news by what you say and how you act. Here are some ways you can share good news.

- Tell someone about Jesus.

- Invite a friend to come to church with you.

- Write a note or draw a picture to cheer up someone who is sad.

- Treat all people with kindness.

- Help someone make a good choice.

- Forgive someone who is sorry for hurting you.

❷ **What are some other ways you can share good news?** Responses will vary.

210

Act It Out Have children role-play situations in which they share good news.

• Invite children to work in small groups to develop their dramatizations.

• Encourage groups to draw ideas from the list on page 210 and the suggestions on the board.

Multiple Intelligence: Interpersonal

CHRISTIAN LIVING SKILLS

Confronting Sharing good news means speaking the truth, even when it is difficult.

• Help children see that that it is possible to stand up to negative peer pressure.

• Remind children that speaking the truth does not mean being rude. Confronting people with the truth and suggesting better choices should always be done with respect and kindness.

Live Your Faith

 Write About Jesus Write words that tell how you feel about Jesus. Use the letters in the word **SAVIOR**.

S

A

V

I

O

R

211

- Read aloud the directions for the activity.
- Write the word SAVIOR vertically on the board or on chart paper, and brainstorm a class example.
- Allow time for children to work independently.

Close

Have children take turns reading aloud their words.

QUICK TIP

Make a Good News Board Give children an opportunity to share good news in the classroom by setting up an ongoing Good News bulletin board or poster. Invite children to add written or artistic descriptions of good news they want to share with their classmates.

OPTIONAL ACTIVITY

Cross-Curricular: Music Share with children a selection of hymns that celebrate Jesus' saving love.

- Use the parish hymnal or invite parish music ministers to teach children one or more songs.
- Help children identify lyrics that describe Jesus as savior.

Multiple Intelligence: Musical

Objective: To praise Jesus the Savior through one of the memorial acclamations

Prepare

Invite children to come up with simple hand gestures to accompany the refrain.

• Call children's attention to the word *Christ* on the page. Explain that Christ is a title given to Jesus, and that he is often called Jesus Christ.

 Use the *Call to Faith 1* CD, track 16, to rehearse the song.

Gather

Invite children to gather in front of the cross in the prayer space.

Pray

A Prayer of Praise

 Let Us Pray   Follow the order of prayer.

• An optional reading includes: *Mark 16:1–6*

• Optional children's acclamations from *Singing Our Faith:* #78 or #79.

 Celebrate

Prayer of Praise

 Let Us Pray

Gather and begin with the Sign of the Cross.

Leader: Christ has died.

All: Christ has died.

Leader: Christ has risen.

All: Christ has risen.

Leader: Christ will come again.

All: Christ will come again.

Sing together the refrain.

Alleluia, alleluia, Alleluia, allelu!

"Alleluia," Traditional

212

 **LITURGY LINK**

Memorial Acclamation   Explain that today's prayer is an acclamation that is sung or said in the middle of every Mass.

• An acclamation is a shout of joy. This one is a memorial acclamation because it recalls Jesus' death and Resurrection.

• Encourage children to sing or say these words at Mass.

LECTIONARY LINK

Break Open the Word   Read last week's Sunday Gospel. Invite children to think about what the reading means to them as they try to follow Christ's example. For questions related to the weekly Gospel reading, visit our Web site at **www.harcourtreligion.com**.

 Visit www.harcourtreligion.com for weekly scripture readings and seasonal resources.

CHAPTER 16
Review

A **Work with Words** Complete each sentence in Column 1 by writing the letter of the correct word from Column 2.

Column 1	Column 2
1. The first humans <u>c (p. 206)</u> God.	**a.** loves
2. God still <u>a (p. 206)</u> his people.	**b.** Savior
3. The <u>e (p. 209)</u> is the name for Jesus' rising from the dead.	**c.** disobeyed
4. Jesus is the <u>b (p. 207)</u>.	**d.** happy
5. God made people to be <u>d (p. 206)</u> with him.	**e.** Resurrection

B **Check Understanding** Circle the correct answers.

6. Adam and Eve made _(p. 206)_ .

   a good choice   (**a bad choice**)

7. Jesus wants you to share _(p. 210)_ .

   (**the good news**)   **sin**

8. Jesus saves people from _(p. 208)_ .

   work   (**the power of sin**)

C **Make Connections** Write a brief response to the question.

How can you share the good news?

_____

- -

_____Responses will vary._____ **213**

Review

A **Work with Words** Have children match answers from Column 2 with sentences in Column 1.

B **Check Understanding** Have children circle the correct response for each sentence.

C **Make Connections** Have children respond briefly to the question.

Assessment

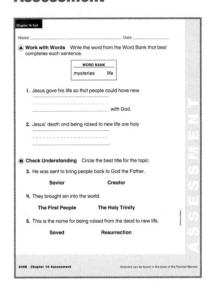

▲ **Chapter 16 Test page 205E**

Answers to the Chapter Test can be found in the back of the Teacher Manual.

 JUSTICE AND PEACE

The Road to Peace In an address on the World Day of Peace, Pope John Paul II said, "There can be no peace without justice, no justice without forgiveness."

- Tell children that Jesus prayed to God the Father to forgive those who hurt him.
- Invite children to think about someone they may need to forgive.

_____

Catholic Social Teaching: Solidarity

 CULTURAL AWARENESS

Symbols Just as the cross is used to represent Christianity, many other religions are associated with symbols of their own.

- The Star of David, for example, is a symbol of Judaism, and the crescent moon represents the Muslim faith.

Family Faith

Remind children to discuss the Family Faith page at home. Encourage children to read the scripture passage.

Activity

- Encourage children to play Honor the Cross with their families.

People of Faith

Tell children about Saint Giuseppina Bakhita.

- Giuseppina was the name Bakhita took as a symbol of her new life in Italy when slavery was abolished. She served the poor and suffering as a nun for fifty years. She helped raise funds to support the missions and was known as a model of holiness and charity.

- Remind children to add Saint Giuseppina Bakhita to their People of Faith albums.

- Encourage them to pray the prayer at home with their families.

 Visit **www.harcourtreligion.com** for weekly scripture readings and seasonal resources.

Unit 6: CHAPTER 16
Family Faith

 Catholics Believe

- God loves you so much that he sent his Son to save you.

- Jesus died and rose to new life.

✝ **SCRIPTURE**

Read John 5:1–11 to see what the Apostle John said about Jesus.

GO ONLINE www.harcourtreligion.com
For weekly Scripture readings and seasonal resources

Activity

Live Your Faith

Honor the Cross The cross is a reminder of Jesus' life, death, and Resurrection. When you're in the car, see who is the first to spot the cross on churches you drive by. As you pass each church, make the Sign of the Cross and say a prayer for all God's people.

People of Faith

In 1869, **Josephine** (Giuseppina) Bakhita was born in the Sudan. At twelve she was kidnapped and made a slave. She became a Catholic nun and a true witness to God's love. She took care of children, comforted people who were poor, and encouraged all who came to her house. Her greatest desire was for everyone to know God. She is the first canonized saint of the Sudan. The Church celebrates her feast day on February 8.

▲ **Saint Giuseppina Bakhita, 1869–1947**

 Family Prayer

Merciful God, help us be like Saint Giuseppina and give comfort to people who are sick or in need of a cheery word. Amen.

In Unit 6 your child is learning about SACRAMENTS.

214 CCC See *Catechism of the Catholic Church* 639–642 for further reading on chapter content.

❓ **HOW DID I DO?**

This week my religion classes were

☐ *some of the best ever!* ☐ *pretty good.* ☐ *in need of improvement.*

In what discussions and activities were children most interested?

_____

What activity did I most enjoy teaching?

_____

In what area do I need to improve?

_____

Name _____ Date _____

Jesus the Savior

Color the figure of Jesus and cut it out. Cut the slits, too.

Put Jesus in every picture. Tell the story of Jesus from the Last Supper to his Resurrection.

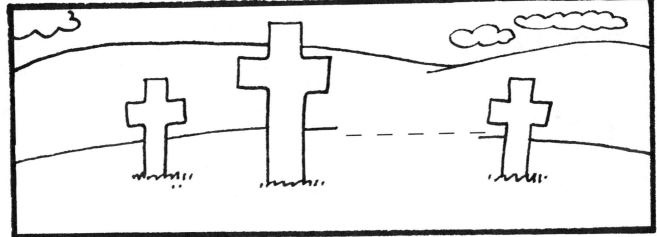

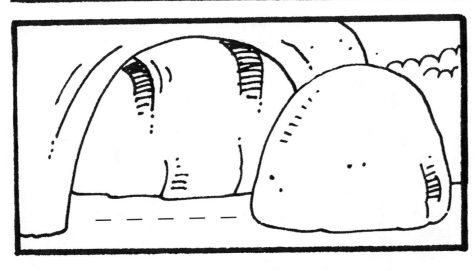

Overview

Faith Focus

- The Church has seven sacraments. They are signs of God's love. *(CCC 1113)*
- Jesus gave the sacraments to make himself present and give a share in his life. *(CCC 1131)*

Catechism Connection

The *Catechism* affirms that the sacraments make people holy, build up the Church, and give worship to God. They also teach, because they are signs. *(CCC 1123)*

GDC Link

Sacraments should be taught within the context of salvation history, the *Directory* suggests, so that the faithful can relive in the liturgy right now the great acts of God that happened in the past. *(GDC 108)*

 "For where two or three are gathered together in my name, there am I in the midst of them."

Matthew 18:20

Jesus and the Sacraments

Jesus' words and actions lay the foundations for the sacraments of the Church. Jesus commissioned his disciples to baptize in the name of the Holy Trinity. He forgave people's sins and healed those who were sick. He was present at the wedding at Cana. He instituted the Eucharist at the Last Supper. After the Resurrection, Jesus sent the Holy Spirit to the Apostles. That Spirit sustains the Church, both in the life of each member and through the ordained ministry.

Sacraments

In order to speak to the whole human person, sacraments engage the senses. God uses words, actions, and material elements from the created world to celebrate the mystery of salvation and convey his grace. The celebration of the sacraments gives glory to God. Sacraments are also for the sanctification of people. They make people holy. Sacraments are not magic. The people who receive the sacraments must have the proper inner attitude in order for the sacraments to be fruitful. Yet in the end all is gift. All is grace.

Reflect   How has your understanding of the sacraments changed over time?

Sacraments

Some children may already be familiar with some of the sacraments. Introduce the idea of signs of God being present in the sacraments.

- Words, actions, and holy things will be seen by young children as signs, or clues, of God's loving presence.

- Take children beyond looking for ordinary signs to being alert to signs of God. Try to use holy water, unconsecrated bread, and unconsecrated wine in your lessons.

- Don't let the lesson end with the class; incorporate simple acts of service for children to perform.

Concrete examples

- Explain to me how objects and words are used as signs and symbols.

- I like to celebrate. Tell me how the sacraments are celebrations.

- I like the way you use concrete examples to teach me about signs and symbols.

Remember Who You Are

You can be overwhelmed by the religious, educational, and emotional expectations of others. Unless you adapt to the challenge of superhuman expectations, you may become fatigued and ineffective.

You may not be able to change others' superhuman expectations of you, but you can practice remembering who you are. This means intentionally reclaiming what you do best and what you care most about.

Remembering who you are encompasses including tasks in your life that come naturally, so that you preserve those sources of fulfillment.

Reflect *Which of your natural talents or interests do you need to remember and reclaim?*

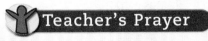
Teacher's Prayer

Lord, may my words and actions be signs of the love and grace you give me. Amen.

Weekly Planner

	Objective	Materials	Prayer & Scripture
DAY 1 Invite	**Sacraments** Page 215	**Objective:** To explore how signs work	☐ Art supplies ☐ *Like a Windy Day* by Frank Asch and Devin Asch (Harcourt, 2002.) ☐ Pencils	🙌 Let Us Pray *Psalm 67:6*
DAY 2 Explore	**Signs of Love** Pages 216–217	**Objective:** To develop an understanding of signs of love	☐ Board or chart paper ☐ Art supplies ☐ Copies of Activity Master 17, p. 224A	🙌 Let Us Pray *Psalm 67:6*
DAY 3 Explore	**Special Signs** Pages 218–219	**Objective:** To describe the sacraments as signs and celebrations of God's presence	☐ Board or chart paper ☐ Art supplies	🙌 Let Us Pray *Psalm 67:6* ✠ **Scripture:** John 14:18–19 ✠ **Scripture Background:** Signs of Love, p. 218
DAY 4 Explore	**Words and Signs** Pages 220–221	**Objective:** To identify the symbols of the sacraments	☐ Board or chart paper ☐ Pencils	🙌 Let Us Pray *Psalm 67:6*
DAY 5 Celebrate	**Prayer of Thanks** Page 222	**Objective:** To pray a prayer of thanks for the gift of the sacraments	☐ Bible ☐ Hymnals ☐ Music CD	🙌 Let Us Pray **Prayer of Thanks** 🙌 **Hymn:** "Sing, Sing, Praise and Sing"

Chapter 17 Wrap-Up: Review and Apply p. 223 • Chapter 17 Assessment p. 215E

Words of Faith

sacraments

Activities	Enrichment
Let's Begin: Many Signs, p. 215 Multiple Intelligence: Visual/Spatial OPTIONAL Children's Literature, p. 215 Multiple Intelligence: Verbal/Linguistic	
Share Your Faith: Think, Share, Act, p. 217 Multiple Intelligence: Visual/Spatial OPTIONAL Guessing Game, p. 216 Multiple Intelligence: Interpersonal OPTIONAL Activity Master 17: Holy Things, p. 217 Multiple Intelligence: Visual/Spatial	• **Reaching All Learners:** Comfort Zone, p. 216 • **Justice and Peace:** Give Comfort, p. 217
Connect Your Faith: Draw a Sacrament, p. 219 Multiple Intelligence: Visual/Spatial OPTIONAL Sacraments Mobile, p. 219 Multiple Intelligence: Visual/Spatial	• **Teacher Background:** Sacraments, p. 218 • **Teacher Background:** Eucharist, p. 219
Live Your Faith: Match the Signs, p. 221 Multiple Intelligence: Visual/Spatial OPTIONAL Cross-Curricular: Language Arts, p. 220 Multiple Intelligence: Verbal/Linguistic	• **Quick Tip:** Visit the Church, p. 220 • **Christian Living Skills:** Celebrating, p. 221 • **Quick Tip:** Share a Video, p. 221
	• **Liturgy Link:** Holy Objects, p. 222 • **Lectionary Link:** Break Open the Word, p. 222

Multimedia Resources

BOOK
Borchard, Therese Johnson. *Taste and See the Goodness of the Lord.* Paulist Press. Mahwah, NJ. 2000. Signs of God's presence as celebrated with the five senses.

VIDEO
The Sacraments (5 videos, 15 min). St. Anthony Messenger Press. Cincinnati, OH. 2002. Children are invited to explore the symbols and celebrations of the sacraments.

 Teacher Resources
www.harcourtreligion.com
• For interactive lesson planner, chapter resources, and activities
• For free materials and information

Home Connection

Chapter 17 Family Faith, p. 224
Take-home activities, chapter content review, saint features and prayer

 For more family activities
www.harcourtreligion.com

Name _____ Date _____

A **Work with Words**   Write the word from the Word Bank that best completes each sentence.

```
┌─────────────────────────────────┐
│           WORD BANK             │
│  ───────────────────────────   │
│  signs              given       │
│                                 │
│            seven                │
└─────────────────────────────────┘
```

1. The sacraments are _____ and celebrations.

2. The Catholic Church has _____ sacraments.

3. The sacraments were _____ by Jesus.

B **Check Understanding**   Circle the best answer for each question.

4. What are the Church's seven signs of God's love?

   commandments   **sacraments**

5. What do all the sacraments have?

   words and actions   **bread and wine**

Answers can be found in the back of the Teacher Manual.

©Harcourt Religion

Chapter 17 Sacraments

 **Let Us Pray**

Leader: God, we thank you for the gift of love.

"May the peoples praise you, God;
may all the peoples praise you!"

Psalm 67:6

All: God, we thank you for the gift of love. Amen.

Activity — Let's Begin

● **Many Signs** Signs are like clues. Leaves, flowers, ice, and snow are signs of some seasons. Some signs tell you what to do. Others may tell you how to think or feel.

• What are some signs of the season you are in now?

_____

- - - - - - - - - - - - - - - - - - -

_____

Draw a Sign Draw a sign or picture that stands for something else. See if your classmates can guess what your sign stands for.

215

OPTIONAL ACTIVITY

Children's Literature A story about the wind that children might enjoy reading is *Like a Windy Day* by Frank Asch and Devin Asch (Harcourt, 2002).

• In this story children can join a little girl as she experiences all the wind is and does.

Like a Windy Day

FRANK ASCH & DEVIN ASCH

Multiple Intelligence: Verbal/Linguistic

Objective: To explore how signs work

Open

 **Let Us Pray** Tell children to move to the classroom prayer space. Read the words to the psalm verse, and have children repeat them.

• Tell children to lift their hands high as they repeat after you each line of the psalm.

Build

Activity

• Read aloud Many Signs.
• Read the question and have children name the current season.
• Call their attention to the photo. Have children identify which seasons are shown in the photo.
• Explain that a sign is something that represents another thing or gives a clue about an event or object (as snow points to winter, or red and yellow leaves to fall).
• Discuss the question.

Extension Activity

• Tell children that they will be drawing a sign that stands for something else.
• Distribute art supplies.
• Have children brainstorm the kind of sign they wish to draw.
• Allow time for children to draw.

Close

Have children discuss what they have learned about signs.

Objective: To develop an understanding of signs of love

Open

 Let Us Pray Invite children to pray the psalm verse on page 215 with you.

Focus **How do you feel and see God's love?** List children's answers on the board or on chart paper.

Build

Signs of Love

Draw a heart on the board and ask children what it is a sign of. love

Ricky the Raccoon

Gather children in a circle (with their books and pencils).

• Read aloud Signs of Love and ask children to listen for what Mama Raccoon said and did to show love.

• Invite children to put an X by the words Ricky's mother said to show Ricky her love. I love you.

❷ **What helps you remember your family's love.** Allow children to discuss the question with a partner.

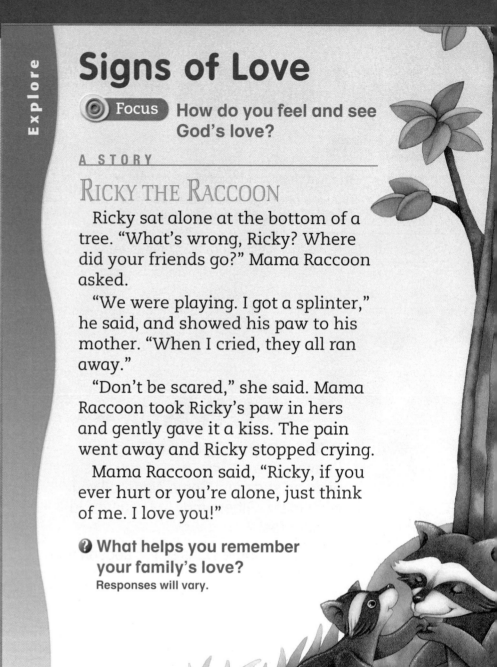

Explore

Signs of Love

Focus **How do you feel and see God's love?**

A STORY

RICKY THE RACCOON

Ricky sat alone at the bottom of a tree. "What's wrong, Ricky? Where did your friends go?" Mama Raccoon asked.

"We were playing. I got a splinter," he said, and showed his paw to his mother. "When I cried, they all ran away."

"Don't be scared," she said. Mama Raccoon took Ricky's paw in hers and gently gave it a kiss. The pain went away and Ricky stopped crying.

Mama Raccoon said, "Ricky, if you ever hurt or you're alone, just think of me. I love you!"

❷ **What helps you remember your family's love?**
Responses will vary.

216

REACHING ALL LEARNERS

Comfort Zone Some children at this age have low self-esteem and feel awkward when singled out. They may feel unsure of themselves and be hesitant to answer a question.

• When asking questions, involve these children by asking for a show of hands, or have children hold up a piece of paper marked "Yes" or "No."

OPTIONAL ACTIVITY

Guessing Game Guessing games make an appropriate tie-in to a lesson about signs as clues.

• Play "Guess the Feeling." Write feeling words (happy, sad) on slips of paper. Ask volunteers to pick a slip and express that feeling by acting out signs that point to it. Have the rest of the class guess what feeling each volunteer is miming.

Multiple Intelligence: Interpersonal

God's Love

Ricky had a sign of his mother's love. God gives you signs of his love, too.

You read about God's love in the Bible. You learn about God's love from Jesus. Jesus healed people as a sign of his Father's love.

The Holy Spirit fills you with God's love. When you show God's love to people, the Holy Spirit is in you.

Activity
Share Your Faith

Think: What are some pictures or items that remind you of God?

Share: Make a list with a partner of things you remember from your church.

Act: As a class walk to the church and play "I Spy." Name the different signs of God in the church.

217

God's Love

Ask children why Ricky's mother gave him a sign of love. Possible responses: Ricky's mother loved him; His mother wanted to help him because he was hurt.

- **Tell** children that God has also given them signs of his love. Ask children what signs of God's love are mentioned in the story.
- **Read** aloud God's Love. Have children identify the signs. Jesus' healings; the acts of love that Christians perform with the help of the Holy Spirit

Activity

- Follow the directions for the "I Spy" game.
- End the game by saying how good it is to know that God loves us.

Close

Tell children that God has given us many signs of his love. Jesus healed people as a sign of God's love. The loving acts that people do with the aid of the Holy Spirit are signs of God's love.

Activity Master 17: Holy Things Distribute copies of the activity on teacher page 224A.

- Tell children to bring their pictures back to class next session to put on display.
- As an alternative, you may wish to send this activity home with children.

▲ **Activity Master 17 page 224A**

✠ JUSTICE AND PEACE

Give Comfort Invite children to show God's love to the homeless.

- Have children trace the outline of one hand onto good paper. Tell each child to cut out the hand and write "God bless you" on it. Ask children to bring new toiletry items to class. Send the messages and toiletries to a homeless shelter.

Catholic Social Teaching: Option for the Poor

Objective: To describe the sacraments as signs and celebrations of God's presence

Open

 Let Us Pray Invite children to pray the psalm verse on page 215 with you.

Focus **What is a sacrament?** List children's answers on the board or on chart paper.

Build

Special Signs
Read aloud Special Signs. Tell children Jesus is with us in special signs called sacraments.

- Ask children if they can name any sacraments. Prompt them to name especially the sacraments of Baptism and Eucharist.

Jesus' Promise
Proclaim the scripture story.

- Ask volunteers to share the promise Jesus made.

❷ **How do you show that God's love is with you?** Encourage children to share what they observed.

Explore

Special Signs

Focus **What is a sacrament?**

God's love is something to celebra[te]. Jesus teaches that God is always with you!

Jesus gave the Church special sign[s] to help people celebrate that he is still here. These signs are called **sacraments**.

 SCRIPTURE John 14:1[8]

 Jesus' Promise

Jesus wanted to remain with his followers even when he returned to God the Father. This is what he said to them.

"I will not leave you orphans; I will come to you. In a little while the world will no longer see me, but you will see me, because I live and you will live."

From John 14:18–19

❷ **How do you show that God's love is with you?** Responses will vary.

218

SCRIPTURE BACKGROUND

Signs of Love Signs of God's love are found throughout the Bible.

- Noah saw a rainbow in the sky after the great flood as a sign of God's love (Genesis 6:11–8:22).
- God sent Jesus to show his love (Luke 2:1–20).
- The Holy Spirit came to the disciples to guide them (Acts 2: 1–12).

TEACHER BACKGROUND

Sacraments The seven sacraments are Baptism, Confirmation, Eucharist, Reconciliation, Anointing of the Sick, Matrimony, and Holy Orders.

- Each of the seven sacraments includes words, actions, and material elements. If received with the proper disposition, each of the sacraments imparts God's grace to the recipient.

igns and elebrations

esus gives us sacraments that we can always know love and care. The tholic Church has seven craments.

he sacraments are signs d celebrations. Every crament has words and tions. When you celebrate e sacraments, the Holy irit is there.

Sacraments of Initiation	• Baptism • Confirmation • Eucharist
Sacraments of Healing	• Reconciliation • Anointing of the Sick
Sacraments of Service	• Matrimony • Holy Orders

Words of Faith

Sacraments are signs of God's love given by Jesus to bring you closer to God.

Activity

Connect Your Faith

Draw a Sacrament
Think of a sacrament that you have taken part in. Draw something from the celebration.

219

Signs and Celebrations

Ask children if they would like to see God standing in the room. Explain that things that you can see, hear, touch, smell, and taste are used to celebrate the sacraments.

• Explain that these holy things are signs that tell you that God—the Father, the Son, and the Holy Spirit—is there with you.

• Read aloud Signs and Celebrations. Introduce each sacrament by name.

Activity

• Have children sit in small groups to work on the activity.

• Invite children to talk about memories of celebrations their families have shared.

Close

Tell children that the seven signs and celebrations of God's love are called sacraments.

✦ TEACHER BACKGROUND

Eucharist In most dioceses, the Sacraments of Reconciliation and Eucharist are celebrated during a child's second grade year.

• Remind children that the word *Eucharist* means "Thanksgiving."

OPTIONAL ACTIVITY

Sacraments Mobile Divide children into seven groups. Give each group a long strip of paper of a different color.

• Assign each group the name of a sacrament to print on the paper and add a picture to illustrate their sacrament.

• Attach the strips of paper to a hanger to make a mobile.

Multiple Intelligence: Visual/Spatial

Words and Signs

Focus What signs are used to celebrate the sacramer

Objective: To identify the symbols of the sacraments

Explore

The Church celebrates seven sacraments. Each sacrament uses words and signs to show God's lov

---

Open

Let Us Pray Invite children to pray the psalm verse from page 215 with you.

Focus **What signs are used to celebrate the sacraments?** List children's responses on the board or on chart paper.

Build

Words and Signs

Invite children to name sacraments with which they are familiar.

- Draw attention to the chart, and read aloud the introduction.
- Invite children to follow along as you go through the chart.
- Read aloud the names of the sacraments, and invite children to respond by reading aloud the names of the signs and what they stand for.

❓ **What signs of the sacraments have you seen?** Discuss the question as a class.

Sacrament	Sign	
Baptism	**Water** God gives new life in Jesus.	
Confirmation	**Holy oil** The gifts of the Holy Spirit are given.	
Eucharist	**Bread and wine** The Body and Blood of Christ are present.	
Penance and Reconciliation	**Outstretched hands** God forgives those who are sorry.	
Anointing of the Sick	**Soothing oil** God helps heal our bodies and spirits.	
Matrimony	**Wedding rings** God blesses the love of a man and a woman.	
Holy Orders	**Holy oil** God calls men to lead and serve the church.	

❓ **What signs of the sacraments have you seen?** Responses will vary.

220

OPTIONAL ACTIVITY

Cross-Curricular: Language Arts Reinforce the children's understanding of symbols by reviewing literary figures of speech.

- Invite children to suggest concrete signs for abstract concepts by asking them to complete sentences such as "Love is like . . ." or "Courage is like . . ."

Multiple Intelligence: Verbal/Linguistic

QUICK TIP

Visit the Church If possible, have the class visit the parish church to examine signs of the sacraments. Arrange for a priest, deacon, or sacristan to show children examples of the vessels used for the sacraments. Tour the baptistery and Reconciliation room.

Activity — ## Live Your Faith

Match the Signs Draw lines to match each sacrament with its sign.

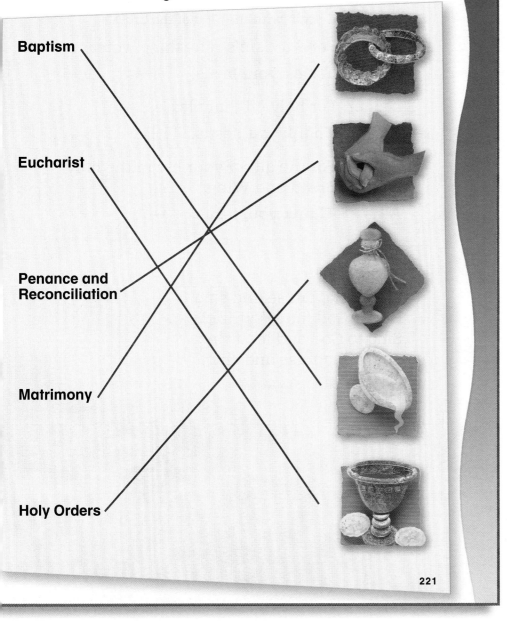

Baptism

Eucharist

Penance and Reconciliation

Matrimony

Holy Orders

221

Activity

- Read aloud the directions for the activity.
- If necessary, review the content of each picture.
- Allow time for children to work independently on the matching activity.
- Review responses by dividing the class into two groups. Have one group read aloud the names of the sacraments, and the other group respond by describing the appropriate signs.

Close

Remind children to look for signs of the sacraments when they attend Mass on Sunday.

 CHRISTIAN LIVING SKILLS

Celebrating Increase children's familiarity with sacramental signs and celebrations by incorporating these ideas into the classroom:

- Use prayers drawn from sacramental celebrations for occasional classroom prayer.
- Note on the classroom calendar any parish or family celebrations of sacraments, such as baptisms or weddings.

 QUICK TIP

Share a Video Children may enjoy watching *A Tour of Our Parish Church* (VHS, 12 min., Ikonographics), in which older students lead young children through the sites of sacramental celebrations.

- Remind children that churches differ in the way they look, but that the sacraments are the same wherever they are celebrated.

DAY 5

Objective: To pray a prayer of thanks for the gift of the sacraments

Prepare

Show children holy water, blessed oil, and bread and wine. Tell them that these are reminders of God's presence. Choose four children to carry the sacramental objects.

 Use the *Call to Faith 1* CD, track 17, to rehearse the song.

Gather

Arrange children in a line at the opposite side of the room from the prayer space.

• Place the four children in front of the line. Have children process to the prayer space.

Pray

A Prayer of Thanks

 Let Us Pray Follow the order of prayer.

• Optional music from *Singing Our Faith:* "You Have Put on Christ," #223.

Celebrate

Prayer of Thanks

 Let Us Pray

Gather and begin with the Sign of the Cross.

Leader: For Baptism's refreshing water,

All: Thank you, Jesus.

Leader: For holy oil that blesses,

All: Thank you, Jesus.

Leader: For the gift of your life in the holy Bread and Wine,

All: Thank you, Jesus.

 Sing together.

Sing, sing, praise and sing!
Honor God for ev'rything.
Sing to God and let it ring.
Sing and praise and sing!

"Sing, Sing, Praise and Sing," Elizabeth Syré
© 2000 GIA Publications, Inc.

222

 LITURGY LINK

Holy Objects Contact the parish to borrow small bottles of holy water and some oil of the sick, some unconsecrated wine, and a few unconsecrated hosts.

• Teach children to handle the objects reverently.

• Explain that the water and oil have been blessed, but the wine and bread have not.

LECTIONARY LINK

Break Open the Word Read last week's Sunday Gospel. Invite children to think about what the reading means to them as they try to follow Christ's example. For questions related to the weekly Gospel reading, visit our Web site at **www.harcourtreligion.com**.

 Visit www.harcourtreligion.com for weekly scripture readings and seasonal resources.

222 Chapter 17

CHAPTER 17
Review

A Work with Words Fill in the letters to complete the sentences.

1. The Catholic Church has _____ sacraments.

___ ___ ___ ___ ___ ___
s   e   v   e   n

2. Sacraments are signs of God's _____.

___ ___ ___ ___ ___
l   o   v   e

3. A sign of Baptism is _____.

___ ___ ___ ___ ___ ___
w   a   t   e   r

B Check Understanding Circle the correct answers.

4. What are the Church's seven signs of God's love?

commandments   (sacraments)

5. God is with you in the sacraments.

(Yes)   No

6. What do all sacraments have?

bread   (words)

7. What did Jesus do for people?

hurt them   (healed them)

8. What are the sacraments?

(celebrations)   stories

9. What sacrament has bread and wine?

(Eucharist)   Baptism

223

Review

A **Work with Words** Invite children to fill in the letters to complete the sentences.

B **Check Understanding** Invite children to circle the correct answer for each question.

Assessment

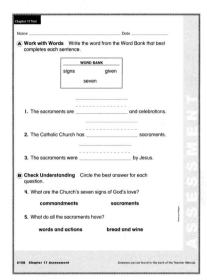

▲ **Chapter 17 Test**
page 215E

Answers to the Chapter Test can be found in the back of the Teacher Manual.

TEACHER BACKGROUND

Seven The number seven has a special significance in Scripture and in Catholic theology. The creation story in Genesis occupies seven days. When Jesus was asked how many times we should forgive a person, he replied, "seventy times seven." The Church celebrates seven sacraments. There are seven deadly sins, seven cardinal virtues, and seven gifts of the Holy Spirit.

TEACHER BACKGROUND

Sacrament The word "sacrament" comes from the Latin word *sacrare*, which means "to consecrate."

- The Church defines a Christian sacrament as "an outward sign of an inward grace instituted by Christ."

Family Faith

Remind children to discuss the Family Faith page at home. Encourage children to read the scripture passage from the Gospel according to Matthew.

Activity

- Tell children they will have the chance to make helping hands with their families.

People of Faith

Tell children about Mary, the mother of Jesus.

- Mary trusted and loved God. We can talk to Mary in prayer and ask her to help us trust God as she did. There is a special prayer to Mary called the Hail Mary.

- Remind children to add Mary to their People of Faith albums.

- Encourage them to pray the prayer at home with their families.

 Visit **www.harcourtreligion.com** for weekly scripture readings and seasonal resources.

Unit 6: CHAPTER 17
Family Faith

 Catholics Believe

- The Church has seven sacraments. They are signs of God's love.

- Jesus gave the sacraments to remind people that he is with them always.

✝ SCRIPTURE

Read Matthew 9:27–31 to learn about Jesus' power to heal.

www.harcourtreligion.com
For weekly Scripture readings and seasonal resources

Activity
Live Your Faith

Make "Helping Hands" Have each family member draw the outline of his her hand on art paper. Then write a loving message on each hand. Save y hands, and give them to a family mem if he or she is having a bad day.

▲ Mary, first century

People of Faith

One day God gave **Mary** a message. "You will have a son. You will name him Jesus." Mary was confused. She said, "How can this be done?" God's messenger said, "The Holy Spirit will come upon you. Your son will be the Son of God." Mary did not know why God had chosen her to be the mother of his Son. She trusted in God's love. Mary became the loving mother of Jesus. She is the greatest of saints.

 **Family Pr**

Blessed Mother pray for us that may always believe in God's great love for us Amen.

In Unit 6 your child is learning about SACRAMENTS.
224 CCC *See Catechism of the Catholic Church 1131–1134 for further reading on chapter content.*

❓ HOW DID I DO?

This week my religion classes were

☐ *some of the best ever!* ☐ *pretty good.* ☐ *in need of improvement.*

In what discussions and activities were children most interested?

_____

What activity did I most enjoy teaching?

_____

In what area do I need to improve?

_____

Name _____ Date _____

Holy Things

Holy things are used in the celebration of the sacraments.

The holy things are signs that God is there.

Use the chart to color the shapes.

See two holy things.

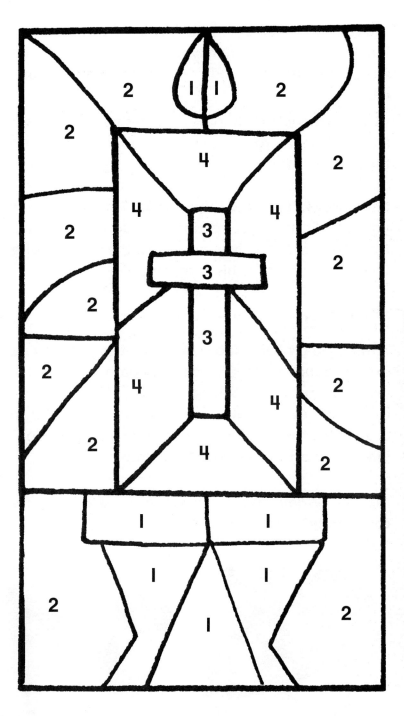

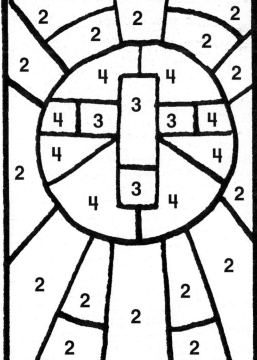

| 1 = yellow |
| 2 = blue |
| 3 = black |
| 4 = white |

Faith Focus

- Your sharing in God's life and love is called grace. *(CCC 1279)*
- Baptism is your welcome into the Church family. *(CCC 1267–1270)*

Catechism Connection

The *Catechism* emphasizes that Baptism forgives all sins and makes a person new. The roots of the whole Christian life are found in Baptism. *(CCC 1263–1266)*

GDC Link

The vocation of the lay catechist arises from the Sacrament of Baptism, according to the *Directory*. The Church helps the individual to discover this gift and calling. *(GDC 231)*

 So whoever is in Christ is a new creation: the old things have passed away; behold, new things have come.

2 Corinthians 5:17

Welcome News

Recall and reflect upon the birth of a new member of the family. How did your family prepare for the arrival of this wonderful gift from God? What did you do to share the good news?

Like a family, the Church welcomes new members with open arms and heart. You became a member of the Church through the Sacrament of Baptism. Baptism is more than a rite that confers membership. Through Baptism, a person is incorporated into Christ's death and burial, and is born into a new life by the power of Christ's Resurrection. Through Baptism, a person is freed from sin and given entry into the new life of grace which Christ opened up for his followers.

Made New

You have probably faced difficult events in your personal existence such as the unexpected death of a loved one, or the loss of a job. Such events can be devastating. These opportunities also hold out new opportunities for spiritual growth. At these times you can find comfort in God's love and in the support of the Church community.

Reflect *When have you most appreciated your faith community?*

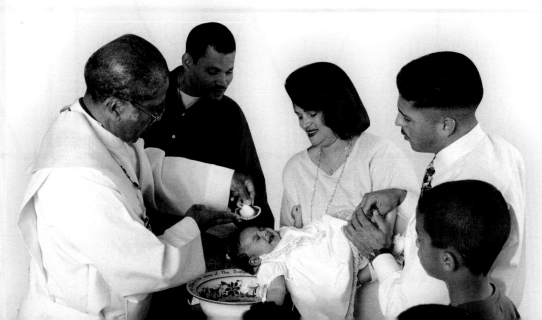

The Sacrament of Baptism

In the sacraments, the Church uses words and actions to show the presence of God. The sacraments work through the senses—through things that are seen, touched, heard, smelled, and tasted. This aspect of the sacraments makes them both accessible and interesting to children, who learn best through their senses.

- Make the lesson about Baptism experiential. Ask someone from the parish staff or the director of religious education to help you obtain holy water, blessed oil, a baptismal candle, and a white baptismal garment—the signs used at a Baptism.

- Treat these items with reverence. Children will observe how you handle them, and will deduce that they are special objects. Allow children to touch the objects. This will help make God's presence more real to them.

- Introduce the children to very basic information about Baptism. In subsequent years, instruction will build on the information you have provided.

Belonging

- I like being part of a group. Explain to me what it means to be part of the Church.

- Help me find ways to thank my family for bringing me to Baptism.

- I learn by example. Show me what it means to be a good Catholic.

Accepting Mediocrity

Acceptance of mediocrity is the quietest and most harmful of all the challenges you face. Accepting mediocrity makes you ineffective and may eventually lead to apathy.

Whether mediocrity is found in colleagues who have lowered expectations, materials that are inadequate, or environments that are in disrepair, its lullaby is the same: "It's good enough."

Testimony is the courageous practice of making a public statement—to one person or many, with words or with actions—that "It's not good enough for me." Even if you don't know how to improve a situation, truthfully testifying that something is not good enough strengthens the fire of your spirit.

Reflect **To what area of mediocrity might you now need to apply the practice of Testimony?**

 Teacher's Prayer

Loving God, help me create a close, generous relationship with these children. Bless me with abundant energy. Amen.

Weekly Planner

		Objective	Materials	Prayer & Scripture
DAY 1 Invite	**Baptism** Page 225	**Objective:** To describe the action of welcoming		**Let Us Pray** *Psalm 100:3*
DAY 2 Explore	**Welcome!** Pages 226–227	**Objective:** To identify Baptism as the sacrament with which the Church welcomes new members	☐ Board or chart paper ☐ A pitcher with water ☐ A bowl ☐ Pencils	**Let Us Pray** *Psalm 100:3* ✝ **Scripture:** Based on Acts 1:5, 8 ✝ **Scripture Background:** The Book of Acts, p. 227
DAY 3 Explore	**Celebrate** Pages 228–229	**Objective:** To examine the rite of Baptism	☐ Board or chart paper ☐ Copies of Activity Master 18, p. 234A	**Let Us Pray** *Psalm 100:3* ✝ **Scripture Background:** Light of the World, p. 228
DAY 4 Explore	**Signs of God's Life and Love** Pages 230–231	**Objective:** To practice living the baptismal call	☐ Board or chart paper ☐ Art supplies	**Let Us Pray** *Psalm 100:3*
DAY 5 Celebrate	**A Blessing Prayer** Page 232	**Objective:** To celebrate a Blessing Prayer	☐ Bible ☐ Hymnals ☐ Music CD	**Let Us Pray** **A Blessing Prayer** 🔥 **Hymn:** "You Have Put On Christ"

Chapter 18 Wrap-Up: Review and Apply p. 233 • Chapter 18 Assessment p. 225E

Words of Faith

Baptisim
grace
godparents

Activities	Enrichment
Let's Begin: The Growing Table, p. 225 Multiple Intelligence: Interpersonal OPTIONAL Choral Reading, p. 225 Multiple Intelligence: Verbal/Linguistic	
Share Your Faith: Think, Share, Act, p. 227 Multiple Intelligence: Verbal/Linguistic	• **Quick Tip:** Giving Directions, p. 226 • **Reaching All Learners:** Up-Close Learning, p. 226 • **Cultural Awareness:** Birth Names, p. 227
Connect Your Faith: Match Game, p. 229 Multiple Intelligence: Visual/Spatial OPTIONAL Being a Light, p. 228 Multiple Intelligence: Visual/Spatial OPTIONAL Activity Master 18: God Is There, p. 229 Multiple Intelligence: Visual/Spatial	• **Teacher Background:** Godparents, p. 229
Live Your Faith: Make Baptism Memories, p. 231 Multiple Intelligence: Visual/Spatial OPTIONAL Renew Baptismal Promises, p. 230 Multiple Intelligence: Bodily/Kinesthetic OPTIONAL Cross-Curricular: Social Studies, p. 231 Multiple Intelligence: Verbal/Linguistic	• **Christian Living Skills:** Goal Setting, p. 230 • **Quick Tip:** Children Who Have Not Been Baptized, p. 231
	• **Liturgy Link:** Bowing, p. 232 • **Lectionary Link:** Break Open the Word, p. 232

Multimedia Resources

 BOOK
Scannell, Anthony J. *Baby's Baptism, Sacrament of Welcome.* Cincinnati, OH: St. Anthony Messenger, 1990. The rite of infant baptism illustrated with photographs.

 VIDEO
The New Birth Day Club: Baptism (13 min). Cincinnati, OH: Ikonographics, 1976. A new member of the family introduces a child to the Sacrament of Baptism.

 Teacher Resources
www.harcourtreligion.com
• For interactive lesson planner, chapter resources, and activities
• For free materials and information

Home Connection

Chapter 18 Family Faith, p. 234
Take-home activities, chapter content review, saint features and prayer

 For more family activities
www.harcourtreligion.com

Baptism 225D

Name _____ Date _____

(A) Work with Words   Write the word from the Word Bank that best completes each sentence.

```
┌─────────────────────────────┐
│       WORD BANK             │
│   parents        water      │
└─────────────────────────────┘
```

1. Your _____ and godparents promised to

   help you live as a child of God.

2. In Baptism _____ is poured on your head

   three times.

(B) Check Understanding   Draw a line to the best ending for each sentence.

3. Baptism makes you   **a.** the new life of grace.

4. Baptism brings you   **b.** a sharing in God's life
                                    and love.

5. Grace is   **c.** a member of the Church.

©Harcourt Religion

Answers can be found in the back of the Teacher Manual.

Chapter 18 Baptism

Let Us Pray

Leader: You give us living water, O Lord.
"Know that the LORD is God,
our maker to whom we belong . . ."
Psalm 100:3

All: You give us living water, O Lord. Amen.

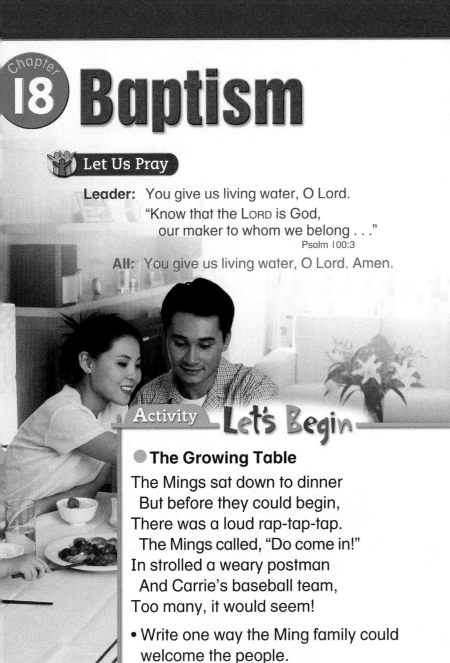

Activity _Let's Begin_

● The Growing Table

The Mings sat down to dinner
But before they could begin,
There was a loud rap-tap-tap.
The Mings called, "Do come in!"
In strolled a weary postman
And Carrie's baseball team,
Too many, it would seem!

• Write one way the Ming family could welcome the people.

_____

– – – – – – – – – – – – – – – – – –

_____

Act It Out With a partner, act out one way your family welcomes visitors.

225

Objective: To describe the action of welcoming

Open

Let Us Pray
Have children move to the classroom prayer space. Pray aloud the psalm verse. Have children pray the response.

• Discuss what living water means in the response.

Build

Activity

• Read aloud The Growing Table.
• Discuss the writing activity at the end of the poem. They make room for everyone; they share their meal.
• Discuss other signs of welcome that children are familiar with.

Extension Activity

• Assign children partners.
• Direct groups to choose one way their families welcome visitors.
• Have children act out how their families welcome visitors.

Close

Have children tell what they have learned about welcoming others.

OPTIONAL ACTIVITY

Choral Reading Have children present a choral reading of the poem.

• Divide children into three groups.
• Assign each group two lines.
• Have each group practice the choral reading.
• Have all read the final line.

Multiple Intelligence: Verbal/Linguistic

DAY 2

Objective: To identify Baptism as the sacrament with which the Church welcomes new members

Open

 Let Us Pray Invite children to pray the psalm verse on page 225 with you.

 Focus **What sacrament welcomes you into the Church?** List children's answers on the board or on chart paper.

Build

Welcome!

Read aloud Welcome! Use index cards to introduce the words *Baptism* and *grace*.

• Ask one child to pour a small amount of water from a pitcher into a bowl. Tell children that at Baptism holy water is poured on a person's head. Explain that Baptism is a welcoming celebration.

❷ **How do you welcome people to your home or classroom?** Write all responses on the board or on chart paper.

Explore

Welcome!

 Focus **What sacrament welcomes you into the Church?**

The Mings welcomed a lot of peopl At their meal, everyone felt like fami

Baptism is your welcome into the Church. God chooses you to be in the Church family.

With Baptism, the Holy Spirit come God makes you his own child. You receive a share in his life. God's life and love in you is called **grace**.

❷ **How do you welcome people to your home or classroom?**
Responses will vary.

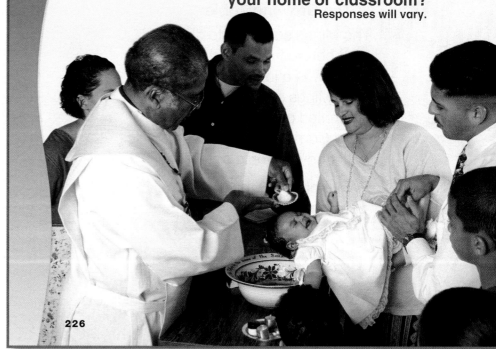

226

 **QUICK TIP**

Giving Directions Clear directions help children stay focused.

• Make sure you have children's attention before giving directions.
• Maintain eye contact.
• Speak in a clear voice.
• Give only one direction at a time.

REACHING ALL LEARNERS

Up-Close Learning Some children may never have seen a celebration of the Sacrament of Baptism.

• In order to give them a better understanding of what happens at a Baptism, make arrangements to teach the entire lesson in church, near the baptismal font.

ollow Jesus

esus said, "You will be baptized
th the holy Spirit. You will receive
wer when the holy Spirit comes
on you. You will be my followers to
e ends of the earth."

Based on Acts 1:5, 8

People who are baptized and who
llow Jesus are called Christians.
ptism helps you do Jesus' work.

You can take part in class and be
ce to others. You can tell others
out Jesus and his love. You can
ow others you care.

What are ways children can do Jesus' work? Possible responses: take part in class; be nice to others; tell people about God's love; welcome others

Words of Faith

Baptism is the sacrament that brings you new life in God and makes you a member of the Church.

Grace is a sharing in God's life and love.

Activity

Share Your Faith

Think: Think about how you might tell others about Jesus.

Share: As a class, make a list of ways.

 Act: Pick one way that you will help others know about Jesus. Fill in the blanks.

_____

- -

I, _____ , promise to

[your name]

_____

- .

227

Follow Jesus

Proclaim the scripture story. Tell children that Jesus' work was to show God the Father's love.

- Invite volunteers to recall some of Jesus' loving actions. Write the actions on the board. Possible responses: helped, forgave, healed, loved, told about the Father

- Have a child slowly pour more water into the bowl. Tell children that the Holy Spirit comes to the person at Baptism and gives him or her power and strength to do Jesus' work.

Activity

- Tell children that following Jesus, doing Jesus' work, and sharing in Jesus' work are all the same.

- Have children fill in their names in the space provided and describe their promise to tell others about Jesus.

Close

Review with children that in Baptism a person is welcomed into the Church, becomes God's child, and receives grace to lead a holy life. God's life and love, communicated to people, is called grace.

 ## CULTURAL AWARENESS

Birth Names The name you receive at birth is usually the name you have at Baptism and throughout your life.

- In Native American cultures names often change as people grow older and reveal talents and strengths. For example, a child's name might be changed to Sings Like A Bird if the child has a beautiful voice.

- Invite children to make up names that describe their talents and interests.

 ## SCRIPTURE BACKGROUND

The Book of Acts The Acts of the Apostles is a continuation of the Gospel according to Luke.

- It describes the early growth of the Church, starting with Jesus' Ascension and the giving of the Holy Spirit on Pentecost.

- The author of Acts was eager to show the various ways that the Holy Spirit was active among the early Christians.

DAY 3

Objective: To examine the rite of Baptism

Open

 Let Us Pray Invite children to pray the psalm verse on page 225 with you.

Focus **What happens in Baptism?** List children's answers on the board or on chart paper.

Build

Celebrate

Invite children to look at the pictures on this page as you read the captions.

- Ask children which person is the one receiving Baptism. the baby Ask them to tell who else is shown in the photos. the baby's parents, godparents, and a priest

- Ask children what objects are used in celebrating Baptism. holy water, a candle, a white garment, blessed oil Explain that the container of water in which people are baptized is called a font.

Explore

Celebrate

Focus What happens in Baptism?

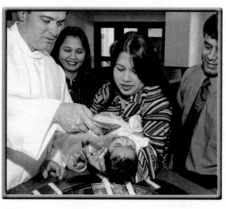
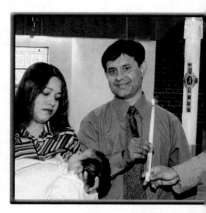

❶ Holy water is poured over you three times while these words are prayed: "[Your name], I baptize you in the name of the Father, and of the Son, and of the Holy Spirit."

❷ You or your parents are giv[en] a lit candle. Light is a sign [of] Jesus. Jesus asks you to b[e] like a light and show his lov[e] to others.

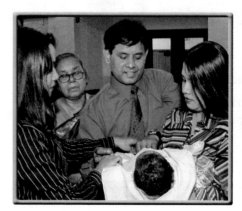

❸ You receive a white garment. It is a sign of your new life in Christ and your membership in the Church.

❹ The priest uses blessed oil to make a cross on your head. It is a sign that you are chosen by God.

228

Being a Light At Baptism, a candle is lit from the Easter candle as a reminder to keep the light of Christ burning in one's heart.

- Draw a candle on a large piece of paper. Invite children to name things they will do to bring God's love to others. Write their ideas on the candle.

Multiple Intelligence: Visual/Spatial

✚ **SCRIPTURE BACKGROUND**

Light of the World From *Genesis 1:3*, when God said, "Let there be light," to *Revelation 22:5*, which states, "Night shall be no more, nor will they need light from lamp or sun, for the Lord God shall give them light," the Bible contains hundreds of references to light.

Your parents and **godparents** are also signs of God's love. They promise that they will help you live as a child of God. The whole community will help you follow Jesus. They will be examples to you and will help you learn about the Church.

Words of Faith

Your **godparents** are chosen by your parents to help you to follow Jesus. They are usually present at your Baptism.

• Read aloud the paragraph.

• Hold up an index card to introduce the word *godparents*. Suggest that when they go home, children ask their families to tell them about their godparents.

Activity

• Read aloud the directions for the match game. Answer any questions children have.

• Give them time to complete the matching exercise.

Activity

 Connect Your Faith

Match Game Draw lines to match the words and the pictures.

Godparents

Light

Holy water

Blessed oil

White garment

229

Close

Tell children that a priest baptizes a person by pouring holy water on his or her head while saying: "I baptize you in the name of the Father, and of the Son, and of the Holy Spirit." A candle, a white garment, and blessed oil are also used in the Sacrament of Baptism.

TEACHER BACKGROUND

Godparents The parents of the child to be baptized generally choose two godparents, one male and one female.

• There must be at least one godparent. This person must be Catholic, at least sixteen, and have celebrated the Sacrament of Confirmation.

• A person from a non-Catholic ecclesial community may be a witness at a Catholic Baptism along with a Catholic godparent.

OPTIONAL ACTIVITY

Activity Master 18: God Is There Distribute copies of the activity on page 234A.

• Tell children to number the pictures to check their understanding of Baptism.

• As an alternative, you may wish to send this activity home with children.

▲ **Activity Master 18 page 234A**

Objective: To practice living the baptismal call

Open

 Let Us Pray Invite children to pray the psalm verse from page 225 with you.

Focus **How can you answer the call of Baptism?** List responses on the board or on chart paper.

Build

Signs of God's Life and Love
Ask children to listen carefully as you read aloud the first sentence.

• Read the next sentence and draw attention to the bulleted list. Have children follow along as you read aloud each item.

• Explain that the chart lists ways to answer the call of Baptism.

• Divide the class into four groups, and have each group read aloud one section of the chart.

❓ **What are some other ways you can be a sign of God's life and love?** Discuss the question as a class.

Explore

Signs of God's Life and Love

Focus **How can you answer the call of Baptism?**

With Baptism, God called you to be a sign of his life and love. Here are some things Go calls you to do.

■ Show that you believe in God—the Father, the Son, and the Holy Spirit.

■ Be like a light and share your goodness.

■ Live a new life in the Church.

■ Love and serve God.

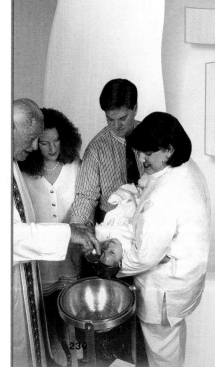

Ways To Answer God's Call

Show You Believe
Pray every day.
Make the Sign of the Cross.

Be Like a Light
Welcome everyone.
Be a good example for younger children.

Live New Life
Go to church with your family.
Give up bad habits that lead to sin.

Love and Serve
Do your chores cheerfully.
Share what you hav

❓ **What are some other ways you c be a sign of God's life and love?**
Responses will vary.

Renew Baptismal Promises Have children make the Sign of the Cross with holy water as a reminder of their baptismal commitment.

• Use a bowl of holy water on the prayer table, or gather children around the holy water container or baptismal font in the parish church.

• Pray the Sign of the Cross.

Multiple Intelligence: Bodily/Kinesthetic

CHRISTIAN LIVING SKILLS

Goal Setting Young children need help recognizing that living out their baptismal commitment is a lifelong process that they take one step at a time.

• Encourage children to set practical, short-term goals for developing good habits.

• Allow time for children to evaluate their own progress on regular occasions.

Live Your Faith

✏ **Baptism Memories** Color the frame and the words. In the frame, draw or glue a picture of your Baptism.

I AM A CHILD OF GOD

231

- Read aloud the directions for the activity.
- Provide art materials, and have children decorate their frames.
- Supply glue or tape for children to insert photos they have brought from home, or allow time for children to draw pictures. Children may also take home their empty frames and invite family members' help in inserting baptismal photos.

Close

Pray together the Apostles' Creed, reminding children that this statement of belief is based on our baptismal promises.

OPTIONAL ACTIVITY

Cross-Curricular: Social Studies Help children research various cultural customs surrounding the celebration of Baptism.

- Guide children in using reference books and appropriate Internet sites.
- Invite children to survey family members about baptismal customs.

Multiple Intelligence: Verbal/Linguistic

 QUICK TIP

Children Who Have Not Been Baptized Be aware that some children in your class may not be baptized, or may come from other religious traditions. Do not draw negative attention to these children's experiences. Invite them to participate, if they so choose, by drawing a generic Baptism picture.

Objective: To celebrate a Blessing Prayer

Prepare

Introduce bowing as a prayerful action. Practice the prayer, bowing at the word "Glory" and remaining bowed through the words "the Holy Spirit."

 Use the *Call to Faith 1* CD, track 18, to rehearse the song.

Gather

Invite children to move to the prayer space and face the prayer leader.

• Stand next to the leader.

Pray

A Blessing Prayer

 Let Us Pray Follow the order of prayer on page 232.

• Optional reading: *John 14:25–27*.
• Optional music from *Singing Our Faith:* "Final Blessing," #287.

Celebrate

Blessing Prayer

 Let Us Pray

Gather and begin with the Sign of the Cross.

 Sing together.

You have put on Christ,
in him you have been baptized.
Alleluia, alleluia.

"You Have Put On Christ," *Rite of Baptism for Children* © 1969, ICEL.

Leader: Glory to the Father,
and to the Son,
and to the Holy Spirit:

All: as it was in the beginning,
is now, and will be for ever.
Amen.

232

 LITURGY LINK

Bowing Bowing is an act of respect that many religions use in their worship.

• You can bow with the head (a reverent nod) or with the whole body (from the waist).

• Catholics often bow to show reverence when they say the "Glory to the Father" doxology used in the service and when they pass in front of the altar in church.

LECTIONARY LINK

Break Open the Word Read last week's Sunday Gospel. Invite children to think about what the reading means to them as they try to follow Christ's example. For questions related to the weekly Gospel reading, visit our Web site at **www.harcourtreligion.com**.

 Visit www.harcourtreligion.com for weekly scripture readings and seasonal resources.

CHAPTER 18
Review

A Work with Words Circle the correct answer.

1. _____ brings you new life in God.

Working **(Baptism)**

2. People who follow Jesus are called _____.

(Christians) family

3. Sharing in God's life and love is called _____.

creation **(grace)**

B Check Understanding Number the steps of Baptism in order.

___2___ You receive a lit candle.

___4___ Your head is marked with blessed oil.

___1___ Water is poured over you three times.

___3___ You are given a white garment.

C Make Connections Write a brief response to the question.

What does Baptism call you to do?

_____

- -
Responses will vary.
_____

- -

_____

233

Review

A **Work with Words** Ask children to complete the sentence by circling the correct answer.

B **Check Understanding** Have children number the steps of Baptism in order.

C **Make Connections** Have children respond briefly to the question.

Assessment

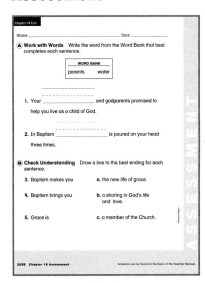

▲ **Chapter 18 Test
page 225E**

Answers to the Chapter Test can be found in the back of the Teacher Manual.

 JUSTICE AND PEACE

Sharing Through Baptism all members of God's family are called to live their faith. The practice of justice and peace begins where you are, here and now.

- You may share a classroom with the parish school. Have children compose a thank you note for others who use the room.

Catholic Social Teaching: Solidarity

 TEACHER BACKGROUND

White In addition to the Sacrament of Baptism, white garments also play an important role in two other sacraments:

- Girls and boys typically wear white garments when receiving their First Communion.
- Brides traditionally wear white for the Sacrament of Matrimony.

Family Faith

Remind children to discuss the Family Faith page at home. Encourage children to read the scripture passage from the Gospel according to Matthew.

Activity

• Encourage children to have their families visit the baptismal font at church.

• Tell them to bless themselves with the holy water as they leave church.

People of Faith

Discuss Saint Moses the Black.

• Moses founded a monastery in the desert of Egypt where monks lived and prayed. He was a very humble man. He never wanted praise for his holiness.

• Remind children to add this saint to their People of Faith albums.

• Encourage them to pray the prayer at home with their families.

 Visit **www.harcourtreligion.com** for weekly scripture readings and seasonal resources.

CHAPTER 18
Family Faith

◎ Catholics Believe

■ God's love and life is called your sharing in grace.

■ Baptism is your welcome into the Church family.

✝ SCRIPTURE

Read Matthew 3:13–17 to find out about the baptism of Jesus.

 www.harcourtreligion.com
For weekly Scripture readings and seasonal resources

Activity
Live Your Faith

Remember Baptism Visit the baptism font at your church after Sunday Mass. Remind your child that the water is blessed. Look for signs of God or of Baptism that decorate the font. On your way out of the church, have each member of the family make the Sign of the Cross with the holy water.

▲ **Saint Moses the Black, fourth century**

People of Faith

During his teenage years, **Saint Moses** was a slave. Many people were frightened of him because he was very, very tall. Moses was unhappy with his life, so he began to search for God. A priest and a farmer told Moses about God and God's love for him. Moses was baptized and later became a priest. He taught others about God's love. He is the patron saint of African Americans. The Church celebrates the feast day of Saint Moses on August 28.

🙌 Family Prayer

Saint Moses the Black, pray for us that we will be peaceful people and show others signs of God's love. Amen.

234 **CCC** *See Catechism of the Catholic Church 1277–1282 for further reading on chapter content.*

? HOW DID I DO?

This week my religion classes were

☐ *some of the best ever!* ☐ *pretty good.* ☐ *in need of improvement.*

In what discussions and activities were children most interested?

_____

What activity did I most enjoy teaching?

_____

In what area do I need to improve?

_____

Name _____ Date _____

God Is There

Write the sentence number under the picture it tells about.

1. Your family brings you to church to be baptized.

2. The priest pours holy water on your head three times. He says, "I baptize you in the name of the Father, and of the Son, and of the Holy Spirit."

3. After the Baptism, the priest makes a cross on your head with holy oil.

4. You are given a white garment.

5. A candle is lit.

Care for God's Creation

Life and Dignity of the
Human Person

Rights and Responsibilities
of the Human Person

Dignity of Work and the
Rights of Workers

Solidarity of the
Human Family

Call to Family, Community,
and Participation

Option for the Poor
and Vulnerable

Faith in Action!
CATHOLIC SOCIAL TEACHING

Connect to Unit 6

This unit's Faith in Action feature teaches first graders the
principle that community involvement is part of living our faith.
It connects to topics covered in this unit.

Children learned that

• Jesus calls us to share the good news of God's saving love.

• the Church celebrates God's love in seven sacraments.

• Baptism makes us members of the Church.

Discover Catholic Social Teaching

Principle: Call to Family, Community, and Participation

Merely belonging to a family or a community is not enough. A
community in which no one participates or works together is
simply a collection of individuals. In order to live in the
communal relationship God intends for humans, we have to
take responsibility for doing our part. We have to give as well as
take, sacrifice as well as celebrate. It is also necessary for our
survival as individuals that we work together.

Catholic tradition calls us

• to recognize that we live in relationship with all members of
the human family.

• to break down walls of selfishness, isolation, and apathy.

• to become fully involved in our families, communities, and
world.

Reflect **How are you answering the call to be fully involved
in your family, your community, and the world?**

Catholic Social Teaching Document

"It is imperative that no one . . . would indulge in a merely individualistic
morality. The best way to fulfill one's obligations of justice and love is to
contribute to the common good according to one's means and the needs
of others, and also to promote and help public and private organizations
devoted to bettering the conditions of life."

From *Gaudium et Spes (Pastoral Constitution on the Church in the Modern World)*, 1965

COVER

ic Social
ng:

Family,
unity,
rticipation

Faith in Action!
CATHOLIC SOCIAL TEACHING

In this unit you learned that you can share the good news of God's love. You can celebrate God's love with the parish family in the sacraments.

You Are Needed

What is a family without family members? What is a community without people? What is a parish without parishioners?

Every group must have members. No group can continue to live and grow unless its members work together.

Your family, your parish, and your community would not be the same without you. You are needed. You can use the gifts God gave you to help in many groups in your community.

❓ **How do you participate in your family's life?**
Responses will vary.

235

DISCOVER
Catholic Social Teaching

Let Us Pray Jesus, you send us to bring light and good news to everyone. Help us do our part at home, in the community, and in the world.

Faith in Action

Ask children to think about what it means to belong to a community.

You Are Needed

Read aloud the first two paragraphs.

- Write the word *participate* on the board or on chart paper, and help children sound it out.
- Read aloud the third paragraph.
- Direct attention to the pictures, and ask how children shown are participating.

❓ **How do you participate in your family's life?** Discuss the question as a class.

💡 QUICK TIP

Families Recognize that children come from families of all kinds.

- Emphasize the love and support family members give one another, not the composition of the individual family.
- Make sure not to ask children for details of their family lives.

OPTIONAL ACTIVITY

Community Web Have children draw community webs showing their links to communities.

- Give children large sheets of chart paper. Have them write their names in the middle of the paper, and begin the web with their families.
- Have children add web links for all organizations, groups, and communities of which they are part— for example, class, school, parish, etc.

Multiple Intelligence: Interpersonal

CONNECT

With the Call to Justice

Wheels for Warmth

Ask children who ride bicycles to tell the longest distances they have biked at one time.

- Invite children to listen carefully as you read aloud the story on this page.

- Explain that a Bike-a-Thon is a way to raise money. People promise to pay the riders a certain amount of money for each mile they ride.

- Make sure children understand that the proceeds of the Bike-a-Thon were used to help pay winter heating bills for families with little money.

❓ **How do you think the people who take part in the Bike-a-Thon feel about what they do?** Discuss the questions as a class.

CONNECT

With the Call to Justice

People can make a big difference when they work together. Let's see how the members of one parish community help keep people warm in winter.

Wheels for Warmt

Winters are very cold in the state c Connecticut. People have to spend a lot of money to keep their houses warm. Some people do not have enough money to heat their homes. So the people in Southbury decided to help.

Every fall this town holds a Bike-a-Thon to raise money. The money the collect helps pay winter heating bills for those in need. Everyone in the community participates. Some peopl ride their bikes and others walk.

The people of Sacred Heart Parish ride and walk. They also do somethii else. Sacred Heart parishioners cook and sell hundreds of hot dogs to the hungry bikers and hikers. The hot dogs are part of a picnic feast that warms everyone's hearts.

❓ **How do you think the people who take part i the Bike-a-Thon feel about what they do?** Possible responses: They fe good helping others; they ar thankful for what they have.

✦ TEACHER BACKGROUND

Tour de Tribury The Bike-a-Thon described in this story is an annual fundraiser sponsored by a number of churches and civic organizations in Southbury, Connecticut.

- You may wish to conduct research on the Internet to find out more about the Tour de Tribury.

OPTIONAL ACTIVITY

Cross-Curricular: Math Help children calculate how much the class might earn in a bike-a-thon if every child participated.

- Suppose each child rides 3 miles, and each child secures three pledges of one dollar per mile.

Multiple Intelligence: Mathematical/Logical

Reach Out!

SERVE
Your Community

Draw Pictures

think about how you take part in your family, your school, and your parish. Draw one way you take part in each group.

Family	School	Parish

Make a Difference

Lend a Hand With your teacher's help, talk about how your class can help to make life better for people n your school, parish, or neighborhood. Make a list. Then choose one thing from the list to work on. If ossible, invite another class to work with you.

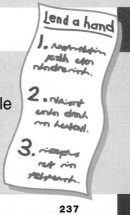

Lend a hand

1. ...
2. ...
3. ...

237

SERVE

Your Community
Reach Out!
Draw Pictures

Activity

- Read aloud the directions for the drawing activity.
- Distribute art materials, and allow time for children to complete their drawings.
- Invite volunteers to share their art work.

Make a Difference

Activity

- Read aloud the directions.
- Brainstorm a list of needs, and help children choose the one they will address.
- Help children choose and carry out a practical project.

Encourage children to share what they have learned with friends, family members, and other classes.

QUICK TIP

Be Practical First graders can generate some imaginative ideas, but will become frustrated if they are unable to carry out their plans. When inviting children to brainstorm ideas for activities, begin with a wide-open approach and gradually narrow the possibilities to those that are practical given children's ages and circumstances.

TEACHER BACKGROUND

Books About Community Help children learn more about community participation by sharing these resources:

- *What Is a Community? From A to Z* by Bobbie Kalman (Crabtree, 2000).
- *It's Our World, Too! Stories of Young People Who Are Making a Difference* by Phillip M. Hoose (Joy Street Books, 1993).

A **Work with Words** Complete each sentence in Column 1 by writing the letter of the correct word from Column 2.

Column 1	Column 2
1. The Resurrection is the name for _c (p. 209)_ rising from the dead.	**a.** Grace
2. Jesus is the _b (p. 207)_.	**b.** Savior
3. _e (p. 218)_ are signs of God's love given by Jesus to bring you closer to God.	**c.** Jesus'
4. _d (p. 226)_ brings new life and makes you a member of the Church.	**d.** Baptism
5. _a (p. 226)_ is a sharing in God's life and love.	**e.** Sacraments

B **Check Understanding** Circle the word that answers the question.

6. Who did God send to save people? (p. 208)

Mary   Mass   (Jesus)

7. Why does Jesus give us sacraments? (p. 218)

(to show love)   to tell stories   to buy things

8. What does Baptism call you to be? (p. 226)

good at sports   smart   (a sign of love)

C **Make Connections** Name a sign of God.

Responses will vary.

© Harcourt Religion

238

239

Unit Review

The Unit Review is designed to prepare children for the Unit Assessment. Have children complete the Review pages. Then discuss the answers as a class. You may wish to review any concepts with which children are having difficulty before the Unit Assessment.

Notes

Name ____________________ Date ____________

Ⓐ **Work with Words** Write the word from the Word Bank that completes the sentence.

WORD BANK
Body
grace
love
seven
words

1. Through the ____________ and actions of the sacraments, you know God's love.

2. The Catholic Church celebrates ____________ sacraments.

3. The sacraments are signs of God's ____________.

4. You received God's ____________ in Baptism.

5. At the Last Supper, Jesus gave his ____________ and Blood.

ASSESSMENT

Answers can be found in the back of the Teacher Manual.

Name _____ Date _____

Ⓑ Check Understanding Circle the word that best completes each sentence.

6. Christians are baptized people who follow _____.

Jesus

Moses

7. With Baptism God makes you his own _____.

slave

child

8. At the Last Supper, Jesus gave his followers the _____.

Eucharist

Church

9. God sent Jesus to save his _____.

people

Bible

10. Savior is a name for _____.

Mary

Jesus

Answers can be found in the back of the Teacher Manual.

©Harcourt Religion

UNIT 7
Forever with God

19 The Mass

What happens during Mass?

20 Life with God

What is heaven?

21 God's Kingdom

How can you help the kingdom to grow?

Faith in Action! Catholic Social Teaching Principle: Option for the Poor and Vulnerable

240

© Harcourt Religion

UNIT 7 OPENER

Preview Unit Content

Tell children that Unit 7 is about happiness forever with God.

- Invite a volunteer to read aloud the chapter title and question for Chapter 19. Ask children what they think they will learn in this chapter.

- Repeat this for Chapters 20 and 21.

- Tell children that at the end of the unit they will learn how two friends helped children in need.

The Mass

CHAPTER BACKGROUND

Faith Focus

- At Mass the Church family celebrates God's love. *(CCC 1359–1361)*
- Jesus gives himself to us in the Eucharist. *(CCC 1374)*

Catechism Connection

The *Catechism* affirms that Mass keeps the Church together and united with God. *(CCC 1325)*

GDC Link

The *Directory* highlights the importance of Mass for ongoing Christian formation. Followers of Jesus are continually nourished both at the table of God's word and at the table of the Eucharist. *(GDC 70)*

 Because the loaf of bread is one, we, though many, are one body, for we all partake of the one loaf.

1 Corinthians 10:17

A Eucharistic People

The word *Eucharist* comes from a Greek word that means to give thanks. Jesus, knowing that the hour of his death was approaching, changed bread and wine into his own Body and Blood. He told his Apostles to do the same in memory of him. The Eucharist celebrates Jesus' great gift of himself poured out so that all could be saved. In praise and thanksgiving, the Mass celebrates this tremendous gift.

Reflect on your Sunday experience—is it a day you look forward to with joy because you are going to Mass? Preparation for this great act of thanksgiving can begin at home. Every Sunday, Catholics gather together in public worship to listen to God's word, to recall the Paschal Mystery (Jesus' suffering, death, and Resurrection), and to be fed with the Body and Blood of Christ. Being kind and charitable to family members or those you meet on the way to Mass can enhance your celebration of the Eucharist.

A Wonderful Gift

The Mass is a wonderful gift. It brings the people who are the Body of Christ together in unity and worship, and sends them out in mission. As a participant in the Eucharist, you provide spiritual support for other members of the Body of Christ. You model faith for the youth of the Church. Your expression of faith becomes a gift for others. So give praise and thanksgiving for God's loving gift, his Son Jesus! Fervently sing a hymn of praise, listen intently, pray from the heart, and extend Christ's peace.

Reflect How does going to Mass help you to be a better disciple?

Eucharist

Help develop the children's Catholic identity by teaching them about the Mass.

- The Mass is a celebration, a joy-filled experience of Jesus' love and special presence. Catholics gather to praise God for his love and thank him every Sunday.

- Help connect children's experiences with celebrations by describing the Mass as a special celebration.

- Children may not understand the word *mystery*, but they can sense God's presence. They can also sense that Mass is more than an ordinary gathering.

Celebrations

- I like being with those who love me. Show me how belonging to the Church is like being part of a loving family.

- I like parties. Tell me how parties connect with Church celebrations.

- Mass is a celebration. Teach me how to act at Mass.

Coming to the Balcony

Pursuing catechetical excellence is increasingly complex. The challenges erode your willingness to shift, evaluate, and grow. As a result, you may find yourself doubting your effectiveness.

In *Leadership Without Easy Answers*, Ronald Heifetz proposes the practice of Coming to the Balcony: occasionally rising above the dance floor to get a better view of the dynamics, interactions, and pace making up the complexity of your catechetical dance. When Coming to the Balcony, seek the Wisdom of the Ratio, which can be found not by choosing one approach over the other but by determining when you are doing too much or not enough of different approaches.

Reflect ***How can you practice Coming to the Balcony?***

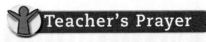
Teacher's Prayer

Dear Jesus, I want to follow you. Bless me with a prayerful disposition and a reflective heart. Amen.

Weekly Planner

		Objective	Materials	Prayer & Scripture
DAY 1 Invite	**The Mass** Page 241	**Objective:** *To learn about celebrations*	☐ Pencils ☐ Art supplies	🙏 Let Us Pray *Psalm 95:6*
DAY 2 Explore	**At Mass** Pages 242–243	**Objective:** *To describe how Catholics celebrate God's love at Mass*	☐ Board or chart paper ☐ Pencils ☐ Index cards ☐ Art supplies	🙏 Let Us Pray *Psalm 95:6*
DAY 3 Explore	**The Eucharist** Pages 244–245	**Objective:** *To learn what is meant by the Sacrament of the Eucharist*	☐ Board or chart paper ☐ Copies of Activity Master 19, p. 250A ☐ Art supplies	🙏 Let Us Pray *Psalm 95:6* ✠ Scripture: *1 Corinthians 11:23–25* ✠ Scripture Background: Right Worship, p. 244
DAY 4 Explore	**At Mass** Pages 246–247	**Objective:** *To identify the people and things you see and do at Mass.*	☐ Board or chart paper ☐ Art supplies	🙏 Let Us Pray *Psalm 95:6*
DAY 5 Celebrate	**Prayer of Praise** Page 248	**Objective:** *To praise God with a special prayer for children*	☐ Bible ☐ Music CD	🙏 Let Us Pray **A Prayer of Praise** 🔥 **Hymn:** "Psalm 89: For Ever I Will Sing"

Chapter 19 Wrap-Up: Review and Apply p. 249 • Chapter 19 Assessment p. 241E

Words of Faith

Mass
Eucharist

Activities	Enrichment
Let's Begin: A Winning Season, p. 241 Multiple Intelligence: Visual/Spatial OPTIONAL Special Gatherings, p. 241 Multiple Intelligence: Visual/Spatial	
Share Your Faith: OPTIONAL Mass, p. 242 Multiple Intelligence: Visual/Spatial Word Scramble, p. 243 Multiple Intelligence: Visual/Spatial OPTIONAL Amen, p. 243 Multiple Intelligence: Visual/Spatial	• **Teacher Background:** Mass, p. 242 • **Reaching All Learners:** Manipulatives, p. 243
Connect Your Faith: Remember Me, p. 245 Multiple Intelligence: Interpersonal OPTIONAL Activity Master 19: I Can Celebrate, p. 245 Multiple Intelligence: Interpersonal	• **Teacher Background:** Giving Thanks, p. 244 • **Teacher Background:** Eucharist, p. 245
Live Your Faith: Draw Yourself at Mass, p. 247 Multiple Intelligence: Visual/Linguistic OPTIONAL Cross-Curricular: Language Arts, p. 246 Multiple Intelligence: Verbal/Linguistic	• **Quick Tip:** Family Involvement, p. 246 • **Christian Living Skills:** Keeping the Lord's Day, p. 247 • **Quick Tip:** Share a Video, p. 247
	• **Liturgy Link:** Movement, p. 248 • **Lectionary Link:** Break Open the Word, p. 248

Multimedia Resources

 BOOK
Nussbaum, Melissa Musick. *My First Holy Communion: Sunday Mass and Daily Prayers.* Liturgy Training Publications. Chicago, IL. 2001. A child's guide to the liturgy of the Christian community.

 VIDEO
What Do We Do at Mass? (17 min). Liturgy Training Publications. Chicago, IL. 1999. Children talk about how they participate in the Eucharistic celebration.

 Teacher Resources
www.harcourtreligion.com
• For interactive lesson planner, chapter resources, and activities
• For free materials and information

Home Connection
Chapter 19 Family Faith, p. 250
Take-home activities, chapter content review, saint features and prayer

 For more family activities
www.harcourtreligion.com

Name _____ Date _____

A **Work with Words**   Circle the word that best completes
each sentence.

1. At Mass the Church family celebrates with stories,
   songs, _____, and a meal.

   gifts   **jokes**

2. At Mass the bread and wine become Jesus' _____.

   Story and Song   **Body and Blood**

B **Check Understanding**   Draw a line to the best title.

3. A word that means   **a.** the Last Supper
   thanksgiving

4. The Church's celebration   **b.** the Mass
   to praise and thank God

5. Jesus' meal with his friends   **c.** Eucharist
   the night before he died

Chapter 19 The Mass

Let Us Pray

Leader: God, we worship you with joy.
"Enter, let us bow down in worship;
let us kneel before the LORD who made us."
Psalm 95:6

All: God, we worship you with joy. Amen.

Activity — Let's Begin

● **A Winning Season** Angela's team practiced and played well. They won the last game and the trophy.

• What was one way the team celebrated their win?

_____

_____

_____

_____

✏ **Draw a Celebration** Draw a picture that shows the best party ever.

241

OPTIONAL ACTIVITY

Special Gathering Have children discuss Thanksgiving and all the festivities associated with that special celebration. Talk about the food, the music, the decorations, and the family members who come together to eat the special meal.

• Have children draw their favorite family celebration.

Multiple Intelligence: Visual/Spatial

Objective: To learn about celebrations

Open

Prayer Space You may wish to have children move to your classroom prayer space. In the space, have a crucifix and a Bible opened to *Psalm 95:6*.

Let Us Pray Ask children to bow from the waist when you pray aloud the first line of the psalm verse and to kneel when you pray aloud the second line. Pray aloud the psalm verse, and ask children to pray the response.

Build

Activity

• Read aloud A Winning Season.

• Have children discuss how they would feel if they were on Angela's team.

• Ask children about the kinds of celebrations their families have. birthdays, anniversaries, holidays.

• Discuss what happens at these celebrations. Possible responses: food, music, gifts.

Extension Activity

• Tell children they will be drawing a picture of the best party ever.

• Distribute art supplies, and ask children to draw one thing they know about Mass.

• Ask volunteers to share their drawings.

Close

Have children tell what they have learned about celebrations.

DAY 2

Objective: To describe how Catholics celebrate God's love at Mass

Open

🌸 **Let Us Pray** Invite children to pray the psalm verse on page 241 with you.

◎ **Focus** **How do you celebrate God's love at Mass?** List children's answers on the board or on chart paper.

Build

At Mass

Read aloud At Mass.

• Ask children what words describe things that happen at celebrations. stories, songs, gifts, meals

• Write the word *Mass* on an index card. Introduce the word to the class.

• Tell children to look at the pictures. Ask what things Catholics do at Mass. gather, sing, pray, listen to stories, receive Jesus in Holy Communion

❓ **What do you know about the Mass?** Arrange the class in small groups to discuss the question.

At Mass

◎ **Focus** How do you celebrate God's love at Mass?

Many families celebrate their love with stories, songs, gifts, and food.

At **Mass**, the Church family gathers to celebrate God's love. There are stories, songs, gifts, and a meal at Mass, too!

❓ **What do you know about the Mass?**
Responses will vary.

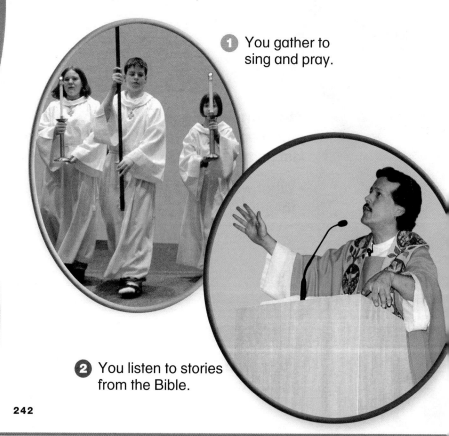

1 You gather to sing and pray.

2 You listen to stories from the Bible.

242

The bread and the wine become the Body and Blood of Jesus.

4 Those who are old enough receive Jesus in Holy Communion.

Words of Faith

The **Mass** is the Church's great celebration of praise and thanks.

Activity — Share Your Faith

Word Scramble Look at the first two letters of each scrambled word. Put them after the other letters to make a word that tells about the Mass. Write the word.

ngsi _____ sing _____

seprai _____ praise _____

ssMa _____ Mass _____

ksthan _____ thanks _____

onCommuni _____ Communion _____

243

• Tell children that family celebrations and Mass have similarities. Tell them Mass is very special because bread and wine become the Body and Blood of Jesus.

• Explain to children that next year they will prepare to receive Jesus in Holy Communion.

Activity

• Have children work as partners to unscramble the words that tell about the Mass.

Close

Tell children that at Mass the Church family gathers to celebrate God's love. Emphasize that Mass is the Church's greatest celebration of praise and thanks to God.

OPTIONAL ACTIVITY

Amen Remind children that the word *Amen* is a Hebrew word that means "So be it."

• Amen is almost always said at the end of prayers.

• Have children write the word *Amen* on a separate sheet of paper and decorate the page.

Multiple Intelligence: Visual/Spatial

★ REACHING ALL LEARNERS

Manipulatives With a little preparation, you can modify the word scramble activity to make it easier for children who would find it difficult to do on the page.

• For the letters, use tiles from a board game.

• Alternately, write the letters you need on index cards cut in half.

• Place the tiles or cards on a table, arranging them as shown in the children's text.

Objective: To learn what is meant by the Sacrament of the Eucharist

Open

 Let Us Pray   Invite children to pray the psalm verse on page 241 with you.

◎ Focus   **Who is present in the holy Bread and Wine?** List children's answers on the board or on chart paper.

Build

The Eucharist

Read aloud The Eucharist.

- Explain to children that an important part of the Mass recalls Jesus' last meal, known as the Last Supper.

The Last Supper

Gather children together to listen for what Jesus did at the Last Supper.

- Proclaim the Scripture.
- Tell children that Jesus promised that he would always be with his friends.

❷ **When do you hear these words at Mass?** Ask volunteers to share responses.

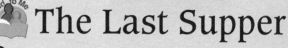

Explore

The Eucharist

◎ Focus   **Who is present in the holy Bread and Wine?**

At Mass, the Church remembers an important night with Jesus. He share a special meal with his followers. Th meal is called the Last Supper.

✝ SCRIPTURE   I Corinthians II:23-

The Last Supper

On the night before he died, Jesus shared a special meal with his friends.

He took the bread, he gave thanks and broke it, and said, "This is my body that is for you. Do this in remembrance of me."

Jesus took the cup and said, "This cup is the new covenant in my blood. Do this as often as you drink it, in remembrance of me."

From I Corinthians II:23–25

❷ **When do you hear these words at Mass?**
Possible responses: before the Lord's Prayer; after the Holy, Holy, Holy

244

 ✝ SCRIPTURE BACKGROUND

Right Worship   One purpose of Paul's first letter to the Corinthians was to denounce the way that some Christians at Corinth were behaving at their worship services.

- In Chapter 11, Saint Paul recalls the words and actions of Jesus at the Last Supper to remind the Corinthians how he had taught them to celebrate the Eucharist.

✳ TEACHER BACKGROUND

Giving Thanks   The word "eucharist" comes from the Greek word *eucharistos,* which means "grateful."

- Christ instituted the Holy Eucharist at the Last Supper, the night before he died.

Thanksgiving

At Mass you celebrate the Sacrament of the **Eucharist**. The word Eucharist means thanksgiving. Catholics are thankful that Jesus is present in the Bread and Wine.

Words of Faith

The **Eucharist** is the sacrament in which Jesus shares himself in the holy Bread and Wine.

Activity

Connect Your Faith

Remember Me Look at the picture on this page. Talk about what is happening in the picture.

245

Thanksgiving

Hold up an index card to introduce the word *Eucharist*. Have children practice pronouncing the word.

- Read aloud Thanksgiving. Tell children that the Eucharist has words and actions that show that Jesus is present.
- Ask children if they recall the words of Jesus that the priest says. Tell children that the priest and people at Mass do what Jesus told the disciples to do at the Last Supper.
- Explain that they share his Body and Blood under the appearances of bread and wine.

Activity

- Have children share their ideas of what is happening in the picture of the Last Supper.

Close

Review with children that the word *Eucharist* means thanksgiving. Jesus gives us himself under the appearances of bread and wine in the Eucharist.

TEACHER BACKGROUND

Eucharist Whenever the Church celebrates Eucharist, it shares the word of God, prays for the needs of everyone, recalls the Last Supper, and receives Jesus in Holy Communion.

- Catholics have an obligation to participate in Mass on Sundays and on holy days.

OPTIONAL ACTIVITY

Activity Master 19: I Can Celebrate Distribute copies of the activity on teacher page 250A.

- Tell children that the activity will help them set goals for themselves at Mass.
- As an alternative, you may wish to send the activity home with children.

▲ **Activity Master 19 page 250A**

Objective: To identify the people and things you see and do at Mass

Open

 Let Us Pray Invite children to pray the psalm verse from page 241 with you.

Focus **What do you see and do at Mass?** List children's responses on the board or on chart paper.

Build

At Mass

Read aloud the introduction to the checklists.

- Have children follow along in their books as you read aloud the lists.

- Pause to describe people, items, and actions as necessary, referring to the pictures where appropriate.

❓ **What else have you seen or done at Mass? Put a check mark (✓) in the boxes next to the things you have seen or done.** Allow time for children to check the lists. Ask the class to find out which items were checked.

Explore

At Mass

Focus **What do you see and do at Mass?**

When you go to Mass, you see many people and things. You do many things, too.

People You Might See at Mass	Things You Might See at Mass	Things You Might Do at Mass
☐ Priest	☐ Altar	☐ Make the Sign of the Cross.
☐ Altar server	☐ Candles	☐ Sing and pray
☐ Song leader	☐ Gospel Book	☐ Share a sign of peace.
☐ Reader	☐ Chalice	☐ Receive Holy Communion.
☐ Extraordinary minister of Holy Communion		

❓ **What else have you seen or done at Mass? Put a check mark (✓) in the boxes next to the things you have seen or done.**

246

OPTIONAL ACTIVITY

Cross-Curricular: Language Arts Have children develop interview questions.

- Invite members of your parish's liturgical team (including older children who act as altar servers) to visit the class and talk about their roles at Mass.

- Have children work in small groups to develop interview questions for the guest speakers.

Multiple Intelligence: Verbal/Linguistic

QUICK TIP

Family Involvement Remember that a first grader's attendance at Mass is dependent upon family involvement in the parish.

- Help children understand that participation in the Sunday Mass is required.

- Do not put children on the spot about their individual attendance; instead, be general and inclusive when discussing participation.

Live Your Faith

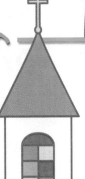

Draw Yourself at Mass In the space, draw a picture of yourself and your family at Mass. See if your classmates can guess which part of the Mass your picture shows.

247

- Share with children the directions for the activity.
- Distribute art materials, and allow time for children to work independently on their drawings.
- Invite volunteers to share their drawings, and encourage the class to guess which parts of the Mass are being depicted.

Close

Encourage children to pay attention to everything they see, hear, and do at Mass this week.

CHRISTIAN LIVING SKILLS

Keeping the Lord's Day Remind children that participating at Mass is only part of fulfilling the commandment to keep the Lord's Day.

- Encourage children to think of ways they can help older family members have time to rest on Sunday.
- Brainstorm ways that family members can relax, pray, and help others on Sunday.

QUICK TIP

Share a Video To help children learn more about the Mass, share the two-part video series *The Mass for Children* (VHS, 20 min., St. Anthony Messenger Press).

DAY 5

Objective: To praise God with a special prayer for children

Prepare

Direct children to look at the prayer page and to find the words of thanks and praise—words that indicate a celebration of God's love.

• Choose two children to read the leader's lines. Allow time for them to practice. Teach the response marked "All" to the rest of the group.

 Use the *Call to Faith 1* CD, track 19, to rehearse the song.

Gather

Display an image of Jesus in the prayer space.

• Gather in the prayer space.

Pray

A Prayer of Praise

 Let Us Pray Follow the order of prayer.

• Optional reading: *1 Corinthians 11:23–25.*

Prayer of Praise

 **Let Us Pray**

Gather and begin with the Sign of the Cross.

Leader: God our Father, we thank you for all the wonderful things you have done.

All: You love us and do great things for us.

Leader: We thank you for the happiness you have given us.

All: We praise you for daylight which lights up our lives.

Sing together.

For ever I will sing the goodness of the Lord.

"Psalm 89: For Ever I Will Sing," *Lectionary for Mass* © 1969, 1981, ICEL.

248

LITURGY LINK

Movement Have children memorize the response used in the prayer service so that they can perform movements as they pray it.

• As they speak the words "You love us," have them cross their arms as if they were giving themselves a big hug. As they say the words "do great things for us," have them hold out their arms wide.

LECTIONARY LINK

Break Open the Word Read last week's Sunday Gospel. Invite children to think about what the reading means to them as they try to follow Christ's example. For questions related to the weekly Gospel reading, visit our Web site at **www.harcourtreligion.com**.

 Visit **www.harcourtreligion.com** for weekly scripture readings and seasonal resources.

A **Work with Words** Complete each sentence in Column I by writing the letter of the correct word from Column 2.

Column I	Column 2
1. Jesus shared the <u>b (p. 244)</u> with his followers the night before he died.	**a.** Eucharist
2. The <u>d (p. 243)</u> become the Body and Blood of Christ.	**b.** Last Supper
3. The <u>e (p. 242)</u> is the Church's greatest celebration of praise and thanks.	**c.** Bible
4. Jesus shares himself in the sacrament of the <u>a (p. 245)</u>	**d.** bread and wine
5. You hear stories from the <u>c (p. 242)</u> at Mass.	**e.** Mass

B **Check Understanding** Circle the correct answers.

6. The word Eucharist means <u>(p. 245)</u> .

(thanksgiving)   **Bible**

7. At Mass, the Church celebrates <u>(p. 242)</u> .

birthdays   (God's love)

C **Make Connections** Write a brief response to the question.

8. What is one thing you are grateful for?

_____

- -

Responses will vary.

249

Review

A **Work with Words** Have children choose an answer from Column 2 to complete the sentences in Column 1.

B **Check Understanding** Have children circle the correct answer.

C **Make Connections** Have children respond briefly to the question.

Assessment

▲ **Chapter 19 Test page 241E**

Answers to the Chapter Test can be found in the back of the Teacher Manual.

 JUSTICE AND PEACE

Love and Serve Tell children that at the end of Mass, the priest or deacon tells the people to go forth to love and serve the Lord.

- We can serve the Lord by serving others.
- Discuss what they can do to show love for all people.

Catholic Social Teaching: Life and Dignity

OPTIONAL ACTIVITY

Thank-You Cards Hand out construction paper and crayons for children to make thank-you cards to God for all of his gifts of creation.

- Children may write or draw their expressions of thanks.
- Gather the cards in a decorative basket and seek permission from the church office to have the notes placed at the altar during next Sunday's Masses.

Multiple Intelligence: Visual/Spatial

Family Faith

Remind children to discuss the Family Faith page at home. Encourage children to read the scripture passage from the Gospels according to Mark and Luke.

- Direct children's attention to the bulleted list on the page. Tell them that the list tells ways families can make their time at Sunday Mass a special time.

People of Faith

Tell children about Saint Angela Merici.

- Angela's Community of Saint Ursula, or the Ursulines, was the first group of religious women to work outside the cloister. It was the first teaching order of women.
- Remind children to add Saint Angela Merici to their People of Faith albums.
- Encourage them to pray the prayer at home with their families.

  Visit **www.harcourtreligion.com** for weekly scripture readings and seasonal resources.

CHAPTER 19
Family Faith

Catholics Believe

- At Mass the Church family celebrates God's love.
- Jesus gives himself to us in the Eucharist.

 SCRIPTURE

Read other descriptions of the Last Supper in Mark 14:22–26 and Luke 22:14–20.

GO ONLINE www.harcourtreligion.com
For weekly Scripture readings and seasonal resources

Activity
Live Your Faith

Live the Mass Make Sunday Mass a special time for your family. Here are some ways.
- Practice the Mass responses.
- Discuss the Scripture readings ahead of time.
- After Mass, talk about the main point of the homily.
- Plan ways to love and serve the Lord all week long.

People of Faith

▲ **Saint Angela Merici, 1474–1540**

Sister Angela lived in Italy. She taught little girls. At that time, only rich children could go to school. Sister Angela changed that. She and her friends began teaching girls who were poor. Sister Angela wanted the girls to be good mothers who told their children about God. Many of the girls chose instead to join Angela's community of religious women. Saint Angela's feast day is January 27.

Family Prayer

Saint Angela, pray for us that we may show our love of God as you did. Amen.

? HOW DID I DO?

This week my religion classes were

☐ *some of the best ever!* ☐ *pretty good.* ☐ *in need of improvement.*

In what discussions and activities were children most interested?

_____

What activity did I most enjoy teaching?

_____

In what area do I need to improve?

_____

Name _____ Date _____

I Can Celebrate

Jesus is at Mass.

You can give Jesus your love.

At Mass people bring gifts to God. Some gifts
are promises to do good. I give a gift.

Draw a picture of your gift.

Life with God

CHAPTER BACKGROUND

We were indeed buried with him through baptism into death, so that, just as Christ was raised from the dead by the glory of the Father, we too might live in newness of life.

Romans 6:4

New Life

The mystery of Christ's death and Resurrection is an experience that plays out over and over again in daily life. How one interprets that experience is the key to following Jesus through death to resurrected glory.

Ponder for a moment some of the illnesses or sufferings you endure—physical, social, emotional, or spiritual ailments. Often the road to recovery is long and difficult, leading many to question: When will it ever end? Yet when recovery is complete, there is a sense of newness.

This is the experience of the Paschal mystery. Dying to your old self in the pain and suffering of illnesses and hardships, you are raised to a new life and a new way of being. These experiences can lead you to appreciate the meaning of Christ's death and Resurrection. By sharing this appreciation with others, you can help to build the Body of Christ.

Sharing Happiness

Eternal happiness is a gift Jesus won for all people. Death is not the end. Jesus assured his Apostles that there is life after death and that there is a heavenly dwelling place. It is a gift that has been offered to you.

Reflect ***How does hope of eternal life color your experience of death?***

Faith Focus

- Heaven is being happy with God forever. *(CCC 1024)*
- All who are friends with God when they die will go to heaven. *(CCC 1023)*

Catechism Connection

The *Catechism* presents union with God, Mary, the angels, and the saints in heaven as "the state of supreme, definitive happiness." *(CCC 1024)*

GDC Link

The *Directory* notes that visible things can help people understand matters that surpass human knowledge. Yet the communication of faith in catechesis is ultimately "an event of grace" and mystery. *(GDC 150)*

Heaven

Jesus the Savior offers eternal life to all God's people. It is a mystery to be grasped in faith, with the help of the Holy Spirit.

- Most children have at least heard the word *heaven*, and may have preconceived notions. Your goal is to lead them to a Christian understanding.

- Teaching about heaven is a balancing act between the abstract and the concrete. Heaven is not a place; it is the life of love with the Holy Trinity. Yet Scripture uses concrete images to explain the mystery of heaven, and you can do so as well.

- You will use the process of discovery to present the material in this chapter. Maintain a sense of enthusiasm because heaven is being happy with God forever.

Imagine That

- I like to discover and explore new things. Tell me more about heaven.

- I like to use my imagination. Can we think aloud about what life forever with Jesus will be like?

- I don't like thinking about death. Help me understand why someone has to die.

Confession

Psychologists tell us that we unconsciously create enemies to avoid responsibility for a problem, to bond closer with the colleagues on our side, or to better define who we are. In catechesis, we can make such an imagined enemy out of parents, the pastor, or a certain group of students.

The struggle to sustain your spirit is difficult enough without carrying such a burden. The courageous practice of Confession enables you to let go of the illusion of an enemy and freely carry on the noble work of catechesis. Your virtuous act of Confession can help you refrain from contributing to the enemy illusion.

Reflect **What enemy comes to your mind as you consider the practice of Confession?**

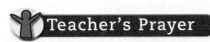

Teacher's Prayer

Lord, sometimes I feel lost and alone. Help me quiet myself to feel your presence, to know your love within me. Amen.

Weekly Planner

		Objective	Materials	Prayer & Scripture
DAY 1 Invite	**Life with God** Page 251	**Objective:** *To explore the concept of life cycles*	☐ Art supplies ☐ Pencils	🙌 Let Us Pray *Psalm 27:13*
DAY 2 Explore	**New Life** Pages 252–253	**Objective:** *To describe the new life that Jesus promised to his followers*	☐ Board or chart paper ☐ Art supplies	🙌 Let Us Pray *Psalm 27:13* ✝ **Scripture:** *John 14:1–3* ✝ **Scripture Background:** My Father's House, p. 252
DAY 3 Explore	**Love and Happiness** Pages 254–255	**Objective:** *To explain how people prepare themselves to share in God's happiness*	☐ Board or chart paper ☐ Copies of Activity Master 20, p. 260A ☐ Pencils	🙌 Let Us Pray *Psalm 27:13*
DAY 4 Explore	**Saying Goodbye** Pages 256–257	**Objective:** *To identify the Christian response to death*	☐ Board or chart paper	🙌 Let Us Pray *Psalm 27:13*
DAY 5 Celebrate	**Pray for the Dead** Page 258	**Objective:** *To pray for those who have died*	☐ Bible ☐ Hymnals ☐ Music CD ☐ Battery-powered candles	🙌 Let Us Pray **Pray for the Dead** 🎵 **Hymn:** "Shout for Joy"

Chapter 20 Wrap-Up: Review and Apply p. 259 • Chapter 20 Assessment p. 251E

Words of Faith

 heaven

Activities	Enrichment
Let's Begin: Life Cycles, p. 251 Multiple Intelligence: Visual/Spatial OPTIONAL Spread Your Wings, p. 251 Multiple Intelligence: Naturalist	
Share Your Faith: Think, Share, Act, p. 253 Multiple Intelligence: Visual/Spatial	• Teacher Background: Mass of Christian Burial, p. 252 • Reaching All Learners: The Subject of Death, p. 253 • Justice and Peace: The New Earth, p. 253
Connect Your Faith: Showing Love, p. 255 Multiple Intelligence: Verbal/Linguistic OPTIONAL Activity Master 20: The Way to Heaven, p. 255 Multiple Intelligence: Verbal/Linguistic	• Teacher Background: Heaven, p. 254 • Quick Tip: Eternity, p. 254 • Cultural Awareness: Honoring the Dead, p. 255
Live Your Faith: Write a Thank-You Letter, p. 257 Multiple Intelligence: Verbal/Linguistic OPTIONAL Make Prayer Cards, p. 256 Multiple Intelligence: Interpersonal OPTIONAL Heaven Collage, p. 257 Multiple Intelligence: Verbal/Linguistic	• Quick Tip: Sensitive Topics, p. 256 • Christian Living Skills: Lamenting, p. 257
	• Liturgy Link: Liturgical Prayers for Children, p. 258 • Lectionary Link: Break Open the Word, p. 258

Multimedia Resources

 BOOK
Sjaz, Kathleen. *I Hate Goodbyes.* Paulist Press. Mahwah, NJ. 1996. A child learns to deal with loss.

VIDEO
My Grandson Lew (13 min). St. Anthony Messenger Press. Cincinnati, OH. 1976. A young boy learns a lesson of hope while mourning the loss of his grandfather.

 Teacher Resources
ONLINE www.harcourtreligion.com
• For interactive lesson planner, chapter resources, and activities
• For free materials and information

 Home Connection
Chapter 20 Family Faith, p. 260
Take-home activities, chapter content review, saint features and prayer

 For more family activities
ONLINE www.harcourtreligion.com

Life with God 251D

Name _____ Date _____

(A) Check Understanding   Circle the best answer to each question.

1. Who will be in heaven with God forever?

   those who show love   **nobody**   **animals and plants**

2. With whom do holy people live forever?

   the whole city   **the Holy Trinity**   **plants and animals**

3. Who said, "There are many rooms in my Father's house"?

   Jairus   **Mary**   **Jesus**

4. What do humans have that plants and animals don't have?

   life forever   **nothing**   **life cycle**

5. What is the name for living in happiness with God forever?

   death   **heaven**   **life cycle**

©Harcourt Religion

ASSESSMENT

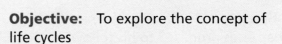

Chapter 20 Life with God

Invite

Let Us Pray

Leader: Loving God, we want to know your love.
"I believe I shall enjoy the LORD's goodness in the land of the living."

Psalm 27:13

All: Loving God, we want to know your love. Amen.

Activity Let's Begin

Life Cycles God lives forever. All other life has a beginning and an ending. Caterpillars become butterflies. They live, and then they die. Seeds become plants. They grow, and then they die. These changes are called life cycles.

- What happens to a plant at the end of its life cycle?

_____

_____

_____

_____

Make a Diagram Draw pictures to show the changes in the life cycle of a tree, a flower, or a butterfly.

251

OPTIONAL ACTIVITY

Spread Your Wings Let children experience the life cycle of a butterfly.

- Have children make a chrysalis out of an empty paper towel roll. Have them cut out and decorate a pre-drawn butterfly.
- Direct children to roll it up inside the chrysalis and then unfurl the butterfly.

Multiple Intelligence: Naturalist

Objective: To explore the concept of life cycles

Open

Let Us Pray Have children move to the classroom prayer space. Have children stand and pray aloud the psalm.

Build

Activity

- Read aloud Life Cycles. Talk with children about creatures that go through life cycles.
- Point to the picture of the chrysalis and butterfly on the tree branch.
- Tell children that the butterfly goes through its life in four stages.
- Explain that an adult butterfly lays an egg on a leaf of a tree. The egg later turns into a fuzzy caterpillar. Explain that the caterpillar forms a chrysalis, and lives in it until it turns into a butterfly.
- Invite children to answer the question at the end of the text.

Extension Activity

- Tell children they will be drawing a diagram of the life cycle of a tree, a flower, or a butterfly.
- Distribute art materials, and allow children time to draw the diagram.
- Ask volunteers to share their diagrams with the class.

Close

Have children tell what they have learned about life cycles.

Objective: To describe the new life that Jesus promised to his followers

Open

 Let Us Pray Invite children to pray the psalm verse on page 251 with you.

Focus **What is heaven?** List children's answers on the board or on chart paper.

Build

New Life

Read aloud New Life.

- Ask children to curl into a ball. Tell them that plants start out as seeds.
- Have children stand, and tell them that plants grow and flowers bloom.
- Ask children to drop to the floor, and tell them that the flower then dies. Remind them that Jesus promised his followers life after death.

Together Always

Ask children to listen for Jesus' promise as you proclaim the Scripture.

❷ **What do you think God's house is like?** Write children's responses on the board or on chart paper.

Explore

New Life

Focus What is heaven?

People have life cycles, too. People [a]re born, they live, and then they die. Bu[t] people are different in a special way[.]

Listen to the promise Jesus made about life after death.

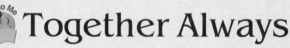

Together Always

Jesus told his followers that he was going to die.

He said, "Don't worry. Have faith in God, and have faith in me. There are many rooms in my Father's house. I am going ahead of you to get a place ready for you. I will come back. When it is time, I will take each of you home to my Father's house. We will be together always."

Based on John 14:1–3

❷ **What do you think God's house is like?** Responses will vary.

252

 ✝ SCRIPTURE BACKGROUND

My Father's House Like an earlier reading, this scripture story is based on Jesus' farewell discourse to his disciples at the Last Supper, as reported by the Gospel according to John.

- In this passage, Jesus explains that the disciples should be happy he is going away because he is returning to his Father's house to prepare a place for them. Because of Jesus, Christians can hope to be united with God forever in the joy of heaven.

 ✦ TEACHER BACKGROUND

Mass of Christian Burial The Church has faith that death is the beginning of a new life with God.

- At a funeral Mass we remember the deceased's union with the Church through Baptism and look forward to the second coming of Jesus, when we will be reunited with our loved ones.

appiness Forever

sus said that he will come back
bring his followers to his
her's house. Jesus said they will
e joy that will never end. After
th, Jesus' followers can have
v life with God. They can be full
happiness. **Heaven** is living and
ng happy with God forever.

**What is Jesus' promise to his
ollowers?**
hat they will be happy; he will come back;
ey will have new life

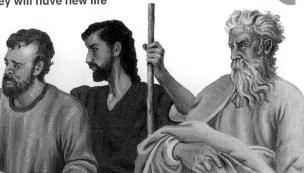

Words of Faith

Heaven is living and
being happy with
God forever.

Activity Share Your Faith

Think: Think about how you might feel with
God in heaven.

Share: In a small group, talk about things
you might draw to show how you
are happy here on earth and how
you will be happy in heaven.

Act: Use your ideas to draw two
pictures. Share your pictures
with the class. Tell how they
are alike and different.

253

Happiness Forever

Read aloud Happiness Forever.

- Hold up an index card of the word
heaven. Explain to children that
heaven is living in happiness with
God and the saints forever.

- Help children understand that the
phrase Jesus uses in the scripture
story—"my Father's house"—is a
metaphor for heaven.

- Ask children why they think house is
a good word to describe heaven.
Lead children to focus on the house
as a setting for family happiness,
rather than as a physical building.

**❷ What is Jesus' promise to his
followers?** Invite children to share
their responses.

Activity

- Have children form small groups to
complete the activity.

- Give them time to draw their
pictures.

Close

Tell children that life and happiness
with God and the saints forever is
called heaven.

⭐ REACHING ALL LEARNERS

The Subject of Death The emphasis of the chapter
is on everlasting happiness. In some children, however,
particularly those who have recently experienced
a death in the family, the text may prompt
sad or scary feelings.

- Be alert to the possibility that
children may have such a
reaction. Be tolerant and
comforting to them.

✝ JUSTICE AND PEACE

The New Earth At the end of time, God will create
a "new heaven and a new earth." (See *Revelation
21:1*.)

- Humans will then possess glorified bodies, like
Jesus after his Resurrection. Nothing underscores
the goodness of God's creation as these doctrines
do.

Catholic Social Teaching: Care for Creation

Life with God   253

DAY 3

Objective: To explain how people prepare themselves to share in God's happiness

Open

 Let Us Pray Invite children to pray the psalm verse on page 251 with you.

Focus **What do you need to do to be happy with God forever?** List children's answers on the board or on chart paper.

Build

Love and Happiness

Read aloud Love and Happiness.

- Tell children that God's love is so great that he wants all people to be happy forever with him after they die.

 Explore

Love and Happiness

Focus What do you need to do to be happy with God forever?

The Holy Trinity lives in love fore All holy people who have died are living in love and happiness foreve with the Holy Trinity.

254

 TEACHER BACKGROUND

Heaven People who are faithful to God's law of love will be welcomed into the everlasting happiness of God's presence which we call heaven.

QUICK TIP

Eternity The concept of forever is a difficult one to grasp by children for whom a week can feel like an eternity.

- Draw a circle on the board or on chart paper, or show children a circular object such as an embroidery hoop or wedding band.
- Explain that, just as a circle has no end, people who embrace God's love and laws will live with him forever.

e Way to Heaven

od wants everyone to be happy
ever, even after they die. Everyone
nvited. Everyone who follows Jesus
l God's laws will be in heaven
h God forever.

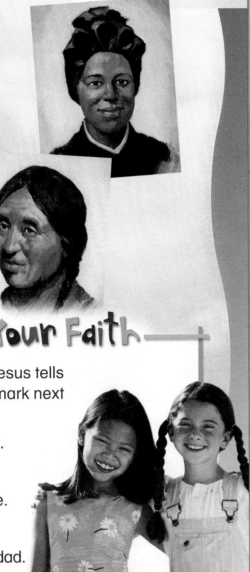

Activity Connect Your Faith

Showing Love In the Bible Jesus tells
now to show love. Write a check mark next
o the actions that show love.

✓ ___ Help someone who is sad.

✓ ___ Pray every day.

___ Call someone a bad name.

✓ ___ Follow God's laws.

___ Talk back to your mom or dad.

✓ ___ Forgive someone.

255

The Way to Heaven

Read aloud The Way to Heaven.

- Share with children the fact that
  whenever they show love for others,
  they get an idea of the happiness
  that is heaven.
- Direct children's attention to the
  photos on the page. Tell them that
  these are pictures of saints who are
  happy in heaven with God.

Activity

- Direct children to put a check next to
  the actions that show love.
- Allow children a minute or two to
  complete the activity, and then go
  over the answers with them.

Close

Remind children that one gets to be in
heaven with God by loving God and
others.

OPTIONAL ACTIVITY

**Activity Master 20: The Way to
Heaven** Distribute copies of the
activity on teacher page 260A.

- Tell children to fill in the boxes
  to learn how to get to heaven.
- As an alternative, you may wish
  to send this activity home with
  children.

▲ Activity Master 20
page 260A

CULTURAL AWARENESS

Honoring the Dead Talk with children about ways
people from other cultures honor their relatives who
have died.

- Explain that Native Americans often commemorate
  the death of a loved one by hosting a giveaway
  during a pow-wow. This tradition exemplifies the
  value of sharing with others. Gifts such as blankets,
  beadwork, and crafts are given to friends and
  visitors.

Objective: To identify the Christian response to death

Open

 Let Us Pray Invite children to pray the psalm verse from page 251 with you.

Focus **What do we do when someone dies?** List children's responses on the board or on chart paper.

Build

Saying Goodbye

Read aloud the introductory paragraph.

- Invite children to listen carefully as you read aloud the list of ways we respond when someone dies.

- Pause after reading each entry, and invite children to restate the information in their own words.

❷ **What kind words can you say to a friend when someone they love has died?** Have children discuss the question in small groups. Invite volunteers to share their responses.

Explore

Saying Goodbye

Focus **What do we do when someone dies?**

When someone we love dies, we sad. We know that we will miss th person. Since we are followers of Jesus, we know that death is not r the end. Even though we miss the person now, we know we will mee him or her again in heaven.

Here are some things the followe of Jesus do when someone dies.

- We let ourselves feel sad. W share how we feel with Go and with other people we l

- We gather for Mass. We th God for giving us this pers to be in our lives.

- We share happy memories with family and friends. We stories about our loved one

- We ask God to take care of person who has died. We a God to welcome him or he heaven.

❷ **What kind words can you say to a friend wh someone they love has died?** Responses will

OPTIONAL ACTIVITY

Make Prayer Cards Have children make prayer cards to give to parishioners who have experienced bereavement.

- Work with children to develop a list of short comforting prayers.

- Have children transfer the prayers to cards and decorate the cards. Give them to your parish bereavement minister.

Multiple Intelligence: Interpersonal

QUICK TIP

Sensitive Topics Be aware that death is a very sensitive topic for most young children, especially for those who have experienced the recent loss of a loved one or a family pet.

- Handle children's questions gently, and respect the privacy of children for whom this topic is too difficult.

Live Your Faith

Write a Thank-You Letter This is a thank-you letter to God. Fill in the blanks with your own words.

Dear God,

I think you are wonderful because

_____

_____

_____

_____

_____ .

Please take care of all those who have died,

_____

especially _____

_____

_____ .

Love,

_____

_____

(Sign your name.)

257

- Share with children the directions for the activity.
- Read through the text of the letter with children, making sure they know where they are to add their own words.
- Allow time for children to work independently on their letters.

Close

Invite volunteers to read their letters aloud as a closing prayer.

Heaven Collage Have children create a collage about what they think heaven might be like.

- Divide children into groups to brainstorm ideas, and then have them draw and cut out their images.
- Have children glue their pictures on a large piece of paper to create a collage.

Multiple Intelligence: Verbal/Linguistic

Lamenting Children who are dealing with death and other losses need to know that it is all right to grieve, and to share their feelings of anger, sadness, or fear with God in prayer.

- Tell children that Jesus cried when his friend Lazarus died. He shared his fear and sadness with his Father in prayer on the night before he died.

DAY 5

Objective: To pray for those who have died

Prepare

Tell children that the Church family includes people who are alive and people who have died.

• Choose a prayer leader.

 Use the *Call to Faith 1* CD, track 20, to rehearse the song.

Gather

Assemble children in two groups facing each other in the prayer space.

• Tell children which group should pray which set of lines (Side 1 or Side 2).

• Explain that both sides pray the sentence marked All.

Pray

Pray for the Dead

 Let Us Pray   Follow the order of prayer.

Pray for the Dead

 **Let Us Pray**

Gather and begin with the Sign of the Cross.

Leader: Those who have died as friends of God are part of our Church family. We pray for them. We ask them to pray for us, too.

Side 1: Lord, our God, we remember those who have died.

Side 2: Bring them home to be with you forever.

Side 1: Gather us all together into your kingdom.

Side 2: There we will be happy forever with the Virgin Mary, Mother of God and our mother.

All: There all the friends of the Lord Jesus will sing a song of joy.

From the Eucharistic Prayer 2 for Children

Sing together the refrain.

Shout for joy, joy, joy!
Shout for joy, joy, joy!
God is love, God is light,
God is everlasting!

"Shout for Joy," David Mowbray © 1982,
Jubilate Hymns, Ltd.
(administered by Hope Publishing Co.)

258

 LITURGY LINK

Liturgical Prayers for Children   Point out to children that the prayer is one said at special Masses for children.

• At every Mass, God's family remembers and prays for those who have died. Direct children to be quiet and respectful when they pray for people who have died.

LECTIONARY LINK

Break Open the Word   Read last week's Sunday Gospel. Invite children to think about what the reading means to them as they try to follow Christ's example. For questions related to the weekly Gospel reading, visit our Web site at **www.harcourtreligion.com**.

 Visit www.harcourtreligion.com for weekly scripture readings and seasonal resources.

CHAPTER 20
Review

A Work with Words Write the correct word from the Word Bank to complete each sentence.

WORD BANK

follow
life
heaven
happy

1. God wants everyone to be

   _____
   -
   _____ happy (p. 255) _____ .

2. Jesus said that after death you would have

   _____
   -
   new _____ life (p. 252) _____ .

3. You can be happy with God when you

   _____
   -
   _____ follow (p. 255) _____ Jesus.

4. You can be happy with God forever in

   _____
   -
   _____ heaven (p. 253) _____ .

B Check Understanding What happens first? Use (p. 253–p. 255) the numbers 1–4 to put the times of life in order.

___4___ We go to heaven. ___3___ We die.

___1___ We are born. ___2___ We live.

259

Review

A Work with Words Have children answer the questions using words from the Word Bank to complete the sentences.

B Check Understanding Explain to children that they will be putting the sentences in the correct order to complete the Christian life cycle.

Assessment

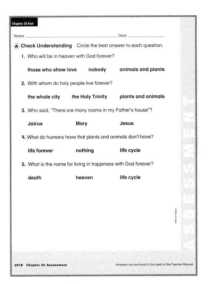

▲ Chapter 20 Test
page 251E

Answers to the Chapter Test can be found in the back of the Teacher Manual.

OPTIONAL ACTIVITY

Give Comfort Some children may wish to do a different version of the Live Your Faith activity.

- Have them look at Jesus' words on page 252. Tell them to decide what their favorite line is and to copy it onto their papers, preceded by the words "Jesus said." Suggest that they decorate their papers.

Multiple Intelligence: Visual/Spatial

TEACHER BACKGROUND

The Holy Trinity Like the number seven, the number three plays an important part in Scripture and in Catholic theology.

- In addition to the three members of the Trinity, there are three members of the Holy Family.
- References to the number three are numerous in the Bible, including the Gospels, which state that Jesus rose on the third day.

Family Faith

Remind children to discuss the Family Faith page at home. Encourage children to read the scripture passage from the first letter to the Corinthians.

Activity

• Encourage children to help their families create a happiness calendar at home.

People of Faith

Tell children about Saint Emily de Vialar.

• Emily bought a large house with money her grandfather left her. She had the Sisters of Saint Joseph of the Apparition live there. Before she died, she founded forty houses where the sisters lived and worked with the poor.

• Remind children to add Saint Emily de Vialar to their People of Faith albums.

• Encourage them to pray the prayer at home with their families.

  Visit **www.harcourtreligion.com** for weekly scripture readings and seasonal resources.

CHAPTER 20
Family Faith

Catholics Believe

■ Heaven is being happy with God forever.

■ God invites all people to heaven. All who follow Jesus and obey God's laws will go to heaven.

SCRIPTURE

I Corinthians 15:50–58 tells what St. Paul said about those who believe in Jesus.

 www.harcourtreligion.com For weekly Scripture readings and seasonal resources

Activity
Live Your Faith

Share Happiness Together create a happiness calendar. Choose one day each week to make a neighbor, friend, elderly family member happy. You can help in the yard, pick up groceries, or invite the person to dinner.

▲ Saint Emily de Vialar, 1797–1856

People of Faith

Emily was born in France. When she was fifteen, her mother died. She took care of her father's house. She devoted her life to prayer. After inheriting some money, Emily and three other young women cared for children who were sick and poor. She founded the Sisters of Saint Joseph of the Apparition to help the sick at home, in hospitals, and in prisons. Her feast day is June 17.

Family Pr

Saint Emily, pre for us that we r be followers of Jesus who care for those who c poor and sick. Amen.

? HOW DID I DO?

This week my religion classes were

☐ *some of the best ever!* ☐ *pretty good.* ☐ *in need of improvement.*

In what discussions and activities were children most interested?

_____

What activity did I most enjoy teaching?

_____

In what area do I need to improve?

_____

Name _____ Date _____

The Way to Heaven

Jesus tells how to love.

Showing love is the way to heaven.

Write the word from the
Word Bank to fill in the blanks.

1. I show love when I _____
   at home.

2. I show love when I _____
   with those who are poor.

3. I show love when I _____

4. I show love when I am _____
   and not mean.

5. I show love when I _____
   others and make up.

Answers can be found in the back of the Catechist Manual.

Overview

Faith Focus

- The signs of God's kingdom are justice, peace, and joy. *(CCC 2819)*
- The Holy Spirit works through Christians here and now to bring his kingdom to its fullness. *(CCC 2818)*

Catechism Connection

The *Catechism* teaches that Jesus calls everyone to enter God's kingdom, especially sinners, the poor, and those who have humble hearts. *(CCC 543–545)*

GDC Link

According to the *Directory*, the good news of God's kingdom includes a "message of liberation" for those who are poor or suffering in any way. *(GDC 103)*

 For the kingdom of God is not a matter of food and drink, but of righteousness, peace, and joy in the holy Spirit.

Romans 14:17

God's Kingdom

Throughout the Gospels, Jesus never directly answered the question "What is the kingdom of God?" but spoke in parables instead. He compared the kingdom of God to the small mustard seed that springs up and becomes the largest of plants. (See *Mark 4:30–32.*) This parable sheds light on the Christian call to hasten the coming of God's kingdom.

Contemplate a world without crime, poverty, and hunger. Think about what the world would be like if it were filled with righteousness, peace, and joy. These qualities mark the kingdom that Jesus proclaimed. Though it is easy to get caught up in the fatalistic, "It is impossible" or "I can't make a difference," Jesus calls his followers to believe in the coming of the kingdom.

Not Impossible

The mustard seed was tiny, but little by little it was transformed into a large shade tree. Through the Holy Spirit, Jesus empowers his followers to further the Father's reign. He calls Christians to participate in his work of transforming the world. As a disciple of Jesus, when you show peace, justice, and love, you bear witness to the kingdom.

Reflect **What action can you take in your community to further the reign of God?**

God's Kingdom

The year's catechesis ends by calling children to welcome the reign of God. God's kingdom corresponds to the deepest longings of the human heart. All Christians, even young children, are invited to foster and be a sign of God's kingdom.

- Merely telling children about their role, no matter how much enthusiasm you show, does not always have a long-lasting effect. By using realistic situations, however, you can inspire children to want to bring happiness into the lives of others through justice, peace, and love.

- The associations children make with concrete objects help them better understand some of the abstract concepts.

- Consider providing balloons with messages for children to take home as reminders to practice justice, peace, and love during their weeks away.

Hopefulness

- I like new ideas and new information. Teach me to use them for a better world.

- I want to help others. Tell me things I can do to help others.

The Promise to Become

Your commitment to catechesis has enabled others to address their promise to become the kind of person God has called them to be. You have given them opportunities to gain knowledge, develop attitudes, and identify behaviors. These things can help them respond spiritually to the Call to Faith.

Reflect **Circle any of the following to revisit and cultivate as you continue to follow your vocational commitments.**

Engagement with Others	Coming to the Balcony
Habits of Mind	Confession
Keeping Company	Moments of Grace
Motivations	Vocational Seasons
Remembering Who You Are	Blessed Assurance

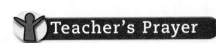 Teacher's Prayer

Creator God, thank you for calling me to serve young children. Care for them during the summer months. Fill me with faith, hope, and love, always ready to trust where you take me. Amen.

Weekly Planner

	Objective	Materials	Prayer & Scripture
DAY 1 Invite	**God's Kingdom** Page 261	**Objective:** To experience and share happiness	☐ Pencils ☐ Art supplies	📖 **Let Us Pray** *Psalm 105:7*
DAY 2 Explore	**God's Kingdom** Pages 262–263	**Objective:** To explore ways of bringing happiness to others	☐ Board or chart paper ☐ A balloon	📖 **Let Us Pray** *Psalm 105:7*
DAY 3 Explore	**Kingdom Workers** Pages 264–265	**Objective:** To identify ways of helping God's kingdom grow	☐ Board or chart paper ☐ Art supplies ☐ Copies of Activity Master 21, p. 270A	📖 **Let Us Pray** *Psalm 105:7* ✚ **Scripture:** Romans 14:17–19 ✚ **Scripture Background** Parable of the Vineyard, p. 264
DAY 4 Explore	**Working for God's Kingdom** Pages 266–267	**Objective:** To practice working for God's kingdom	☐ Board or chart paper ☐ Art supplies ☐ *Faces of Hope: Children of a Changing World* by Allison Wright (New World Library, 2003)	📖 **Let Us Pray** *Psalm 105:7*
DAY 5 Celebrate	**Asking Prayer** Page 268	**Objective:** To pray for the coming of God's kingdom	☐ Bible ☐ Music CD	📖 **Let Us Pray** **An Asking Prayer** 🔔 **Hymn:** "Bring Forth the Kingdom"

Chapter 21 Wrap-Up: Review and Apply p. 269 • Chapter 21 Assessment p. 261E

Words of Faith

Activities	Enrichment
Let's Begin: Happy Signs, p. 261 Multiple Intelligence: Interpersonal OPTIONAL Crown the King, p. 261 Multiple Intelligence: Visual/Spatial	
Share Your Faith: Think, Share, Act, p. 263 Multiple Intelligence: Bodily/Kinesthetic OPTIONAL Happiness at Home, p. 262 Multiple Intelligence: Interpersonal OPTIONAL Act Out Classroom Solutions, p. 263 Multiple Intelligence: Interpersonal	• Justice and Peace: Justice, p. 262 • Quick Tip: Acting with Justice, p. 263
Connect Your Faith: Make a Membership Card, p. 265 Multiple Intelligence: Verbal/Linguistic OPTIONAL Activity Master 21: Help God's Kingdom Grow, p. 264 Multiple Intelligence: Visual/Spatial	• Reaching All Learners: Advance the Kingdom, p. 265 • Teacher Background: The sign of peace, p. 265
Live Your Faith: Imagine, p. 267 Multiple Intelligence: Visual/Spatial OPTIONAL Act It Out, p. 266 Multiple Intelligence: Bodily/Kinesthetic OPTIONAL Cross-Curricular: Art, p. 267 Multiple Intelligence: Visual/Spatial	• Christian Living Skills: Social Analysis, p. 266 • Quick Tip: A Summer Mission, p. 267
	• Liturgy Link: Sign of Peace, p. 268 • Lectionary Link: Break Open the Word, p. 268

Multimedia Resources

BOOK
Conan, Sally Anne. *God's Best Gift.*
Paulist Press. Mahwah, NJ. 1997.
Children reflect on God's unconditional love.

VIDEO
The Gospel with a Smile: Hope
(18 min).Paulist Press. Mahwah, NJ.
1997. Stories and songs celebrate God's
faithfulness to his promises.

 Teacher Resources
www.harcourtreligion.com
• For interactive lesson planner, chapter resources, and activities
• For free materials and information

Home Connection

Chapter 21 Family Faith, p. 270
Take-home activities, chapter content review, saint features and prayer

 For more family activities
www.harcourtreligion.com

Name _____ Date _____

(A) Check Understanding   Draw a line to the best ending for each sentence.

1. God's kingdom

    a. you help God's kingdom grow.

2. Every time you say the Lord's Prayer,

    b. began with Jesus.

3. When you show love, peace, and justice,

    c. you pray for the coming of God's kingdom.

(B) Make Connections   Write two ways you can help God's kingdom grow.

4. _____

    _____

5. _____

    _____

ASSESSMENT

©Harcourt Religion

Answers can be found in the back of the Teacher Manual.

chapter 21 God's Kingdom

 Let Us Pray

Leader: God, guide us in working for your kingdom.
"The LORD is our God
who rules the whole earth."

Psalm 105:7

All: God, guide us in working for your kingdom.
Amen.

Activity Let's Begin

● **Happy Signs** There are many things that make you happy. There are many ways to show you are happy.

Stand in a circle. Sing the song "If You're Happy and You Know It." Everyone in the circle can take a turn showing a sign of happiness.

• What is one thing that makes you happy?

_____

- -

_____

✎ **Make a List** Write three ways you can make someone else happy. Share your list with a partner. **Responses will vary.**

261

OPTIONAL ACTIVITY

Crown the King Invite children to make a crown for God.

• Supply each child with crayons and a piece of construction paper with the points of a crown already cut on one of the short sides.

• Have them decorate the crown and then tape the ends together.

Multiple Intelligence: Visual/Spatial

Objective: To experience and share happiness

Open

Let Us Pray Invite children to move to your classroom prayer space. Have children stand and pray the psalm verse together three times, beginning in a whisper and getting a little louder each time.

Build

Activity

• Have children form several circles so the activity occurs simultaneously.

• Read aloud the first two sentences of Happy Signs. Ask children to think about ways they show they're happy.

• Have children sing the song "If You're Happy and You Know It" until each child has a chance to show a sign of happiness.

Extension Activity

• Tell children they will be making a list.

• Ask a volunteer to read the question.

• Have children write three ways they can make someone else happy.

• Allow time for children to share their lists with a partner.

Close

Have children tell what they have learned about making someone else happy.

DAY 2

Objective: To explore ways of bringing happiness to others

Open

 Let Us Pray Invite children to pray the psalm verse on page 261 with you.

Focus **How can you make others happy?** List children's answers on the board or on chart paper.

Build

God's Kingdom

Read aloud the first paragraph of God's Kingdom.

- Blow up a balloon part way. Tell children that the world would be so happy if everyone worked to be more peaceful.

- Blow up the balloon a little more. Explain that the world would be even better if everyone worked for justice.

- Finish inflating the balloon and tell children that God's kingdom grows when people show love to others.

- Ask children what they can do to make the classroom a happy place.

God's Kingdom

Focus **How can you make others happy?**

Imagine people showing happiness every single day. What a wonderful world that would be! When followers of Jesus act with peace, justice, and love, they help the kingdom of God grow.

Suppose you are in charge of happiness in the classroom. Choose the best way for the children to act.

> Some quiet or shy children don't get picked as partners.
>
> Kindly ask one of them to be a partner. This is spreading peace.

262

Happiness at Home Ask children how they could use their suggestions on how to promote peace, justice, and love in the classroom at home.

- Ask children to illustrate one of their suggestions.
- Invite volunteers to share their ideas.

Multiple Intelligence: Interpersonal

✚ JUSTICE AND PEACE

Justice Tell children that justice is a way of acting by which we give God and people what is due them. Ask questions, and have children answer "some people" or "all people." Who should be treated with kindness? Who should have enough food to eat? Lead children to conclude that all people should be treated with justice.

Catholic Social Teaching: Life and Dignity

me children don't want to share.

are and give others what they need.
is is acting with justice.

en the teacher isn't looking, children
teasing and calling names.

ow care for others, even if it's hard.
is is love.

Share Your Faith

Think: How could you make a happy playground?

Share: In small groups discuss ways to bring peace, justice, and love to your playground.

Act: Act out different ways to make a happy playground.

263

- Have children work individually or in small groups.
- Direct children to read the three classroom situations and decide what to do to produce peace, justice, and love in the classroom.
- Have volunteers share their work.
- Have the whole class clap to show their happiness after each presentation is made.
- Adapt the activity by using the playground instead of the classroom.

Close

Tell children that God's kingdom is a kingdom of justice, love, and peace. Remind them that you work for God's kingdom by your just, loving, and peace-making actions.

OPTIONAL ACTIVITY

Act Out Classroom Solutions   Invite three small groups to act out their solutions to the problems of the imaginary classroom.

- One group should take peace, a second justice, and a third love.
- Allow time for each group to practice.
- Have groups present solutions to the class.

Multiple Intelligence: Interpersonal

QUICK TIP

Acting with Justice   Justice means being as generous to others as God has been with us. It is more than simple fairness. We are called to work for true justice by respecting others. Jesus shows the perfect example of generosity and justice.

- Have children draw a picture of something they would like to change in the world like poverty, war, and hunger.

Objective: To identify ways of helping God's kingdom grow

Open

 Let Us Pray Invite children to pray the psalm verse on page 231 with you.

Focus **How can you help God's kingdom grow?** List children's answers on the board or on chart paper.

Build

Kingdom Workers
Read aloud Kingdom Workers.

• Gather children together, and tell them they will hear how Saint Paul described God's kingdom.

Christian Living
Proclaim the scripture story.

• Have children list some of the things Saint Paul says about God's kingdom.

❷ **What have you done today to bring happiness to other people?** Have small groups discuss responses.

Explore

Kingdom Worker

Focus How can you help God kingdom grow?

The Bible tells us how to have tru happiness. The Bible teaches how t do this.

Every Christian tries to bring mor peace, justice, and love to the worlc When you do this, you help God's kingdom grow.

SCRIPTURE Romans 14:

Read to Me Christian Living

God's kingdom isn't about eating and drinking. God's kingdom is about living in justice, peace, and joy. These things come from the Holy Spirit. If you serve Jesus Christ in this way, then you please God. People will respect you. Let us do all we can to live at peace.

Based on Romans 14:17–19

❷ **What have you done today to bring happiness to other people?**
Responses will vary.

264

SCRIPTURE BACKGROUND

Parable of the Vineyard In this parable, Jesus compares God to the owner of a vineyard who gives freely and generously to everyone.

• In God's kingdom, everyone is rewarded the same: eternal life with God. (See Matthew 20:1–15.)

OPTIONAL ACTIVITY

Activity Master 21: Help God's Kingdom Grow Distribute copies of the activity on teacher page 270A.

• As an alternative, you may wish to send the activity home with children.

▲ Activity Master 21 page 270A

arn from Jesus

od's kingdom on earth began with
us. Read some things Jesus said
did.

Jesus forgave people over and over
again. Jesus brought peace.

Jesus treated others as he would like
to be treated. Jesus brought justice.

Jesus fed people who were hungry.
Jesus showed love.

Activity **Connect Your Faith**

Make a Membership Card
Write your name in the
pace. Talk about
ways you can help
God's kingdom grow.

God's Kingdom

265

Learn from Jesus
Read aloud the first line of Learn from
Jesus. Tell children that Jesus' actions
reveal to Christians how to work for
God's kingdom.

- Read aloud the rest of the text.
- Ask children to sum up Jesus' actions
  in their own words.

Activity

- Have children make their own
  membership cards to the kingdom.
  Have tape on hand so children can
  wear their cards home.

Close

Remind children that Jesus began
God's kingdom on earth. All Christians
work for God's kingdom when they
bring more love, justice, and peace to
the world.

★ REACHING ALL LEARNERS

Advance the Kingdom   By the time your class
reaches this chapter, summertime is close by.

- During the summer, children might forget the moral
  lessons you have tried to teach them.
- You may want to have children draw up a list of
  specific things they can do in the summer to help
  the kingdom of God.

✦ TEACHER BACKGROUND

The Sign of Peace   In the 16th century, the Council
of Trent reformed the liturgy to restrict the Sign of
Peace to the celebrant and the ministers at the altar.

- The Second Vatican Council reinstated the Sign of
  Peace as a part of the Mass shared by the entire
  congregation.

Objective: To practice working for God's kingdom

Open

Let Us Pray Invite children to pray the psalm verse from page 261 with you.

Focus **How can you work for the kingdom of God?** List children's responses on the board or on chart paper.

Build

Working for God's Kingdom

Read aloud the introductory paragraph.

• Draw attention to the text on the banners.

• Invite volunteers to read aloud the bulleted items on each banner.

❷ **What other things can you do to work for God's kingdom?** Brainstorm responses as a class, and add suggestions to the list on the board or on chart paper.

Explore

Working for God's Kingdom

Focus How can you work for the kingdom of God?

God's kingdom grows whenever people show justice, love, and peac Here are some ways you can work for God's kingdom.

To bring **JUSTICE**
- Play fair.
- Share what you have with others.
- Don't leave anyone out.
- Help people get the food and clothing they need.

To bring **LOVE**
- Show family members and friends that you care about th
- Be happy when good things h to others.
- Help those who are hurt or lo
- Don't gossip or call people na

To bring **PEACE**
- Be patient.
- Try to settle an argument so everyone wins.
- Don't always try to get your way.
- Be the first to say "I'm sorry" and "I forgive you."

❷ **What other things can you do to w for God's kingdom?** Responses will var

266

Act It Out Invite children to dramatize ways to work for God's kingdom.

• Divide the class into three groups, and assign each group one of the three qualities of the kingdom— justice, love, and peace.

• Have each group act out one way to work for its assigned quality.

Multiple Intelligence: Bodily/Kinesthetic

CHRISTIAN LIVING SKILLS

Social Analysis Young children are already sensitive to situations of injustice. Remind children that they can help work for God's kingdom when they

• make sure everyone is treated fairly.

• learn about the needs of others, and help meet them.

• get involved to make a positive difference at home and in school.

Live Your Faith

Imagine Think about what the world would be like if everyone worked together to bring God's kingdom justice, love, and peace. Draw a picture that shows your idea of this wonderful world.

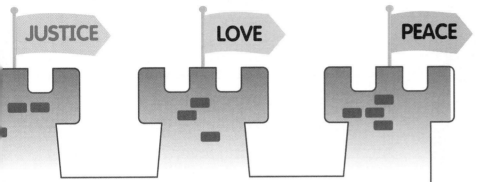

JUSTICE   LOVE   PEACE

267

- Read aloud the directions for the activity.
- Allow time for children to plan their drawings.
- Distribute art materials, and have children work independently on the activity.
- Display finished artwork in the classroom.

Close

Pray together the Lord's Prayer, inviting children to pay special attention to the phrase "Your kingdom come."

OPTIONAL ACTIVITY

Cross-Curricular: Art   To inspire or complement children's art work, share the following picture book on the theme of making a better world:

- *Faces of Hope: Children of a Changing World* by Alison Wright (New World Library, 2003)

Multiple Intelligence: Visual/Spatial

 QUICK TIP

A Summer Mission   Invite children to think of ways they can continue working for God's kingdom over the summer. List ideas on the board or on chart paper, and encourage children to copy the list into their faith journals or notebooks.

Objective: To pray for the coming of God's kingdom

Prepare

Select one child as the prayer leader.

• Practice the responses to the prayer.

 Use the *Call to Faith 1* CD, track 21, to rehearse the song.

Gather

Assemble children in the prayer space.

Pray

An Asking Prayer

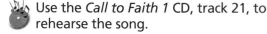 Follow the order of prayer.

• Sing together the refrain.

Celebrate

Asking Prayer

 Let Us Pray

Gather and begin with the Sign of the Cross.

Leader: God, we want to do your will.

All: Help us bring peace.

Leader: God the Father, we want to do your will.

All: Help us bring justice.

Leader: God the Father, we want to do your will.

All: Help us bring love.

Sing together the refrain.

Bring forth the kingdom of mercy,
Bring forth the kingdom of peace;
Bring forth the kingdom of justice,
Bring forth the City of God!

"Bring Forth the Kingdom," Marty Haugen © 1986 GIA Publications, Inc.

268

 LITURGY LINK

Sign of Peace Tell children that Catholics share a sign of peace with each other during Mass. People usually shake hands and say "Peace be with you."

• Ask children how they exchange a sign of peace with their family members at Mass and have them practice with each other in the classroom.

 LECTIONARY LINK

Break Open the Word Read last week's Sunday Gospel. Invite children to think about what the reading means to them as they try to follow Christ's example. For questions related to the weekly Gospel reading, visit our Web site at **www.harcourtreligion.com**.

 Visit www.harcourtreligion.com for weekly scripture readings and seasonal resources.

CHAPTER 21
Review

Work with Words Write the correct word from the Word Bank to complete each sentence.

WORD BANK

love
peace
justice

1. When you settle problems with kindness,

you bring _____peace (p. 266)_____.

2. When you give God what he deserves and give

others what they need, you bring ____justice (p. 266)____.

3. When you care, even if it's hard, you bring

_____love (p. 266)_____.

Make Connections Put an X by things you can do to help God's kingdom grow.

___X___ love your parents

_____ tease

___X___ be a good friend

_____ fight

___X___ pray

___X___ help others

___X___ share

269

Review

Ⓐ **Work with Words** Tell children to fill in the sentences with words from the Word Bank.

Ⓑ **Make Connections** Ask children to place an X by the things they can do to help God's kingdom grow.

Assessment

▲ **Chapter 21 Test page 261E**

Answers to the Chapter Test can be found in the back of the Teacher Manual.

Counting Blessings Have children make a large poster showing God's blessings.

- Help them find photos of things for which they are thankful (pets, parents, food, house) in old magazines.

- Have them paste the pictures on a large piece of poster board under the heading, "God's Blessings."

Multiple Intelligence: Visual/Spatial

 QUICK TIP

Helping the Kingdom Inquire at the parish office if there are any opportunities for young children to share their time or talent.

- If your parish contributes to a food bank or homeless shelter, for example, children may be able to collect food, clothing, or toys from home to donate.

HOME CONNECTION

Family Faith

Remind children to discuss the Family Faith page at home. Encourage children to read the scripture passage from the book of Deuteronomy.

Activity

- Encourage children to get their families involved in justice activities.

People of Faith

Tell children about Blessed Pedro Calungsod.

- The Church has given Pedro the title Blessed because he led a holy life. Pedro always went to confession, Mass and Communion before he went on mission trips.
- Remind children to add Blessed Pedro Calungsod to their People of Faith albums.
- Encourage them to pray the prayer at home with their families.

 Visit **www.harcourtreligion.com** for weekly scripture readings and seasonal resources.

CHAPTER 21
Family Faith

◎ Catholics Believe

- Justice, peace, and love are signs of God's kingdom.
- Christians work here and now to help God's kingdom grow.

 SCRIPTURE

Read Deuteronomy 16:18–20 as a reminder to act with justice.

GO ONLINE www.harcourtreligion.com For weekly Scripture readings and seasonal resources

Activity
Live Your Faith

Work for Justice Every community needs God's justice. Look into parish or neighborhood opportunities to find ways you can help others, such as by taking food to a food bank or serving food to the homeless. Volunteer to help as a family. Discuss the importance of being generous with your time and love.

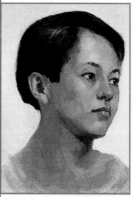

People of Faith

Blessed Pedro Calungsod was born in the Philippines. At fourteen he became a lay missionary. Pedro was a painter, singer, and catechist as he worked with the Jesuit missionaries. His greatest desire was to spread Jesus' message of love. He died while protecting a priest from men who hated Christianity. Pedro is the patron of Filipino children. The Filipino Church celebrates his feast day on April 2.

▲ **Blessed Pedro Calungsod, 1654–1672**

🎁 Family P:

Dear God, help use our talents serve you. Help share your lov with everyone meet. Amen.

270 **CCC** See Catechism of the Catholic Church 2816–2821 for further reading on chapter content

---

❓ HOW DID I DO?

This week my religion classes were

☐ *some of the best ever!* ☐ *pretty good.* ☐ *in need of improvement.*

In what discussions and activities were children most interested?

_____

What activity did I most enjoy teaching?

_____

In what area do I need to improve?

_____

Name _____ Date _____

Help God's Kingdom Grow

The children in the pictures need your help.

Draw a new picture in each space. Show justice, peace, or love.

Seven Principles of CATHOLIC SOCIAL TEACHING

▶ Care for God's Creation

▶ Life and Dignity of the Human Person

▶ Rights and Responsibilities of the Human Person

▶ Dignity of Work and the Rights of Workers

▶ Solidarity of the Human Family

▶ Call to Family, Community, and Participation

▶ Option for the Poor and Vulnerable

Faith in Action!
CATHOLIC SOCIAL TEACHING

Connect to Unit 7

This unit's Faith in Action feature teaches first graders the principle that those who are poor and vulnerable deserve special efforts on their behalf. It connects to topics covered in this unit.

Children learned that

- we celebrate God's love at Mass.
- God wants all people to be happy with him forever.
- we are called to work for God's kingdom of peace and love.

Discover Catholic Social Teaching

Principle: Option for the Poor and Vulnerable

At first glance, the Church's longstanding policy of the preferential option for the poor may seem "unfair" to young children, who are used to defining justice in terms of strict equality. Truth to tell, we adults sometimes have as much difficulty with this concept as children do. The justice of God's kingdom calls us to redress the injustices of this world, which means tilting the scales in favor of those most in need.

Catholic tradition calls us

- to recognize that all blessings are gifts of God.
- to work for the just distribution of those blessings.
- to defend those deprived of a voice in society.

Reflect **How are you sharing your blessings with those most in need?**

Catholic Social Teaching Document

"The prime purpose of this special commitment to the poor is to enable them to become active participants in the life of society. . . The 'option for the poor,' therefore, is not an adversarial slogan that pits one group or class against another. Rather it states that the deprivation and powerlessness of the poor wounds the whole community . . ."

From *Economic Justice for All,* U.S. Catholic Bishops, 1986, #88

Faith in Action!
CATHOLIC SOCIAL TEACHING

In this unit you learned that we celebrate God's love at Mass. At Mass you are reminded to work for God's kingdom of peace and love.

People in Need

One day Jesus was teaching a big crowd about God's love. Late in the afternoon, people started getting hungry, but they had no food. Jesus wasn't sure what to do.

A boy offered to share his lunch. He had five small loaves of bread and two pieces of fish. Jesus blessed the food. He gave it to his friends. Jesus told them to give everyone some food. Many, many people ate until they were full. There were even twelve baskets of leftovers! (Based on John 6:1–13)

We are called to be like Jesus and the boy. We should try to share what we have.

 What are some things that people in your school and community need?
Possible responses: food, clean clothing, shoes, friends

271

DISCOVER
Catholic Social Teaching

Let Us Pray Jesus, you showed us that loving God means sharing what we have with those in need. Help us to grow in love.

Faith in Action
Summarize the content of this unit by reading aloud the first paragraph.

People in Need
Invite children to listen carefully as you read aloud the story of the feeding of the multitudes (the first two paragraphs).

- Ask children what the people in the crowd needed, and how Jesus helped them.
- Read aloud the concluding paragraph.
- Direct attention to the pictures, and ask children to talk about the similarities between them.

 What are some things that people in your school and community need? Discuss the questions as a class.

QUICK TIP

Children's Literature Share with children the classic folk tale *Stone Soup* by Marcia Brown (Scribner, 1947), which explores themes of sharing and community that parallel those of the Gospel story.

SCRIPTURE BACKGROUND

John 6:1–13 The story of Jesus' miraculous feeding of the crowd appears in all four gospels. In the Gospel according to John, the story is intended to evoke a direct connection with the Eucharist, in which we are fed with the "living bread" of Christ's Body and Blood. Familiarity with this account is an important part of children's preparation for First Communion.

CONNECT

With the
Call to Justice

One Great Summ

CONNECT

With the Call to Justice

One Great Summer

Have children listen carefully as you read aloud the story on this page.

- Refer to the picture to help children follow the story.

- Remind children that helping one another goes both ways. Talk about what the children of Mississippi might have shared with Anne and Anna.

 **How are Anne and Anna like Jesus and the boy who shared his food?**
Discuss the question as a class. Help children note the girls' recognition of the children's needs and their willingness to share.

Jesus asks us to care for the needs of others. Let's look at how two friends went out of their way to help children in need.

Anne and Anna are best friends. They go to the same high school in New York. During summer vacation they like to do the same fun things.

Last year, Anne and Anna heard about some children whose summe are difficult. These children live in a very poor part of Mississippi. There no summer school programs, activiti or playgrounds. Their parents work hard during the hot summer days. The children are bored and lonely. Sometimes they get in trouble, beca they have nothing to do.

Anne and Anna spent las summer trying to help. The girls flew to Mississippi and made new friends. They played games with the children. They taught then swim and to speak Spanish

Anne and Anna had a great summer, and so did the children they helped.

 How are Anne and Anna like Jesus and the boy v shared his food?
Possible responses: They share love; they help others.

272

TEACHER BACKGROUND

Anne and Anna The girls profiled in this story participated in a shared mission project of the Sisters of the Holy Names of Jesus and Mary, who run the Academy of the Holy Names in Albany, New York, where Anne and Anna went to school.

QUICK TIP

Children's Literature The award-winning novel *Roll of Thunder, Hear My Cry* by Mildred D. Taylor (Phyllis Fogelman Books, 2001) provides a vivid portrait of life in the Mississippi Delta.

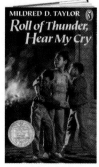

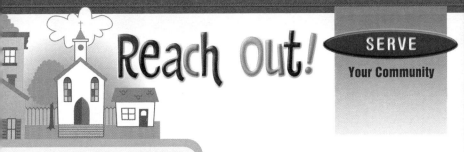

Reach Out!

SERVE
Your Community

What Can You Do?

...w it is your turn to pay attention to what
...ple need. Look at each picture and read
...words. Write what you will do.

...onely.
...l you do?

I have no friends.
What will you do?

_____

- -

_____

...ke a Difference

...mer Savings Make a bank from a jar or a
...ee can. Over the summer, save your pennies.
... your family to save their pennies, too. When
...time to go back to school, count and wrap
... pennies. Give the money to a group that
...s people in need.

SERVE

Your Community

Reach Out!

What Can You Do?

Activity

- Read aloud the directions for What Can You Do?
- If necessary, read aloud each of the speech balloons.
- Allow time for children to work independently on the activity.
- Invite volunteers to share their work.

Make a Difference

Activity

- Read aloud the directions.
- Provide craft materials, and help children make and decorate their banks.

Encourage children to share what they have learned with friends, family members, and other classes.

273

OPTIONAL ACTIVITY

Cross-Curricular: Mathematics   Show children
how to count and wrap pennies.

- Explain that 50 pennies make a roll.
- Tell children that 100 pennies make one dollar, and ask how many rolls of pennies they need to equal a dollar.

Multiple Intelligence: Mathematical/Logical

QUICK TIP

Commission Children   Acknowledge children's
year-long exploration of the seven themes of social
justice by commissioning them to put what they
learned into practice.

- Give each child a Faith in Action certificate listing the seven themes.
- Compose your own commissioning prayer, asking the Holy Spirit to support children as they go out to live their faith.

Ⓐ Work with Words Write the correct word from the Word Bank to complete each sentence.

1. Jesus shared the
   _____
   ⎯ ⎯ ⎯ ⎯ ⎯ ⎯ ⎯ ⎯ ⎯ ⎯ ⎯ ⎯ ⎯
   Last Supper (p. 244)
   with his followers the night before he died.

2. At the Mass, the bread and wine become the
   _____
   ⎯ ⎯ ⎯ ⎯ ⎯ ⎯ ⎯ ⎯ ⎯ ⎯ ⎯ ⎯ ⎯
   Body and Blood of _____ Jesus (p. 243) _____.

3. ⎯ ⎯ ⎯ ⎯ ⎯ ⎯ ⎯ ⎯ ⎯ ⎯ ⎯
   _____ Heaven (p. 252) _____ is living and being
   happy with God forever.
   _____

4. God wants _____ everyone (p. 255) _____ to be
   happy with him.

5. Jesus asks his followers to act with
   _____
   ⎯ ⎯ ⎯ ⎯ ⎯ ⎯ ⎯ ⎯ ⎯ ⎯ ⎯ ⎯
   _____ peace (p. 265) _____.

© Harcourt Religion

Ⓑ Check Understanding Draw a line to match the words on the left with the definition on the right.

(p. 245) Eucharist — life after death

(p. 253) Jesus' promise — used at Mass

(p. 242) Gospel book and candles — living in peace, justice, and love

(p. 262) God's kingdom — sacrament celebrated at Mass

Ⓒ Making Connections How can you make others happy? Draw a picture.

© Harcourt Religion

274

275

Unit Review

The Unit Review is designed to prepare children for the Unit Assessment. Have children complete the Review pages. Then discuss the answers as a class. You may wish to review any concepts with which children are having difficulty before the Unit Assessment.

Notes

Name _____ Date _____

(A) Work with Words Write the words from the Word Bank that best complete the sentences.

1. Jesus gave his life so that people could have

_____

_____ with God.

2. _____ is happiness with God forever.

3. Every _____ works for the

kingdom of God.

Use the Word Bank to help you answer the question.

4. What is another name for the Mass?

_____

_____

5. What did Jesus say when he blessed the bread?

_____

_____

Answers can be found in the back of the Teacher Manual.

©Harcourt Religion

Name _____ Date _____

B **Check Understanding** Trace the line to the best ending for each sentence.

6. Jesus saved people ------------------ from friends.

------------ from the power of sin.

7. Jesus being raised from ---------- the Resurrection.

the dead is called ------------------ Easter.

Draw a line to the best title.

8. Celebrates Jesus' presence in the holy Bread and Wine

heaven

9. Being happy with God forever

grace

10. God's life and love in you

Eucharist

Answers can be found in the back of the Teacher Manual.

©Harcourt Religion

CATHOLIC SOURCE BOOK

HOW TO USE Topics covered in each of the sections will enrich the content in the student book.

During class time you may wish to invite children to use the Catholic Source Book to clarify or discuss some of the topics of interest in a given lesson.

ACTIVITIES In the first five sections of the teacher's edition for the Catholic Source Book, you will find Optional Activities for each page of the student book. This activity is located beneath the reproduced student pages in your teacher edition.

You may wish to use these activities during class as enrichment activities or, if appropriate, as homework.

WORDS OF FAITH The Glossary section contains all of the Words of Faith found in the student book as well as other important faith words that are introduced in the text.

Encourage your children to refer to the Catholic Source Book when they want to learn more about a topic.

The Catholic Source Book for *Call to Faith*—which includes the four pillars of the Catechism of the Catholic Church—is organized in six sections.

Scripture	p. 276
Creed	p. 278
Liturgy	p. 284
Morality	p. 298
Prayer	p. 300
Words of Faith	p. 302

CATHOLIC SOURCE BOOK

The Bible

The **Bible** is the word of God. Another word for the Bible is **Scripture**, which means "writing."

The Bible has two parts. Christians call the first part the **Old Testament**. They call the second part the **New Testament**.

What Is in the Bible

In the Bible there are many kinds of stories. Some of the most important stories are found in the **Gospels** in the New Testament.

The Gospels

The Gospels include stories about Jesus' birth and life. They also include stories Jesus told that are called **parables**. He told these special stories to help people better understand God's love. For example, Jesus told the parable of the Prodigal Son as a way to show God's great love and forgiveness.

Faith Fact

The first book of the Bible begins with the words, "In the beginning." The last word in some Bibles is "Amen."

© Harcourt Religion

© Harcourt Religion

276

277

OPTIONAL ACTIVITY

Main Parts of the Bible   To help children visualize the Bible's two main parts, illustrate it in the following manner on the board or on chart paper:

Old Testament + New Testament = The Bible

- Gather children in a circle around a large Bible.
- Help them locate the Old and New Testaments and then the four Gospels.

OPTIONAL ACTIVITY

The Good Shepherd Parable   Usually one of children's favorite Gospel parables, the story of the Good Shepherd can teach a wonderful lesson about Jesus and his love for us.

- Read the story of the Good Shepherd aloud to children.
- Provide each child with a cardboard cutout of a sheep, cotton balls, and glue sticks. Have each child glue the cotton balls to the sheep outline and draw in its eyes, nose, and mouth.
- Have children bring their sheep home to remind them of how much Jesus loves them.

The Trinity

- God the Father is the Creator of all things.
- Jesus Christ is the Son of God and our Savior.
- God the Holy Spirit is God's gift of love to the Church.

The **Trinity** is God the Father, God the Son, and God the Holy Spirit—Three Persons in one God.

When you make the Sign of the Cross and say, "In the name of the Father, and of the Son, and of the Holy Spirit," you are telling your belief in the Trinity.

278

The Church

The **Church** is the community of the People of God. The Church gathers to worship and praise God, especially at the celebration of the Mass.

Each member of the Church has been **baptized** and welcomed into God's family. Christians have a **mission** to share God's message of love with others.

In order to carry out this mission, Christians receive the gift of the **Holy Spirit**. Jesus' followers received the Holy Spirit at Pentecost. Pentecost is the birthday of the Church.

The Holy Spirit gave each of the disciples the courage to spread the good news of Jesus to other people. The Holy Spirit also makes you strong.

279

© Harcourt Religion

© Harcourt Religion

The Sign of the Cross   Point out to children that when we make the Sign of the Cross, we are praying to the Holy Trinity.

- Print the Sign of the Cross on sheets of bright paper.
- Print the words *Father*, *Son*, and *Holy Spirit* in trace-over letters.
- Duplicate the prayer and give each child a copy. Have children trace over the names of the three Persons in one God.
- Pray the Sign of the Cross together.

Who Is the Church?   Play the finger game "Here's the Church" with children.

- Interlock fingers of both hands with palms facing down. Begin the finger play, "Here's the Church."
- Bring two index fingers to form the steeple while saying, "And here's the steeple."
- Open two thumbs as if opening doors and say, "Open the doors."
- Turn remaining fingers over and wiggle them while saying, "And see all the people."
- Remind children that the Church is all who have been baptized and follow Jesus.

I Believe

The **Creed** tells the faith of the Church. It brings together the Church's most important beliefs about

■ God the Father, the Creator of all that is.

■ Jesus, God's Son and the Savior.

■ God the Holy Spirit, Giver of God's gifts.

■ The Church, the Body of Christ in this world.

Apostles' Creed

This creed gives a summary of the Apostles' beliefs. It is sometimes used at Masses for children and is part of the Rosary.

The Apostles' Creed

I believe in God, the Father almighty,
creator of heaven and earth.
I believe in Jesus Christ, his only Son,
  our Lord.
He was conceived by the power of the Holy
  Spirit,
and born of the Virgin Mary.
He suffered under Pontius Pilate,
was crucified, died, and was buried.
He descended to the dead.
On the third day, he rose again.
He ascended into heaven,
and is seated at the right hand of
  the Father.
He will come again to judge the living
  and the dead.
I believe in the Holy Spirit,
the holy Catholic Church,
the communion of saints,
the forgiveness of sins,
the resurrection of the body,
and the life everlasting. Amen.

▲ Pope
Benedict XVI
1927–

© Harcourt Religion

© Harcourt Religion

280

281

The Apostle Peter's Faith   Tell children Peter was blessed by Jesus after he confessed that Jesus was the Messiah and Son of God.

• Read Matthew 16:13–19 from a children's bible.

• Ask children what others said about Jesus.

• Ask children what Peter said about Jesus.

• Ask children how Jesus then blessed Peter.

Apostles' Creed   Help children connect the Apostle's Creed to the faith of the twelve Apostles.

Explain to students that the Apostles' Creed is a faithful summary of what they believed. There are twelve Apostles and twelve articles of the Apostles' Creed.

• Help children identify the twelve main beliefs or articles in the creed.

Mary, the Mother of God

Mary is the Mother of God. She is also Mother of the Church. Mary is a very special saint. All her life, Mary said "yes" to the things God asked of her.

Mary Prays for Us

At the Annunciation the angel Gabriel came to Mary to tell her she was going to give birth to the Savior, whom she should call Jesus. Because Mary said "yes," all people have been saved from the power of sin and everlasting death.

282

Mary is a good role model for the Church. The People of God often ask Mary to pray for them so that they have the courage to say "yes" to God, especially when it is difficult.

The Church honors Mary in many special ways. Special prayers, such as the **Rosary**, are said. Feast days, such as **Our Lady of Guadalupe**, are celebrated. These prayers and feasts remind people that Mary was willing to serve God.

283

The Story of the Annunciation   This Scripture story is often a favorite of children.

- Read aloud the story of the Annunciation.
- Help children understand that the story's message for us is to show us how to say "yes" to God when he asks hard things of us.
- Provide children with drawing paper and crayons. Have them draw their version of the Annunciation story.

Show a Video   To reinforce children's understanding that the Church honors Mary with special feast days, show children a video about Our Lady of Guadalupe or another feast.

- Check with your director of religious education or diocesan religious education office for an appropriate video.
- If a video needs to be purchased, there are many Catholic publishers who offer such videos for first graders.

The Sacraments

Baptism

Baptism joins you to God in a loving closeness. You become a member of the Church.

Confirmation

Confirmation celebrates the help of the Holy Spirit.

Eucharist

Jesus shares himself in the Eucharist.

© Harcourt Religion

284

Reconciliation

You say you are sorry. God forgives you in Reconciliation.

Anointing of the Sick

In the Anointing of the Sick, a priest blesses the very sick with holy oil. God gives comfort and peace.

Marriage

In Marriage God blesses married love. Married love is the heart of a family.

Holy Orders

In Holy Orders God blesses leaders who serve the Church.

© Harcourt Religion

285

OPTIONAL ACTIVITY

Attend Parish Baptism   Provide children with an experience of Baptism as it is celebrated in your parish.

- Arrange to have children attend a parish Baptism, whether during a Sunday liturgy or at another time designated for Baptisms at your parish.
- Afterward, talk with children about what they saw and heard.
- Emphasize how God shares his love and life with us through the sacrament of Baptism.

OPTIONAL ACTIVITY

Signs of God's Love   Reinforce that the sacraments are signs of God's love given by Jesus to bring people closer to God.

- Remind children that signs of God's love are all around us. The sacraments are signs of God's love, too.
- Provide children with paper, glue, and a variety of pre-cut symbols such as hearts, flowers, gift boxes, and so on. On each symbol, print *Signs of God's love are all around me!*
- Have children create collages with their symbols.

Special Things in Church

Altar

The **altar** is the table that is used to celebrate the Mass.

Tabernacle

The **tabernacle** is a very special box where the Body of Christ, the Blessed Sacrament, is kept.

Vestments

The priest wears special clothing called **vestments**. Some of the vestments that he wears are different colors for the different seasons of the Church year. The priest wears special clothing because he represents Jesus at Mass.

Faith Fact

Sometimes at Mass you might hear the ringing of bells a couple of times during Mass. This is a reminder that a very important part of the Mass is about to take place.

286

287

OPTIONAL ACTIVITY

Design a Tabernacle Use this activity to strengthen children's appreciation for containing the presence of Jesus in the Blessed Sacrament in a very special receptacle.

- Challenge children to design their own tabernacles.
- Provide them with drawing paper and crayons, and ask them to draw illustrations of tabernacles that would be special enough to hold Jesus in the Blessed Sacrament.

OPTIONAL ACTIVITY

Conduct a Church Tour Strengthen children's knowledge of their parish church and its special things by taking them on a tour of the church.

- Make arrangements to bring children to church for a tour.
- Be the tour guide yourself or invite a parish staff member to guide children.
- Point out to them the items listed on pages 286–289.

Crucifix

A **crucifix** is an image of Jesus on the cross. A crucifix is usually hung somewhere near the altar or is carried in procession as Mass begins.

Holy Water

As you enter the church, you dip your hand in **holy water** from the baptismal font or holy water font and make the Sign of the Cross to remind you of your Baptism.

© Harcourt Religion

288

Candles

Candles light the darkness. They are a sign of the presence of God.

© Harcourt Religion

Faith Fact

Some churches have special candles called vigil lights. They are usually blue, red, or amber. These candles are lit when people ask for special prayers.

Paschal Candle

At Easter, the **Paschal candle** is lit to remind the Church that Jesus is the light of the world. This candle is a very large candle from which many other baptismal candles are lit.

289

Invite a Speaker Enrich children's knowledge and understanding of crosses and crucifixes by inviting a guest speaker to class.

- Consider inviting a parish priest or parish staff member to class to speak to children about crosses and crucifixes. Consider inviting a person who is knowledgeable about icons.

- Explain to the speaker beforehand that children are learning about the cross and the crucifix and their role in the Catholic faith. Ask him or her to bring several examples of crosses and crucifixes for children to hold and examine.

Tabernacle Vigil Light Explain to children that in honor of Jesus in the Blessed Sacrament, a constant light is kept burning near the tabernacle. Tell them that in some churches this light is a candle, while in other churches this light is an oil lamp.

- Take children to church to see the tabernacle lamp, or show them a picture of such a light.

The Mass

There are four parts to the Mass.

❶ The **Gathering Rite**

- A procession by the priest, deacon, and servers begins the Mass.
- The Church asks for God's mercy with the prayer: Lord, have mercy. Christ, have mercy. Lord, have mercy.
- A song of glory and praise comes after that.

Faith Fact

God's family participates in the Mass in various ways: as servers, cross bearers, singers, readers, and extraordinary ministers of Holy communion. Someday you can choose to be one of these people.

❷ The **Liturgy of the Word** is the first main part of the Mass.

- The community listens to a reading from the Old Testament and one from the New Testament.
- The priest or deacon reads the Gospel and gives a homily.

During Mass Jesus is present. Christ is present in

- the assembled community.
- the word of God.
- the presiding priest.
- his Body and Blood.

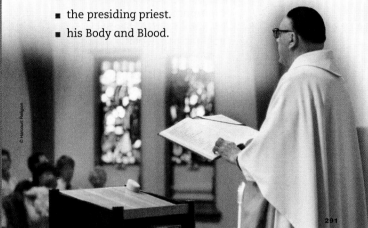

290

291

OPTIONAL ACTIVITY

Read a Book   There are many books available for young children that explain the Mass. Consider reading one of these books aloud to children or suggesting the titles to children's families.

- *I Can Pray the Mass!* by Mary Terese Donze ASC (Liguori Publications, 1993)
- *A Child's Guide to the Mass* by Sue Stanton (Paulist Press, 2000)
- *The Mass for Children* by Jude Winkler (Catholic Book Publishing Company, 1997)

OPTIONAL ACTIVITY

Write a Class Epistle   Talk with children about the letters, or epistles, of Paul. Explain how important these letters were as reminders of how the followers of Jesus should live.

- Guide children in writing an epistle to another class.
- Have them include the Christian behaviors that every follower of Jesus should live out.
- When children's ideas are completed, print the letter on chart paper.

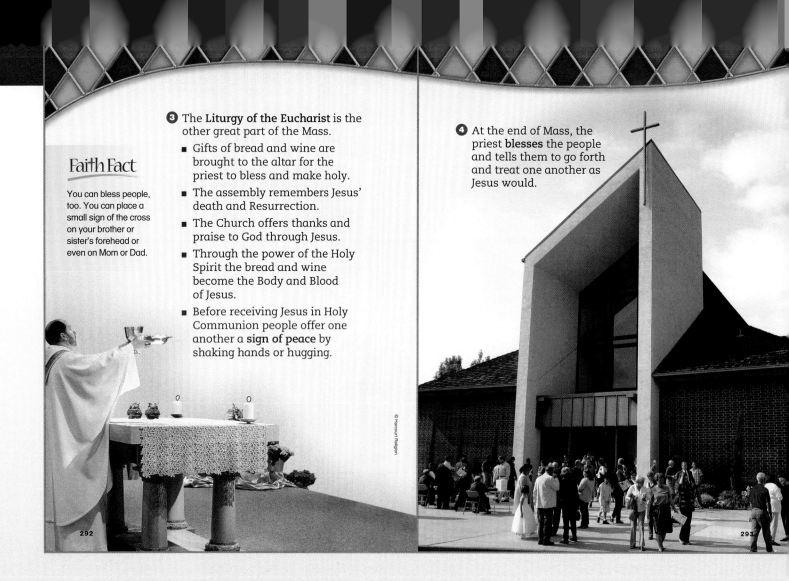

3 The **Liturgy of the Eucharist** is the other great part of the Mass.

- Gifts of bread and wine are brought to the altar for the priest to bless and make holy.
- The assembly remembers Jesus' death and Resurrection.
- The Church offers thanks and praise to God through Jesus.
- Through the power of the Holy Spirit the bread and wine become the Body and Blood of Jesus.
- Before receiving Jesus in Holy Communion people offer one another a **sign of peace** by shaking hands or hugging.

Faith Fact

You can bless people, too. You can place a small sign of the cross on your brother or sister's forehead or even on Mom or Dad.

4 At the end of Mass, the priest **blesses** the people and tells them to go forth and treat one another as Jesus would.

© Harcourt Religion

292

293

Make a Mass Mural   Reinforce children's knowledge of the Mass by having them create a Mass mural.

- Provide children with a long sheet of butcher paper and crayons or markers.
- Assign small groups of children various Mass parts.
- Challenge children to draw their images of those parts of the Mass.

Make Collages   To reinforce children's learning that the Mass is continued with our loving actions throughout the week ahead, have them make collages that show people loving and serving one another.

- Provide children with old magazines.
- Have them find pictures that show people at service to others.
- Ask children to cut out those pictures and arrange them on art paper.
- Instruct children to glue the pictures on the art paper.

Liturgical Seasons and Colors

The Church has many seasons. Each season is marked by a special color or colors that decorate the church and the vestments.

Advent

Advent is the beginning of the Church year and is marked by the color violet. Advent is about four weeks long; it looks forward to the return of Jesus at the end of time, and it leads up to Christmas. It is a time of waiting.

Christmas

Christmas is celebrated with the colors white and gold. Gold can be used instead of white for special Church holy days. At Christmas the Church remembers the birth of Jesus and looks forward to the return of Jesus at the end of time.

Ordinary Time

Ordinary Time celebrates the words and works of Jesus and is marked by the color green.

Lent

During **Lent** Christians recall their baptismal promises to change their life and act more like Jesus. As a sign of preparation for Easter, Lent is marked by the color violet.

Easter Triduum

The Easter **Triduum** is the season that lasts for three days and is the most holy season of the Church year. It celebrates Jesus' passing through death to life. The holy days of Triduum are Holy Thursday (white or gold), Good Friday (red), and Holy Saturday (white or gold), and Easter Sunday (white or gold).

Faith Fact

The butterfly is a symbol for new life. This reminds us of the Resurrection of Jesus and life after death.

Easter Season

The **Easter** season starts on the night of Easter Sunday. Vestments are brilliant white for new life because the Easter season celebrates Jesus' Resurrection. Easter also celebrates the new life Jesus' resurrection brings to all.

294

295

© Harcourt Religion

© Harcourt Religion

OPTIONAL ACTIVITY

Read the Nativity Story   Children this age really enjoy listening to the story of the Nativity.

- Choose a children's Bible version of the story or one of many trade book versions available at local bookstores or libraries.
- Take some class time to read the story with enthusiasm.

OPTIONAL ACTIVITY

Loving Lenten Crosses   Talk with children about the loving sacrifices we make during the season of Lent to prepare to celebrate Jesus' Resurrection at Easter.

- Provide children with prepared crosses made from white construction paper. Section off each cross with a "stained-glass pattern" of boxes.
- Explain to children that each time they do a kind or unselfish act during Lent, they are to color in one of the spaces on their crosses.
- Challenge them to fill in each space with bright colors by Easter.

Mary Around the World

Many countries celebrate Mary in different ways.

■ In Mexico, Latin America, and the United States, the people honor **Our Lady of Guadalupe**. She appeared to Juan Diego on his way to Mass. A church was built on that site. Pope John Paul II named Our Lady of Guadalupe the Patroness of the Americas.

296

■ In France, people honor **Our Lady of Lourdes**. Mary appeared to a young peasant girl, Bernadette. A spring of water flows at that spot. To this day it has healing power. People from all over visit the site.

■ In Poland, the people honor the image of **Our Lady of Czestochowa**. Pope John Paul II has a special devotion to this image of Mary, who is named queen of Poland. He visited her shrine just after becoming pope in 1979.

297

OPTIONAL ACTIVITY

Read the Story   Provide children with more information about Juan Diego and Our Lady of Guadalupe by reading them a classic version of this story of faith.

- Read the book *Lady of Guadalupe* by Tomie de Paolo (Holiday House, Inc., 1980).

OPTIONAL ACTIVITY

The Holy Family   Remind children that the Holy Family is made up of Joseph, Mary, and Jesus.

- Jesus honored and obeyed his earthly parents.

- Jesus' love for his human parents teaches us how we should treat those in our families who care for us.

- Invite children to suggest ways in which their families care for them as Mary and Joseph cared for Jesus.

Morality

God knows it is sometimes difficult to make good choices. He gave his people the Ten Commandments to help guide them. He wants you to make good choices, too.

THE TEN COMMANDMENTS

1. I am the Lord your God. You shall not have strange Gods before me.

2. You shall not take the name of the Lord your God in vain.

3. Remember to keep holy the Lord's day.

4. Honor your father and your mother.

5. You shall not kill.

6. You shall not commit adultery.

7. You shall not steal.

8. You shall not bear false witness against your neighbor.

9. You shall not covet your neighbor's wife.

10. You shall not covet your neighbor's goods.

© Harcourt Religion

Jesus' Command to Love

Jesus taught that the Great Commandment and the law of love sum up the Ten Commandments.

298

The Great Commandment

"You shall love the Lord your God with all your heart, with all your soul, with all your strength, and with all your mind, and your neighbor as yourself."

Luke 10:27

Law of Love

"This is my commandment: Love one another as I have loved you."

John 15:12

Faith Fact

Saint Thérèse of the Little Flower of Jesus said, "I will spend my heaven doing good on earth. I will let fall a shower of roses." That is why she is often pictured with a crucifix covered with roses.

299

Moses   Provide children with a deeper understanding of the giving of the Ten Commandments by reading to them the story of Moses.

- *The Story of the Ten Commandments* by Patricia A. Pingry (Ideals Publications, 1999), and *Moses: The Deliverance of Israel and God's Commands* (Master Books, 2001) are two examples of the wonderful books available for children of this age.

- Read the story of Moses to children. Invite their reviews.

Memorize the Law of Love   Challenge children to memorize *John 15:12*.

- Provide each child with the scripture verse written on an index card.

- Tape the cards to their desk and have them read the verse often until they have memorized it.

Sign of the Cross

In the name of the Father, and of the Son, and of the Holy Spirit. Amen.

The Lord's Prayer

Faith Fact

Some people make the sign of the cross from right to left instead of left to right. That is because they are Eastern-rite Catholics.

Our Father,
who art in heaven,
hallowed be thy name;
thy kingdom come,
thy will be done on earth
as it is in heaven.
Give us this day our daily bread;
and forgive us our trespasses
as we forgive those who trespass
  against us;
and lead us not into temptation,
but deliver us from evil. Amen.

Hail Mary

Hail, Mary, full of grace.
The Lord is with you!
Blessed are you among women,
and blessed is the fruit of your womb,
  Jesus.

Holy Mary, Mother of God, pray for us sinners,
now and at the hour of our death.
Amen.

Glory to the Father

Glory to the Father, and to the Son,
  and to the Holy Spirit:
as it was in the beginning, is now,
  and will be for ever. Amen.

Grace Before Meals

Bless us, O Lord, and these your gifts
which we are about to receive from
  your goodness,
through Christ our Lord. Amen.

Grace After Meals

We give you thanks for all your gifts,
  almighty God,
Living and reigning now and for ever.
Amen.

© Harcourt Religion

© Harcourt Religion

300

301

The Sign of the Cross   Tracing the cross on one's own body or the forehead of another has been a common Christian gesture since the early centuries of the Church.

- Take time during prayer to have children practice this ancient custom.
- Show them how to trace the cross on another person's forehead. Then allow them to do the same.
- Encourage children to "sign" their family members with the sign of Jesus.

Glory to the Father   This ancient prayer is known as a *doxology*, or "words of praise." It is part of the Rosary and is traditionally used to conclude the praying or chanting of a psalm in the Liturgy of the Hours.

- Teach children this ancient prayer.
- Use the phrase "as it was in the beginning, is now, and will be forever" to remind children that God is eternal.

WORDS OF FAITH

A

Advent The season of four weeks before Christmas. During Advent the Church prepares to celebrate the birth of Jesus. (10)

B

Baptism The sacrament that brings you the new life in God and makes you a member of the Church. (227)

Bible God's word written down by humans. (27)

C

caretaker A person who treats everything with care and respect. (49)

Christians People who are baptized and who follow Jesus. (227)

Church The community of all baptized people who believe in God and follow Jesus. (137)

commandment A law that God made for people to obey. (111)

consequence The result of a choice. (183)

creation A word for everything God made. All that God made is good. (47)

Creator A name for God. It means that God made everything. (27)

E

Easter The Church's celebration of the Resurrection of Jesus from the dead. (20)

Eucharist The sacrament in which Jesus shares himself and the bread and wine become his Body and Blood. (245)

F

faith The gift of believing in God and all that he has told about himself. (100)

family A group of people related by birth or adoption. (72)

follower A follower of Jesus is someone who believes in Jesus and lives by his teachings. (173)

© Harcourt Religion

302

303

forgive To agree to put aside what someone has done and not hold it against him or her. *(193)*

free will God created you to be free. You can choose to obey God or disobey God. *(182)*

God the Father God the Father is the first Person of the Holy Trinity. *(64)*

godparents Two people chosen by your parents to help you to follow Jesus. They are usually present at your Baptism. *(229)*

grace Sharing in God's life and love. *(227)*

304

Great Commandment Jesus' law that tells you to love God above all else and to love others the way you love yourself. *(111)*

guide Someone who leads us and teaches us. The Holy Spirit guides Jesus' followers. *(143)*

heaven Living and being happy with God forever. *(253)*

holy To be filled with the Holy Spirit and to serve God with all your heart. *(155)*

Holy Communion Jesus received in the Sacrament of the Eucharist, the holy Bread and Wine. *(243)*

© Harcourt Religion

© Harcourt Religion

Holy Family The name for the human family of Jesus, Mary, and Joseph. *(75)*

Holy Spirit The third Person of the Holy Trinity. *(145)*

Holy Trinity God the Father, God the Son, and God the Holy Spirit are the Holy Trinity, the three Persons in one God. *(65)*

Jesus The name of the Son of God. Jesus is also human. *(65)*

Joseph The name of the foster father of Jesus. *(74)*

justice Giving God and other people what is due them. Justice is a sign of the kingdom of God. *(262)*

kingdom of God The world of love, peace, and justice that God wants. *(137)*

Last Supper The special meal Jesus shared with his friends the night before he died. At the Last Supper Jesus gave himself in the holy Bread and Wine. *(244)*

305

Lent The season of forty days during which the Church gets ready for Easter. (16)

Lord's Prayer The prayer Jesus taught. It is also called the Our Father. (121)

Mary The mother of Jesus, the Mother of God. She is also our mother and the Mother of the Church. (8)

Mass The Church's great celebration of praise and thanks. (243)

New Testament The second part of the Bible. It tells about Jesus and his followers. (85)

Old Testament The first part of the Bible. It tells about the times before Jesus was born. (85)

parable A story Jesus told that teaches something about God. (85)

peace When people settle problems with kindness. Peace is a sign of the kingdom of God. (262)

praise Giving God honor and thanks because he is good. (37)

prayer Listening to and talking with God. (119)

Resurrection The name for Jesus being raised from the dead to new life. (209)

sacraments Signs of God's love given by Jesus to bring you closer to God. (219)

saints People who lived a good life and loved God. (155)

Savior God the Father sent Jesus to save people and bring them back to God. (207)

serve To help give others in a loving way what they need. (171)

sin To choose to disobey God and do wrong. (191)

Son of God A name for Jesus. The Son of God is the second Person of the Holy Trinity. (65)

Ten Commandments The Ten Commandments are God's laws. They tell how to love God and others. (181)

306

307

Boldfaced numbers refer to pages on which the terms are defined.

A

Adam, 26, 48, 206
Advent, 10-11, 294, **302**
Albert the Great, Saint, 54
almsgiver, 116
altar, **286**
Angela Merici, Saint, 250
angels, 208, 255
Anointing of the Sick, 219, 220, 285
Apostles, 64
Ash Wednesday, 16

B

Bakhita, Saint Josephine, 214
Baptism, 219, 220, 226, **227**, 279, 284, **302**
Benedict, Saint, 156
Betancur, Saint Pedro de San Jose, 152
Bethlehem, 10, 12
Bible, 26, **27**, 90, 120, 154, 242, 264, 276-277, 291, **302**
   parts of, 85, 86, 276
Blessed Virgin Mary (BVM), 296
blessing, 232, 292, 293
Blood of Christ, 243, 292
Body of Christ, 243, 286, 292
Boy Jesus, The, 75

C

Cabrini, Saint Frances, 188
Calungsod, Blessed Pedro, 270
candles, in church, 228, 289
caretaker, **49**, 54, **302**
   caring for God's gifts, 45-50, 55-57
Casey, Venerable Father Solanus, 178
Catholic Source Book, 276-301
choices, making, 179-183, 190, 193, 194, 206
Christ. See Jesus Christ
Christian, **227**, 279, **302**
Christian Living, 264
Christmas, 12-13, 294
Church, **137**, 142, 279, **302**
   Holy Spirit as guide of, 146
   members of, 235-237
   seasons of, 6-7, 294-295
church, liturgical, 294-295
Come Join Me, 136
commandments, **303**
   Great, **111**, 112, 116, 298-299, **304**
   Ten, **181**, 182, 184, 188, 298, **307**
Communion, 243, 244-246, 292, **304**
community members, 235-237
Confirmation, 219, 220, 221, 284
consequence, 183, **303**
creation, **47**, **303**
   of world, 25-27, 29, 30, 34, 36, 37, 44, 46, 47, 54, 64
Creator, 25-27, 29, 30, 34, 36, 37, 44, 278, **303**
creed, 278-283
crucifix, 288

D

death
   of Jesus, 20, 208, 209, 214, 252
   life with God after, 251-256, 260
   prayer for the dead, 258
Diego, Saint Juan, 296
Dominic, Saint, 162

E

Easter, 20-21, 209, 289, 295, **303**
Elizabeth (Mary's cousin), 80
Elizabeth Ann Seton, Saint, 157
Emily de Vialar, Saint, 260
Eucharist, 219, 220, **245**, 284, **303**
   Sacrament of, during Mass, 244-245, 250
Eve, 26, 48, 206

F

Faber, Frederick William, 126
faith, **100**-101, 106, 109, **303**
family, 71-76, **303**
   of Jesus (Holy Family), 74-75, 76, 80, 282, **305**
   love of, 71-73, 111, 216-217
   prayer of, 120
   of saints, 155
Father, God as, 64, 65, 119, **304**
First Humans, The, 26
   followers of Jesus, 172-**173**, 227, 253, 255, 260, 283, **303**
forgive, 16, **189**-193, 198, 277, 304
Frances Cabrini, Saint, 188
Francis, Saint, 14
free will, 182, **304**
friends
   God as, 28, 64, 118, 190, 206
   of God, 154, 158, 162

G

Gabriel, angel, 280
gifts, 91-93
   from God, 30, 35-40, 44, 45-50, 54, 55-57, 181
   of life, 91
   of love, 108-109
Glory to the Father, 301
God
   as Creator, 25-27, 29, 30, 34, 36, 37, 44, 278, **303**
   as Father, 64, 65, 119, **304**
   as friend, 28, 64, 118, 190, 206
   friends of, 154, 158, 162
   gifts from, 30, 35-40, 44, 45-50, 54, 55-57, 181
   kingdom of, 136-137, 142, 261-266, 270, 283, 305
   life with, 251-256, 260
   listening to and talking with, 117-122
   love for, 111, 112, 116, 181, 184
   love of, 26, 28, 44, 64, 66, 74, 75, 83, 90, 98, 99, 100, 102, 206, 216-220, 224, 230, 234, 277, 278
   obeying, 182-183, 190
   praising, 32, 36, 37, 42, 68, 248, **307**
   promise of, 134-135

as Son, 64, 65, 66, 70, 74, 80, 208, 214, 278, 307
   thanking, 49, 52, 119, 124, 245
   Word of, 78, 114
God the Father (Scripture story), 64
godparents, **229**, **304**
Good Friday, 18, 295
good news, 210, 279
Good Shepherd, 84-85
Gospels, 276-277, 291
grace, 226, **227**, 301, **304**
Great Commandment, **111**, 112, 116, 298-299, **304**
guide, 143-146, **304**

H

Hail Mary, 300-301
happiness, 253-255, 260, 262, 264
Have Faith, 101
healing, 97-102, 104, 106
heaven, **253**-256, 260, **304**
helping others, 62-63, 169-174, 178
holy, **155**, **304**
Holy Communion, 243, 244-246, 292, 304
Holy Family, 74-75, 76, 80, 282, **305**
Holy Orders, 219, 220, 285
Holy people, 153-158, 162, 281
Holy Saturday, 18, 295
Holy Spirit, 22-23, 66, 70, 120, **145**, 146-148, 152, 158, **305**
   Baptism and, 226, 227
   Christian Living and, 264
   God's love and, 217, 278, 279
   as guide, 143-146, 304
   help from, 148, 194
Holy Thursday, 18, 295
Holy Trinity. See Trinity
holy water, 228, 288
homily, 291
hope, 109
How to Pray, 120
human rights and responsibilities, 127-128
hymns, 126

I

"I'm sorry," saying, 189-194, 198
Initiation, Sacraments of, 219, 284

J

Jesus Christ, **65**, **305**
   birth of, 10-13
   Body and Blood of, 243, 286, 292
   death of, 20, 208, 209, 214, 252
   followers of, 172-173, 227, 253, 255, 260, 283, 305
   as Good Shepherd, 84-85
   Great Commandment of, 111, 112, 116, 298-299, 304
   as healer, 100-102
   at Last Supper, 244-245, 305
   light of, 12-13
   love of, 265
   message of, 137
   parables of, 82-85, 90, 277, 306
   presence during Mass, 291
   promises of, 146, 218, 224, 252

Resurrection of, 20-21, 208, 209, 295, 307
   presence of Jesus during, 291
   reading of Bible during, 242, 291
   ringing of bells during, 287
   Sacrament of the Eucharist during, 244-245, 250
Matrimony, Sacrament of, 219, 220, 285
Merici, Saint Angela, 248
Michelangelo, 34
mission, 279
morality, 298-299
Moses, and Ten Commandments, 181, 182
Moses the Black, Saint, 234

N

Nazareth, 74, 75
need, 271
neighbors, 199-200
New Testament, 85, 86, 276, 277, 291, **306**
Nicholas, Saint, 44
Noah Says "Yes," 134-135

O

obedience, to God, 182-183, 190
Old Testament, **85**, 86, 134, 276, 291, **306**
Orders, Holy, 219, 220, 285
Ordinary Time, 8-9, 14-15, 295
Our Lady of Czestochowa, 297
Our Lady of Guadalupe, 281, 296
Our Lady of Lourdes, 297

P

parable, 84-**85**, 90, 277, **306**
Paschal candle, 289
Patrick, Saint, 70
peace, 262, 264, 265, 266, 270, 271, 292, **307**
Pedro Calungsod, Blessed, 270
Pedro de San Jose Betancur, Saint, 152
Pentecost, 22-23, 279
people of God, 153-158, 162
Philip, Saint, 156
praise, 32, 36, **37**, 42, 68, 117, 215, 248, **307**
prayer, 117-118, **119**-122, 126, 300-301, **307**
Prodigal Son, 277

R

Reconciliation, Sacrament of, 219, 220, 285
respect, for workers, 163-164
Resurrection, 20-21, 208, **209**, 214, 295, **307**
rights, human, 127-128
rosary, 281

S

Sacraments, 218-**219**, 220, 224, **307**
   of Healing, 219, 220, 285
   of Initiation, 219, 220, 284
   of Vocation and Service, 219, 220, 285

parts of, 290-293

Jesus Lives, 208
Jesus Promises the Holy Spirit, 146
Jesus Serves, 170
Jesus' Promise, 218
John the Baptist, 80
John Paul II, Pope, 296, 297
John XXIII, Pope, 90
Joseph (foster father of Jesus), 74, 75, 80, 282, **305**
Josephine (Giuseppina) Bakhita, Saint, 214
justice, 262-266, 270, 305

K

Kateri, Blessed, 157
kingdom of God, 136-**137**, 142, 261-266, 270, 283, **305**

L

Last Supper, 244-245, **305**
law of love, 299
Lent, 16-17, 295, **306**
Leo, Pope, 188
liturgical seasons and colors, 6-7, 294-295
Liturgy, 284-297
Lord's Prayer, **121**, 122, 126, 300, **306**
Lost Sheep, The, 82
Louise de Marillac, Saint, 106
love, 109, 264, 265, 266, 270, 271
   of family, 71-73, 111, 216-217
   gifts of, 108-109
   for God, 111, 112, 116, 181, 184
   of God, 26, 28, 44, 64, 66, 74, 75, 83, 90, 98, 99, 100, 102, 206, 216-220, 224, 230, 234, 277, 278
   Jesus' teachings about, 110-111, 170-174, 178
   law of, 299
   of saints, 156-157
   serving others and, 170-174, 178
   signs of, 216-220, 230, 234
Loving Others, 110

M

Marillac, Saint Louise de, 106
Martin, Saint, 156
Mary, Mother of God, 8-9, 74, 80, 280-281, 282, **306**
   celebrations for, 296-297
   prayer to, 300-301
   as saint, 156, 224
   saying "yes" to God, 138
Mass, 241-**243**, 244-246, 250, **306**
   Liturgy of the Eucharist during, 292
   Liturgy of the Word during, 291

saints, 154-**155**, 156-158, 162, **307**
   family of, 155
   feast days of, 14, 44, 54, 70, 106, 116, 152, 162, 188, 198, 214, 234, 250, 260
   kinds of, 156-157
   prayer of, 160
Savior, 10, 205-**207**, 208-209, 214, 278, **307**
Scripture, 276-277. See also Bible
seasons, liturgical, 6-7, 294-295
serve, 170-**171**, 172-174, 178, **307**
Seton, Saint Elizabeth Ann, 157
sharing, 263
sick, healing of, 97-102, 104, 106, 219, 220, 285
Sign of the Cross, 5, 300
sin, 190-**191**, 193, 206, 208, **307**
Sistine Chapel, 34
Son of God, 64, 65, 66, 70, 74, 80, 208, 214, 278, **307**. See also Jesus Christ
sorrow, showing, 191
"sorry," saying, 189-194, 198
star of Bethlehem, 12
stories, of Jesus, 81-86, 90, 277

T

tabernacle, 286
Ten Commandments, **181**, 182, 184, 188, 298, **307**
Teresa of Calcutta, Mother, 98-99, 100
Teresa of Jesus of the Andes, Saint, 198
thanking
   God, 49, 52, 119, 124, 245
thanksgiving, 245
Theresa of the Child Jesus, Mother, 142
Thérèse of the Little Flower, Saint, 299
Thomas of Villanova, Saint, 116
Together Always, 252
Triduum, 18-19, 295
Trinity, Holy, 65-66, 70, 254, 278, **305**
Two Men Who Prayed, 191

V

vestments, 287, 294-295
Vialar, Saint Emily de, 260
Villanova, Saint Thomas of, 116

W

What God Made, 37
workers, respect for, 163-164
world
   caring for, 45-50, 54, 55-56
   creation of, 25-27, 29, 30, 34, 36, 37, 44, 46, 47, 54

Y

"yes," saying to God, 8, 133-138, 140, 142, 280

Z

Zechariah, 80

© Harcourt Religion

308

309

308 and 309 Catholic Source Index

Illustration Credits

Martha Aviles 62-63, 216; Paige Billin-Frye 84-85; Simone Boni 12-13, 264-265; Hector Borlasca 144-145; Nan Brooks 42-43; Dan Brown 252-253; Nancy Cassidy 181; Olivia Cole 79, 137, 159, 207; Jane Conteh-Morgan 26-27; Carolyn Croll 28-29, 146-147, 182-183; Roman Dunets 82-83, 190-191; Allen Eitzen 134-135; Patrick Girouard 110-111; Nick Harris 20-21; Pamela Johnson 136-137; Barbara Kiwak 208-209; Dennis Lyall 22-23; Patrick Merrell 72-73; Kathyrn Mitter 170-171; Moria Maclean 74-75; David Opie 39-40; Frank Ordaz 280; Pat Paris 218-219; Mick Reid 64-65, 76, 120-121; Bill SMITH STUDIO 16-17, 66, 165, 257, 280; Joel Spector 228-229; Arvis Stewart 206-207; Matt Straub 30, 31, 34, 40, 41, 53, 57, 59, 67, 67, 67, 70, 77, 79, 86, 87, 93, 93, 99, 103, 106, 109, 111, 113, 116, 119, 123, 125, 126, 128, 135, 138, 139, 148, 149, 174, 175, 184, 186, 198, 201, 203, 211, 219, 224, 229, 231, 237, 247, 249, 265, 266, 267, 271, 283; Susan Swan 100-101, 280; Peggy Tagel 37-38, 303; Lois Woolley 34, 44, 54, 70, 80, 90, 106, 116, 126, 142, 152, 162, 178, 188, 198, 214, 224, 234, 250, 260, 270; The Curator Collection, Ltd. 8-9.

Photo Credits

iii (t), Mel Yates/Getty Images; iii (tc), Polak Matthew/Corbis Sygma; iii (bc), Banana-Stock/BananaStock, Ltd./PictureQuest; iii (b), Peter Griffith/Masterfile; 1 (l), Com-stock Images; 1 (r), Rubberball Productions; 2, Digital Vision; 6, Randy Miller/Masterfile; 7, Father Gene Plaisted, OSC; 10, Ted Spiegel/Corbis; 14, Réunion des Musées Nationaux/Art Resource; 16, 18, Father Gene Plaisted, OSC; 24 (t), Digital Vision/Getty Images; 24 (c), Ian Mckinnell/ Getty Images; 24 (b), Michael Pole/Corbis; 25, Digital Vision/Getty Images; 27, Tom Stewart/Corbis; 32, Wayne Eardley/Master-file; 35, Ian Mckinnell/Getty Images; 37 (tl), Bluestone Productions/Getty Images; 37 (brc), Father Gene Plaisted, OSC; 37 (blc), Kaz Chiba/Getty Images; 37 (bl), Mel Yates/Getty Images; 37 (br), Tim Davis/Corbis; 40 (br), BananaStock/Banana-Stock, Ltd./PictureQuest; 40 (tr), Dennis Gottlieb/Foodpix; 40 (bl), Jan Oswald/Food-pix; 40 (tl), Photos.com; 42, David Mendel-sohn/Masterfile; 44, Tom & Dee Ann McCarthy/Corbis; 45, Michael Pole/Corbis; 48, Doug Menuez/Getty Images; 49 (t), Kevin Dodge/Masterfile; 49 (rbc), Kevin Laubacher/Getty Images; 49 (br), Michael Newman/Photo Edit; 49 (rtc), Tony Free-man/Photo Edit; 50 (tl), David Young-Wolff/Photo Edit; 50 (br), SW Productions/ Getty Images; 51 (tl), Bill Bachmann/Photo Edit; 51 (bl), Catherine Ledner/Getty Images; 51 (br), Image Source/Picture-Quest; 51 (tr), Jim Cummins/Corbis; 52, Michael Newman/Photo Edit; 54, Henryk T. Kaiser/Index Stock; 55 (lc), Myrleen Ferguson Cate/Photo Edit; 55 (b), Stuart Pearce/AgeFotostock; 55 (tl), Tom Stewart/ Corbis; 55 (tl), Tom Stewart/Corbis; 56, David Young-Wolff/Photo Edit; 60 (c), Digital Vision/Getty Images; 60 (b), Joel Sartore/Getty; 60 (r), SuperStock; 61, SuperStock; 65, Father Gene Plaisted, OSC; 66, Hutchings Photography; 68, Hutchings Photography; 71, Digital Vision/Getty Images; 75, Stockbyte/SuperStock; 78, IT Int'l/ eStock Photo/ PictureQuest; 80, CLEO Photography/Photo Edit; 81, Joel Sartore/Getty; 83, Randy Lincks/Masterfile; 85, Myrleen Ferguson Cate/Photo Edit; 90, Charles Gupton/Corbis; 91, Ariel Skelley/Corbis; 92, Owen Franken/Corbis; 93 (t), Digital Vision/Fotosearch; 93 (b), Omni Photo Communications Inc./Index Stock; 96 (t), Britt Erlanson/Getty Images; 96 (b),

Erlanson Productions/Getty Images; 96 (c), Stephen Simpson/Getty Images; 97, Britt Erlanson/Getty Images; 98, Polak Matthew/Corbis Sygma; 99, CORBIS SYGMA; 102 (t), Myrleen Ferguson Cate/ Photo Edit; 102 (b), SW Production/Index Stock; 104, Father Gene Plaisted, OSC; 107, Stephen Simpson/Getty Images; 108, Hutchings Photography; 109, Jerome Tisne/Getty Images; 112 (l), Bill Wittman; 112 (r), Mary Kate Denny/Photo Edit; 114, Ariel Skelley/Corbis; 117, Erlanson Productions/Getty Images; 118, Ariel Skelley/Corbis; 119, Gregory Kramer/Getty Images; 122, Jeff Greenberg/Photo Edit; 124, Ron Chapple/Getty Images; 127 (b), Cindy Charles/Photo Edit; 127 (t), Eye Wire; 128 (l), Myrleen Ferguson Cate/Photo Edit; 128 (bg), Photodisc; 129, Jose Luis Pelaez, Inc./ Corbis; 132 (b), Lori Adamski Peek/Getty Images; 132 (t), LWA-Sharie Kennedy/ Corbis; 132 (c), Richard Hutchings/Photo Edit; 133, LWA-Sharie Kennedy/Corbis; 137, Zephyr Picture/Index Stock; 140, PIXAL/Age-Fotostock; 142, David Young-Wolff/Photo Edit; 143, Richard Hutchings/Photo Edit; 145, Bill Wittman; 147 (bg), Jose Luis Pelaez, Inc./Corbis; 147(c), Hutchings Photography; 148, RubberBall Productions/RubberBall Productions/ Picture-Quest; 150, Rommel/Masterfile; 152, Tony Hopewell/ Getty Images; 153, Lori Adamski Peek/ Getty Images; 154, Kevin Dodge/Masterfile; 155, Doug Mazell/Index Stock Imagery/PictureQuest; 156 (tl), Andrea Jemolo/Corbis; 156 (bl), Father Gene Plaisted, OSC; 156 (tr), 156 (br), Seraphic Icons; 157 (r), Father John Giuliani; 157 (l), Seraphic Icons; 158 (lc), Burke/Triolo Productions/Getty Images; 158 (b), Myrleen Ferguson Cate/Photo Edit; 160, Arte & Immagini/Corbis; 162, LWA-Dann Tardif/Corbis; 163 (b), Bill Miles/Corbis; 163 (t), Rubberball Productions; 164 (blc), 164 (brc), Digital Vision; 164 (l), Mary Stein-bacher/Photo Edit; 164 (r), Photodisc; 165, Photodisc; 168, Corbis Images/PictureQuest; 168 (c), Corbis Images/Picture-Quest; 168 (b), Digital Vision/Getty Images; 168 (t), Digital Vision/PictureQuest; 169, DigitalVision/PictureQuest; 171, Jonathan Nourok/Photo Edit; 172 (bl), 172 (br), BananaStock/BananaStock, Ltd./Picture-Quest; 172 (tr), Myrleen Ferguson Cate/ Photo Edit; 173, Tom & Dee Ann McCarthy/ Corbis; 176, Myrleen Ferguson Cate/Index Stock; 178, Brad Wrobleski/Masterfile; 179, Corbis Images/PictureQuest; 180, Banana-Stock/BananaStock, Ltd./PictureQuest; 185 (b), Buccina Studios/Getty Images; 185 (tl), Myrleen Ferguson Cate/Photo Edit; 185 (tr), Royalty-free/Corbis; 186, BananaStock/ BananaStock, Ltd./PictureQuest; 189, Digital Vision/Getty Images; 192, Antony Nagelmann/Getty Images; 193, Tony Free-man/Photo Edit; 194 (tl), CLEO Photo-graphy/Photo Edit; 194 (bl), Laura Dwight/ Photo Edit; 194 (br), Myrleen Ferguson Cate/Photo Edit; 194 (tr), Ryan McVay/ Getty Images; 196, Ronnie Kaufman/ Corbis; 199 (b), Paul Barton/Corbis; 199 (lc), Robert Frerck/Getty Images; 200, Myrleen Ferguson Cate/Photo Edit; 201, Photospin; 204 (b), Reed Kaestner/Corbis; 204 (t), Stewart Cohen/Getty Images; 204 (c), Walter Schmid/ Getty Images; 205, Stewart Cohen/Getty Images; 210, Myrleen Ferguson Cate/Photo Edit; 212 (b), Bill Wittman; 212 (t), Photos.com; 214, Robert Frerck/Getty Images; 215, Walter Schmid/Getty Images; 217, Bill Wittman; 222, Myrleen Ferguson Cate/Photo Edit; 225, Reed Kaestner/Corbis; 226, Michael Newman/Photo Edit;

228, Bill Wittman; 230, Myrleen Ferguson Cate/Photo Edit; 232, Ariel Skelley/Corbis; 234, Myrleen Ferguson Cate/Photo Edit; 235 (t), David Young-Wolff/Photo Edit; 235 (b), Royalty-Free/Corbis; 236, Warren Morgan/Corbis; 240 (c), IFA/ eStock Photo/ PictureQuest; 240 (b), Rolf Bruderer/ Masterfile; 240 (t), Tim Pannell/Corbis; 241, Tim Pannell/Corbis; 242 (r), Bill Wittman; 242 (l), Father Gene Plaisted, OSC; 243 (r), Bill Wittman; 243 (l), Michael Newman/Photo Edit; 245, Bill Wittman; 246 (t), Myrleen Ferguson Cate/Photo Edit; 246 (b), Tony Freeman/Photo Edit; 248, Father Gene Plaisted, OSC; 250, Bill Wittman; 251, IFA/ eStock Photo/ PictureQuest; 253 (b), Dam Lim/Masterfile; 253 (t), Luc Beziat/Getty Images; 254, OVASTOCK/Photo Edit; 255, Mike Hamel/Masterfile; 256, Arthur Tilley/Getty Images; 258, Terry Vine/Getty Images; 260, Lars Klove Photo Service/Getty Images; 261, Rolf Bruderer/Masterfile; 262, Jim Craigmyle/Masterfile; 263, Peter Griffith/ Masterfile; 268, Jack Hollingsworth/Getty Images; 270, Michael Newman/Photo Edit; 271, Myrleen Ferguson Cate/Photo Edit; 272, Peter Byron/Photo Edit; 273 (l), Mark Richards/Photo Edit; 273, Myrleen Ferguson Cate/Photo Edit; 276, Hutchings Photography; 278, Réunion des Musées Nationaux/Art Resource, NY; 279, Michael Newman/Photo Edit; 281, Steve Cole/Getty Images; 282, Photos.com; 286, Richard Cummins/Corbis; 287, Father Gene Plaisted, OSC; 288 (b), Bill Wittman; 288 (t), PhotoSpin; 289, 290, 291, 292, Father Gene Plaisted, OSC; 293, Spencer Grant/Photo Edit; 294, Father Gene Plaisted, OSC; 295, Photos.com; 297, Archives Charmet/ Bridgeman Art Library; 299, PhotoDisc; 300, Thinkstock/Getty Images; 302 (r), Comstock; 302 (l), Hutchings Photography; 303, zefa/Masterfile; 304, Bill Wittman; 305, Dave Bartruff/Corbis; 306, Steve Skjold/Photo-Edit; 307, Rubberball Productions/Getty Images

Acknowledgments

For permission to reprint copyrighted material, grateful acknowledgment is made to the following sources:

The Copyright Company, Nashville, TN: Lyrics from "Alleluia No. 1" by Don Fishel. Lyrics © 1973 by Word of God Music. International Copyright secured.

Hope Publishing Co., Carol Stream, IL 60188: Lyrics from "Spirit-Friend" by Tom Colvin. Lyrics © 1969 by Hope Publishing Co. Lyrics from "Shout for Joy" by David Mowbray. Lyrics © 1982 by Jubilate Hymns, Ltd. Lyrics from "When Jesus the Healer" by Peter D. Smith. Lyrics © 1978 by Stainer & Bell Ltd.

International Commission on English in the Liturgy: From the English translation of "You Have Put on Christ" in *Rite of Baptism for Children.* Translation © 1969 by International Committee on English in the Liturgy, Inc. From the English translation of the Psalm Responses for "Psalm 25: Teach Me Your Ways," "Psalm 89: For Ever I Will Sing," "Psalm 98: Sing to the Lord a New Song," "Psalm 113: Blessed Be the Name," and "Psalm 119: Happy Are They" in *Lectionary for Mass.* Translation © 1969, 1981, 1997 by International Committee on English in the Liturgy, Inc. (ICEL).

Scott Treimel New York: "A Moment in Summer" from *River Winding* by Charlotte Zolotow. Text copyright © 1970 by Charlotte Zolotow.

Teacher's Notes

_____

_____

_____

_____

_____

_____

_____

_____

_____

_____

_____

_____

_____

_____

_____

_____

_____

_____

_____

Teacher's Notes

_____

_____

_____

_____

_____

_____

_____

_____

_____

_____

_____

_____

_____

_____

_____

_____

Teacher's Notes

_____
_____
_____
_____
_____
_____
_____
_____
_____
_____
_____
_____
_____
_____
_____
_____
_____
_____

Activity Master Answer Key

Activity Master 2

CAT

RABBIT

OCTOPUS

FEATHER

CRAB

COW

DUCK

BIRD

CARROT

LOAF OF BREAD

APPLE

TURTLE

SNAKE

FROG

FLOWER

Activity Master 8

1. SAY "I'M SORRY."

2. PICK UP YOUR TOYS.

4. PRAY.

6. HELP AT HOME.

7. GO TO MASS.

8. HELP A CLASSMATE WHO IS SAD.

Activity Master 10

Activity Master 17

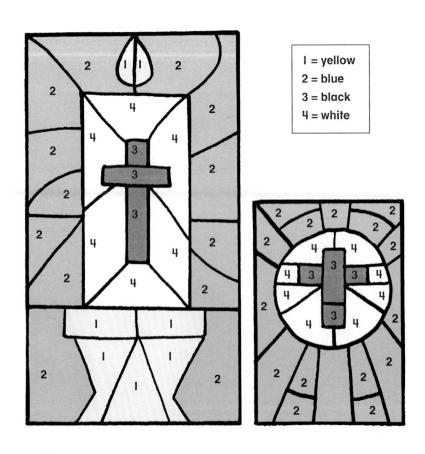

I = yellow
2 = blue
3 = black
4 = white

3

5

2

1

4

1. HELP
2. SHARE
3. PRAY
4. KIND
5. FORGIVE

Name _____ Date _____

(A) **Work with Words**   Write the word from the Word Bank that completes the sentence.

WORD BANK

loves

Creator

good

1. God is the ____Creator____ who made everything.

2. Everything God made is ____good____.

3. God knows and ____loves____ everyone.

(B) **Check Understanding**   Circle the best answer.

4. Everything around you is a _____ from God.

   person   (gift)

5. The story of creation is in the _____.

   (Bible)   box

6. God is our loving _____.

   Angel   (Father)

Name _____ Date _____

(C) **Make Connections**   Draw a line to the best title for each picture.

7. Bible

8. praise

9. Adam and Eve

10. creation

the first humans

God's word

everything God made

give honor and thanks to God

Notes _____

_____

_____

_____

_____

_____

_____

_____

_____

_____

_____

_____

_____

_____

A4   Answer Key for Unit 1 Tests

Name _____ **Date** _____

(A) Work with Words Write the word from the Word Bank that best completes the sentence.

WORD BANK

Great

Our Father

law

1. The _____Great Commandment_____ Commandment tells you to love God and other people.

2. The Lord's Prayer is also called the _____Our Father_____.

3. A commandment is a _____law_____ that God made.

(B) Check Understanding Draw a line from each picture to the best title.

4. talking and listening to God

Jesus

5. the one who taught the Lord's Prayer

prayer

6. Jesus' healing actions

God's power and love

Name _____ **Date** _____

(C) Make Connections Trace the words to answer the questions.

7. What is one way to show love for others?

share

8. How should you love God?

with all your heart

9. How should you love others?

as you love yourself

10. What is the gift of believing in God?

faith

Notes _____

_____

_____

_____

_____

_____

_____

_____

_____

_____

_____

_____

_____

_____

_____

_____

_____

Answer Key for Unit 2 Tests A5

Name _____ Date _____

A **Work with Words** Write the word from the Word Bank that completes the sentence.

WORD BANK		
Holy Family	love	Bible
New	Jesus	

1. Jesus, Mary, and Joseph are called the

_____
- - - - - - - - - - - - - - - - - - - -
      Holy Family
_____ .

2. The _____ New _____ Testament tells stories about Jesus.

3. Jesus' stories tell about God's _____ love _____ .

4. In the parable in this chapter, _____ Jesus _____ is the Good Shepherd.

5. Stories about God's love are in the _____ Bible _____ .

Name _____ Date _____

B **Check Understanding** Circle the best answer.

6. The Bible is the Church's holy _____.

building   (**book**)

7. The Old Testament is the _____ part of the Bible.

(**first**)   **second**

Draw a line to the best ending for the sentence.

8. Jesus used parables ——————— a parable.

9. Jesus is the Good ——————— cares for all
   Shepherd. He   God's people.

10. The Good Shepherd story is ——————— to teach people
                                         about God.

Notes _____

_____

_____

_____

_____

_____

_____

_____

_____

_____

_____

_____

_____

_____

A6   Answer Key for Unit 3 Tests

Name _____ Date _____

Ⓐ Work with Words Write the word from the Word Bank that best completes the sentence.

WORD BANK

peace

Holy Spirit

Church

_____

1. The _____Church_____ is made up of people who follow Jesus.

_____

2. The kingdom of God is the world of love, _____peace_____, and justice.

_____

3. The _____Holy Spirit_____ is your guide and helper to follow God.

Ⓑ Check Understanding Draw a line to the best ending for the sentence.

4. When you were baptized,   loved God.

5. Saints lived good lives and   you became a member of the Church.

6. The sign of God's promise to Noah was   Jesus.

7. The people of the Church believe in God and follow   a rainbow.

Name _____ Date _____

Circle the best answer.

8. Jesus told the story of the rich man's _____.

(party)   bed

9. Those who are holy love God with all their _____.

(hearts)   hands

10. The Son of God is _____.

Noah   (Jesus)

Notes _____

_____

_____

_____

_____

_____

_____

_____

_____

_____

_____

_____

_____

_____

_____

_____

Answer Key for Unit 4 Tests   A7

Name _____ Date _____

(A) Work with Words Write the word from the Word Bank that best completes the sentence.

WORD BANK
good
God
forgives
choice
serve

1. Jesus shows you how to _____serve_____ others.

2. The Ten Commandments help you make _____good_____ choices.

3. Every _____choice_____ has a consequence.

4. God _____forgives_____ you when you are sorry.

5. When you serve others, you serve _____God_____.

Name _____ Date _____

(B) Check Understanding Choose the best ending for each sentence.

6. God's love for you   to be free.

7. A consequence can be   good or bad.

8. God created you   never ends.

9. A follower of Jesus treats people   God's laws.

10. The Ten Commandments are   the way Jesus did.

ASSESSMENT

Notes _____

_____

_____

_____

_____

_____

_____

_____

_____

_____

_____

_____

_____

A8   Answer Key for Unit 5 Tests

Name _____ Date _____

Ⓐ Work with Words Write the word from the Word Bank that completes the sentence.

WORD BANK
Body
grace
love
seven
words

1. Through the _____words_____ and actions of the sacraments, you know God's love.

2. The Catholic Church celebrates _____seven_____ sacraments.

3. The sacraments are signs of God's _____love_____.

4. You received God's _____grace_____ in Baptism.

5. At the Last Supper, Jesus gave his _____Body_____ and Blood.

Name _____ Date _____

Ⓑ Check Understanding Circle the word that best completes each sentence.

6. Christians are baptized people who follow _____.

(Jesus) Moses

7. With Baptism God makes you his own _____.

slave (child)

8. At the Last Supper, Jesus gave his followers the _____.

(Eucharist) Church

9. God sent Jesus to save his _____.

(people) Bible

10. Savior is a name for _____.

Mary (Jesus)

Notes _____

_____
_____
_____
_____
_____
_____
_____
_____
_____
_____
_____
_____
_____
_____
_____
_____

Answer Key for Unit 6 Tests   A9

A Work with Words Write the words from the Word Bank that best complete the sentences.

1. Jesus gave his life so that people could have

_____

_ _ _ _ _ _ _ _ _ _ _ _ _ _ _
                new life
_____ with God.

2. _____ _ _ _ _ _ _ _ _ _ _ _ _ _ _ _
            Heaven   is happiness with God forever.

_____

3. Every _ _ _ _ _ _ _ _ _ _ _ _ _ _ _ works for the
                Christian

   kingdom of God.

WORD BANK

Sacrament of the Eucharist

"This is my Body."

Use the Word Bank to help you answer the question.

4. What is another name for the Mass?

_____

_ _
        Sacrament of the Eucharist

5. What did Jesus say when he blessed the bread?

_____

_ _
            "This is my Body."

©Harcourt Religion

B Check Understanding Trace the line to the best ending for each sentence.

6. Jesus saved people ----------- from friends.

   from the power of sin.

7. Jesus being raised from   the Resurrection.

   the dead is called ------------ Easter.

Draw a line to the best title.

8. Celebrates Jesus' presence   heaven
   in the holy Bread and Wine

9. Being happy with God forever   grace

10. God's life and love in you   Eucharist

©Harcourt Religion

Notes _____

_____

_____

_____

_____

_____

_____

_____

_____

_____

_____

_____

_____

_____

Name _____ Date _____

Ⓐ Work with Words Write the word from the Word Bank that best completes each question.

WORD BANK
God
Creator

1. Who made you?   God

2. What is one name for God who made everything?

          Creator

Ⓑ Check Understanding Draw a line to the best ending for each sentence.

3. God's word written down by humans is the   **a.** Bible.

4. God created the   **b.** good.

5. Everything God made is   **c.** world.

Name _____ Date _____

Ⓐ Work with Words Circle the word that best completes each sentence.

1. God's gift to you is the _____.

   sea   (world)   [globe]

2. The _____ tells that God made the world.

   (Bible)   HOLY BIBLE   arithmetic book

3. God made the _____ to give light at night.

   sun   (moon)

Ⓑ Check Understanding Draw a line to the best ending for each sentence.

4. God created the world to show his   **a.** good.

5. Praise God because he is   **b.** love.

Notes _____
_____
_____
_____
_____
_____
_____
_____
_____
_____
_____
_____
_____
_____
_____
_____
_____

Name _____ Date _____

(A) Work with Words Write the word from the Word Bank that best completes each sentence.

```
┌─────────────────────────┐
│        WORD BANK        │
│  everything    creation │
└─────────────────────────┘
```

1. Creation is _____ everything _____ God made.

2. You can care for all God's _____ creation _____ .

(B) Check Understanding Put an X next to the three things a good caretaker would do. [1 POINT FOR EACH CORRECTLY CHECKED ITEM]

____X____ 3. Be kind to pets.

_____ 4. Throw away a dull pencil.

_____ 5. Dump milk in the lunch garbage.

____X____ 6. Save water.

____X____ 7. Recycle cans.

_____ 8. Throw out cardboard boxes.

ASSESSMENT

Answers can be found in the back of the Teacher Manual.

Name _____ Date _____

(A) Work with Words Write the word from the Word Bank that best completes the sentence. [1 POINT FOR EACH BLANK]

1. The three Persons in the Holy Trinity are

```
┌──────────────┐
│  WORD BANK   │
│  Son         │
│  Father      │
│  Holy Spirit │
└──────────────┘
```

_____

God the _____ Father _____ ,

_____

God the _____ Son _____ ,

_____

and God the _____ Holy Spirit _____ .

(B) Check Understanding Your teacher will help you read the sentences. Circle the answer that best completes each sentence.

2. The Holy Trinity is _____ Persons in one God.

two 2   (three) 3

3. The Holy Spirit helps you know and love _____ and the Father.

books   (Jesus)

ASSESSMENT

Answers can be found in the back of the Teacher Manual.

Notes _____

_____

_____

_____

_____

_____

_____

_____

_____

_____

_____

_____

_____

_____

Name _____ Date _____

A **Work with Words** Unscramble the words to name the three people in the Holy Family.

1. essJu
   Jesus

2. yMra
   Mary

3. Jpesho
   Joseph

B **Check Understanding** Circle the best ending for each sentence.

4. Jesus is a man and ——————— **a.** God.

5. The Holy Family is ——————— **b.** the name for the human family of Jesus.

ASSESSMENT

Name _____ Date _____

A **Work with Words** Draw a line to a good title for each sentence.

1. It tells about times before Jesus was born. — New Testament

2. Jesus loves and cares for all people. — Bible

3. A kind of story that teaches something important. — Parable

4. It tells about Jesus' life and teachings. — Old Testament

5. God's word was written down by humans. — The Good Shepherd

ASSESSMENT

Notes _____

_____

_____

_____

_____

_____

_____

_____

_____

_____

_____

_____

_____

_____

Answer Key for Chapter Tests A13

Name _____ **Date** _____

(A) **Work with Words** Write the word from the Word Bank that best completes each sentence.

1. Mother Teresa knew that God's

_____

— — — — — — — — — — — — — — — — — —
goodness

is in all people.

WORD BANK
goodness
faith
power

2. _____ faith _____ is the gift of believing in God.

3. Jesus' healing actions show God's

_____

— — — — — — — — — — — — — — — — — —
power   and love.

(B) **Check Understanding** Trace the line to the best way to complete the sentence.

4. Jesus healed people. ———————— God's love.

This was a sign of ———————————— bad things.

5. Jesus told Jairus to have ——————— food.

——————— faith.

Name _____ **Date** _____

(A) **Work with Words** Write the word from the Word Bank that best completes the sentence. [1 POINT FOR EACH BLANK]

WORD BANK		
Great	others	love

1. The _____ Great _____ Commandment

teaches you to _____ love _____ God and

to love _____ others _____ .

(B) **Check Understanding** Circle the word that best completes each sentence.

2. You show love for God when you _____.

talk   **pray**

3. A commandment is a law that God made for _____ to obey.

plants   **people**

Notes _____

_____

_____

_____

_____

_____

_____

_____

_____

_____

_____

_____

_____

_____

A14   Answer Key for Chapter Tests

Name _____ Date _____

(A) Work with Words Write the word from the Word Bank to complete the first part of the Lord's Prayer. [1 POINT FOR EACH BLANK]

```
┌─────────────────────────────┐
│         WORD BANK           │
│  heaven          name       │
└─────────────────────────────┘
```

1. Our father, who art in _____heaven_____ ,

   hallowed be thy _____name_____ .

(B) Check Understanding Draw a line to the best ending for each sentence.

2. Prayer is   a. two ways to pray.

3. The Lord's Prayer is   b. listening and talking to God.

4. Ask and thank are   c. the prayer Jesus taught.

Answers can be found in the back of the Teacher Manual.

Name _____ Date _____

(A) Work with Words Circle the word that best completes each sentence.

1. Noah said _____ to God's invitation.

        no   (yes)

2. Sharing _____ is a way to say yes to God.

        sadness   (love)

3. The _____ tells people about God and his kingdom.

        (Church)   ark

(B) Check Understanding Draw a line to the best ending for each sentence.

4. The kingdom of God is ——— a. the world of love, peace, and justice that God wants.

5. God invites all people ——— b. into his kingdom.

Answers can be found in the back of the Teacher Manual.

Answer Key for Chapter Tests A15

Name _____ Date _____

A) Work with Words Circle the word that best completes each sentence.

1. Jesus promised to send the _____.

Church   (Holy Spirit)

2. The Holy Spirit guides the _____.

(Church)   bears

B) Check Understanding Draw a line to the best ending for each sentence.

3. The Holy Spirit

4. The Holy Spirit will help you

5. The Holy Spirit fills

a. your heart with God's love.

b. make good choices.

c. will guide you.

Answers can be found in the back of the Teacher Manual.

ASSESSMENT

Name _____ Date _____

A) Check Understanding Draw a line from the saint to something about that person.

1. Blessed Kateri

2. Saint Elizabeth Ann

a. opened schools for girls.

b. was a Native American.

Trace the line to the best ending for each sentence.

3. Saints are ------------- sad people.

Holy people.

4. Those who are holy ----- serve God with all their hearts.

----- do whatever they feel like doing.

5. Saints are filled with ------- themselves.

the Holy Spirit.

Answers can be found in the back of the Teacher Manual.

ASSESSMENT

Notes _____

_____

_____

_____

_____

_____

_____

_____

_____

_____

_____

_____

_____

_____

_____

_____

Name _____ Date _____

Ⓐ Work with Words Circle the word that best completes each sentence.

1. Jesus washed his friends' feet. He showed them how to
_____.

        (serve)   play

2. When you serve others, you show your _____ for God.

        hope   (love)

3. To serve is to help give others what they need in a _____ way.

       (loving)   selfish

Ⓑ Check Understanding Put an **S** on the line if the person is serving. [1 POINT FOR EACH CORRECT S]

_____ **4.** Elena sees her teacher carrying books. Elena walks away.

___S___ **5.** A child is hurt on the playground. Trevor leads the crying child to a teacher.

_____ **6.** It snowed all night. Cassie sleeps in while her dad cleans the sidewalk.

___S___ **7.** Kyle carries groceries for a neighbor who uses a cane.

Name _____ Date _____

Ⓐ Work with Words Write the word from the Word Bank that best completes each sentence.

___WORD BANK___
right
choices

_____

1. Some ____choices____ can help or hurt others.

_____

2. When you choose what is ____right____, you grow closer to God.

Ⓑ Check Understanding Trace the line to the best ending for each sentence.

3. The Ten Commandments   — laws.
   are God's   ---- stories.

4. You are free to make   — choices.
   good or bad   ---- laws.

5. God gave the Ten   — Jesus.
   Commandments to   ---- Moses.

Notes _____

_____

_____

_____

_____

_____

_____

_____

_____

_____

_____

_____

_____

_____

_____

_____

_____

Name _____ Date _____

Ⓐ Work with Words Write the word from the Word Bank that best completes each sentence.

WORD BANK
sin
forgive

1. To ___sin___ is to choose to disobey God and do wrong.

2. To ___forgive___ is to put aside what someone has done to hurt you.

Ⓑ Check Understanding Circle the word that best completes each sentence.

3. When you sin, you hurt your _____ with God.

(friendship)   neighbor

4. You can start over with God by saying, "_____."

(I'm sorry)   Thank you

5. God _____ gives you another chance to change.

never   (always)

Name _____ Date _____

Ⓐ Work with Words Write the word from the Word Bank that best completes each sentence.

WORD BANK	
mysteries	life

1. Jesus gave his life so that people could have new ___life___ with God.

2. Jesus' death and being raised to new life are holy ___mysteries___.

Ⓑ Check Understanding Circle the best title for the topic.

3. He was sent to bring people back to God the Father.

(Savior)   Creator

4. They brought sin into the world.

(The First People)   The Holy Trinity

5. This is the name for being raised from the dead to new life.

Saved   (Resurrection)

Notes _____

_____
_____
_____
_____
_____
_____
_____
_____
_____
_____
_____
_____
_____
_____

Name _____ Date _____

Ⓐ Work with Words Write the word from the Word Bank that best completes each sentence.

```
         WORD BANK
signs              given
        seven
```

1. The sacraments are ___signs___ and celebrations.

2. The Catholic Church has ___seven___ sacraments.

3. The sacraments were ___given___ by Jesus.

Ⓑ Check Understanding Circle the best answer for each question.[1 POINT FOR EACH CORRECT CIRCLE]

4. What are the Church's seven signs of God's love?

   commandments   (sacraments)

5. What do all the sacraments have?

   (words and actions)   bread and wine

Name _____ Date _____

Ⓐ Work with Words Write the word from the Word Bank that best completes each sentence.

```
         WORD BANK
parents            water
```

1. Your ___parents___ and godparents promised to help you live as a child of God.

2. In Baptism ___water___ is poured on your head three times.

Ⓑ Check Understanding Draw a line to the best ending for each sentence.

3. Baptism makes you   a. the new life of grace.

4. Baptism brings you   b. a sharing in God's life and love.

5. Grace is   c. a member of the Church.

Notes _____

_____

_____

_____

_____

_____

_____

_____

_____

_____

_____

_____

_____

_____

_____

Answer Key for Chapter Tests A19

Name _____ Date _____

(A) Work with Words   Circle the word that best completes each sentence.

1. At Mass the Church family celebrates with stories, songs, _____, and a meal.

   (gifts)   jokes

2. At Mass the bread and wine become Jesus' _____.

   Story and Song   (Body and Blood)

(B) Check Understanding   Draw a line to the best title.

3. A word that means thanksgiving   a. the Last Supper

4. The Church's celebration to praise and thank God   b. the Mass

5. Jesus' meal with his friends the night before he died   c. Eucharist

Name _____ Date _____

(A) Check Understanding   Circle the best answer to each question.

1. Who will be in heaven with God forever?

   (those who show love)   nobody   animals and plants

2. With whom do holy people live forever?

   the whole city   (the Holy Trinity)   plants and animals

3. Who said, "There are many rooms in my Father's house"?

   Jairus   Mary   (Jesus)

4. What do humans have that plants and animals don't have?

   (life forever)   nothing   life cycle

5. What is the name for living in happiness with God forever?

   death   (heaven)   life cycle

Notes _____

_____
_____
_____
_____
_____
_____
_____
_____
_____
_____
_____
_____
_____
_____

A20   Answer Key for Chapter Tests

Chapter 21 Test

Name ______________________ Date ____________

Ⓐ **Check Understanding** Draw a line to the best ending for each sentence.

1. God's kingdom — b. began with Jesus.
2. Every time you say the Lord's Prayer, — c. you pray for the coming of God's kingdom.
3. When you show love, peace, and justice, — a. you help God's kingdom grow.

Ⓑ **Make Connections** Write two ways you can help God's kingdom grow. [1 POINT EACH]

4. ______________________

5. ______________________

ASSESSMENT

Answers can be found in the back of the Teacher Manual.

Notes ______________________

Illustration Credits

1 Linda Mordan; 5A Kate Flanagan; 25E Kate Flanagan, Rusty Fletcher; 30 Vicki Wehrman; 35E (t) Kate Flanagan, (bl) Rusty Fletche 35A David Opie; 43 Matt Straub; 50 Susan Nethery; 61E(t) Kate Flanagan, (b) Yvette Banek; 61A Mick Reid; 62 Matt Straub; 66 (bl) Artville/Imspace Systems Corporation; 71 Amoria McLean; 78 Matt Straub; 81A Paige Billing Frye; 81B Olivia Cole; 97A Susan Swan; 97B Meryl Treatner; 101 Dan Brown; 107E Kate Flanagan; 107A Patrick Girouard; 115 Elizabeth Brandt; 117A Mick Reid; 121 Caroly Croll; 123 Matt Straub; 133A Allen Eitzen; 141 Claude Martinot; 143A Carolyn Croll; 151 Matt Straub; 169A Kathryn Mitter; 179A Nancy Cassidy; 181 Matt Straub; 183 Tuko Fujisaki; 189A Roman Dunets; 190 Matt Straub; 196 Susan Swan; 205A Barbara Kiwak; 215A Pat Harris; 219 Matt Straub; 220 Bernard Adnet; 222 Susan Swan; 225B (br) Matt Straub; 228 Matt Straub; 231 Matt Straub; 241A Joel Spector; 246 Ruth J. Flanigan; 251A Dan Brown; 266 Mits Katayama/Artville.

Photo Credits

iv Getty Images; v (b) Eric Camden; vii (tr) Jim Whitmer Photography; xi (br) Sonny T. Senser; xviii Rubberball Productions; xxi (br) Getty Images; xxii (bl) Getty Images; xxiii (bc) Eric Camden; 1 Digital Vision/Getty Images; 2 Digital Vision/Getty Images; 3 Steve Cole/Photodisc/Getty Images; 4 L. Hobbs/Photolink/Photodisc/Getty Images; 5 Photolink/Photodisc/Getty Images; 6–7 Randy Miller/Masterfile; 8A The Curator Collection LTD.; 8 Steve Cole/Photodisc/Getty Images; 9 Corbis; 10A Ted Spiegel/Corbis; 10 Michae Matisse/Photodisc/Getty Images; 11 Siede Presis/Photodisc/Getty Images; 13 Fototeca Storica Nazionale/Photodisc/Getty Images; 14A Myrleen Ferguson Cate/Photo Edit; 14 Geostock/Photodisc/Getty Images; 15 Corbis; 16A Father Gene Plaisted; 16 Father Gene Plaisted; 17 Father Gene Plaisted; 18A Father Gene Plaisted; 18 Corbis; 19 Bill Whittman; 22 Corbis; 25A Tom Stewart/Corbis; 25B (t) PhotoDisc, (bl) Corbis; 25 Nicola Sutton/Life File/Photodisc/Getty Images; 26 Corbis; 31 Corel Stock Photo Library; 32 Myrleen Ferguson Cate/Index Stock; 35B (bl) Corbis, (t) Corbis; 37 Corbis; 45A (br) Doug Menuez/Getty Images; 45B (bl) Corel Stock Photo Library, (t) Digital Vision/Getty Images; 45 (bl) Myrleen Ferguson Cate/Photo Edit; 46 Photodisc; 47 Corel Stock Photo Library; 52 (bl Ryan McVay/Photodisc/Getty Images; 55A Corbis; 56 (br) Andrew Ward/Life File/Photodisc/Getty Images; 62 Siede Preis/Photodisc/ Getty Images; 63 Steve Cole/Photodisc/Getty Images; 64 Father Gene Plaisted, OSC; 67 Corbis; 69 Photolink/Photodisc/Getty Images; 70 Bill Whittman; 71B (bl) Corbis, (t) Corbis; 71 Superstock; 72 Corbis; 73 Photolink/Photodisc/Getty Images; 76 (bl) Rubberball Productions; 77 Fototeca Storica Nazionale/Photodisc/Getty Images; 77B Corbis; 79 Corbis; 81B Corbis; 82 (bl) Photolink/Photodisc/ Getty Images; 88 Bill Whittman; 91A Corbis; 98 (bl) Father Gene Plaisted, OSC, (br) Sygma/Corbis; 102 Corbis; 103B Doug Menuez/Photodisc/Getty Images; 105 Corbis; 107B (bl) D. Berry/Photolink/Photodisc/Getty Images, (t) C Squared Studios/Photodisc/ Getty Images; 109 Keith Brofsky/Photodisc/Getty Images; 112 Rubberball Productions; 117B (bl) Corbis, (t) Corbis; 117 Corel Stock Photo Library; 119 Corbis; 125 Corbis; 127A Corbis; 128 Mel Curtis/Photodisc/Getty Images; 129 Digital Vision/Getty Images; 134 (bl) David Buffington/Photodisc/Getty Images, (br) Robert Glusic/Photodisc/Getty Images; 135 Digital Vision/Getty Images; 138 Annie Reynolds/Photolink/Photodisc/Getty Images; 139 Corbis; 143B (bl) Photolink/Photodisc/Getty Images, (tr) Digital Vision/Getty Images 145 (bl) D. Berry/Photolink/Photodisc/Getty Images; 147 Richard Hutchings/Photo Edit; 148 (bl) Rubberball Productions, (br) Photolink/Photodisc/Getty Images; 150 C Squared Studios/Photodisc/Getty Images; 153A Kevin Dodge/Masterfile; 153B Corbis; 155 Corbis; 157 (bl) Paul Bachem, (br) S. Solum/Photolink/Photodisc/Getty Images; 158 Ryan McVay/Photodisc/Getty Images; 159 Richard Lentz/Robert Lentz; 160 (bl) The Crossiers/Father Gene Plaisted,OSC; 163A Corbis; 169B (tr) Photolink/Photodisc/Getty Images; 169 Bill Whittman; 173 Corbis; 179B (bl) Nicola Sutton/Life File/Photodisc/Getty Images, (tr) Ryan McVay/Photodisc/Getty Images; 180 (b Photodisc; 184 (bl) Rubberball Productions; 185 Corbis; 186 Photodisc; 189B (bt) Roger Tulley/Getty Images, (tr) Digital Vision/Getty Images; 189 Corbis; 191 Digital Vision/Getty Images; 192 Corbis; 194 Barbara Penoyar/Photodisc/Getty Images; 197 Corbis; 199A Rya McVay/Photodisc/Getty Images; 201 Michael Newman/Photoedit; 205B (bl) Corbis, (tr) Siede Preis/Photodisc/Getty Images; 206 Corb 211 Steve Cole/Photodisc/Getty Images; 215B (bl) Father Gene Plaisted, OSC, (tr) Bill Whittman; 216 Photolink/Photodisc/Getty Images; 217 Corbis; 218 Michael Newman/Photo Edit; 220 Rubberball Productions; 221 Corel Stock Photo Library; 225A Michael Newman/Photo Edit; 225B (tr) Father Gene Plaisted, OSC; 226 (bl) Corbis; 230 Myrleen Ferguson Cate/Photo Edit; 233 Corbis; 235A Corbis; 235 Rim Light/Photolink/Photodisc/Getty Images; 237 Geostock/Photodisc/Getty Images; 241B (bl) Father Gene Plaisted, OSC (tr) Ariel Skelley/Corbis, 241 Corbis; 242 Bill Whittman; 245 Photolink/Photodisc/Getty Images; 248 Michael Newman/Photo Edit; 24! Corbis; 251B (bl) Digital Vision/Getty Images, (tr) Corbis; 251 Pat Powers and Cherryl Schafer/Photodisc/Getty Images; 252 Tomi/Photo Link/Photodisc/Getty Images; 253 Digital Vision/Getty Images; 256 (bl) Corbis; 257 Adobe Image Library; 259 Geostock/ Photodisc/Getty Images; 261A Simone Boni; 261B (bl) Corbis, (tr) Corbis; 262 Michael Newman/Photo Edit; 263 Photo Link/ Photodisc/Getty Images; 265 Corbis; 268 Kevin Dodge/Masterfile; 271A Keith Brofsky/Photodisc/Getty Images; 271 John A. Rizzo/Photodisc/Getty Images; 273 Corbis.

Acknowledgements

Teacher's Notes

_____

_____

_____

_____

_____

_____

_____

_____

_____

_____

_____

_____

_____

_____

_____

_____

_____

_____

_____

Teacher's Notes

_____

_____

_____

_____

_____

_____

_____

_____

_____

_____

_____

_____

_____

_____

_____

_____

_____

_____

Teacher's Notes

_____
_____
_____
_____
_____
_____
_____
_____
_____
_____
_____
_____
_____
_____
_____
_____
_____
_____
_____
_____

Teacher's Notes

_____

_____

_____

_____

_____

_____

_____

_____

_____

_____

_____

_____

_____

_____

_____

_____

_____

_____

_____

Teacher's Notes

Teacher's Notes

Teacher's Notes

_____

_____

_____

_____

_____

_____

_____

_____

_____

_____

_____

_____

_____

_____

_____

_____

_____

Teacher's Notes